IN THE COMPANY OF SISTERS:
CANADA'S WOMEN IN THE WAR ZONE,
1914–1919

In the Company
of Sisters

CANADA'S WOMEN IN THE WAR ZONE,

1914–1919

DIANNE GRAVES

ROBIN BRASS STUDIO

Published 2021 by Robin Brass Studio Inc.
www.robinbrassstudio.com

ISBN 978-1-896941-76-9

Printed and bound in Canada by Marquis, Montmagny, Quebec.

Library and Archives Canada Cataloguing in Publication

Title: In the company of sisters : Canada's women in the war zone, 1914-1919 / Dianne Graves.

Names: Graves, Dianne, author.
Description: Includes bibliographical references and index.
Identifiers: Canadiana 20200304410 | ISBN 9781896941769 (softcover)
Subjects: LCSH: World War, 1914-1918 – Women – Canada. | LCSH: World War, 1914-1918 – Medical care – Canada. | LCSH: World War, 1914-1918 – War work – Canada. | LCSH: World War, 1914-1918 – Women – Canada – Biography.
Classification: LCC D639.W7 G73 2021 | DDC 940.3082/0971 – dc23

This book is dedicated to the women of Canada who were part of the war effort at home and overseas during the years 1914 to 1919.

It is also in memory of my late friend Margaret Sankey (1916–2012), the daughter of Captain Nisbet V. Sankey of the 58th Battalion, Canadian Expeditionary Force.

Sisters in the Aegean. This photograph of the nursing staff of No. 1 Canadian Stationary Hospital was taken in the summer of 1916 at Salonika (modern-day Thessaloniki). Having served at Lemnos, the unit was based in Greece from March 1916 to September 1917. It then returned to Britain, where it became No. 13 Canadian General Hospital at Hastings, Sussex, until its demobilization in June 1919. (Canadian War Museum 20070103-014_Lpb, George Metcalf Archival Collection)

Contents

Introduction

In the summer of 2014, as the centenary of the outbreak of the First World War approached, work was already well in hand at Britain's Tower of London to create a tribute to the fallen of that conflict. Volunteers from around the world planted ceramic poppies that gradually formed a vast sea of red around the site's historic White Tower. Each poppy – and there were 888,246 in all – represented a British or Commonwealth serviceman or woman killed in the conflict and a name on a war memorial or grave at one of the Commonwealth War Graves Commission cemeteries in Europe and farther afield. Of this total, 59,544 were Canadians.

When Britain declared war against Germany on 4 August 1914, Canada as a member of the British Empire was automatically at war. The conflict soon dominated every aspect of life in the Dominion and led to the federal government intervening in the country's economic, social and military affairs to an unprecedented degree. Regulations reminded Canadians of the need to contribute to the war effort, whether at home or in active theatres of war, and the part they played is a tale of courage, resilience and unstinting service on the part of a young nation that had celebrated only forty-three years of official existence. Quite apart from the troops who went into action on the battlefields, a significant aspect of Canada's First World War story belongs to those who worked behind the scenes to support them. Much of their endeavour took place on the home front, where a huge effort was mounted, but a significant contribution was also made by Canadian women who chose to "do their bit" abroad, in some cases undertaking special missions that earned them well-deserved recognition.

In the Company of Sisters focuses on this latter group of women. The idea for the book came about nearly a decade ago when I was researching at Library and Archives Canada in Ottawa. While looking for images, I came across a reference to the First World War paintings of the Canadian artist Mary Riter Hamilton and her activities on the Western Front a matter of months after the war ended. One thing led to another, and I was soon studying other women who were part Canada's overseas military effort and the ways in which they chose to be of service in the war zone. To clarify the term "war zone," I have taken it to include all the campaign theatres where opposing troops fought, Allied territory which came under attack from German ships and aircraft, and the seas on which the *Kaiserliche Marine* (the Imperial German navy) waged unrestricted submarine warfare against Allied shipping.

Fortunately, a number of the women who spent their war years away from Canada left diaries, letters, memoirs and, in several cases, published accounts that enable us to follow what happened to them. The impact of the conflict was undeniable, for although it occupied only a short period in their lives, all who experienced it lived, in the words of author Sandra Gwyn, "more fully and more intensely than they ever did before, or ever will do again." Their papers and records make clear the impact of the war, the enormous number and seriousness of casualties, the needs of the troops away from the front line, the concerns of their families back home, and the predicament of those civilians who lost their homes, families and livelihoods in areas where fighting took place.

With so many problems to be addressed far from home and amid the unpredictable conditions of war, all possible help – voluntary and otherwise – was needed. Getting things done in a male-dominated world was invariably not easy and took resolve, dedication and determination. Among Canada's women who were part of this effort and who, for the purposes of this book, include those from Newfoundland, which was still an independent colony at that time, there were nurses, war workers and many others who volunteered with a variety of organizations. Their knowledge, ability and willingness to be of service at a critical time saw them taking on work some of which had hitherto been the preserve of men.

The reality of women breaking new ground challenged societal norms and conventional ideas of gender roles, and their appearance in a variety of uniforms and regulation clothing provoked reactions ranging from amusement to outrage. However, the impact of these ladies proving themselves capable of doing responsible and, at times, hazardous work, widened the appreciation of their potential. It was further reinforced after female war workers returned from France with accounts of what they had witnessed and been able to achieve.

In the midst of these new activities, exceptional and pioneering women emerged. Some had already completed professional training that prepared them for the work they wanted to undertake, while others from wealthy families were determined to use their advantages to good effect. Background, education, self-assurance and familiarity with the wider world enabled them to set up and run their own projects. With contacts, enterprise and leadership skills, they came to the fore as people who could achieve their goals in ways that benefited troops and civilians alike.

Necessity, the driving force behind so many wartime initiatives, brought with it changes that would lead to greater gender equality in employment and to more freedom of choice. The efforts of Canada's women at home and abroad during the First World War gained them support for political advances such as women's suffrage, and by 1922 seven of the nine Canadian provinces had granted them the right to vote in provincial elections. Federally, the franchise came in three stages, beginning in 1917 with nurses serving overseas in the armed forces.

Despite such progress and the efforts of women during the war years, when it ended and the troops returned home the majority of female workers were expected to give up their wartime jobs in favour of their male colleagues. By 1929 women employed outside the home only formed about twenty per cent of the Canadian labour force and progress in terms of education remained slow. Yet despite this tardy momentum, a door had opened on the long road that would lead, via increasing opportunities and changing attitudes, to greater equality and to women achieving their potential. Few of them in 1914 could have imagined that later, the nursing and social work professions would be looking at the need to attract more men, nor that as more time went by, qualified women would be appointed as engineers, senior scientists, surgeons, pilots and the like, and would occupy high positions in industry, commerce, government and the professions.

2020 marks the centenary of the year the Treaty of Versailles came into effect – an event regarded by many as marking Canada's coming of age – and *In the Company of Sisters* seeks to pay tribute to the First World War generation of Canadian women, their place in the nation's history and their legacy. In doing so, it highlights their contribution to the national overseas effort from 1914 to 1919 and recognizes their courage and selfless spirit in tackling the unpredictable and at times dangerous conditions of life in the war zone. Their example and their many achievements stand as an inspiration to subsequent generations and their experiences, to which official records provide clues but which in many cases have remained part of local or family history, are woven into the fabric of the nation and the places where they served. Canada's First World War record, on and off the battlefield, is remembered not only at home but also by communities in Britain and mainland Europe where Canadians trained, worked, fought and died.

At this unprecedented time of upheaval caused by a pandemic, it is important to remember that a century ago Spanish influenza swept the world from February 1918 to April 1920, causing an estimated death toll of between 17 and 50 million. The present Covid-19 virus against which, at the time of writing, there is no vaccine yet available, has already claimed over a million lives. It links us to those who experienced the worst of the Spanish influenza pandemic, and as we struggle to combat the current global emergency, their ordeal can be felt across the years.

As I turn to the process of writing the book, I would like to mention that its title, *In the Company of Sisters*, is taken from *Censored Letters*, a modern collection of poems by novelist and poet Betsy Struthers. The phrase seemed to me to convey a sense of comradeship that undoubtedly bound together the women who were part of the war effort. The term "sisters" could be taken literally, especially as several chapters discuss the work of Canada's nursing sisters, but in this instance it is intended metaphorically to include all the remarkable Canadian women who served overseas in a variety of very different ways.

Almost all the verses that form the epigraphs at the start of each chapter are from *Canadian Poems of the Great War*, an anthology of poetry written by Canadians who were inspired by their country in its time of trial. Of the seventy-three contributors, twenty-six were women and included a literary and drama critic, a teacher, a journalist, a translator, an editor and book reviewer, and well-known novelists Lucy Maud Montgomery and Mazo de la Roche. John Garvin, who edited the anthology, believed it was not only "the poetic expression of a young nation, involved for the first time in a life and death struggle," but it was also "unique" and "worth preserving."

As I conducted my research, I consulted a wide range of sources that included various helpful studies and, in several cases, biographies of women I had earmarked for inclusion. As someone with a long-held interest in the First World War, it was gratifying to find that the centenary of the conflict had generated new scholarship that will be of interest to students in the future.

I now come to the important task of acknowledging the help I received from institutions and individuals during the writing of *In the Company of Sisters*. In expressing my gratitude to the staff of all the research facilities I approached, I wish to make special mention of the assistance I was given by Carol Reed, Fiona Anthes and Shannyn Johnson at the Military History Research Centre, Canadian War Museum, Ottawa; Dr. Heather McNabb, Anne-Frédérique Beaulieu-Plamondon and Roxanne Drouin of the McCord Museum of History, Montreal; Jodi Aoki of the Trent University Archives,

Peterborough; Christopher Coutlee of the Special Collections Department, Toronto Public Library; Jeannie Hounslow of the City of Vancouver Archives; Andrew Webb of the Imperial War Museum, London; and the archivist of the *Kenniscentrum*, In Flanders Fields Museum, Ypres, Belgium. I also thank the personnel of the Joseph S. Stauffer Library, Queen's University, Kingston, and Michael Rikley-Lancaster, Executive Director of the Mississippi Valley Textile Museum, Almonte, and his staff.

Special thanks are due to Jacques Ryckebosch of Flanders Battlefield Tour, Poperinghe, Belgium, whom I first met in 1992 when he was the curator of Talbot House, a building in that town that served as a club offering rest and recreation to Allied troops during the First World War. Jacques was kind enough to meet me in Ypres and together we visited a number of locations in the former Ypres Salient, enabling me to update my experience of that very significant part of the Western Front.

Jackie Sansom of Accor Hotels made it possible to access photographic material, and historian René Chartrand shared images from his personal collection. Michael Whitby, Chief Naval Historian, Department of National Defence, was kind enough to assist with research queries and information, while Alex Hughes and Barry and Anne Roxburgh – Alex and Anne being great-nephew and great-niece of Nursing Sister Dorothy Cotton – were good enough to provide information about their great aunt and her family. Barry and Anne also shared items from their own research and enabled me to access photographs from the family collection. I am indebted to them for their generosity, interest and support throughout the project.

I am most grateful to Dr. John Moses and his mother, Helen Moses, who is a daughter of Edith Anderson Monture, for permission to include a photograph of Edith and extracts from her wartime diary. Ron Riter, a nephew of Mary Riter Hamilton, was good enough to supply photographs of her and I appreciated very much his interest and assistance. In England my friend Heather Hole made my visit to Polesden Lacey, the Surrey home of the Honourable Margaret Greville, extra special, and Sue and Lindsay Court allowed me to quote from the memoir of Colonel R. McLeod. I would also like to thank Debbie Marshall, author of *Firing Lines*, a fascinating account of three Canadian women journalists during the First World War, for her help and encouragement.

While I was working on the early drafts of the manuscript my neighbour Christina Hunink helped me with proof-reading, and I thank her for her efforts. I was also fortunate to have the interest of several other friends. Kitty Cairns kindly shared books from her collection, while Chris Hume, Terry Sarchuk and Aud Karin Sund were a source of support and encouragement at those inevitable times when the road ahead still appeared long and unending.

When it came to the task of putting the book together, I am extremely grateful to my publisher, Robin Brass. I feel fortunate to have been able to work with him once again, especially during what has been a challenging year for us all, and his expertise, painstaking efforts and unfailingly high standards have led to another beautifully produced publication.

In conclusion, I thank my husband, historian Donald E. Graves, for his advice, suggestions and the care with which he reviewed the page proofs. His help with them, and with other aspects of the book, has been greatly appreciated. I also wish to mention my furry friend Pippi the cat, whose company is always a joy. She is the latest in a series of feline companions who have brightened my days, whether researching, writing, proof-reading or waiting for inspiration.

The result of all this endeavour is a story that matters deeply to me. I hope I have been able to do it justice.

DIANNE GRAVES
Thanksgiving, 2020

Note to the Reader

Several of the early chapters in the book chronicle the experiences of nurses in various theatres of war from the Western Front to hospital ships. For the benefit of those who may not be familiar with nursing titles in use a century ago, the Canadian Army Medical Corps appointed qualified women to its nursing service during the war as officers with the rank of lieutenant and the title "Nursing Sister." They were employed in a variety of positions from staff nurse to charge nurse, and managed the day-to-day matters involved in running one or more wards. Matrons, who were in overall charge of hospitals or other medical units and the nursing staff of each, held the rank of captain. Their British counterparts in the Queen Alexandra's Imperial Military Nursing Service did not, at that time, have officer status and held ranks from staff nurse to sister, senior sister (later assistant matron) and matron. Those Canadian nurses who served with the French Flag Nursing Corps were, according to the organization's 1916 report, referred to as "Sister." Volunteers with the United States Army Nurse Corps held no formal rank or commission.

A married woman or widow being known by her husband's first and second names, e.g. Mrs. John Smith, was regarded by many in the early twentieth century as the only correct form. Instances in this book of a woman being referred to in this manner derive from sources consulted. Where research has revealed a first name, it has been used. – DG

Organizations and Abbreviations

I t has been estimated that more than thirty thousand Canadian women were in Britain, western Europe, the Balkans, the Mediterranean, the Middle East and Russia during the war. Many served in a wide variety of organizations, as indicated in the following list (which is by no means comprehensive). Some of these were purely military, such as the Canadian Army Medical Corps, while others were entirely civilian, and some combined features of both. The First Aid Nursing Yeomanry, for example, was a civilian organization whose members wore uniforms, held ranks and came under military command. Military organizations listed are marked "M," civilian organizations are marked "C," while those that were a combination of both are designated "C/M." Abbreviations, where used in the book, are also shown.

AEF	American Expeditionary Forces (M)
USANC	— United States Army Nurse Corps (M)
	American Red Cross (C)
	Amputation Club of British Columbia (C)
	Anglo-Russian Hospital (C/M)
	Anglo-Russian Field Hospital (M)
	Army and Navy Canteen Board (C)
ANZAC	Australia and New Zealand Army Corps (M)
	— Australian Auxiliary Hospital (M)
ASH	— Australian Stationary Hospital (M)
	Belgian Canal Boat Fund (C)
	British Army Corps of Clerks (M)
BRCS	British Red Cross Society (C)
CAMC	Canadian Army Medical Corps (M)
CAT	— Canadian Ambulance Train (M)
CCCS	— Canadian Casualty Clearing Station (M)
CGH	— Canadian General Hospital (M)
CSH	— Canadian Stationary Hospital(M)
CFCC	Canadian Field Comforts Commission (C)
	Canadian Pay and Records Office (M)
	Canadian Imperial Voluntary Aid Detachment (C/M)
CRCS	Canadian Red Cross Society (C)
	— Information Bureau (C)
CWCA	Canadian War Contingent Association (C)
	Clarence House Convalescent Hospital (C)

	Comité Britannique (C)
	Concerts at the Front (C)
FANY	First Aid Nursing Yeomanry (C/M)
FFNC	French Flag Nursing Corps (C/M)
	French Red Cross (C)
	Independent constituent organizations:
	— *L'Association des Dames Françaises* (C)
	— *La Société de Secours aux Blessés Militaires* (C)
	— *L'Union des Femmes de France* (C)
	Ford International Peace Commission (C)
FWEF	French War Emergency Fund (C)
HMCHS	His Majesty's Canadian Hospital Ship (M)
HMHS	His Majesty's Hospital Ship (M)
IODE	Imperial Order Daughters of the Empire (C)
	Lady Ridley's Hospital for Officers (M)
	Manitoba War Relief Fund (C)
	Maple Leaf Clubs (C)
	Motor Transport Volunteers (C/M)
	Navy and Army Canteen Board (C/M)
	Ouvroir pour les Blessés (C)
	Order of St. John of Jerusalem (C)
	— St. John Ambulance Brigade (C)
	Perkins Bull Hospital (M)
QAIMNS	Queen Alexandra's Imperial Military Nursing Service (M)
RAMC	Royal Army Medical Corps (M)
BGH	— British General Hospital (M)
	— British Stationary Hospital (M)
CCS	— Casualty Clearing Station (M)
	Russian Red Cross (C)
SWH	Scottish Women's Hospitals (C)
	Serbian Red Cross (C)
	Service des Blessés et des Réfugiés (C)
	Soldiers' and Sailors' Families Association (C/M)
	South of France Relief Association (C)
	St. Dunstan's Hostel for Blinded Soldiers and Sailors (M)
VAD	Voluntary Aid Detachment (C/M)
WAAC	Women's Army Auxiliary Corps (M)
WEC	Women's Emergency Corps (C)
WHC	Women's Hospital Corps (C)
WI	Women's Institute (C)
WRAF	Women's Royal Air Force (M)
WRNS	Women's Royal Naval Service (M)
WVR	Women's Volunteer Reserve (M)
YMCA	Young Men's Christian Association (C)
YWCA	Young Women's Christian Association (C)

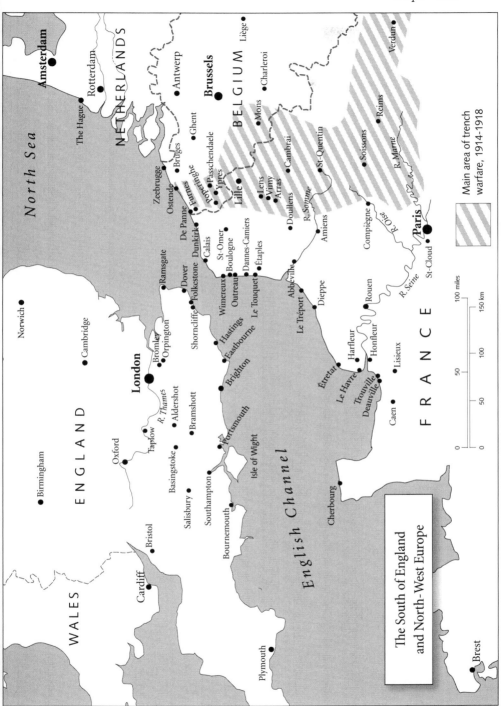

The South of England
and North-West Europe

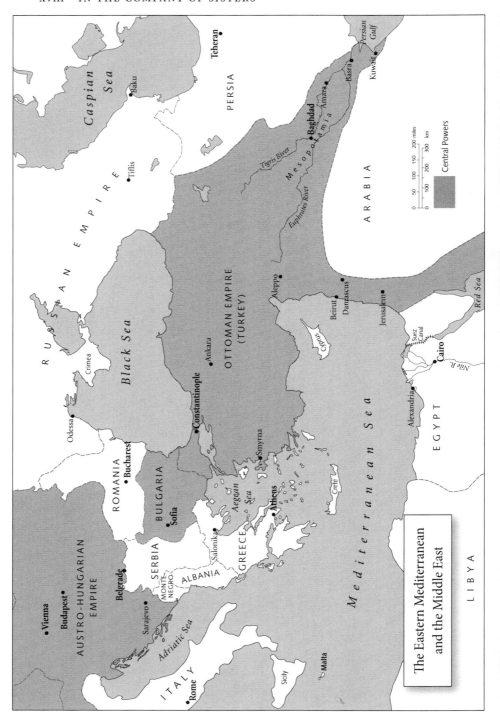

The Eastern Mediterranean and the Middle East

The Balkans, Gallipoli
and the Greek Islands

The Eastern Front,
1915–1918

Central Powers

0   50   100   150   200 miles
0   100   200   300 km

SWEDEN

FINLAND

Helsinki

Stockholm

Tallinn

Petrograd
(St. Petersburg)

Pskov

Riga

Baltic
Sea

Moscow

Front line
July 1917

Polotsk

Front line Feb. 1918.
Maximum penetration
by the Central Powers

Königsberg

Vilna

Maladzyechna

GERMANY

Front line
Jan. 1915

Minsk

Vistula R.

Varapaeva

R U S S I A

Warsaw

Brest-
Litovsk

Stokhod R.

Lodz

Lutsk

Kiev

Kharkov

Lemberg

Dnieper R.

AUSTRO-HUNGARIAN
EMPIRE

Budapest

Odessa

Kronstadt

Crimea

Danube R.

Danube R.

ROMANIA

Belgrade

BULGARIA

Black Sea

SERBIA

Bucharest

CHAPTER 1

Prelude to Armageddon

The Coming of War, 1914

> *Blood of your best you gave us, gave it that we might live,*
> *Blood of our best we offer, the best of our youth we give.*
> *The price of a nation's manhood we offer to pay the debt –*
> *Did you dream, O Mother of Nations, that Canada would forget?*[1]

The summer of 1914 and its golden days before the storm of war broke was as lovely in Britain as it was in Canada. The world "on the verge of its catastrophe was very brilliant," recalled Winston Churchill, and it was not just the exceptional weather that added a special lustre to life. There seemed to be a pervasive feeling that everything was "easy and light, as if the atmosphere had something electric and gay in it."[2] Britain had been basking in the benefits of a long period of peace which it had, with few interruptions, enjoyed since the end of the Napoleonic Wars in 1815. It took pride in its empire which spanned much of the globe, but its imperial authority was being challenged and eroded by the ambitions of other nations, notably Germany. As events unfolded and international tension mounted, that last glorious summer of 1914 would be remembered with nostalgia as a "vanished world," that "seemed most beautiful just before it disappeared."[3]

The threat of an approaching conflict had for some time been mooted in well-informed circles, but the outbreak of war in August 1914 came as a "real bolt from the blue" to most people, who had not grasped the portents that preceded it.[4] Like their British counterparts, Canadians were enjoying "the loveliest summer," with the usual round of outdoor activities such as walking, swimming, boating, gardening, or relaxing at summer cottages with companions and family.[5] Ottawa socialite Ethel Chadwick was staying with friends at Blue Sea Lake in Quebec's Gatineau Hills. "Heavens it was beautiful," she wrote in her diary, sensing, as the international situation deteriorated, that "war was blowing all over the world." Even so, she found it hard to accept that "on such an evening in such a place," hostilities could be imminent, for "such terrible things seem so far away."[6] Author Lucy Maud Montgomery, at home in Leaskdale, Ontario, was horrified at the prospect of all-out conflict but recalled how Canada's governor-general, Earl Grey, had warned her in 1910 that war was "surely coming in a few years" and "we must get ready for it."[7]

The origins of the impending cataclysm could be traced back to the Franco-Prussian War of 1870-1871, from which Prussia had emerged victorious, and the creation of the new nation of Germany, which brought together many hitherto independent German states. France, resolved to exact revenge for her defeat, allied herself defensively with Russia whilst Germany made a similar alliance with the Austro-Hungarian empire. As the twentieth century dawned, Germany's fast-growing economy, her status as the leading military nation in continental Europe, and her decision to build a fleet that would rival that of the Royal Navy, were viewed collectively as a serious threat. When, in 1904, Britain concluded an *entente cordiale* – an alliance in all but name – with France, it effectively divided Europe into two rival power blocs and meant that any incident affecting a member of either would inevitably involve all the others. In such circumstances, it would be easy to trigger a chain reaction that could drag all the nations concerned into a war.

The Balkans were the most likely place for such an incident to take place. The region was made up of fiercely nationalistic states that had won their freedom from the Ottoman Empire in a series of struggles and revolutions.[8] Serbia was the most powerful and enjoyed the protection of Russia, such that when Austria-Hungary arbitrarily annexed Bosnia-Herzegovina in 1908 – lands regarded by Serbia as part of her territories – tension between Russia and Austria-Hungary worsened. Crises in that part of the world recurred between 1908 and 1913, but a major European conflict was averted. By 1914, however, astute observers and those in political and diplomatic circles recognized that the western world was heading for disaster.

Events were set in motion on 28 June 1914 when the heir to the throne of the Austro-Hungarian empire, Archduke Franz-Ferdinand, and his wife, Sophie, were assassinated by a Serbian militant, Gavrilo Princip, during an official visit to the Bosnian capital, Sarajevo. Given that previous troubles had been resolved, Canadian newspapers duly reported the event and then switched to topics closer to home, but the tension that resulted from the assassination grew steadily worse and Austria-Hungary, with Germany's support, issued an ultimatum to Serbia on 23 July 1914. Despite Serbian agreement to almost all the points in that document, on 28 July Austria-Hungary chose to declare war on Serbia. Russia mobilized the following day in support of Serbia, and when Germany, which had begun assembling her troops, asked the Russians to cease mobilization and received a refusal, Germany

The shots that sparked a war. On 28 June 1914 in Sarajevo a Serb militant, Gavrilo Princip (lower left), shot and killed the Archduke Franz Ferdinand, heir to the throne of Austria-Hungary, and his wife, Countess Sophie. The assassination started a train of events that led to the outbreak of the First World War a little over a month later. (Author's collection)

declared war on Russia on 1 August. France, as Russia's ally, mobilized that same day and forty-eight hours later Germany declared war on France.

Britain had worked hard to bring the crisis to an end through negotiation. However, when Germany asked for free passage of her troops through Belgium – a nation whose neutrality Britain was bound by an earlier treaty to protect – and Belgium refused, German troops crossed that country's frontier. Britain presented Germany with an ultimatum that if her troops were not withdrawn from Belgian territory by 11 P.M. London time on 4 August 1914, a state of war would exist between the two nations. Crowds gathered in the British capital on that memorable evening and cheers rang out when Big Ben, the famous clock at the Houses of Parliament, struck eleven times amid silence from Berlin.

As the news of war reached eastern Canada, where it was early evening, telegraph wires transmitted it across the nation. In scenes that were unprecedented, crowds cheered, sang patriotic songs, waved flags and toasted what they hoped would be a victorious contest for Britain and her allies. As one woman remembered it, "our young nation realized that the cause was just, and with serious enthusiasm men declared themselves ... ready to stand with King and Empire."[9] Within twenty-four hours of Britain's declaration of war Canada had issued her own, reminding people of the fact that in 1910 the then prime minister, Sir Wilfrid Laurier, had declared that "when Britain is at war, Canada is at war. There is no distinction."[10]

Wednesday, 5 August 1914, was a day marked by militia units parading in front of enthusiastic onlookers in Vancouver, crowds besieging Government House in Winnipeg, and thousands taking to the streets of Ottawa in scenes not witnessed since the outbreak of the South African War in 1899.[11] Newspapers, which only a month earlier had been offering women readers details of potions "to ward off summer complexion ills" or tempting them with the prospect of transatlantic travel aboard the Cunard liner *Franconia*, scheduled to sail from Boston on the fateful 4 August, now busily trumpeted the fact that there were "wild scenes in Toronto," Calgary was going "military mad," and people in Quebec City had mounted "a display of loyalty and patriotism" unlike any seen before. "All Europe is mobilizing," announced the *Winnipeg Free Press*, with the reminder that Canada now faced a "State of War for First Time since Becoming a Nation."[12] Most people believed the whole thing would be over by Christmas.

Some Canadians on vacation in Europe were caught unawares by the new state of affairs. Dinah Meredith of Toronto was travelling with her mother in the French Alps and faced a journey by road from the resort town of Aix-les-Bains. After what Dinah described as a "dash for life through France," they reached England in mid-August 1914 and found London "in an uproar, full of soldiers."[13] Mary Tuer, from Port Hope, was touring with friends in Germany's Rhine valley at the end of July 1914. On 30 July she had her first sighting of Germans in uniform as she watched "about 2000 soldiers march past," but her group hastened on to Heidelberg and Freiburg. The guard on their train informed them that war was imminent and "it was our last chance of getting out of Germany as a full mobilization of troops had been ordered." On 1 August "most disquietening reports" were circulating in Freiburg, and Mary and friends were advised that "we stay quietly here." On 4 August "we hear of the arrests of spies," she wrote, "and the town is in a perfect ferment."[14] After Britain's declaration of war, all British subjects (which included Canadians at that time) had to leave Germany, and having reached Baden-Baden Mary recorded that she and her travel companions hoped "to be sent on to England any day."[15]

Among other Canadian women in Europe were three journalists: Beatrice Nasmyth from Stratford, Ontario, Mary MacLeod Moore from La Prairie, Quebec, and Elizabeth Montizambert of Quebec City. Elizabeth was based in Paris for the *Montreal Gazette* while Beatrice and Mary were in London,

Beatrice as assistant editor of the *Vancouver Province's* women's page and Mary as a columnist for both the London *Sunday Times* and *Saturday Night* magazine. At that time there were few Canadian women doing such work, and as events moved towards war, the three began recording what they were witnessing. Elizabeth Montizambert reported from Paris on the "quiet, orderly demeanor of the crowds" and the "extraordinary courage and devotion shown by the women in this terrible crisis." She clearly admired the "splendid solidarity" of the French people and the "marvellous network of charities" that sprang up quickly under the direction of the *Assistance Publique*, a state system that provided welfare services.[16] In London Mary MacLeod Moore applauded "the magnificent unity of the whole British race in the face of adversity," as the United Kingdom prepared for the conflict that lay ahead. Behind the stoicism, however, Mary could feel a "terrible tension" and foresaw the "dark shadow of coming mourning and privation."[17]

Although they were established journalists, these Canadian women were new to war reporting, which in Britain was subject to strict regulations resulting from the Defence of the Realm Act. This recently-enacted legislation made it illegal to publish anything that directly or indirectly aided the enemy, and it stipulated that stories "not in the national interest" would result in prosecution.[18] Editors were subject to tough constraints and individual reporters faced many obstacles. Censorship and vetting of news and material prior to publication were strictly enforced; reporters were banned from entering a military zone around the troops who formed the British Expeditionary Force, while dispatches from France had to be approved by the British War Office before they could be published. Official policy also excluded women journalists from the war front, regarding them as "too emotionally and physically fragile to withstand its effects."[19] These restrictions notwithstanding, the three Canadian women set out to establish a professional niche for themselves in the world of wartime journalism, and found they were among a "small cadre of females breaking new ground and changing the rules."[20]

Although the population of Canada in 1914 was still a relatively small eight million, the government under Prime Minister Robert Borden pledged to send an expeditionary force to join Britain and its allies. Canada's governor-general, the Duke of Connaught, sent a message to King George V that the nation was ready "to uphold the honour and traditions of our Empire."[21] This phrase fitted a time when the British Empire consisted of self-governing dominions, colonies, protectorates and other territories that were important in maintaining not only Britain's economic dominance s in the world but also an effective military presence. As citizens of one of those dominions, many

English-speaking Canadians favoured stronger ties with the mother country through imperial federation. "The Empire is my country. Canada is my home," was how Lady Julia Drummond, a prominent member of Montreal society, described her feelings on the matter.[22] In August 1914 she and others like her were aware that British sovereignty and all that it stood for was about to be put to the test.

Canada had an active militia, well enough established to form the basis of wartime military expansion, and a Minister of Militia, Sam Hughes, who was an ebullient, larger-than-life figure. He quickly launched a programme of recruitment that, by sidestepping the mobilization plan, went directly to militia unit commanders across the country. They were given authority to recruit physically fit volunteers for overseas service aged between eighteen and forty-five years of age, and so positive was the response that within three weeks nearly 45,000 men had come forward. Preference was given to those who were unmarried but married men were also considered, subject to an order issued from Ottawa on 14 August 1914 that "no married man will be authorized to proceed to Valcartier without the written consent of his wife."[23]

Valcartier, Quebec, had been chosen as the site for an enormous and hastily constructed camp where the volunteers would muster and train. In early September 37,000 of them prepared to travel there, and at train stations across the nation there were emotional scenes as people said their farewells. The camp was located on a plateau fifteen miles from Quebec City, and on arrival the men found tented accommodation and facilities sufficient to house all those who assembled there. After medicals and other formalities the conscripts, who would form the First Canadian Contingent, began their training. Among them were a high proportion of Britons who had emigrated to Canada prior to 1914, and a large number of outdoorsmen who were tough, physically fit, good shots with a rifle and very self-sufficient. As they were put through their paces feelings were buoyant, and there was widespread enthusiasm to get into the war as soon as possible. One among them later recalled that there was "not the vaguest thought" that they would not return to Canada.[24]

In Belgium and France, meanwhile, events were unfolding in dramatic fashion. The Germans had mounted a huge offensive involving some 800,000 troops based on a plan devised by Field Marshal Alfred von Schlieffen, a former Chief of the German General Staff. It involved a rapid attack through Belgium and northern France in a wheeling movement that would pass around and behind Paris and was intended to take and defeat French forces from the rear before Russia had completed her mobilization. "No one really

Off to Valcartier. In the early evening of 22 August 1914, men from the Royal Grenadiers, a Toronto militia unit, march through the streets to board a train bound for Quebec City and Valcartier camp. As members of the newly-formed Canadian Expeditionary Force, they are being given a rousing send-off by friends, family and supporters. (Library and Archives Canada, PA-005122)

expects that the Germans will be able to get as far as Paris," Elizabeth Montizambert reported to her *Montreal Gazette* readers on 28 August 1914, but a month later enemy troops had advanced to within nearly twenty-five miles of the city. Many Parisians left for safer quarters, and those who had decided to remain gathered anxiously in cafés to discuss the situation. As she walked the largely empty city streets, Elizabeth found there was a beauty in the "strange, silent, deserted spaces shimmering in the warm sunshine" of those tense, late September days of waiting and wondering.[25]

Fortunately, determined opposition from the French and the men of the small but highly professional British Expeditionary Force succeeded in stalling the German advance and their forces withdrew to a defensive position along the River Aisne. After this unsuccessful first phrase in their plan the German high command switched their main attack to French and Belgian ports on the English Channel coast that were vital to the Allied chain of communication and supply. At the front line, given the lethality of the weapons being used and the high casualty rates being sustained by both sides, troops began to dig trenches for shelter and protection. The result was the creation of a trench line that stretched from the English Channel to the Swiss border, and the beginning of a mode of warfare that would forever be associated with the First World War.

As people in Canada started to understand more about the nature of the fighting in Europe, they also began to question "how long a war could last in this industrial age."[26] This was a thought that preoccupied Grace Morris of Pembroke, Ontario, daughter of an engineer and a thoughtful, intelligent young woman. She grasped the fact that the scientific and technical developments of the past decades had made it possible to create powerful and dangerous new weapons that were wreaking havoc on the armies fighting in Europe. The age that had produced the internal combustion engine, trains, battleships, airplanes, industrial manufacturing of metals and machinery, and speedier communication by telegraph and telephone, had also created the potential for huge destructive power. As for the opposing forces, Germany was one of the most advanced industrialized countries in the world, France was highly militarized, Russia had vast manpower and Britain possessed a mighty navy and the resolution to do all that was necessary to protect her people and her empire. The German chancellor, Theobald von Bethmann-Hollweg, had warned the country's ruler, Kaiser Wilhelm II, that even though Germany was most efficient at waging war and a leader in tactical innovation, it would be a long and exhaustive struggle. All in all, the prospects were chilling.

Novelist Lucy Maud Montgomery was among those closely following the progress of hostilities. She was under no illusions about the implications and believed that the war would be "no paltry struggle in an out-of-the-way corner … but a death grapple" that was destined to be "awful beyond anything ever known in the world before."[27] In London, Lady Ottoline Morrell, a British aristocrat and pacifist, also foresaw "the horror of what it meant" and was deeply concerned that the conflict would bring about a changed world in which "poverty, want, suffering, chaos" would overtake all that had gone before.[28] In Madison, Wisconsin, Julia Grace Wales, a young Canadian academic at the state university, was so worried that she began to consider how the conflict might be settled, not by military means but by discussion and mediation.

For the Canadian troops at Valcartier, however, there was little time for reflection. They were working hard to prepare for war, but nothing could prepare them or any of the Allied armies for what they would face in this new, industrialized conflict. One historian has left a telling image of Canada a few years before 1914, likening the young nation to "a happy child swinging a five-cent scribbler in one hand and a shiny new pencil-box in the other on the way to the first day of school."[29] Not yet fifty years old when the First World War began, Canada was nevertheless eager to play its part.

The country was prospering by world standards. An economic policy aimed at increasing investment in the Canadian economy, a positive attitude towards business and a decline in freight rates had enabled it to enjoy the fruits of an industrial revolution. Exploitation of vast natural resources had brought the growth of new industries, the development of hydro-electric power and the formation of major new conglomerates. These assets, together with a substantial wave of immigration, seemed to underpin another statement by Sir Wilfrid Laurier that "Canada shall build the twentieth [century]."[30]

Within this optimistic society, life for women, irrespective of their social class, remained largely concerned with marriage, motherhood and domesticity. However, by the last decade of the nineteenth century a new woman began to emerge – independent, self-supporting, and mostly to be found in the upper echelons of society where upbringing and financial resources opened the way to greater freedom. At the same time, improved education was widening the scope of employment generally. Female paid labour was on the increase, and many women were attracted to the shorter hours and better wages offered by commercial companies, manufacturers, businesses, and the retail sector. Those in a position to pursue a professional qualification in fields such as teaching or nursing found it was increasingly regarded as an important step towards the kind of independence that a growing number of young women were seeking.

As workers (mostly men) attempted to organize themselves and call for better employment conditions across the industrialized world, women began to channel their efforts into the struggle for basic rights – especially the right to vote. They lent their support to feminists campaigning internationally and to organizations that could help them extend their position and influence in society. In Canada these included the National Council of Women, the Dominion Women's Enfranchisement Association and the Young Women's Christian Association.[31] Canadian writer and reformer Nellie McClung, "with her gift for oratory, her energy and her delightful sense of humour," was a well-known voice for the women's suffrage movement.[32] In Quebec the battle was harder and more protracted than in English-speaking Canada, but French-Canadian women also began to actively support desired reforms through institutions such as the National Council of Women.[33]

In 1914, as Canada began to mount its war effort on the home front, women were poised to make a substantial contribution through voluntary organizations, and by helping to fill the wartime labour shortage caused by men serving overseas. As the war progressed, they were to be found on farms, in offices and at factories involved in industrial production and munitions. One group in particular knew that while there was work to be done at home, there would be great need of their skills overseas. The country's nurses expected that they would form a part of Canada's war effort and that medical assistance would be of vital importance. Sir Edward Kemp, Canada's Minister of Overseas Military Forces, believed that it was "impossible to divorce the Medical Services from the rest of the military machine." In terms of nursing, the existing Canadian Army Medical Corps (CAMC) included qualified staff to cover the needs of local militia regiments in each province. They participated in summer training camps, but with the exception of twelve Canadian nurses who had served in the South African War, the CAMC was "essentially untried in actual warfare." That small number, which included two very experienced nurses, Margaret Macdonald from Nova Scotia and Georgina Pope from Prince Edward Island, had been appointed to the CAMC with the special rank of "nursing sister."[34] When the First World War broke out there were still only five nurses (one matron and four sisters) in the permanent force and a further fifty-seven nurses in a reserve force made up of suitably qualified civilian staff. Some of them had attended a course of instruction in military nursing, and all worked to rules and regulations based on those governing the British military nursing service.

On 17 August 1914, Margaret Macdonald was appointed Matron-in-Chief to take charge of Canada's wartime nursing service, and was immediately inundated with letters from nurses at hospitals and training schools across Canada and the United States. Macdonald's mandate was to mobilize women who were members of the Army Medical Corps reserve and those whose civilian qualifications and experience were deemed most suitable. Applicants were expected to be serious, not just about their work but also about serving overseas, and to fulfill other criteria. They had to be between the ages of twenty-one and thirty-eight, British subjects, graduates of a recognized nursing training programme, physically fit and able to display dignified deportment and first-class moral character. The standard of those who applied was high, perhaps not surprisingly given that according to one history of the war, nursing in Canada was already attracting committed young women "of birth and education who had too much independence of character and self respect to waste their lives in the social merry-go-round."[35]

According to plans, several medical units would accompany the first contingent of Canadian troops going overseas from Valcartier, together with a nursing staff of some one hundred sisters.[36] On 16 September 1914 the order to mobilize the successful nursing applicants was received, and each was sent a telegram with orders to report a week later at Quebec City. The nurses were billeted at an immigration hospital with somewhat basic accommodation that consisted of wire bunks in "a huge draughty space." In addition, the hospital's location on the main road to Valcartier meant that the noise of "artillery wagons or marching troops" passing by often interrupted sleep during the night. It was an introduction to the less than ideal conditions of military life that these women could expect to encounter in the future.[37]

For the first time since nursing had been organized as a profession in Canada, the nurses selected were officially enrolled in the CAMC. Among them were Mabel Clint from Quebec City, Florence Hunter from Orono, Ontario, Katharine Wilson from Chatsworth, Ontario, and Clare Gass from Shubenacadie, Nova Scotia, all of whom documented their time at Quebec. The new arrivals underwent a medical examination, completed the necessary paperwork and became acquainted with military procedures and parlance. As they mixed with other nurses from across Canada, Mabel Clint saw that "the lure of adventure was uppermost in the minds of some" while "experience and mass-action appealed to others." But above and beyond individual reasons for volunteering, she believed the overriding factors common to most, were patriotism and "a chance to serve."[38] The desire to be a part of their country's war effort overseas was, for many, likely to be bound up in notions of honour, loyalty, and support of Canada's forces and the British Empire.

Quebec City itself was new to many of the women, and its striking position overlooking the St. Lawrence River proved memorable, especially at dusk when "the last lights in the sky made a scene like fairyland," noted Clare Gass.[39] During the day all was hustle and bustle as uniforms and equipment were amassed, travel trunks were procured, kit bags made ready and instructions given and often countermanded. Florence Hunter managed to find time for some shopping and a visit to the city's famous Chateau Frontenac hotel with its views over the river and surrounding countryside. "Had tea with Major Bennett, Captains Greer, Jones at Chateau," she wrote in her diary.[40] Florence and her officer companions enjoyed the pleasant pastime of a formal tea on the hotel terrace consisting of "scones with jam and whipped cream, followed by cake-fingers and puff-pastries with good English-brew tea." One soldier described it as "a most popular rendezvous; at every table, drab khaki alternates with pretty, summery, floor-length dresses

The Château Frontenac. Overlooking the St. Lawrence at Quebec City, the Château Frontenac (today Fairmont Le Château Frontenac) was one of the first grand hotels built by the Canadian Pacific Railway. The photograph, taken soon after its completion, shows the original main building and the Dufferin Terrace. The central tower, a distinguishing feature today, was completed in 1924. (Courtesy AccorHotels)

surmounted by wide-brimmed, soft straw hats adorned with gay ribbons or artificial flowers."[41]

"Rumours, excursions and alarums kept us agog during the last days of September," remembered Mabel Clint, and as departure time approached the nurses witnessed a continuous procession of men from Valcartier who, having completed their training, were being moved to ships waiting at anchor in the St. Lawrence to transport them to Europe. Thirty-three vessels had been procured for the purpose, and such a large convoy made a deep impression on troops and civilians alike. One woman, moved by the sight of newly-minted soldiers going off to war, described the "sea of brave, earnest young faces, with their khaki uniforms." She offered up the hope and prayer that "God bless the dear boys. May every one of them come back to Canada! Vain, futile hope!"[42]

After the embarkation of men, horses, artillery and supplies was completed, on 1 October 1914 it was the turn of the nurses. They were travelling with Matron-in-Chief Margaret Macdonald on the *Franconia*, flagship of the convoy, and the women were cheered aboard by the men of the 90th Winnipeg Rifles who would be sharing the journey with them. A number of other women were also going with the contingent, including the wives of several

Going overseas. The nursing sisters selected to join the Canadian Army Medical Corps in 1914 travelled to Britain with the First Canadian Contingent aboard the SS *Franconia*. In this photograph taken by Colonel Lamb of 1st Canadian Division, a number of them can be seen mingling on the boat deck. (Library and Archives Canada, PA-005561)

officers of the Princess Patricia's Canadian Light Infantry (PPCLI), a new regiment raised by millionaire Andrew Hamilton Gault of Montreal. They were joined by two others, Mary Plummer and Joan Arnoldi of the Canadian Field Comforts Commission (see Chapter 8), who were tasked with setting up and running the organization's British depot. When loading was completed, the ships weighed anchor one by one and began to move down the St. Lawrence towards Gaspé Bay. Among the many onlookers was Lady Julia Drummond of Montreal, whose son, Lieutenant Guy Drummond, was going overseas as an officer with the 13th Battalion, Royal Highlanders of Canada. Julia very much wished she was travelling with the departing troops, for

> truly the thought and wish were in my heart as I stood on the shore at Quebec to see the First Canadian Contingent sail away ... I think many of the wives and mothers who waved "Farewell" from the shore, forcing the brave semblance of a smile, must have had the longing to go too, so that they might be near their men in the hour of trial, so that they might mother not only their own but all who were destined to suffer in the Great War.[43]

The following day, 2 October, was one of those beautiful Canadian autumn days, with "the surrounding hills and woods forming a background of brilliant colour" and "a warm purple haze hanging over the ships."[44] As the con-

voy reached Gaspé Bay, the sight of all the vessels with their Red Ensigns* flut-
tering and the sound of bugle calls ringing out across the calm water, contributed to making it "a never to be forgotten event in the lives" of those who were
there.[45] Last letters to loved ones were written and sent ashore, among them
a note from Guy Drummond to his "dearest Mother" in which he told her,
"I know I'll see you in England if you can square it with your conscience."[46]
On 3 October 1914, with final preparations completed, one ship after another
headed out into the Atlantic leaving "a golden sunset sinking behind them."
The great expedition was finally on the move.[47]

At home in Pembroke, Ontario, engineer's daughter Grace Morris thought
of her brother, Ramsey, who was somewhere in that great armada. "To most
Canadians" she wrote, "it was a proud moment, for we were now taking part
in the defence of the Empire."[48] Ottawa socialite Ethel Chadwick, who had
returned from her summer break at Blue Sea Lake, could not help wondering whether "some of these soldiers as they sailed out of the St. Lawrence
... would ever see it and Canada's shores" again. "I hope they do," she said,
thinking of those she knew personally. Having decided to volunteer with the
Canadian Red Cross she busied herself cutting out garments for the soldiers
and knitting socks which, she admitted, was "my first real attempt in years
on four needles."[49]

As the First Contingent crossed the Atlantic, conditions were cramped
but the men tolerated overcrowding, poor ventilation and seasickness, and
managed to enjoy card games, songs around the piano and complaining
about the food. Aboard the RMS *Royal Edward*, the PPCLI officers' wives
whiled away the days and accompanied their husbands to dinner each evening to the sound of bagpipes. Not all the officers approved of their presence,
and a certain captain decided firmly that "women are a mistake aboard a
troopship." He described one wife, a Mrs. McKinery, as having "a very limited range of conversation," while another, a Mrs. Colquhoun, was "full of
views for the betterment of mankind and future generations, most of them
unworkable in Men's hands." As for Marguerite Gault, wife of the regiment's
founder, he thought she was "very nice generally, she has just missed being
quite pretty, sings a bit."[50]

Having been diverted from its original destination of Southampton due
to rumours of a German submarine in the English Channel, the Canadian
convoy was directed to the port of Plymouth, Devon. Its sudden appearance

---

* The Red Ensign flag was the Canadian national standard from the late nineteenth century until 1965,
when it was replaced by the current flag.

Arriving at Plymouth. As the ships carrying the 33,000-strong Canadian Expeditionary Force to Britain arrived at Plymouth on 14 October 1914, they were greeted
warmly by enthusiastic crowds. Taken from the shore, this photograph shows some
of the transports in what was the largest troop movement by sea up to that time.
(Library and Archives Canada, PA-022708)

early on 14 October 1914 was a surprise to the local people but large crowds
soon gathered to welcome the Canadians with cheers, sirens, hooters, bagpipes and a band playing "The Maple Leaf Forever." It was a "magnificent
spectacle" reported the *Times* newspaper, and as the Canadians began disem-
barking one journalist remarked on their appearance of "strength and rude
health" and their independent attitude. They quickly "became the talk of the
country," and the same journalist was certain that "men here can never forget
the coming of the men of Canada. They have lit an Imperial beacon in the
land which will not now go out."[51]

The Canadians had arrived in a country where the sound of artillery in
France, often heard in the towns, villages and fields of the southeastern coun-
ties, was a stark reminder of the battlefields in France and Belgium. As in
many wars, there was an energy and an urgency to life in Britain which kept
it moving at an intense rate, especially in those early months of the conflict.
With the sacrifice of men killed and missing in action, longer working hours,
the prospect of shortages of food and other essentials, and the palpable sense
that tough, uncertain times lay ahead, people came together to support one
another.

Women demonstrated their willingness to contribute to the war effort on
the home front through voluntary work and by taking over jobs previously

done by men, even though many of them had little or no training and experience in the kind of employment they might be asked to cover. A huge effort was also under way to help Belgian refugees who had fled the advancing
Germans, and by early October 200,000 of them had arrived in Britain. They
were welcomed and housed, and those who ended up at the town of Torquay,
Devon, unwittingly proved inspirational to a certain volunteer nurse helping
at the local hospital. Agatha Christie was the nurse in question and she created her famous character Hercule Poirot, the Belgian detective who was to
solve so many crimes in her future books.[52]

At Oxford, another city that welcomed the Belgians, support was organized by a number of volunteers among whom was Lady Grace Osler, wife of
the university's Regius Professor of Medicine, Sir William Osler. The Canadian doctor, one of the most revered members of his profession, was at the
forefront of medical work and was an indefatigable member of the British
Medical Association's War Emergency Committee. Grace Osler arranged assistance for those arriving from Belgium and ran a workroom to make hospital garments. Both felt deeply the tragedy of this new war in which they
were already hearing of "friends being mown down" along with "all the youth
and glory of the country, the young men we have known." Both were also in
agreement that "work is the only salvation."[53]

The main body of the Canadian contingent that had disembarked at Plymouth was transported by train to Salisbury Plain in southern England,
where the troops would spend the autumn and early winter undergoing further training. Of the medical staff, the nurses were taken to London's St.
Thomas's Hospital, where they were accommodated and escorted on visits
to other medical units. While they waited to be posted to Salisbury Plain, or
temporarily to British hospitals, the Canadian women enjoyed the opportunity to explore the city and visit some of its famous landmarks.

London in October 1914 was a very different place from a year earlier,
when one account described it as the "gayest, richest and largest capital in
the world." There had been an aura of power and excitement about the place
as a centre of international commerce, politics and diplomacy and a focus of
literary, artistic and social activity.[54] After 4 August 1914, however, it was as if,
according to one British officer, all that had made London great and glamorous was suddenly obscured beneath the "nightmare cloud" of war.[55] On the
streets, the flags of the Allies could be seen in shop windows, over doorways
and on cars. Recruiting posters covered hoardings and shop windows, and
nearly all taxi cabs carried notices calling for men to volunteer at newly-
opened recruitment offices. Parks were taken over to assemble transport

for military use and as camps and drilling areas for soldiers. One woman described how "you had to be careful in walking across the open space by Marble Arch, or you suddenly found yourself up against a solid wall of Kitchener's Army." *[56]

As they explored the city, the Canadian nurses could not help but notice that "London was in uniform." They themselves attracted attention in their outfits, which consisted of a light blue cotton dress with two rows of brass buttons down the front and shoulder epaulettes fitted with two stars denoting their military rank of lieutenant.[57] There was also a white fitted apron, a leather belt with two brass buckles and a sheer white veil worn on the head so that the back hung down over the shoulders. A navy blue dress uniform, complete with matching hat, a long navy military-style coat, and a navy cape lined with scarlet, completed the ensemble. Thus attired, the smart-looking nurses from Canada were the envy of their British counterparts in the Queen Alexandra's Imperial Military Nursing Service (QAIMNS), who did not hold commissioned rank and whose grey uniforms looked subdued by comparison.

Journalist Beatrice Nasmyth noticed her fellow countrymen and countrywomen in uniform and concluded that the Canadian soldiers she saw in London were "a little bit taller and straighter and more efficient than any of the other thousands of uniformed figures which throng the streets."[58] She described the long lines of men of different nationalities marching to the sound of popular and patriotic songs and the khaki-painted motor buses with large red crosses painted on them, preparing to help transport the wounded from France. Beatrice felt that few of the civilians who seemed to go calmly about their business had yet realized "the depths of the devastation" those buses would later represent.[59]

It was after dark that London's thoroughfares were the most noticeably transformed. Prior to the war, Britain's capital had always come alive at night and its theatres, music halls and restaurants had provided many an evening of gaiety and enjoyment. Now, with the imposition of a black-out, shops had to obscure their outside lights, neon signs were turned off, street lamps were dimmed and tramcars travelled unlit. Such measures were deemed vital to public safety as the Germans had developed Zeppelin airships capable of reaching and bombing parts of southern and eastern England.[60] One Canadian airman who visited London remarked that in the evening at street

---

* "Kitchener's Army" referred to the all-volunteer army formed in the United Kingdom from the outbreak of the First World War onwards. It took its name from Field Marshal Herbert Kitchener, a senior British Army officer who was appointed Secretary of State for War in 1914.

level, the city was "so dark I could hardly see anything," and "all blinds must be kept shut … under penalty of a fine."[61] By early September 1914 dozens of searchlights began sweeping the sky every night for any sign of enemy air activity, and many citizens made their own preparations for raids that, alas, were only a matter of months away.[62]

As October 1914 progressed, news from the war front told of a fierce battle taking place in Belgium. The Germans had seized the port of Antwerp and fighting was now raging "from Ostend to Lille." One British nurse working on an ambulance train sent to evacuate casualties described how many of them were "dangerously and seriously wounded" and "bleeding faster than we could cope with it." The "'carnage' is appalling," she recorded, and it was only after an "absolute hell of a journey" that her train finally reached Boulogne.[63] Reports arrived of the fall of Antwerp, of British troops having retreated to the medieval city of Ypres in Flanders, of villages and churches "a blaze of fire against an inky sky" and "the continuous flash and vicious crack of shrapnel overhead" as fighting continued and the first enemy shells started to hit Ypres.[64] In London long queues of women waited outside the War Office at all hours hoping for news of their loved ones, while the realization that the conflict was dispensing death and destruction "undreamed of among the rank and file" was now touching civilians and war workers alike.[65]

Early in November the first of the Canadian nurses to be posted to France prepared for departure. A number of them were due to join No. 2 Can-

Louvain in ruins. As German troops crossed Belgium in 1914, they inflicted damage on Belgian cities and communities in their path. The old university city of Louvain, with its world-famous library, suffered severely as this image shows. (Library of Congress)

Raising funds for the war. At one of countless fund-raising events held across the country, women from Montreal's "Square Mile" gathered in the early months of the war for a bridge party at Ravenscrag, the home of Sir Montagu and Lady Marguerite Allan. Within the year, Lady Allan had sailed for England to help set up and run a convalescent home for Canadian officers. (Notman Photographic Archives, McCord Museum, Montreal, VIEW 14013)

adian Stationary Hospital,* which was transferring from Salisbury Plain with a clear sense of what its staff were likely to face. The remaining medical units and nurses would continue to provide care for the Canadian troops on the Plain, who were not due to complete their training for a further three months and were having to endure extremely wet, miserable conditions.[66]

Back home in Canada, more women had been making plans to go overseas. Some undoubtedly wanted closer involvement with what was going on in Europe, while others were anxious to be nearer relatives and their menfolk on active service. There were also those who felt they had a definite plan, calling or mission to fulfill as part of the war effort, and who were in a position to make their own individual contributions. Sea travel was the only way to

---

* See Chapter 2 for further information on Canadian medical units.

cross the Atlantic and before the First World War the cost meant that it was mainly the prerogative of the wealthy. The conflict opened up more opportunities in this respect, and with transatlantic liners still sailing to British and French ports in the latter months of 1914, a steady stream of wives, mothers, sisters and daughters left Canada for Europe.

On 17 December 1914 Britain was made painfully aware that it was now part of the war zone when a force of German cruisers bombarded the northeast coast towns of Scarborough, Whitby and West Hartlepool, killing over a hundred civilians, including children. As people adjusted to the reality of the German menace reaching their shores, a British housewife who recorded her comments on the war remarked that "it is horrible to think such things can take place in these enlightened (?) days."[67] The attack heralded a very different Christmas from those celebrated in peacetime, especially with many loved ones putting their lives on the line at the war front. "With all the horrors of war, no one could feel 'Christmassy,'" declared the same housewife as she struggled through a holiday season in which few people "wanted to be merry."[68] New Year's Eve was a subdued affair, as one officer discovered when he made his way to London's Piccadilly Circus on a "glorious night," with a full moon "brightly white." As twelve o'clock struck, instead of the usual celebrations there was only "a little shudder among the crowd and a distant muffled cheer" to mark the moment.[69]

In Canada thoughts turned inevitably to those serving overseas, and to what 1915 held in store. At her home Ottawa socialite Ethel Chadwick pondered sadly the events of the past few months, while Lucy Maud Montgomery reflected on the fact that the old year "which rose fairly has set in blood" and she dreaded what lay ahead – a time that she foresaw as "freighted with such awful possibilities."[70] So began another year of war in which, as Winston Churchill described it, "all the horrors of the ages" were being unleashed. In the allied countries, many may well have agreed with the sentiments of a poem published in the *Daily Telegraph* newspaper, and from which these lines are taken:

> *And the prayer that the Empire prays to-night –*
> *O Lord of our destiny! ...*
> *We have stood for peace, and we war for right;*
> *God give us victory!*[71]

CHAPTER 2

"How will it all end and what will become of us all?"

MEDICAL SERVICE – THE WESTERN FRONT AND ENGLAND, 1914-1915

How can we give enough – since they have died?
Since they have lived – shall we not greatly live
And know in life or death with holy pride
No wealth of service is too much to give?[1]

"I FEEL AS IF I HAVE STRAYED INTO A NEW WORLD":
THE WARTIME MEDICAL SYSTEM

The First World War, as the Reverend Albert Woods of Winnipeg told his wife during his time overseas, was a conflict in which "on the one hand it is science straining every nerve to accomplish man's destruction, on the other hand it is science working overtime to save his life."[2] The main European theatre of war, known as the Western Front, was opened in 1914 by the German invasion of Belgium and for almost the next four years the fighting that took place in that theatre was nearly static. Although both sides established their own trenches to provide protection from the devastating power of the new weapons being used, the unprecedented numbers of casualties meant that the military authorities had to develop an efficient system for evacuating and treating wounded men.

The first step in handling casualties began with the work of the medical officer of an army unit who was responsible for the health of his men in action and away from the front line. During an offensive a medical officer was usually to be found at his Regimental Aid Post (RAP) not far behind the front line, where stretcher bearers would bring casualties as soon as conditions allowed. They were then classified: the lightly wounded were treated and sent to the rear, and the more seriously wounded were divided into those expected to die, those who could be stabilized and evacuated for further treatment, and those who required additional attention before they could be moved. Efforts were made to keep all casualties warm with blankets and hot drinks and to ease their pain with morphine, since experience had proved that administering it early, "accompanied by quiet and warmth," was the most effective method of saving lives.[3]

Once evacuated from an RAP, the wounded entered successive stages of an established system of medical treatment. They were first taken to a Relay Point and then to an Advanced Dressing Station for further evaluation, and emergency surgery if required. After that they were transported by vehicle to a Casualty Clearing Station (CCS), located beyond the range of enemy artillery, where treatment was more elaborate and operations were carried out by surgeons. Medical personnel at an RAP or Advanced Dressing Station worked under the imperative of getting wounded men to a CCS as swiftly as possible. As the most significant stage of the evacuation system, the aim was to ensure that "there would be no need to disturb the patient again, on his journey."[4]

Only the most serious cases were kept for more than a few days at a CCS, the remainder being transferred by ambulance train or alternatively by river barge to base hospitals that were usually located on or near the English Channel coast. On reaching its destination a train or barge would be met by an ambulance convoy that took patients to hospital or, if necessary, directly to a ship bound for Britain, where advanced or specialist medical care was available. It was a system which the Reverend Alfred Woods likened to "an endless chain propelled by an unseen power; there is no confusion under the most severe stress. Every ounce of energy is used to the best advantage." In his opinion, no other part of the "vast complicated Military Machine" was "better organized, more efficiently managed, or has produced better results" than the Canadian Army Medical Corps.[5]

Canadian nurses were part of this "machine," from casualty clearing stations to hospitals and treatment centres in Britain. With few among them having undergone specific training in military nursing before enlisting, and fewer still having any experience of overseas service in wartime conditions, it is little wonder that it took time to adjust to such a different working environment. "I feel as if I have strayed into a new world," wrote Nursing Sister Sophie Hoerner on her arrival in Britain in May 1915, and it was a world that offered not only the fascination of foreign travel and the satisfaction of being able to serve king and country, but also nursing duties and experiences that would test her and all her colleagues to the utmost.[6]

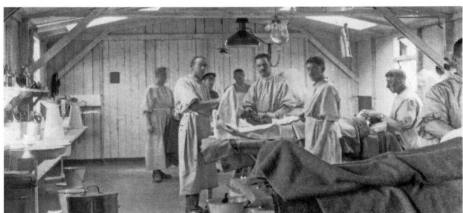

Treating the wounded. The chain of evacuation for wounded men on the Western Front involved several stages, including an advanced dressing station, a casualty clearing station and, if necessary, transport by hospital train, or possibly barge, to hospitals near the north French coast. Those needing further treatment could be taken to England. These photographs show an advanced dressing station, an operating theatre at a casualty clearing station, and an ambulance train. (Library and Archives Canada, PA-000029, PA-000104, PA-000975)

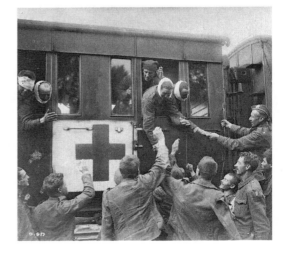

"SO DIFFERENT FROM A CIVIL HOSPITAL": WARTIME NURSING

Those women accepted by the nursing service of the CAMC became commissioned officers with the title of Nursing Sister. As such, it gave them a higher status than their counterparts in Britain's QAIMNS (Queen Alexandra's Imperial Military Nursing Service). Nurses from Canada could also apply to serve with the "QAs," as they were often known, and after newspapers published a request from the British government for additional nursing assistance from the dominions, the *Daily Telegraph* of Saint John commented that the opportunity "should no doubt satisfy the desires" of suitably qualified nurses who had not yet gone overseas and were keen to do so.[7] Applications from women who were twenty-five or over had to be made via the Royal Victoria Hospital, Montreal, and several hundred Canadians submitted their details. QAIMNS contracts were available for one year or for the duration of the war, with uniforms provided, but the successful applicants were responsible for their own travel costs.[8]

Canadians were also to be found with the USANC (United States Army Nurse Corps), the FFNC (French Flag Nursing Corps) and the Red Cross. Numerous women joined the latter and, as an example, Margaret MacFarlane from Alberta was the first nurse from her province to work with the organization in Malta and France. Those who enrolled with the USANC did so under the auspices of the American Red Cross and served with American hospitals and mobile units in Belgium and France.[9] The nurses who signed up with the FFNC were part of a collaborative effort between the French government and two prominent British nurses to recruit qualified women from Canada, Britain, Australia and New Zealand to work in French hospitals. In the latter half of 1914 about 250 nurses from Canada joined the FFNC, among whom were a group supervised by Helen McMurrich, a former instructor at Montreal General Hospital, who sailed from Saint John, New Brunswick, to join an FFNC unit in Belgium.[10]

What made a good nurse? In addition to her qualifications and general demeanour, she was expected to display adherence to military discipline, a high sense of duty, devotion to work and patients and absolute loyalty to the nursing service of which she was a member. Those without specific military nursing training were expected to adapt swiftly to wartime conditions and to a system in which the intake, treatment and release of patients was subject not only to their condition and needs but also to other war-related factors. Nurses had to be prepared to move locations, sometimes at short notice if help was urgently required elsewhere, and to work in new, unfamiliar and, at times, improvised surroundings. Other positive qualities are summarized in the following reference, written in 1916 for Nursing Sister Alice Isaacson of the CAMC: "Miss Isaacson is one of the very best nurses I have come across – not only is she thoroughly acquainted with every branch of her profession, skilful, energetic and reliable, but she is also possessed of great self reliance, initiative and organizing capacity."[11]

Over the next four and a half years, Canada's nurses proved themselves well able to face the demands of their work, which fell into two categories: medical and surgical. Medical work involved the treatment of illnesses and problems that resulted from the conditions in which the troops had to fight. These could include respiratory troubles, influenza, meningitis, gastro-intestinal complaints, exposure to poison gas, fevers of various sorts, and nervous exhaustion or what today would be termed post-traumatic stress disorder. The strain of battle, the constant noise of artillery fire and explosions, sleep deprivation for days on end and the combination of terrain and bad weather that many soldiers had to endure, all contributed to physical and mental problems. Solutions such as a bath, a meal and undisturbed rest could work wonders for some, but those severely affected required further treatment at specialist hospitals. The nature of combat in the First World War meant that challenges were constant, and as one historian has written, "only individual courage, endurance, a reward system, and an efficient medical apparatus could keep a fighting force from degenerating into a mob of madmen."[12]

Surgical work involved dealing with major and multiple wounds resulting from the weapons in use. Among these were explosive artillery shells, poison gas, flame throwers, mortars, machine guns and mines laid with charges. The physical damage was often horrific, and it was no surprise that one Canadian nurse later wrote, "I can never see anything worse and hope I'll never have to."[13] Treatment often required operations for a variety of reasons, including repairing damage, controlling bleeding, amputation of limbs or diseased areas of the body, and the removal of foreign bodies such as bullets, shrapnel or debris. Surgical treatment posed the greatest challenges due to the sheer number and nature of wounds sustained, and the possibility of further complications such as shock, hemorrhaging, infections and gangrene at a time before antibiotics were available. With so many potential problems and the constantly changing nature of life in a war zone, it was necessary to come to terms with "the chaos that accompanied the great machine of healing," and focus instead on creating "a semblance of order," efficiency and the best patient care achievable.[14]

Whether serving in France or England, there was vital work to be done, some of which involved finding new solutions to the kind of problems noted above. It is little wonder that urgent necessity led to new inventions such as the Thomas splint, introduced in 1916 on the Western front and originally designed some forty years earlier by British surgeon Hugh Owen Thomas. It reduced the rate of mortality from fractures, in particular fractures of the femur, from eighty to twenty per cent. Blood transfusions during the war refined techniques already in use, and the introduction of the Carrel-Dakin treatment helped to solve the problem of deep wounds contaminated with mud. French surgeon Alexis Carrel came up with a mechanism to irrigate this type of wound, which looked much like a modern intravenous drip, while British chemist Henry Dakin created the sterilizing solution used. The treatment dramatically reduced infection and the need for amputation, and was encouraging for both patients and medical staff alike.

Surviving diaries and letters written by nurses on overseas service give a sense of their lives on and off the hospital wards, and how they handled the challenge of wartime nursing. For many of them the idea of working in a war zone, and at times relatively close to the front line, would have been hard to imagine prior to 1914. Nor could they have foreseen the sheer numbers of casualties they would be treating or the nature of the suffering that had to be faced daily. Working in a military environment where "everything was bugle calls and red tape" felt "so different from a civil hospital," according to Sophie Hoerner, who had trained at Montreal General Hospital and had sixteen years' experience.[15] Some nurses apparently found the changes and new methods difficult to assimilate, and Lieutenant-Colonel John McCrae, Head of Medicine at No. 3 Canadian General Hospital (CGH), commented that "I find the nursing sisters hard to suit. They think everything should be right before anything can be done and some of them do not realize that things have to be done the best way one can, or even left undone."[16]

By the end of the war Canada's nurses would have served with medical units that included British casualty clearing stations, general and stationary hospitals, French military hospitals, the eight Canadian stationary hospitals and sixteen general hospitals located in France and England, and a number of other facilities. A general hospital had a basic capacity of 520 beds and could be extended to as many as 2,000 beds or more when required, while a stationary hospital could increase its 200-bed capacity to 650 beds or more – in 1918 one such unit extended to 1,090 beds.[17] In England, Canadian medical units were situated mainly in the southeast at centres on or within easy reach of the coast such as Brighton, Bramshott, Hastings, Eastbourne, Taplow and Orpington. A further eight specialist hospitals treated particular conditions such as injuries to the eyes, orthopedic problems, venereal disease and tuber-

Granville Hospital, Ramsgate. The Granville Hospital, a specialist orthopedic unit run by the CAMC, occupied this building on the Kent coast from September 1915 to October 1917 before moving to Buxton, Derbyshire. Today, it houses St. Lawrence College, a day and boarding school. (Photograph by Dianne Graves)

culosis. As examples, patients with orthopedic complications were handled by the Granville Special Hospital at Ramsgate, Kent, while those with tuberculosis were taken to a special centre not far away at Lenham.

There were also eight convalescent hospitals, one of which was at Bromley, north Kent, in a former hotel surrounded by pleasant gardens. Canadian soldier Jack Davey was one of its patients and wrote to a friend at home that it was "a fine place here & we get looked after alright." The townspeople took a considerable interest in the recuperating Canadians and one newspaper account mentions them being involved in local events such as a soccer match against the local police.[18] Other rehabilitation units included a sanatorium at Hastings in Sussex and units for other ranks at Sandgate and Walmer in Kent. As the war moved on, a Red Cross hospital opened further north at Buxton, Derbyshire, in the heart of picturesque countryside with "high moors" and "alternating valleys." It was an environment which, according to Nursing Sister Mabel Clint, provided an "entire and healthful change of scene for all."[19]

"STRANGE IN THIS NEW WORLD OF WAR": 1914

Although they faced many pressures, crises and at times, dangers, Canadian nursing sisters not only wanted to be part of the enormous task of caring for soldiers; they were also "anxious to serve in forward medical units" when the opportunity arose, and to experience what they regarded as "real war nursing."[20]

When the First World War began in August 1914, the majority of them were working in Canada but a few happened to be in Europe and were by chance the first on French soil after hostilities were announced. Mabel

Lindsay, a nurse from Montreal's Royal Victoria Hospital, was vacationing in Paris at the time while Agnes Warner, from Saint John, New Brunswick, chanced to be at the French resort town of Divonne-les-Bains, close to the Swiss border. She was working privately for an American family, and as church bells rang to mark the onset of hostilities she witnessed how "gardeners, porters, all classes of men stopped work immediately and rushed to the city hall," where mobilization of troops began.[21] "The awful war we have all been dreading is upon us," Agnes lamented in a letter to her mother, noting that within twenty-four hours, "five hundred men had gone, they know not where." She was "filled with admiration and respect" for the local people and began to do all she could to help them and their community, which she regarded as courageous and "remarkable."[22]

Of the Canadian nurses in Britain who arrived with the First Canadian Contingent, those posted to Salisbury Plain began their experience of field nursing in October 1914. Under the supervision of Acting Matron Myra Goodeve, No. 1 CGH was set up in marquees before acquiring more permanent premises. Throughout a wet, chilly autumn of troop training, the nurses handled mainly medical problems that included outbreaks of influenza, enteritis and cerebro-spinal meningitis. During their time off, they were able to visit local towns such as Salisbury or plan excursions to other places of interest. Among the hospital staff was Margaret Parks, one of a number of nurses from Saint John, New Brunswick, and a rarity inasmuch as she was also a qualified physician. As a graduate of Trinity College, University of Toronto, Margaret had worked as an anesthetist before the war but the gender barrier was still a considerable obstacle to women in the medical profession, who, it was thought, did not have "the stamina, mental or physical" to be doctors. Dr. Parks decided to set aside her professional work and volunteered for service as a nurse with the CAMC.[23] She remained with No. 1 CGH for the first two years of the war and was not the only Canadian woman doctor to choose this path: Dr. Margaret MacKenzie of Middle River, Nova Scotia, joined the CAMC nursing service in 1915.[24]

Among the first Canadian nurses to transfer to France with No. 2 Canadian Stationary Hospital (CSH) in November 1914 were Nursing Sisters Alexina Dussault from Montreal, Edith Hudson from Pictou, Nova Scotia, and Mabel Clint, who was fed up with "waiting around while there was so much to be done." Accompanied by Matron Ethel Ridley of Hamilton, Ontario, the group finally arrived in Boulogne but, after a further delay, Mabel's "impatience to be at work" reached its limit.[25] The inactivity ended when she and her colleagues were directed to the resort town of Le Touquet, some twenty-five miles distant, where the former Golf Hotel had been made available for the new hospital. On arrival, everyone worked hard to transform the building: they scrubbed it thoroughly from ceiling to floor, unpacked supplies, set up an operating theatre, prepared the wards and arranged a schedule of duties. Its purpose as a stationary hospital was to accept patients from casualty clearing stations who needed longer-term care or more extensive surgery. The daily routine would have been not unlike that described by a nurse attached to another similar hospital. The morning began with a bugle call at 6.45 A.M., followed by breakfast at 7.30 A.M. Dinner was at noon, tea at 4 P.M., supper at 6.P.M. and "lights out" was at 10.30 P.M.[26] As it prepared for its first intake of 200 patients in early December 1914, Edith Hudson hoped that No. 2 CSH, the nation's first hospital on the Western Front, would be seen as a worthy example of "Canadian efficiency" and organization.[27]

Nurses who served at Canadian medical units established over the next few years in France, lived and worked mainly at towns on or near the north French coast such as Le Touquet, Boulogne and Wimereux. They were also to be found at Étaples, Trouville and Le Tréport, at Rouen, Harfleur and Le Havre in the Normandy region, at Saint-Cloud and Troyes near Paris, and later in Dunkirk, close to the Belgian border. CAMC nurses could be sent to help at other Allied hospitals, as in the case of Nursing Sister Constance Bruce from Toronto, who was seconded from No. 2 CSH to No. 14 British Stationary Hospital (BSH) at Wimereux, an attractive coastal town close to Boulogne. No. 14 was also housed in a former hotel, the Grand, and the time she spent there formed part of her early impressions of working in the war zone.

At Wimereux Constance could not help reflecting on how much things had changed from a couple of months earlier when tourists must have

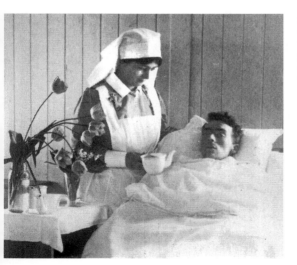

No. 2 Canadian General Hospital. One of the first Canadian medical units to cross to France in February 1915, this hospital was located at Le Tréport, on the north French coast. Here a nursing sister is giving a drink to a patient. (Library and Archives Canada, MIKAN 3607161)

"thronged the hotel, and bands played through the summer evenings!"[28] She was on duty when a large convoy of men arrived from the front, leaving the passageways and ground floor rooms of the hospital "literally strewn with wounded" whose uniforms were caked with mud and "stiff with blood." She noticed how many men slept with their heads covered as they had done in the trenches, fearful of "an imaginary enemy," and remembered how the faces of her patients at night were illuminated by searchlights that constantly swept "sea and sky." The appreciation shown by the men, no matter how seriously wounded, of even the smallest kindnesses touched Constance Bruce deeply.

Back at No. 2 CSH, the nursing staff were doing their best to demonstrate the high standard expected of CAMC nurses by their Matron-in-Chief, Margaret Macdonald. Her appointment as head of Canada's overseas nursing service was the first of its kind undertaken by a woman in the British Empire, and the local newspaper in her home town of Pictou, Nova Scotia, proudly informed its readers that Major Macdonald's "former experience will be of inestimable benefit to her in this war."[29]

From her London office Margaret Macdonald, who reported to the Director-General of Canadian Medical Services, set out in the autumn of 1914 to run a highly efficient and professional organization. In managing her nursing staff, her views and intentions were made abundantly clear. She was quick to comment on whatever displeased her, be it slackness in dealing speedily with official communications or any deviation from standards. She made a point of inspecting medical units in Britain and on the Western Front whenever possible. Hospital matrons were left in no doubt as to what she expected of them, as illustrated in the following instructions given to a nurse newly appointed to the position: "You will exercise the necessary discipline over all the Sisters under your charge; they must conform to the rules of the house, and you must see that they do not disregard these in any manner."[30]

While she may not have been present to see medical staff coping with convoys of wounded men or the intense pressure of work during and after an offensive, Margaret Macdonald concentrated on maintaining proper staffing levels and nursing standards and on supporting the health, welfare and efficiency of the women under her charge. She took pains to ensure they had decent, hygienic living conditions and supported the benefits of having a life away from the wards.

Given the social constraints of the time, British nurses were not permitted to dance with officers but Matron-in-Chief Macdonald steadfastly upheld the right for her Canadian nurses to do so. She seldom missed opportunities to promote the importance of nursing work, emphasizing that it was carried

The matron-in-chief at her desk. Major Margaret Macdonald, head of the Canadian nursing service, is seated at her desk and surrounded by members of her staff. From her London office she managed a complex and vital professional operation with characteristic efficiency and discipline. (Library and Archives Canada, MIKAN 3382663)

out "cheerfully, devotedly and willingly."[31] The high standard of nursing was undoubtedly a significant component in the success achieved by Canadian hospitals during the First World War, which achieved excellent results and low death rates.

As 1914 drew to a close, the Canadian nurses caring for the troops on Salisbury Plain were still seeing patients suffering from illnesses exacerbated by the difficult weather conditions. In addition, price increases, shortages of basic foods and other effects of wartime were impacting everyday life in Britain. London continued to be busy with troops, and the number of soldiers she saw prompted Canadian journalist Mary MacLeod Moore to describe it as "a khaki winter." Now that the flag-waving and ebullience of the summer of 1914 were past, most of the men she observed were "intent, quiet and efficient," whether new recruits or seasoned troops. When the time came for them to leave for France, they slipped away, she said, "without bands or flags or loud farewells," seen off from train stations by women who would "smile to the last and wave as the train pulls out."[32] What Mary witnessed strengthened her resolve to document events in the lives of Britain's civilians and to keep her readers as well informed as she could. Her Canadian colleagues, Beatrice Nasmyth and Elizabeth Montizambert, were of similar mind.

In the French town of Divonne-les-Bains Canadian nurse Agnes Warner continued to work for her American family, who would soon be returning to New York. In her spare time she had been helping at a local hospital set up by the Red Cross and had made up her mind that after completing her current job she would offer her services to France. As she told her mother, "I would be a coward and a deserter if I did not do all I could for these poor, brave people."[33]

By mid-December as she went about her duties, Agnes observed the local inhabitants preparing for their first wartime Christmas, a *Fête de Noël* unlike any other most of them could remember. In the north of the country at Le Touquet, the staff of No. 2 CSH were trying to do the same, as were the doctors and nurses on Salisbury Plain. The Canadian medical staff working far from home did all they could to make Christmas as cheerful as possible for their patients, while those lucky enough to get leave enjoyed time with colleagues, friends or relatives. Even though the war overshadowed everything, it was a welcome chance to step back from a reality that few could have envisaged six months earlier.

"HOW WILL IT ALL END, AND WHAT WILL BECOME OF US ALL?": 1915

In February 1915 the main body of Canadian troops in England completed their training and crossed to France. The medical staff followed, setting up No. 1 and No. 2 Canadian General Hospitals at the coastal towns of Étaples and Le Tréport respectively. A new Canadian base and training camp was established at Shorncliffe on the Kent coast, and Beatrice Nasmyth visited it to document the experiences of men on their way to the front. Among the camp's facilities, a disused barracks building was designated as a hospital even though it was "in bad repair, extremely dirty and most inconvenient" in layout. Much hard work was required to bring it to an acceptable standard and the task was allocated to the staff of No. 3 CSH, a new medical unit organized in London and posted to Shorncliffe from May to August 1915. The nursing staff under their matron, Jessie Jaggard, helped to transform the facilities into the Moore Barracks Hospital and to make it well equipped and efficient.[34]

That spring another Canadian stationary hospital, No. 1 CSH, was established near Wimereux "in a lovely spot, amidst hills" which in spring and early summer were a mass of colour with "bluebells and poppies vying with each other in richness of colour." This description was left by Constance Bruce, who joined the new unit from No. 14 BSH and loved the area. With its cottages and farms, undulating fields and attractive views, she appreciated the fact that "peace seems to reign everywhere."[35] Also joining the hospital staff was Nursing Sister Helen Fowlds from Hastings, Ontario, who was delighted to find there were several colleagues she already knew, including

Gateway to the Western Front. Watched by local citizens, men of the British 51st Highland Division march from the harbour into Boulogne. Such scenes were commonplace in 1914-1918 as were the convoys of ambulances bringing the wounded to ships waiting to transport them to England. (Library of Congress)

Constance. As she told her mother, among them were "Hunter and Blewett and Miss Squires [Squire] of Norwood, so you see I am well surrounded by friends … Also Miss Hammell and Miss Bruce of the T[oronto].G[eneral]. H[ospital]. And we have many friends in common." Helen also enjoyed the fact that Boulogne was nearby and she could get "a real English meal at the Folkestone Hotel a swell British place."[36] As for her patients, they were apparently "in one constant spasm of delight over their present comfort" and were "full of admiration" for "the generosity, cheerfulness, adaptability etc." of the Canadian medical staff.[37]

While the nurses at No. 1 CSH grappled with their workload, the inclement spring weather and Zeppelin scares, Easter was approaching and women in Boulogne gathered baskets of forget-me-nots, violets, pansies and other flowers to decorate the graves of Allied soldiers at the local cemetery. Constance Bruce was at a service there on Easter Sunday, attended by nurses, doctors, orderlies and convalescent patients. "What a memory for those who were present!" she wrote, recalling the hymns they sang and the fact that "all the crosses and flowers were covered in glistening raindrops" after a shower.[38]

In April 1915, two more hospital units from Canada were preparing to set off for France: No. 3 CGH, raised and staffed by doctors and medical students from Montreal's McGill University, and No. 4 CGH from the University of Toronto. Sophie Hoerner was joining No. 3 CGH as one of its senior nursing staff, and while waiting for the new unit to arrive she was posted temporarily to No. 2 CSH. It was her first experience of sleeping in a tent "with the moon and stars gazing at me," and the sight of "a lighthouse across the Bay twinkling every minute." As Sophie took stock of her surroundings, she knew that her decision to serve overseas was the right one. "I am so glad I am here," she wrote to a friend a few weeks later.[39]

The enjoyment of the coastal locale was shared by other nurses at No. 2 CSH, among them Wilhelmina Mowat from Brandon, Manitoba, who arrived at about the same time as Sophie Hoerner. However, there would be little time for reflection because on 22 April 1915 the Germans launched a major offensive against the Ypres Salient, a bulge in the Allied front line around the medieval Belgian city of Ypres. They deployed a terrible new weapon, poison gas, the use of which directly contravened the Hague Conventions of 1899 and 1907,* and Canadian troops helping to hold the line in the Salient were among the first to experience it. Two Canadian medical officers decided the gas was probably chlorine, and realizing the men had no protection against it other than what could be hastily improvised, Captain Francis Scrimger instructed them to "urinate on your pocket handkerchief [and] tie it over your mouth."[40] This emergency measure, which caused the chlorine to crystallize, saved many lives over the next few days.

Among the base hospitals placed on standby, the staff at No. 2 CSH received orders on 22 April to pitch extra marquees in front of their building and raise the unit's 300-bed capacity to 615. Nursing Sister Edith Hudson described how "everyone was called on duty," and as each ambulance arrived with casualties from what came to be known as the Second Battle of Ypres, word quickly spread of friends and colleagues killed or seriously wounded

---

* The Hague Conventions were treaties adopted at Peace Conferences held in The Hague, Netherlands, in 1899 and 1907. They were the first multilateral treaties that addressed the conduct of warfare, and they defined the rules that must be followed by belligerents during hostilities.

Devoted service. Sophie Hoerner (centre) served overseas with the CAMC from 1915 to 1919. She was assistant matron of No. 3 Canadian General Hospital for much of that time, and her surviving letters contain moving accounts of her work, her patients and her reactions to what she witnessed. (Library and Archives Canada, PA-006783)

in the fighting. The shock and anxiety was such that "we all fell silent," said Edith as they faced the gruelling work and heartache that lay ahead.[41]

Gas casualties from the battle were described by a nurse working in a Belgian hospital at Furnes, northwest of Ypres. "There they lay," she said, "fully sensible, choking, suffocating, dying in horrible agonies. We did what we could, but the best treatment for such cases had yet to be discovered, and we felt almost powerless."[42] Agnes Warner, who by now was planning to join the French Flag Nursing Corps, later on also handled many gassed patients. She described their ordeal as "the worst thing I have seen yet, much worse than the wounded," and felt that caring for them was "awfully hard, for they cannot be left a moment until they are out of danger."[43]

Chlorine gas damaged the respiratory system, skin and mucous membranes. As the lungs became swiftly congested, they "failed to take in oxygen and the victims suffocated as they drowned in their own fluids."[44] "This fiendish mode of warfare," as one nurse described it, was "without doubt the most awful form of scientific torture."[45] Immediate treatment was largely limited to "rest and oxygen," but it still involved intensive and exacting work.[46] Mabel Clint remembered one very bad case at No. 1 CSH of a man who for nearly two weeks "breathed only from oxygen cylinders" and had "two special nurses assigned for his care" who substituted "one tank for another without a break."[47]

As convoys of casualties arrived under cover of darkness to safeguard them from the enemy, nurses became accustomed to what one of them de-

In transit. Wounded men, having received treatment at various stages in the medical chain, might well require more specialized care. Such cases were taken by ship to England, and this photograph shows patients from No. 3 Canadian General Hospital being tended by nurses while awaiting evacuation. (From R. C. Fetherstonhaugh, ed., *No. 3 Canadian General Hospital (McGill), 1914-1919*)

scribed as "a ghastly enough procession," bearing in mind the state of many of the men on the stretchers.[48] When Nursing Sister Clare Gass was on temporary duty at No. 1 CGH, she never forgot the sound of the ambulances arriving. "I cannot go to sleep for hours," she recorded, "listening & thinking what it all means & of the condition of these poor lads."[49]

The use of gas and other new weapons seemed to be taking suffering to a new level. One medical officer treating wounded men from the Second Battle of Ypres commented that as far as he and his fellow doctors were concerned, "I must confess we needed all our training this morning ... The condition of the wounds was indescribable." The situation was not helped by the fact that with the heavily manured soil of the Belgian countryside those same wounds became "septic at once unless treated thoroughly."[50] Sophie Hoerner wrote movingly about the men she looked after, describing them as "so patient, and sweet to each other ... Some of the wounds are so dreadful that one's most vivid imagination couldn't even faintly picture them." She went on to explain that those caused by "bursting shrapnel are most severe," for "it rips, tears, lacerates and penetrates the tissues in a horrible manner. The doctor tries to repair and make good the best he can, but our best is often of little value." Sophie freely admitted that she had never seen "such courage and spunk" as that displayed by her brave, uncomplaining young patients, for whom she felt she "could never do enough."[51]

Within the limits of what was possible, the knowledge and ability that enabled medical staff to ease pain and make patients comfortable, was recognized. Adelaide Plumptre, a prominent member of the Canadian Red Cross Society, believed it meant a very great deal to be in a position to "relieve human suffering which at the present time is greater than ever before in the world's history." This statement was borne out by the first intake of patients at No. 3 CGH when it opened its doors at Dannes-Camiers, just north of Étaples, in August 1915. They told the nurses that as far as they were concerned, it was "like coming from hell to heaven."[52]

In England, meanwhile, Canadian nurses were also seeing wounded men whose condition required their best nursing skills. Bertha Forsey from Newfoundland, who was with the QAIMNS at Catterick Military Hospital in Yorkshire, described how she assisted in the operating room, treated German prisoners-of-war and cared for a continuous stream of young men "broken in body and spirit."[53] Further south, Nursing Sister Laura Holland, recently arrived from Vancouver, was beginning her overseas nursing at the Duchess of Connaught's Canadian Red Cross Hospital at Taplow, Buckinghamshire. It was situated on the estate of American millionaire Waldorf Astor and his wife, Nancy, and was a popular posting that another Canadian, Anne E. Ross, described as "the happiest I spent overseas."[54] Laura Holland was still adjusting to the nature of wartime nursing with its peaks and troughs in numbers of patients, its changing schedules and the welcome "in-between" periods when the work quietened down. Typical was the day when royalty were visiting and Laura found herself in the midst of frantic activity as a new intake of 200 wounded soldiers arrived. All of them had to be bathed and put to bed in double-quick time before King George V and Queen Mary arrived, both of whom were, according to Laura, "awfully nice to the men."[55]

Canadian nurses at medical units in England, where conditions were regarded as easier than in France, generally believed themselves to be fortunate even though they had to contend with the risk of air attacks by German airships and aircraft, which began in 1915. These took place mainly in the east and southeast of the country, areas within range of German air bases in Belgium. Raids on Tyneside and East Anglia were launched in the spring of 1915 while Londoners' first experiences of a Zeppelin bombing raid took place on 31 May and 1 June 1915. Further attacks ensued, both on the British capital and on other locations not always of military importance. This airborne violence had a shocking impact on ordinary British people, who realized their vulnerability to the new danger and the fact that the enemy was deliberately targeting their towns and cities. The civilian population was anxious, and one Canadian officer visiting the south coast resort of Brighton reported that "the people seem to spend their time mainly in being afraid of Zeppelins."[56]

Whatever the challenges of working overseas in wartime, Canadian women were proving they could handle the demands put upon them. When Nursing Sister Katherine Wilson arrived in France to join No. 1 CGH, she was immediately ordered to go on duty as a night supervisor. This was a daunting prospect given that the hospital had nearly doubled its original capacity of 520 beds to 1,000. Necessity, however, meant that Katharine had to very quickly learn "the lay of the land."[57] In Flanders, meanwhile, QAIMNS nurse Maysie Parsons wrote to her father in Newfoundland that she was working within six miles of the trenches near Ypres and that "we can hear the guns and see the flashes" every one of which "means so many deaths."[58]

Some Canadians were tackling nursing duties in a rather different environment, among them Mabel Joice from Cobourg, Ontario. She had chosen to apply to the FFNC, and in the summer of 1915 she was attached to a French military hospital near Bordeaux, on the Atlantic coast. Mabel had fulfilled the FFNC requirements that, in addition to her professional qualifications, she had to be a minimum of twenty-eight years of age with a good knowledge of French. She was feeling her way in her new work and discovering that while some things were different from what she was accustomed to, others clearly transcended language and nationality. "We have many touching scenes in connection with our work here," she wrote to her local newspaper in Cobourg, explaining that one of her patients was a young Belgian soldier who was about to return to the trenches "for the fourth time." She felt deeply for him, knowing that "his brothers have been killed in the war. His home has been destroyed, and his people captured by the Germans … He is so very sad, it makes one's heart ache."[59]

When she finally had some free time, Mabel travelled to meet Canadian colleagues serving at the base hospitals in the north of the country. "They tried to make quite a heroine of me," she said modestly, on account of the fact that "I had been all to-gether with foreign people for so long." However, having joined the FFNC, Mabel had little choice in the matter for it was "a case of *'parlez-vous français'* or nothing."[60] There were inevitably times when she felt rather alone, and that sense of separation was also shared by Mary Burns, a Canadian nurse with the QAIMNS who was posted to No. 5 British General Hospital (BGH) at Rouen. Mary confessed that "sometimes we long for our own people. We seem so isolated … scattered in two's around the different hospitals."[61] Mabel Joice may well have sympathized with such feelings, but she believed that the need to be of service was more important than personal considerations. "War time is not the time to think of being lonely," she said, "so I will have to dismiss it from my mind." Besides which, Mabel had to admit that there was "always something happening, even in our busiest days, to make us laugh."[62] From the French perspective, it seems that the Canadian nursing sisters more than won their spurs through their dedication and the high standard of their work. "Their well directed energy" and "self-sacrifice," wrote one doctor, "never wavered."[63]

In September 1915 hospitals in northern France were alerted to expect higher numbers of casualties, and on 25 September the British launched an offensive at Loos, not far from the French city of Lille. It marked their first use of poison gas, much of which unfortunately blew back over their own lines. This and another new weapon, the flamethrower, which inflicted horrible wounds, meant that 1915 was producing a level of casualties beyond anything previously envisaged. Wounded men from the battle told the nurses caring for them that "the slaughter is terrible," further proof that in spite of some Allied gains, the overall cost in lives was very high.[64]

Once the autumn settled in, the weather began to create problems for the Allied hospitals in France, especially those which were housed in tents and marquees. Equinoctial gales were so violent that rain burst through the flimsy structures and soaked the beds. Nurses dressed for the elements and at No. 3 CGH Sophie Hoerner described how she wore "rubberboots, and my skirts pinned up to my knees, three sweaters on and rain-coat and hat."[65] On several occasions the tents were flattened by the wind and on 26 October 1915 a storm along the north French coast created havoc. The matron of No. 3, Katherine MacLatchy, recorded that she "nearly blew out of bed last night" and leaking hospital tents led to "pools of water all over the camp."[66] Clare Gass described how many of the wards proved unsafe and patients had to be moved – no easy job over muddy ground. Everything became "sodden with rain" and nurses on night duty had to struggle from one marquee to another in the dark, often tripping over guy ropes and ending up covered in mud.[67] When Nursing Sisters Willett and Wilson came off duty at No. 1 CGH late one evening and returned to their sleeping quarters, they awoke later that night to find cold air swirling around them. The guy ropes of their tent had given way on one side but judging by the screams and laughter they heard nearby, the same thing was happening to their neighbours. At that moment, "away went the tent pole, and we were buried under a sheet of clammy wet canvas," recalled Katherine Wilson.[68] Yet in spite of the bad weather, nurses also remembered the good times when mornings were clear and sunny and there were "breathtaking" views of the coastline, the deserted sand dunes and fishing smacks out at sea.[69]

As time went on, life away from the wards became ever more important and the simple pleasure of some quiet time by the sea or in the country took on a therapeutic quality. "Went down on the shore with Ruth to see the sunset," wrote Clare Gass, who shared a love of walking and cycling with her friend and colleague Ruth Loggie.[70] Being somewhere tranquil and unspoilt made it "hard to realize that not far from us is fierce fighting," wrote Sophie Hoerner, who also treasured her coastal walks.[71] Clare Gass, Ruth Loggie and Sophie Hoerner, along with the other medical staff at No. 3 CGH, were fortunate to be in an attractive area where forays into the countryside were a delight. During their wanderings, they discovered a quiet wooded valley with a stream which was known to the local people as the Vallée du Denacre. The Canadian girls renamed it "Happy Valley" and loved its "peace & quiet."[72] Such moments proved to be precious interludes in a war that was far from over.

Among their other off-duty activities were shopping, sewing, tea parties, gardening, bicycling and visiting colleagues at other hospitals. In the local towns they discovered busy markets, cafés and restaurants which tempted customers with good meals and good coffee. Helen Fowlds enjoyed browsing in Boulogne and described how she and two friends had a splendid afternoon that began with a luxurious bath at one of the town's hotels. They then purchased "a wonderful cake" and inspected most of the shop windows. "The lingerie shops are a great temptation," Helen told her mother, "and I must lay in a stock while I am over here."[73] Among the more fashion-conscious, it was clear that French garments, even in wartime, were sought after.

Canadian nurses could meet and mix with male officers as part of a group, enjoying "the tennis court and the occasional dances," but officially they were not permitted to go out alone with a male colleague to any public place.[74] There are accounts of medical staff of both sexes going on group picnics and other outings during the war, and attending plays, concerts and other entertainments. The group ruling could be set aside in certain circumstances, however, as was the case for Sophie Hoerner after her promotion to Assistant Matron in the autumn of 1915. She was then able to report that "I may

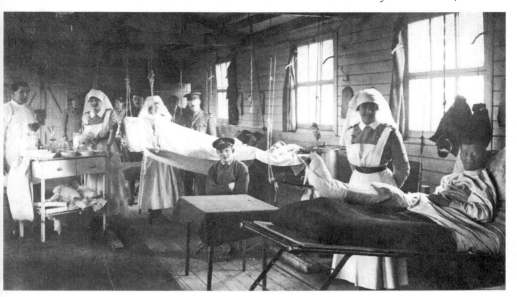

On the wards. This view taken at No. 3 Canadian General Hospital shows a well-staffed ward with patients comfortably and spaciously accommodated. To the rear can be seen the uniformed figure of senior medical officer Lieutenant-Colonel Frances Scrimger, VC, MD. (McGill University Archives, PR028737)

be allowed to walk with a Major," which was no doubt a concession to her seniority.[75]

While Sophie and her colleagues continued to brave the elements during that stormy autumn on the north French coast, far to the southwest at Divonne-les-Bains, Agnes Warner had completed her private nursing assignment and been accepted for service with the FFNC. She received orders to travel to Paris – now very quiet and full of wounded French officers – and from there to Dunkirk. By October 1915 she was on the staff of *Ambulance Mobile No. 1,* an FFNC surgical unit based at Roesbrugge, near the Belgian town of Poperinghe. It was an active area of the war zone and from the start Agnes knew she was likely to be far closer to the fighting than many other medical workers. She described how "the guns roared all night" and German shells were landing close enough to her accommodation that "everything in our little shanty rattled." She also witnessed an air battle between German and French airplanes, her first sighting of aerial combat and another sobering reminder of danger from the air as well as on the ground.[76]

For company, Agnes had "four English, three American, and three French nurses here" and all were kept busy tending their patients and trying to keep them warm and comfortable in the unseasonably wet and chilly weather. When Agnes went to collect supplies from Dunkirk, the target of a recent German bombardment, she saw evidence of the damage to the town. Houses had been "simply crushed like a pack of cards," and other medical personnel who had been there at the time of the bombardment told her that "the noise was the most terrifying part of it all," something she already understood from her own experience of artillery fire.[77]

With the year drawing to a close, a move was in prospect for the staff of No. 3 CGH. In the wake of the autumn storms it was decided to relocate the hospital to more permanent accommodation at a former Jesuit college outside Boulogne. Breaking up the unit involved a great deal of "shifting around" and disruption, with temporary staff postings to other units, packing of equipment and supplies, and evacuation of patients. A flexible approach in wartime was essential, and this was borne out not only by the need to respond to changing conditions but also by the number of postings that nurses could be asked to undertake. Records show that nine or ten was not uncommon during the war, and in the case of Assistant Matron Janet Mac-Donald from Nova Scotia the total ran as high as thirteen.[78] So many changes could pall at times and led one Canadian nurse to admit that she had grown "weary of this eternal moving."[79]

With another wartime Christmas approaching, the search began for holly, mistletoe, yew and other greenery to brighten hospital wards. At No. 1 CSH Constance Bruce noted with humour that one flirtatious French cleaning woman was discovered holding "a spray of mistletoe over her head with one hand, while she scrubbed the floor vigorously with the other" in the hope of getting a Christmas kiss.[80] Meanwhile, at No. 3 CGH the nursing staff had other things on their minds as they prepared to transfer to England for a few weeks during the hospital's temporary closure. While there, they provided additional help for the Canadian hospitals at Shorncliffe and Taplow, and over the holiday one group of nurses stayed at a hotel in London. They made the most of the chance to do some shopping, see a West End show and tour the city "on [the] tops of buses."[81]

On Christmas morning, Clare Gass of No. 3 CGH and her nursing colleague Margaret Woods were among the congregation at St. Paul's Cathedral for "the most beautiful service I have ever heard," noted Clare in her diary. As far as she was concerned, it was almost the end of "a sad year," and Assistant Matron Sophie Hoerner felt much the same. "How changed all the world seems," Sophie wrote to a friend, wondering at the same time, "what it all means and how it will all end and what will become of us all."[82]

CHAPTER 3

"A hospital alone shows what war is"

MEDICAL SERVICE – THE WESTERN FRONT AND ENGLAND, 1916-1919

This is Our Crusade –
To waken hope once more
In that sad People, helpless at our door;
To send swift healing where our wounded are;[1]

"OUR NATION IS IN MORTAL COMBAT FOR THE CAUSE OF TRUTH AND LIBERTY": 1916

"Surely this terrible war will soon be over" was the hope of one Canadian nurse on the last day of 1915, but it soon became clear that this was wishful thinking.[2] February 1916 saw the beginning of a terrible battle of attrition at Verdun, where German forces began a siege of the fortress town that had long stood as a symbol of French resistance to foreign aggression. While that battle was raging, Canadian nurse Agnes Warner, who continued to serve with the FFNC *Ambulance Mobile No. 1*, was working at full stretch to handle casualties amid the din of "cannonading without ceasing" and airplanes overhead "almost as thick as the motors" passing in convoys on the road. The wounded were nearly all brought in after dark, "so we have our hearts and hands full," she noted in her diary.[3]

Agnes was grateful for additional help from two newly-arrived Canadian nurses who, like her, had opted to serve with the FFNC. She found them "a joy to work with, for they have had splendid training and are the kind that will go till they drop." The hospital was only fourteen miles from Ypres and received casualties from around the region. News of its work spread and the staff were honoured by a visit from Queen Elisabeth, wife of Belgium's reigning monarch, King Albert. As Agnes recorded, Her Majesty was kind enough to speak "highly of the Canadians and of the splendid work they had done."[4]

During the spring and early summer of that year, Canada's troops were involved in local operations in the Ypres Salient. Rumours of their presence were soon confirmed by the numbers of men arriving at the base hospitals

from Mount Sorrel, where an attack was made on 2 June 1916 against German-held high ground. The battle lasted until 13 June and Canadian medical
staff heard how their countrymen had been "simply mown down without
hope of resistance" by enemy artillery fire. As Nursing Sister Clare Gass listened to "the tales of loss of life" that increased each day, she and her fellow
nurses gained a deeper understanding of what she described as "a ghastly
affair."[5]

German air attacks were now hitting Allied targets around Boulogne and
Étaples, while across the Channel London was also suffering aerial bombardment. With high Allied casualties on the Western Front that would continue
to increase with the coming battles of the summer, it was already proving a
gruelling year.

More Canadian hospitals arrived in France, including No. 7 CGH from
Queen's University, Kingston, and No. 7 CSH from Dalhousie University,
Halifax. Three Canadian casualty clearing stations were now in operation
and one of them, No. 2 CCCS, was located close to the Ypres Salient at
Poperinghe. When British officer Lieutenant B. W. A. Massey of the Royal
Field Artillery was taken there with serious wounds, he paid tribute to the
skilled treatment and excellent care he received. "*Everybody* is so good and
gentle here," he wrote to his wife, acknowledging his gratitude to the "surgeons, the sisters, and the orderlies," all of whom contributed to his recovery.[6]
The presence of an increasing number of Canadian medical units in France
and Belgium was timely, as Allied troops would soon be engaged "in mortal
combat for the cause of Truth and Liberty."[7]

In late June 1916 the base hospitals were instructed to prepare for a rush,
and all leave was cancelled ahead of a major new offensive in the Somme
region of France. Launched on 1 July 1916, it was originally planned as a
joint French-British action but with almost every able-bodied French soldier drawn into the fighting at Verdun, the task eventually fell to the British
armies. The main attack was preceded by a massive artillery bombardment
intended to annihilate German defences and make it possible for British
troops to cross the region's open downland and take enemy positions without much resistance. Unfortunately, the British artillery failed to dislodge
enemy troops, their machine guns and barbed wire defences, and on 1 July
as wave after wave of British infantry crossed open ground, they were mowed
down by accurate fire. At the end of the first day of the battle British casualties totalled 57,470, marking the worst single day in British military history.
The Newfoundland Regiment was part of this offensive and tried to attack a
German position near the hamlet of Beaumont Hamel. It, too, was slaugh-

tered and of 801 men, just 68 survived. In proportion to numbers, no single unit at the Somme suffered more heavily.

For Allied medical staff, so many troops needing treatment meant hours of frantic work, and Nursing Sister Alice Swanston of Calgary described how "there were tragic days during each 'big push' when the stream of wounded … seemed endless."[8] The resources needed to provide adequate medical help during major battles such as the Somme led to the creation of mobile surgical teams consisting of a surgeon, a nursing sister, an anesthetist (who might be a nurse with special training) and an orderly. Taken from base hospitals or casualty clearing stations, they went wherever they were needed and one of the surgeons praised the women assisting him for "the very cheerful way in which they put up with the long, fatiguing hours." Their "steady nerves and calm demeanour" while working to the sound of German planes overhead and "the shrieking of dropping bombs," were a tribute to their professionalism.[9]

One account of the work of No. 7 CGH contains a description of a typical CCS nurse. She was said to be "generally in a hurry, always busy … doing dressings, taking temperatures – preparing patients for the theatre, looking after fresh arrivals." It also describes how such women needed endless patience, an "infinite capacity for hard work" and an "infinite sense of humour" to help them cope with their duties and living conditions. The reality of CCS work, in which it was necessary to "nurse under fire" in "the din of air raids" and "to face the dangers of a soldier's life," was regarded as "no novelty nowadays," because CCS nurses came closer than most to the reality of actual combat.[10]

Among those nurses who volunteered for casualty clearing station duties that summer was Katherine Wilson. She was sent to No. 44 British CCS and soon after arriving, she awoke in the night to the sound of "an explosion that was repeated" and followed by "other terrific blasts." It was her first taste of artillery fire at close range, and she was warned that "the enemy might make a push forward." During the Somme offensive, Katherine was on night duty in charge of "a ward of horrors!" Of her forty-eight patients, she thought that "ten might live to see the base hospital," and she knew she had to be prepared for an emergency at any time. Among them was a young German prisoner-of-war she found to be "more like a frightened schoolboy" than a soldier, and his youth and helplessness "wiped away all hate."[11] When she returned to her normal duties at No. 3 CGH, any risk from enemy air attacks seemed to matter little after what she had experienced behind the front line. It was perhaps not surprising that she was found one morning outside the hospital, seemingly unconcerned as she watched anti-aircraft guns blasting away at a German plane overhead.[12]

Throughout that tragic summer of 1916, surgeons, physicians, nurses and orderlies faced the daily sight of damaged bodies and the awful effects of gas gangrene, an infection whereby bacteria flourished in the dirty wounds of men who had lain untended for some time before they could be evacuated. When microbes flourished in dirt-impregnated wounds, they could produce "a bacteria-generated gas with a nauseating stench, monstrous swelling, and a dreadful death." Control of gas gangrene could only be managed by cutting away all the affected flesh and irrigating the wound, which could be several inches in width and depth. "Constant nursing" was required to oversee the tubes and pumps required for irrigation and to ensure regular re-dressing of affected areas.[13]

One Canadian doctor described how "we are fearfully busy, as our people are coming in every hour of the 24."[14] Assistant Matron Sophie Hoerner admitted that what she saw often reduced her to tears, and she told a friend, "no one could imagine the horrors of a war like this, unless they are here and could see for themselves."[15] One of her medical colleagues, Canadian surgeon Dr. Edward Archibald, expressed admiration for his young patients and the way many coped with their dreadful injuries and the possibility of death. "When I see these men, cheerful still, or at least uncomplaining," he said, "I come near to tears, and count myself as nought."[16]

Hospitals were taking in hundreds of casualties at a time, and at No. 4 BGH, Étaples, where Emmeline Robinson from Minden, Ontario, was working as a QAIMNS nurse, the pressure was intense. She had joined that particular service only a few months earlier and despite the heavy workload, the rigidity of British hospital regulations and the usual differences in attitude between British and Canadian nurses, Emmeline felt sufficiently committed to her work that she planned to renew her contract for a further year.[17]

Devoted nurses, irrespective of nationality, remained after their shifts had ended to write letters on behalf of wounded men and to do whatever they could for their comfort. For many of the patients a cheery word, a little humour and small treats such as "fruit-cake, beer and stout," made a difference to men who expected so little. One soldier had been a professional dancer in civilian life and arrived in hospital with "a terrible gunshot wound in his knee." His leg had to be amputated and "my heart ached," wrote Katherine Wilson, who discovered that before the war he had appeared in a popular London musical entitled "Tonight's the Night." With grim humour the young man in question remarked, "There goes my old job."[18]

As the Somme offensive continued into the autumn of 1916, British and Canadian troops had to contend with seasonal rain that reduced the ground to the consistency of a bog. By the time the fighting ground to a halt in November, conditions had become so bad that, in the words of one senior Canadian artillery officer, "they would have revolted the stomach of a decent woodchuck."[19] Back in London, hospitals were full to overflowing with men needing further or specialized treatment and journalist Beatrice Nasmyth met one of them. He was a young Canadian pilot, Captain Fred Sutton, who had been shot down during the fighting and he told her what it was like to endure the dangers of the war in the air, with "the huge shells of the German howitzers pointing at us" and the difficulty of landing his plane "under a pelting rain of bullets." In spite of his injuries Captain Sutton maintained he was better off than the men on the ground who, as far as he was concerned, "haven't a chance in the world."[20]

Also in search of material for her regular column in the *Montreal Gazette,* journalist Elizabeth Montizambert arranged to visit one of two new French-Canadian medical units near Paris. No. 6 CGH had been offered by Laval University and was at Joinville-le-Pont, while No. 4 CSH, founded and financed by Montreal physician and philanthropist Lieutenant-Colonel Arthur Mignault, was in operation at Saint-Cloud. Mignault believed that wounded men would be more comfortable being treated by those who spoke their mother tongue and the Canadian government gave its approval for both hospitals, seeing it as an opportunity to enhance Canada's medical contribution in France.

It was agreed that No. 4 CSH would treat French wounded exclusively, and on 5 July 1916 the hospital's status was changed when it became No. 8 CGH. As Elizabeth Montizambert toured its wards she found it hard to maintain her composure on seeing what soldiers had suffered in battle as a result of the use of flamethrowers. The weapon, which used flammable oil, projected a stream of fire and in addition to terrorizing troops its effects included third-degree burns and suffocation resulting from searing the lungs and air passages. Treatment, to prevent infection and heal the damage to the respiratory system, had to be carefully handled. Elizabeth wished fervently that "every pro-German in the world" could see the suffering inflicted, which "no treatment, alas, will ever restore," and then ask themselves "what should be done with men who fight with such a devil-fired weapon as liquefied tar on fire."[21]

Most of the thirty-three nurses working at No. 8 CGH were from Quebec where, given the social, religious and moral values that governed the lives of

"Oiseau bleu." Nursing Sister Blanche Lavallée from Montreal served at what became No. 8 Canadian General Hospital, near Paris, from 1915 to 1917. In this sketch by artist R. G. Mathews in June 1916 she is seen in her uniform, the dress of which was a distinct blue and led to the CAMC nurses being known as "bluebirds" or "*oiseaux bleus.*" (Courtesy Department of National Defence PMR-C-86-419)

French-Canadian women at that time, it required determination to embark on a career such as nursing.

One among them was Blanche Lavallée, a recent graduate from Montreal's Hôtel-Dieu nursing school. During her overseas service she received regular communications from her mother, Marie Lavallée, who seems to have been a sensible, practical person and proud of her daughter's contribution to the war effort. "What work! What times you are having!" wrote Madame Lavallée, who described No. 8 CGH as "a mini-Canada in the heart of France" and wished Blanche "lots of courage … do well for those who are suffering."[22] Madame Marie appeared to be glad that her daughter was in France rather than England, as "you will be more at home and it will be good in every way." Having a serving nurse in the Lavallée family also meant that "the war and all its events seems alive to us now." "Be brave my dear Blanche," urged her mother, adding that "the war will end and your merit alone will remain with you."[23]

In June 1916 Blanche Lavallée was given permission to sit for a portrait by war artist R. G. Mathews. He had enlisted in the CEF and was on special duty in France that summer. One of his commissions was on behalf of the Canadian Red Cross Society, for whom he was completing portraits that might be suitable for use on postage stamps. It was with this in mind that while visiting No. 8 CGH, he decided to undertake a striking pastel drawing of Blanche that later brought her celebrity. Mathews succeeded in capturing not only her beauty, but also a pensive quality that conveyed something of the impact the war was having on nurses like Blanche.

Elsewhere, efforts to provide additional care for men needing further treatment at Canadian hospitals in Britain resulted in the opening of a new unit

Lieutenant Roberta MacAdams. Alberta, in 1916, was one of the first provinces in Canada to grant women the right to vote. Albertans elected two women to their Legislative Assembly – political activist Louise McKinney and armed forces representative Roberta MacAdams, who served during the war as a dietitian at No. 16 Canadian General Hospital, Orpington, England. They were the first women to be elected to any British or Canadian parliament or assembly. (Provincial Archives of Alberta A.13, 185)

at Orpington, Kent. The Ontario Military Hospital, later redesignated No. 16 CGH, was funded by the Ontario provincial government and housed in huts with views over the Kent countryside. Its twenty wards contained a total of 1,040 beds and facilities for the nurses included a sitting room, rest room, writing room and their own mess with separate kitchen and serving staff.[24] Nursing Sisters Emma Murton from Port Hope and Sarah Might from Millbrooke, Ontario, were among the staff, as was Roberta MacAdams from Edmonton.

MacAdams was a qualified dietitian supervising meal production for staff and patients. Beyond her professional work Roberta had become interested in the politics of her province, where that year women were granted the right to vote. Alberta was also offering the chance for two soldier representatives to be elected to the provincial legislature and journalist Beatrice Nasmyth, who was a suffragist* and a cousin of the province's premier, Arthur Sifton, was determined a woman would enter the contest. Lieutenant MacAdams proved to be the perfect candidate and behind the scenes Beatrice, whom Roberta referred to as her "silent partner," guided and helped to publicize her electoral campaign. Under the slogan "Give One Vote to the Man of Your Choice and the Other to the Sister," Roberta MacAdams won a seat, making her one of the first women to be elected to a legislature in the British Empire.[25]

---

* In an effort to gain the right to vote, women's suffrage societies formed to advance that cause. Those involved in the first wave of the campaign were known as suffragists and they believed in peaceful, constitutional methods to gain their objective. After they failed to make significant progress, a new generation of activists emerged, known as suffragettes. They were prepared to take direct, militant action in support of their cause.

Another woman from Alberta who trod new ground that year was Dr. Evelyn Windsor, a graduate of the Women's Medical College, Toronto, who had worked in the United States. She enlisted in the CAMC in October 1916 as a nursing sister, but once the credentials of this "brilliant scholar" were known, she was transferred to the Endell Street Military Hospital in London.[26] Prior to 1915 the British military authorities did not accept qualified women doctors, but as the country's medical men were called up, the gaps they left prompted the War Office to change tack. The Women's Hospital Corps (WHC), an organization led by two former suffragettes, Dr. Flora Murray and Dr. Louisa Garrett Anderson, had been doing excellent work in France and was invited to run a medical facility in London. They set up the Endell Street Military Hospital in a renovated former workhouse and the unit went on to pride itself on its "independent and individual character" and ability to deliver "innovations and strategies of its own." As a member of the all-female staff, the personable Evelyn Windsor, with her striking looks and "slightly casual manner," was soon a "great favourite" with everyone. Among the hospital's achievements were ground-breaking work in surgery, the warming of the general public to the idea of men being treated by women, and a greater acceptance of women in medicine.[27]

Taking time off from medical work during a year like 1916 was recognized as important for well-being but, as always, subject to workloads. Some nurses in France chose Britain as their leave destination, but enemy air attacks were on the increase and the largest Zeppelin raid on British soil took place during the night of 2-3 September 1916. London was the main target, and Laura Holland and her friend and colleague Mildred Forbes were in the city. Laura admitted that danger in the skies was "always more or less un-consciously on our minds," and the two nurses were ready, if necessary, to evacuate their hotel.[28] Clare Gass was also on leave in England and enjoyed a tour of Shakespeare's Warwickshire. She arrived in London two days after the September raid, relieved to have missed it and cheered to find that her hotel, the Kingsley, was "full of Canadian nurses recently arrived from Canada."[29]

While the average nurse was no doubt glad to get away from the war front, air raids notwithstanding, there were some who felt differently. Mabel Joice, who was still with the French Flag Nursing Corps, was delighted to be moved to No. 41 Military Hospital near Lisieux, Normandy, and to be "so much nearer the firing line." Seemingly seeking more of a challenge, she found her work at No. 41 "much better than we had at Bordeaux," and she appeared to thrive on the idea of being closer to the action. As she embarked on her new work, she paid tribute to her French patients, who bore their "sufferings bravely, always manifesting a cheerful spirit."³⁰

With the war continuing to take a grim toll, recreational events offered diversion at a difficult time. Hallowe'en in 1916 was an opportunity for an evening in fancy dress, and the prospect of Christmas seemed cheering in some ways but bittersweet in others, especially given that the conflict was proving "more deadly than ever."³¹ As in previous years, no effort was spared to make it as pleasant as possible for men in hospital, and at Boulogne it proved to be "such a happy, happy day" for the "lads" being cared for at No. 3 CGH.³² In London, Laura Holland was now working at a CAMC special hospital for officers in Hyde Park Place while Mildred Forbes was assisting at the office of Matron-in-Chief Macdonald. On Christmas Day, after spending time with the patients at Laura's hospital, the two nurses were invited to dine with Margaret Macdonald at her apartment. Laura found her "clever & wonderfully good company" and pronounced the festivities a success even though as she pointed out, the only "absolutely satisfactory place" to spend the holiday was at home in Canada.³³

"OUR LITTLE CEMETERY IS FILLING UP WHERE WE LAY OUR HEROES": 1917
In northern France 1917 began with bitterly cold weather, which made life more difficult for everyone. The effects of that harsh winter were felt in French cities, where people queued for food including their much-loved pastries and gateaux, and endured fuel shortages. The Allied base hospitals were admitting patients with pneumonia and chest complaints, and having to make do with limited supplies of coal for heating. At No. 3 CSH, Doullens, Nursing Sister Anne E. Ross described how "each two sisters were allowed 1 bucket of coal a week" and often ended up combining their allocation with others to maximize warmth.³⁴ When it snowed at Le Tréport, Nursing Sister Beatrice Kilbourn from Owen Sound, who was with No. 2 CGH, had to resort to a coat and a "coarse brown blanket" to keep warm at night. The combination of freezing conditions and the constant rush of work left tempers in "a frazzle" wrote one medical officer, "and we all actually suffer somewhat by the intensity of the weather."³⁵

In London there were grand plans afoot for Laura Holland, who was one of several Canadian nurses selected to receive the Royal Red Cross, an award for exceptional services to military nursing.³⁶ Early in March 1917 Laura attended her investiture at Buckingham Palace along with other recipients, and found it all "intensely interesting, even to get one's nose inside the Palace." Afterwards, all the award winners were invited to tea at the residence of

Queen Alexandra, mother of King George V, who appeared in "a black, tight, tailor-made suit, a funny little hat & heavy veil," and was "most gracious" as she shook hands with each of them.[37]

Militarily, preparations were going on for a major Canadian offensive under the leadership of General Arthur Currie, appointed to overall command of the four army divisions that now formed the Canadian Corps. With meticulous planning, an attack on Vimy Ridge near Lens, France, was set to take place on Easter Monday, 9 April 1917, and when the time came the troops, with the support of the Canadian Field Artillery, advanced "amid the chilling sleet of that deafening Easter dawn."[38] The combination of tactics, training and co-operation produced an outstanding victory for the Canadians and one that kept casualties lower than the very high numbers that had become the norm in major attacks. Even so, hundreds of lightly wounded men were admitted to the base hospitals the following day, with the more serious cases starting to arrive twenty-four hours later. So many men requiring treatment meant that bed capacity was filled to overflowing, and the medical services faced considerable pressure.

Alice Isaacson reported from No. 2 CGH that the hospital admitted 1,810 patients on 11 April 1917 alone, with "all staff working overtime" and the operating room "running all night." No. 2 had to erect an additional eight marquees to cope with less seriously wounded men who, although they did not require a bed, certainly needed to be treated and monitored.[39] At No. 5 CGH, Beatrice Kilbourne described night duty on a surgical ward where more seriously wounded patients were "all very sick and sore. Any one of them liable to hemorrhage any minute," she said, admitting that "the strain and anxiety" was worse than "any amount of work. We who thought we were hard worked at home knew not what work really was."[40]

The news of the Canadian victory and of America's recent declaration of war against Germany on 6 April 1917, were causes for optimism. A few weeks later there were more encouraging tidings of a British victory at Messines, Belgium, which lifted spirits in the face of continuing German air raids and the use of a more dangerous poison gas, phosgene. That same year the Germans introduced mustard gas, which proved to be even worse in its effects. It could kill by blistering the lungs and throat if inhaled in large quantities and Alice Isaacson first observed its effects among a convoy of patients in July 1917. It seemed to take effect imperceptibly at first, and then "in a few moments the victim discovers that his nose, throat and eyes are dreadfully burned." QAIMNS nurse Edith Appleton noticed how the damage spread throughout the mucous membranes, including the eyes, and described how men arriving at her hospital were "extremely ill, breathing like a person dying from bronchitis with a horrible discharge pouring from nose and mouth."[41] Mustard gas patients required extensive support during their lengthy and painstaking treatment.

Handling these and other gas complications, according to one recent study, revealed not only "the intricacy" of the necessary treatment; it also made very clear, in the words of the *British Journal of Nursing*, that the use of such appalling methods of warfare put at stake "the right to live ... and we mean to secure that God-given right at all costs."[42] Sophie Hoerner at No. 3 CGH would doubtless have agreed with this conclusion; she had to handle "terrible gas and gangrene cases," with the sad result that "our little cemetery is filling up where we lay our heroes," she said.[43] Two years after gas had first been used at the Second Battle of Ypres, the fact that medical officers and nurses could still only give limited relief for its effects was distressing to the point that, as one Canadian nurse admitted," it broke our hearts."[44]

As the weeks passed the workload eased somewhat, and at No. 8 CGH, near Saint-Cloud, Nursing Sister Blanche Lavallée had time to correspond with an admirer, French-Canadian officer Lieutenant Henri Trudeau. Henri had been seconded from the Royal Canadian Regiment to serve with the Royal Flying Corps, and was an Air Officer with No. 3 Squadron. Before the war he had qualified as a doctor in Montreal and may have met Blanche there or in England while she was awaiting orders to proceed to France. Henri was someone who clearly enjoyed flying, despite all the risks involved in those early days of aviation. At the same time, he expressed his admiration of Blanche for the "devotion and relief that you are able to give to these poor brave souls who are suffering terribly," and reminded her that "we will be better able to savour the peace because it is we who will have obtained it."[45]

Henri regaled his *"chère amie"* with tales of his flying missions and encouraged her to make the most of her free time, wishing only that "you should have been with me."[46] Romance in the midst of such a war seemed an unlikely prospect, yet the conflict brought people together who would otherwise almost certainly never have met. Among the younger nurses there was "lots of flirting going on," according to one assistant matron, and Canadian nurse Edna Howey described how at her unit, No. 7 CGH, everyone was "very friendly" and "more or less went around a bit together." It was fortunate for Edna and her colleagues that their matron was a "pretty good sport" about it.[47]

Although relationships were discouraged in wartime, love did blossom in unlikely circumstances, and when Katherine Wilson went on sick leave to London after a bout of influenza, she little suspected that she would meet her future husband, Captain Robert Simmie. In the case of Florence Hunter, who was invalided back to Britain from the eastern Mediterranean suffering from malaria, she renewed her friendship with an officer she had met earlier. Before the end of 1917 Florence married Major Howard Ridout at St. Margaret's Church, Westminster.

As enemy air activity increased over the Allied base areas in France during the late summer and early autumn of 1917, the main action was under way further east in Flanders, where the British launched an offensive aimed at breaking through the German front line and capturing enemy submarine bases on the Belgian coast. Just as they had at the Somme, the British used a preparatory artillery barrage which forewarned the Germans and destroyed the drainage systems vital to the terrain of the region. With the start of the attack came heavy rains that transformed the ground into a quagmire, and the wet weather continued through the months that followed. The troops in Flanders had to endure appalling conditions and British journalist Philip Gibbs described how they "hung on grimly in their isolated bog."[48] The danger of slipping and drowning in water-filled shell holes or disappearing in the mud was ever present, and a more desolate place than the battlefield in Flanders during the latter months of 1917 was hard to imagine.

After Canadian troops finally captured the village of Passchendaele in early November, the Third Battle of Ypres as it was known, came to an end. It would forever be associated with the mud, dreadful casualty figures of almost half a million men and the sacrifice of brave soldiers. Mary MacLeod Moore paid tribute in her *Saturday Night* column to the 15,654 Canadians killed or wounded in the fighting. "With pride, but in anguish," she wrote, "the names have been read in Canada of those who died for others, who have not counted the cost, who have forgotten self, and happiness and love and future joys that they might offer themselves for the greater good."[49]

Throughout this time, Mildred Forbes was acting matron of No. 2 Canadian CCS, only a few miles from the Ypres Salient. "One realizes the horrors of war more than ever in this place," she wrote to a friend. Although she was in a high-risk area, Mildred reminded herself that "we all have to take our chance – & when one sees the splendid men thrown away – one feels why should we value our lives."[50] What she experienced that autumn made her more than ever convinced that people in Canada had "*no idea* what the soldiers are going through for them."[51]

At No. 3 Canadian CCS near Poperinghe, Nursing Sister Luella Denton from Bradford, Ontario, was of similar mind and felt her own concerns were "as nothing compared to the boys." Caring for large numbers of casualties left her little time to think of danger during the day, but in the evening she had a chance to reflect. As she told a friend frankly, "imagine going to bed and saying to your roommates, 'well good night. I wonder if we will be here in the morning.'"[52] Being within range of the Salient during the latter months of 1917 was perilous, as Canadian FFNC nurse Madeleine Jaffery from Galt, Ontario, discovered when she sustained a shrapnel wound that resulted in the amputation of part of her foot.

American medical units were now arriving in France, and with them Canadian nurses who had joined the United States Army Nurse Corps (USANC). Ontarians Ella Mae Bongard of Picton and Hannah Lister of Hanover, Grey County, were among them and had both trained at New York City's famous Presbyterian Hospital. Ella Mae was posted to Base Hospital No. 2 at Étretat on the Normandy coast, while Hannah was with Base Hospital No. 8, mobilized in July 1917 and established at the town of Savenay in southern Brittany. Her unit began to receive patients from the military camps at the port of St. Nazaire, and over the next few months in "little old Savenay," Hannah nursed a lot of men with "rheumatism, acute fractures and appendicitis," numerous cases of meningitis, measles, scarlet fever, and a "whole ward full of mumps." She could not help feeling envious of other nurses who managed to obtain a pass to go within three miles of the French front line and who returned with tales of "exciting experiences and thrilling escapes."[53]

At Étretat Ella Mae Bongard was keeping a diary in which she recorded some of her early experiences in the autumn of 1917: the cold, drenching rain; nursing German prisoners-of-war; and wounds the like of which she had never imagined. Her first few months overseas were rounded off by the arrival on 9 December of a Canadian officer from Le Havre, who arranged for her to cast her vote in the Canadian general election. Military nurses were among the first to enjoy this new right for women, and Ella Mae admitted that "I feel quite important now."[54]

At almost the same time Canadian journalists Mary MacLeod Moore, Beatrice Nasmyth and Elizabeth Montizambert, and Florence McPhedran, a Canadian doctor's wife determined to be a war correspondent, were about to break new ground.[55] They had been given permission to tour the Allied lines of communication on the Western Front, which consisted of a vast network of facilities including hospitals, transportation, supply depots, military camps and other services essential to the war effort, and which were linked by railways, roads, rivers and canals. Accompanying them was Roberta

Casting their vote. In December 1917 Canadian nurses, whether serving at home or overseas, were able to vote in that year's federal election for the first time. Here they can be seen at an improvised polling station on the Western Front preparing to exercise their new right. (Library and Archives Canada, PA-002279)

MacAdams, who intended to visit her Albertan soldier constituents serving in that part of the war zone. Mary MacLeod Moore had decided it was "easier for a camel to go through the eye of a needle than for any unauthorized person to go to France during war-time," and she realized that some important strings must have been pulled for a temporary doorway to open for her and her colleagues.[56] Beatrice Nasmyth was glad of the opportunity to make the "dark impenetrable curtain" that stood between the men serving on the Western Front and their families back home, "just a little less impenetrable."[57]

Starting at Boulogne, the women saw for themselves how the vast operation of war fitted together, from the post offices that mailed and received letters, to trains and barges that carried the troops, and medical units that treated them. Their busy schedule included visits to warehouses full of hospital supplies and comforts for the soldiers; casualty clearing stations; an ambulance convoy where they met the women drivers; hospitals in the base areas; a rest home for nurses; troop training facilities; and a special unit for sick and wounded horses, whose presence in hauling guns and supplies had become almost as important to the military as the soldiers themselves. Troops from different parts of the British Empire were a constant source of interest to the journalists, and on their final stop in Paris the Canadian women were pre-

Journalists on tour. Canadians Beatrice Nasmyth (back row, left), Elizabeth Montizambert (front row second from the left) and Mary MacLeod Moore (possibly the tall figure in the fur coat, front row) were among a group of women correspondents permitted to tour the Allied lines of communication on the Western Front in December 1917. Also in the photograph is Roberta MacAdams (back row, right), who had been elected to the Alberta Legislature. (Collection of Monica Newton, courtesy of Debbie Marshall)

sented to General Sir Arthur Currie, commanding officer of the Canadian Corps. The tour left many lasting impressions and helped to establish professional camaraderie and respect.[58]

The fourth Christmas of the conflict brought with it "a wonderful hoarfrost over trees & earth this morning" that made the countryside "like Fairy land," recorded one nurse. It set the scene for what everyone hoped would be a quieter end to the year and at Étretat Ella Mae Bongard watched as a procession of doctors and nurses carrying torches sang Christmas carols in the wards and on the streets, making a "very pretty" scene.[59] Canadian hospitals in England and France tried to bring some cheer to their patients at the end of what, in many ways, was a year that marked the low point of the war. With the terrible casualties of the Third Battle of Ypres, feelings of general war-weariness and the worry of an increasing number of enemy air attacks on clear nights, spirits needed a lift. Hospital patients received a traditional Christmas meal with treats such as "nuts, raisins, oranges, and tobacco or cigarettes," thanks to generous gifts from Canada.[60] On a bright New Year's Eve, the Germans heralded the start of 1918 with "a little air raid" on some of the hospitals that began at 11.30 P.M. and went on past midnight.[61] It was hardly surprising that by now there were those who wondered if they would ever enjoy moonlight again.

"WAR IS WAGED ON SO GIGANTIC A SCALE": 1918–1919
In the base hospital area 1 January 1918 proved to be quieter than the previous evening, and something of an anti-climax for Nursing Sister Alice Isaacson. She described a feeling of "monotony behind the trenches" and a daily routine that had "become a bit of a bore," but it was unlikely to last long.[62] Even when hospitals were not working under pressure there were few days without medical challenges, as QAIMNS nurse Bertha Forsey could attest. She was looking after men suffering from contagious diseases at a British stationary hospital and knew that even without the complications of wound trauma, her patients still required the attention and "skilled nursing care" that she was able to give them.[63]

Elsewhere, the New Year began in livelier fashion and for Ella Mae Bongard at American Reserve Base Hospital No. 2, Étretat, there were few spare moments. She had 157 patients under her charge and when the pressure eased she was glad to take a day's leave. She chose to visit the port city of Le Havre, some thirty kilometres distant, in the company of two other nurses and lunched at the Hotel Normandie before browsing in the shops. Ella Mae decided the downtown area was "a very good place to get things" and her various purchases included several bunches of violets, bought at the flower market because "they looked so spring-like and so like home."[64]

At rural Savenay, Hannah Lister received news of her transfer to another American unit, Evacuation Hospital No. 1 near Toul, in north-eastern France, where she was appointed head nurse. Asked about her "willingness to go into the danger zone," Hannah had volunteered without hesitation, not knowing that the Germans were planning to launch a massive offensive, codenamed Operation MICHAEL, in March 1918 as an attempt to land a decisive blow that would bring the Allies to the peace table before American troops were fully trained and ready to enter the fighting.

When the German attack began, Clare Gass was serving with No. 2 Canadian CCS at Rémy Siding, north of Ypres. By 19 March everyone was aware of increased enemy activity and the build-up of what seemed to be something very significant. Clare described continuous shelling in the vicinity of her unit and its hasty evacuation to a safer location out of range of enemy artillery.[65]

The offensive began on 21 March 1918 and there was news of a "desperate" German effort "all along the line," with long-distance shelling of towns that had hitherto escaped bombardment.[66] The medical units in the area were overcrowded with wounded and Nursing Sister Gass and her colleagues waited, tense and discouraged, as they heard reports of enemy gains. "The rush of ambulances here is tremendous," she reported on 10 April as the Allies fought hard to stop the German momentum. No 2 Canadian CCS re-opened in mid-April at the village of Esquelbecq, just inside the French border, and learned that its former site near Poperinghe had been "knocked to pieces." The medical team had to cope with "many, many hundred[s]" of patients and became exhausted from the continuous and extremely heavy workload.[67]

With German troops advancing towards Paris and Amiens, orders came to evacuate some of the larger hospitals and Nursing Sister Anne E. Ross was put in charge of a group of nurses sent to the relative safety of No. 1 CGH and No. 7 CGH at Étaples. Amid widespread concern, Ella Mae Bongard wrote in her diary on 31 March 1918 that "the war is looking very serious indeed. Last night we got a convoy of 400 terribly wounded cases. They are right from the front as the CCSs have been either captured or destroyed."[68] On 1 April she reported that all her unit's "regular operating rooms & some extras" were working day and night, and she clearly felt the gravity of the situation. Even so, Ella Mae refused to believe that "the worst can happen" and decided that no matter what happened she would "prefer to stay and 'stick it.'" She made her decision, not because of any sort of "bravado or hero stuff," but simply because she wanted to be "in the midst of things that's all & so does everyone else here."[69] Finally, on 7 May 1918, the news was better and according to Clare Gass, "the British line now seems to be holding firmly with its allies the French."[70]

Allied base hospitals were at full stretch and Matron Ethel Ridley, who had been appointed Principal Matron, Canadians in France, had her work cut out with casualties averaging about 10,000 per week and an outbreak of influenza that was starting to sweep across Europe. At No. 1 CGH Nursing Sister Katherine Macdonald from Brantford, Ontario, reported that "we are simply rushed, we get patients from the field since the C.C.S. was bombed … Poor fellows they have some awful wounds." The overall situation meant that medical staff were working under intense pressure, but nurses like Katherine remained committed to the safety and recovery of those in their care.[71]

During what was proving a very stressful period, Elizabeth Montizambert wrote from Paris describing the city under daylight enemy bombing raids and bombardment from a long-range German siege gun. Nevertheless, she observed that the spirit of the people was "tempered to a fine endurance," which fuelled her determination to carry on with her own work. Elizabeth remained in the French capital, venturing out on personal errands when it was safe to do so and visiting a canteen at the Gare du Nord where people could get "a good meal served by American and French women." As the German offensive continued and enemy troops marched further into France, the journalist recorded how brave individuals helped one another during those deeply troubled days. She applauded the work of doctors, housing and transportation coordinators, and ambulance drivers – some of them Canadian – who ferried refugees, the sick and the wounded to hospitals and shelters for rest and treatment.[72]

The force of the German attacks brought their troops to within sixty miles of Paris by early June 1918, but the proud citizens of the French capital continued to stand firm "with cool heads and passionate hearts," and the city was even "jauntily opening her first Spring [fashion] Salon since the war," wrote a delighted Elizabeth Montizambert in her *Montreal Gazette* column.[73] A steady build-up of new American troops was now providing much-needed reserves, and although the Allied armies reeled and retreated they did not collapse. Things were heating up in the vicinity of Evacuation Hospital No. 1 at Toul, where Canadian head nurse Hannah Lister discovered that the Germans were targeting nearby towns by means of guns mounted on a train that "moved up and down the line shelling everything in sight." Worrying as it was, Hannah continued to treat wounds, the severity of which she had never before encountered, and victims of concentrated gas attacks, all of whom were "suffering terribly."[74]

Only some forty-three miles south of Hannah's hospital lay the spa town of Vittel, where another Canadian nurse was living through the impact of those dramatic weeks. Working at U.S. Army Base Hospital 36 was Charlotte Edith Anderson, usually known as Edith, who was from the reserve of the Six Nations of the Grand River in Ontario. Following her graduation from Brantford Collegiate Institute, Edith Anderson had decided to pursue a career in nursing despite the fact that the Federal Indian Act was a barrier to native women entering Canadian nursing programmes. Embarking on a path that set her apart from other women on her reserve was challenging, but Edith was accepted at New Rochelle Nursing School, New York, and her subsequent qualification meant that she became the first indigenous registered nurse in Canada.

With America's entry into the war Edith volunteered with the United States Army Nurse Corps and in early 1918 she set off for "goodness knows

A pioneer among her people. Charlotte Edith Anderson was a Canadian nurse who served with the American Expeditionary Forces during the First World War. As a member of the First Nations, this remarkable woman became the first indigenous woman from Canada to serve overseas in the First World War. She left a diary documenting her experiences, and after the war she married, raised a family and continued to work as a nurse for many years. (Photograph by kind permission of Helen Moses)

where."[75] By June she was working fourteen-hour shifts at Vittel and handling both Allied and German patients. At her hospital, the wards were "filled to the doors" with patients, said Edith, most of whom were suffering from the effects of gas. Some among them found a special place in the hearts of those caring for them, and in Edith's case it was a young American named Earl, who had been shot in the neck. Despite the best treatment he died on 21 July 1918 and was, by all accounts, a fine young man. "My heart was broken," wrote Edith in her diary, describing how deeply affected she was by the loss of her patient.[76]

A series of major German attacks were launched against Allied formations in the areas of Ypres, Reims and Soissons, and journalist Mary MacLeod Moore followed events from London. She recognized how hard it was for the average person to grasp what was happening and told her *Saturday Night* followers, "We read, only half realizing what it means, of the tremendous number of German divisions massed against our men and we dimly understand what the conditions must be like when war is waged on so gigantic a scale."[77] Mary continued her morale-boosting columns, describing how everyone was carrying on stoically and without panic. She expressed her "wonder and admiration" at the efforts of the British and Allied troops holding their own "splendidly" while the Germans appeared to have the upper hand.[78]

The Allies were finally able to stem the German advance and in late July 1918 the tide began to turn in their favour. Ella Mae Bongard made a note in her diary that "it looks as if Fritz might be starting for home but it's a little early to crow yet."[79] By this time plans were nearing completion for a major Allied offensive to be launched using the element of surprise, and a new strategy aimed at breaking the deadlock of trench warfare. It began on

8 August 1918 with attacks east of Amiens, and the Australian and Canadian Corps – by now two of the finest Allied fighting formations – played a crucial role. As the medical services braced for what lay ahead Dr Margaret Parks, who was still nursing at No. 1 CGH, was seconded to help at several British casualty clearing stations where her expertise could be put to good use during the early part of the offensive.[80]

For Canada, the period from 4 August to 11 November 1918 became known as "the Hundred Days," and as the Allies continued to advance into territory that had been held by the enemy their success cheered everyone. Hannah Lister was outside her hospital at dawn on 12 September and was privy to a sight she would never forget. Ahead in the distance was the line of battle "well defined in a big half circle of light," she said, and from the thunder of artillery it sounded as though "every gun must be firing at the same instant."[81]

A sense of what it was like to handle large numbers of wounded during those critical weeks was provided by Anne E. Ross who, as a night supervisor at No. 1 CGH, described how "Night always brought dread of hemorrhages – 36 wards – 40 pts [patients] in each ward. Overflow in tents, up to 700 in August. Gas attacks."[82] One casualty of that difficult time was Nursing Sister Georgina Pope, who was the first permanent nurse to join the CAMC and had served with Matron-in-Chief Margaret Macdonald in the South African War. By the outbreak of the First World War she was fifty-two years of age and remained on training duties in Canada, but in 1917 she went to France and joined the staff of No. 2 CSH at Outreau. Having survived the pressures of the autumn of 1917 and the spring of 1918, Nursing Sister Pope had to be hospitalized in August 1918 and according to her service record she was suffering from "nervous debility." After a period of rest and treatment at the Buxton Red Cross Special Hospital, this distinguished nurse was subsequently given a medical discharge.[83]

The CAMC now included mobile units in the form of two ambulance trains which it taken over from the British. One of them, No. 4 Canadian Ambulance Train (CAT), began its work on 15 August 1918, initially serving parts of the Somme region. After somewhat basic beginnings ambulance trains were by then composed of purpose-built cars, normally fifteen or more per train, providing comfortable travel for patients. Berths were made up as beds and facilities included an isolation ward, a dispensary, an operating room, an office, quarters for staff and a van for stores.[84] These trains, which functioned under the direction of Britain's Royal Army Medical Corps, generally carried 400 patients, a staff of two or three medical officers, four nursing sisters and subordinate personnel. They could be loaded in twenty-five minutes and were organized and managed as hospital units with staff on duty for the entire train journey. A train would stop at various stations until it was full, and then travel at a speed of twelve miles per hour to its destination.[85]

Nursing Sister Gertrude Gilbert, from St. Thomas, Ontario, joined No. 4 CAT in August 1918 and straightaway began to handle "very badly wounded" men. Trains often travelled at night as a protection against enemy air attacks and even then, on occasion, Sister Gilbert mentioned many German "machines" overhead during the hours of darkness. As the days passed she described the rigours of long shifts and working in hot weather within the confined space of the train. Her first encounter with wounded German patients merited a special note in her diary, as did leisure time in Boulogne that included a visit to a hotel for a "wonderful bath" and a walk along the English Channel shoreline. Even if she had taken such things for granted in the past, she now clearly appreciated them.[86]

In late August 1918 the train began a series of journeys to the front line area beyond Amiens, where Gertrude Gilbert saw badly shelled towns and "trenches and barbed wire and dugouts in the ground as thick as hives." With heavy firing at times and a "tremendous amount of transport on the roads," it was the closest to the front line that No. 4 CAT had been thus far and Gertrude managed to find "a tank shell case" and a bayonet as souvenirs.[87] Picking up men recently evacuated from the fighting meant she was dealing daily with large numbers of "very sick cases," who required non-stop care on their way to the base hospitals, and she was always very happy if, on arrival, she found "all patients alive."[88] From their perspective it was, said one man, "such a relief and comfort to be in a clean, comfortable bed." He remembered being settled in his berth and given some food before the train moved off late at night. The next thing he knew, "we were awakened about six a.m. to find

Messing about on the river. A few months before she joined No. 4 Canadian Ambulance Train, Nursing Sister Gertrude Gilbert and two colleagues from No. 6 Canadian General Hospital at Joinville-le-Pont went rowing on the Marne. Gertrude (centre) is the one doing all the work. (Library and Archives Canada, MIKAN 5065801)

our train standing at Wimereux station" with ambulances waiting nearby.[89] For the nurses, the long unsocial hours, danger of enemy air activity, regular loading and unloading of wounded and sick men, and changes of schedule at short notice, were offset by the value of the work they were doing.

As the Allied armies continued their advance the news was optimistic, and the liberation of French and Belgian cities made it clear that the war could not last much longer. On board No. 4 CAT, the relentless pace of work and the arduous nights of tending very sick men, were starting to tell on the nurses. "We are getting very fed up on this run," recorded Gertrude Gilbert who was glad to be given a short period of leave from No. 4 CAT. With the Canadian base hospitals struggling to cope with increasing numbers of influenza cases, she volunteered to help, knowing that every skilled pair of hands was needed.[90]

From 23 October until the war ended on 11 November 1918 Gertrude Gilbert and her colleagues with No. 4 CAT followed the advancing Allied troops through France and Belgium. From their train they saw towns "very badly smashed," countryside "full of fresh shell holes and barbed wire," and the presence of German signs and graves left by retreating enemy troops. The sound of artillery was at times "very near – we are the first train up here," wrote Gertrude, mentioning also that the "railway bridges are blown up and tracks have been mined." When No. 4 CAT reached an area where gas had been used only four days earlier, it was ordered to withdraw and the medical staff were "not allowed out without our gas masks."[91]

The worst situations the train encountered at this stage were "several big explosions" that occurred while it picked up patients at Cambrai, and a nightmare journey back to the base hospitals during which it almost ran off the tracks. It was clear that the end of hostilities was close and "there was a new thrill to be had every day," wrote Hannah Lister from Toul. At a small hotel in the Jura mountains, Laura Holland and Muriel Forbes were well away from the war front but not from medical problems, for they were looking after men of the Canadian Forestry Corps suffering from influenza. Mildred described how it was "terrible & the deaths appalling," as the disease spread relentlessly.[92] Over the coming days there was much talk of an armistice and "great excitement over the rumor that [the] Kaiser has abdicated," noted Gertrude Gilbert in her diary entry for 10 November. The following day at 11 A.M. the order to "cease fire" was given to all troops on the Western Front, and the fighting came to an end after more than four years of a titanic struggle and untold suffering.

The work of the medical units on the Western Front, however, was not yet over. The base hospitals continued to receive sick and wounded men and to treat prisoners-of-war after they were brought back from camps in France, Belgium and Germany. Taking part in these mercy missions No. 4 Canadian Ambulance Train passed through areas that were still "mined and marked dangerous," and the medical staff heard tales from their patients of brutal treatment and poor food that was often little better than "cabbage and water."[93] In January 1919 Gertrude Gilbert and her colleagues went to Cologne in Germany to bring back British prisoners who were "too ill to be sent out." There were, she recorded, "about 2000 not accounted for yet" and the rescue work lasted until all were hospitalized or repatriated. Doctors and nurses on both sides of the English Channel continued their duties until ordered to demobilize, and for Gertrude Gilbert that order came on 3 March 1919. Her diary entry for that day stated simply, "England tomorrow. Very tired after months of loyal service."[94] Many other Canadian nurses who had remained overseas with their medical units to care for wounded and recuperating soldiers, or to nurse men who had contracted the influenza that was claiming so many lives, could no doubt say much the same.

"SHE WAS A BRAVE GIRL AND SO DEVOTED TO HER DUTY"

Surviving records provide information about Canadian nurses who died during their service overseas. Among those who passed away as a result of illness were Nursing Sisters Victoria Hennan, Matilda Green and Evelyn McKay, who succumbed to pneumonia in October 1918 during the influenza epidemic.[95] Sister Lena Davis was working at No. 4 CGH at Basingstoke in England when she became dangerously ill and died in February 1918 from blackwater fever, a complication of the malaria she had contracted in the eastern Mediterranean. At Calais, Sister Anna Whitely was with No. 10 CSH when she was diagnosed with an abdominal tumour that led to her death on 21 April 1918.

A few weeks later a major German aerial bombing campaign targeted Allied installations in France including ammunition dumps, railways and the docks at coastal ports. The Allied base hospitals found themselves under serious attack and Nursing Sister Mabel Clint, with No. 3 CGH, noted that Boulogne and surrounding areas were hit almost nightly, mainly to destroy civilian morale and to disrupt the British lines of communication. She described it as a "nerve-wracking time" and "an appalling ensemble," so much so that Canadian Prime Minister Sir Robert Borden, who happened to be visiting the Canadian hospitals at that time, ordered timbered dug-outs to be prepared for the nurses. Despite the danger the enemy air attacks "did not succeed in breaking our spirit," wrote Mabel Clint.[96]

Some hospitals escaped with only shrapnel damage or narrowly missed bombs that fell nearby, but on 19 May 1918 No. 1 CGH at Étaples was not so fortunate. According to the unit's war diary, "at the close of what had been a peaceful Sunday, enemy aircraft came over the camp in large numbers:– viz. at 10 P.M. It concluded that the raid was "obviously planned to take place in relays."[97] Bombs hit the sleeping quarters of the medical orderlies and started fires which "offered a splendid target for the second part of the attack." German planes then flew over the officers' and sisters' quarters, parts of which were "completely wrecked by a bomb, the inmates being killed and wounded." The raid continued while the casualties were being rescued and two hospital wards received direct hits that killed eight patients and wounded a further thirty-one.

Those nurses on duty never wavered during the crisis and others who were not working rushed to help. One medical officer, one nursing sister and fifty-one other ranks were killed. The nurse in question was Katherine Macdonald from Brantford, Ontario, who was wounded by a piece of shrapnel that severed a femoral artery. According to her fiancé, Captain T. W. Ballantyne, "she died from shock."[98] Seven other nurses were wounded, among whom were Gladys Wake, originally from Esquimalt, British Columbia, and Margaret Lowe, who had enlisted at Winnipeg. The day before her death Katherine Macdonald wrote her last letter home using words that seemed especially poignant in the light of what followed. It was "another nice day," she said, "my, the weather is grand … I suppose we shall have another big push again … but don't worry we are far from harm."[99]

The tragedy at No. 1 CGH made Katherine Macdonald the first Canadian nurse to be killed on active service and among the letters received by her mother was one from Matron-in-Chief Margaret Macdonald, who wrote that "we hear nothing but the highest praise of the manner in which the Sisters carried on their work regardless of personal danger, – their first consideration in every instance being for their patients.[100] Katherine's fiancé, who was stationed in England at the time, paid tribute to her as follows:

> She was a brave girl and so devoted to her duty in the cause of justice and relief to the suffering, that she has made the supreme sacrifice. Her heart and soul were in her work… our love meant much to us … to me she was ideal in every respect … her memory will always be one to inspire me to higher ideals.[101]

A poem published in memory of Nursing Sister Katherine Macdonald commemorates her and the other nurses who died on overseas service.

For her heart's perennial gladness,
For the years untouched by sadness,
For the duty dared and done,
For the Crown of Life well won
We thank thee Lord.[102]

Katherine was buried on 21 May 1918, the same day her colleague Gladys Wake died of her wounds. Nursing Sister Margaret Lowe, who had serious injuries to her chest and skull, also subsequently died. Five other nurses who suffered wounds in the German air attack were fortunate to survive.[103]

On 30 June 1918, the hospital's nurses went to the local cemetery to lay wreaths and "decorate Canadian graves for Dominion Day."[104] Sadly, the danger was not over and before the day's end a few miles away at Doullens, No. 3 CSH was attacked. A bomb smashed through the main building and claimed more lives including three nurses. Agnes Macpherson from Brandon, Manitoba, and Eden Pringle from Vancouver died immediately when the operating room was hit and Dorothy Baldwin of Toronto, who was on ward duty, was also killed. The heroic conduct of two other nurses, Eleanor Thompson from Valleyfield, Quebec, and Mary Hodge of Hamilton, Ontario, resulted in both women being awarded the Military Medal.[105]

A life given in service. Nursing Sister Katherine Macdonald was one of three nurses killed when the Germans bombed No. 1 Canadian General Hospital at Étaples, France, on 28 May 1918. This studio portrait of her was taken shortly before the start of the First World War. (Canadian War Museum, George Metcalf Archival Collection, Acc 19970030-005)

A nurse's funeral. Nursing Sister Gladys Wake was injured in the German air attack on No. 1 Canadian General Hospital and died a few days later. This photograph shows her funeral procession, formed by the staff and nurses of her unit. She and a third victim, Nursing Sister Margaret Lowe from Binscarth, Manitoba, were buried beside Nursing Sister Macdonald, and their colleagues decorated their graves with flowers. (Library and Archives Canada, PA-002562)

During their years of service Canada's medical staff in England, France and Belgium saw the worst that war was capable of inflicting. The work they did was an indispensable part of the chain of medical care provided in the First World War, the effectiveness of which is typified by the statistics of No. 3 Canadian General Hospital (McGill). During its four years of operation in France, it handled 143,762 admissions and registered 986 deaths, less than one per cent of the total number of its patients.[106] These figures represented thousands of hours of skilled and dedicated work by those who served there, and everyone who was part of the great machine of healing would surely have agreed with a comment made by a young German soldier in Erich Maria Remarque's novel *All Quiet on the Western Front*. After witnessing the deaths of brothers-in-arms and finally his best friend, he concluded that, "A hospital alone shows what war is."[107]

CHAPTER 4

"A chapter, unique in its joys and sorrows"

Medical Service in the Eastern Mediterranean

Out there, where'er they be,
Wasting with fever by some southern sea,
Braving the heights where mind and senses reel,
Death's icy fingers clutching at the wheel.[1]

"NO PLACE FOR SISTERS": LEMNOS

During the First World War Canadian nurses served beyond the Western Front in various parts of the Mediterranean and the Middle East. In these regions there were five main theatres: Gallipoli; Mesopotamia; Sinai and Palestine; the Caucasus (between the Black Sea and the Caspian Sea); and Persia (modern-day Iran). Several minor campaigns included one at Salonika in Greece, where Allied forces fought troops of the Ottoman Empire,* Bulgaria, Germany and Austria-Hungary.

"I simply can't realize that I am away off here in the East," wrote Nursing Sister Laura Holland to her mother in August 1915.[2] Like most Canadian nurses, Laura had not envisaged working in a distant region where there were no Canadian troops in action, but a British plea for additional medical assistance was sufficiently pressing to persuade Canada's Director of Medical Services, Major-General G. Carleton Jones, to send three stationary hospitals to the eastern Mediterranean. Thus, in the summer of 1915, some seventy Canadian nurses were ordered at short notice to a destination yet to be revealed.

The story behind the nurses' hasty departure began in the summer of 1914. As war became increasingly likely, the Ottoman Empire signed a secret treaty with Germany and on 29 October 1914 it entered the conflict on the side of that nation and its allies. Ottoman lands spanned large parts of the Middle East and Arabia, and with German support including intelligence gathering

---

* The Ottoman Empire, created by Turkish tribes in Anatolia (Asia Minor), became one of the world's most powerful states during its 600-year existence. It came to an end after the First World War in 1922 when the Turkish Republic replaced it.

and subversive activity, the Ottoman high command aimed to sever Russian access to the Caspian Sea and its vital natural resources. It was also intent on recovering areas in the Caucasus region lost in an earlier war against Russia. If the Ottoman plan succeeded the Russians would be forced to divert troops away from other war fronts to deal with these threats. Britain had particular interests in Mesopotamia (corresponding to part of modern-day Iraq) and Persia, where there were vital petroleum deposits, but it was a stretch of land bordering a major sea route to Russia that became the focus of one of the most significant campaigns of the early part of the war.

In January 1915 Grand Duke Nikolai Nikolaevich, commander-in-chief of the Russian armies, sent an urgent request to the War Office in London asking if it might be feasible to "arrange for a demonstration of some kind against the Turks," either military or naval, that would draw Ottoman troops away from their fight against the Russians in the Caucasus.[3] Planning began for a campaign against the Ottomans on the Gallipoli peninsula, which formed the northern shore of the Dardanelles – the narrow waterway connecting the Mediterranean Sea to the Black Sea. Germany and Austria-Hungary having closed the other major routes between Britain and France and their Russian ally, the entrance to the Black Sea was of strategic importance.

The Ottoman Empire had shut and mined this vital sea passage, and Britain and France decided to launch an operation aimed at forcing a way through the Dardanelles and capturing Constantinople, the Ottoman capital and now known as Istanbul. Winston Churchill, Britain's First Lord of the Admiralty, proposed a naval attack on the Dardanelles in the hope that other countries such as Greece and Bulgaria (at the time still neutral) would be drawn into the war on the Allied side. The first action began on 18 March 1915 and was repelled. The Allies then assembled ground units whose task would be to storm the rocky heights of the Gallipoli peninsula and eliminate the Turkish mobile shore artillery. On 25 April 1915 French, British, Australian and New Zealand troops tried to gain a foothold on the beaches at Gallipoli but were halted by Turkish forces firing from the high ground. It was the start of eight months of fighting, during which the Allies made repeated assaults in terrible conditions. Lack of water, poor food, flies and high temperatures, resulted in widespread disease and unrelenting misery for the soldiers, which continued into the autumn and winter of 1915 as colder weather brought gales, flooding, blizzards and exposure.

With the focus of attention on military operations, less thought had been given to the provision of medical facilities and the handling of sick and wounded men. With enemy resistance preventing Allied troops at Gallip-

Gallipoli. The Gallipoli peninsula was the scene of a campaign that lasted from the spring of 1915 until early 1916. The enemy, soldiers of the Ottoman Empire, were in a strong position on the heights overlooking beaches such as this one, and for the Allies it became a battle for survival against not just their opponents, but also heat and disease. Many men had to be evacuated for hospital treatment at Lemnos, Malta and Egypt. (Author's collection)

oli from advancing beyond the beach areas, no hospitals could be set up there. Evacuation of casualties was therefore necessary but it proved difficult and risky as they had to be carried over rough terrain under hostile fire. If they reached the beaches, lighters (flat-bottomed barges) transported them to ships that would take for treatment as far away as Cairo, Alexandria and Malta. Medical facilities nearer to Gallipoli were urgently needed, prompting Britain's request for additional help. Canada's answer was the deployment of three CAMC hospitals in the eastern Mediterranean.[4]

The first selected for service were No. 1 CSH, one of the base hospitals in France, and two new stationary hospitals that arrived from Canada in the spring of 1915: No. 3 CSH, raised in London, Ontario, and No. 5 CSH, organized by Queen's University, Kingston, and staffed by nurses from eastern Ontario. When they received their orders, No. 1 CSH was at Wimereux, near Boulogne, while No. 3 CSH was temporarily at Moore Barracks, Shorncliffe, and No. 5 CSH was nearby at St. Martin's Plain, a British training camp. Nursing Sister Mabel Clint, now serving on the staff of No. 1 CSH, learned on 30 July 1915 that "we were under orders to sail for Egypt in two days!" The initial reaction of Mabel and her colleagues, who had "thought of the war in terms of the western front," was one of "consternation" and "sadness" at leaving their more familiar surroundings, but they were coming to appreciate "the vast scale of operations" in different theatres of war.[5] Anne E. Ross was one Canadian nurse who took a pragmatic approach to the prospect of a distant posting at short notice. "We can expect to be sent anywhere & everywhere," she said, in the knowledge that it was "what we enlisted for."[6]

In early August 1915 the three medical units sailed from the British port of Southampton aboard His Majesty's Hospital Ship *Asturias*, which had on its previous voyage handled "1500 patients, 150 operations and buried 60 patients at sea," with the staff working eighteen-hour days.[7] When they reached the Egyptian port of Alexandria, No. 5 CSH was despatched to Abbasieh, a few miles outside Cairo, while Nos. 1 and 3 CSH were soon taken aboard a smaller ship, the SS *Delta*, and sailed north towards an island in the northern Aegean some thirty miles from the Dardanelles, which had been chosen as an advanced Allied base.

The island was called Lemnos, and the Canadians found it to be a largely barren and mountainous place with, according to Anne E. Ross, "sand sand everywhere."[8] The principal harbour, Mudros, was on a large bay that provided a forward anchorage wide enough for warships. Its accessibility to Gallipoli had obviously influenced its selection, but Lemnos unfortunately lacked adequate military facilities for handling large numbers of troops and the poor water supply made it anything but ideal as a base for hospitals. There was a sense of remoteness about the island, and when British Voluntary Aid Detachment nursing assistant Vera Brittain stopped there in September 1916 on her way to Malta, she was struck by its isolation "in the rich desolation of the Aegean."[9]

The news that the Canadian nurses were going to such a solitary, primitive-sounding location came as a surprise to them. Laura Holland and her friend Mildred Forbes were among those selected, and after leaving England Laura told her mother,

> you can't imagine the shock, for while it had been whispered as a possibility when in London, the officers on this boat said it was an impossibility, for no women could be sent there. They told us fearful things about the place.[10]

When the two hospital units arrived at Mudros on 16 and 17 August 1915, it was oppressively hot. At first sight a British camp was visible on a slope beyond the harbour, an assortment of destroyers, minesweepers and other vessels filled the bay, and gangs of Egyptian workers could be seen "making roads."[11] Beyond lay barren countryside with its "irregular ridges, and rocky mounds … in the clefts of which white, square-roofed villages clustered." As for the local people, it was disconcerting to learn that they were "popularly supposed to be taking money from both sides" in the war, and to have "various ways of notifying the Turks of departures from the harbour."[12]

While stores and baggage were unloaded and the bell tents and canvas huts of the hospitals were erected, the nurses awaited orders to disembark from their ship. As they learned more about what they were facing, they realized that they were "six weeks from base and with communication over dangerous seas." They also learned about the nature of the casualties from Gallipoli, the difficulties involved in evacuating and treating them, and an apparent lack of organization that characterized operations during the campaign.[13] An example of this was the fact that "tramp steamers and cattle boats" arrived at Mudros with stretcher cases "practically unattended" and in dreadful conditions, while doctors on Imbros, another Greek island nearer to Gallipoli, were "kept inactive" as casualties bypassed them.[14] Lemnos was a base for ANZAC (Australian and New Zealand Army Corps) troops as well as those from Britain and Newfoundland. No. 1 Australian General Hospital (AGH), had arrived only a week earlier and, like other Allied units already on the island, it had no

Bound for Lemnos. In this photograph, Nursing Sister Helen Fowlds seems to have her sea legs as she poses for a photograph. She and the other Canadian nurses posted to the island of Lemnos left Egypt on the SS *Delta* and arrived at their destination in mid-August 1915. (Helen Fowlds Marryat Papers, Trent University Archives)

The first day. When the Canadian medical staff arrived at Lemnos in August 1915, they found conditions primitive. Tents were pitched and in this photograph nurses at No. 3 Canadian Stationary Hospital can be seen having their first cup of tea in their new surroundings. (Helen Fowlds Marryat Papers, Trent University Archives)

nursing sisters. The sudden appearance of the Canadian women, therefore, caused quite a stir and led to the comment that Lemnos was "no place for sisters."[15]

As the Canadian medical staff set up their camp a mile or so to the west of Mudros, it was clear that they would have to take care of all their requirements from scratch. There were only two local wells, one of which had dried up and the other required the addition of chlorine to make the water safe to drink. Wood had to be imported along with other supplies, and there was no sanitary provision whatsoever. The next few weeks were "a time of acute misery," according to Mabel Clint, who decided that "never was a Florence Nightingale more needed" than on Lemnos.[16]

The hospital personnel discovered they were strictly limited to one quart of water per person per day for washing and drinking. Fresh quantities had to be brought on a cart, and this problem lasted for a couple of months until engineers could sink new wells. In the meantime, the summer heat gave rise to dust and plagues of flies which added to the daily troubles. To cap it all, the Canadians could not even look forward to appetizing meals, food being "scarce and unsuitable" for the medical staff and "impossible for patients." As the official historian of the CAMC described it, the arduous conditions and the suffering of those being treated at Lemnos were to prove reminiscent of "the events of Crimean days," a reference to the earlier war of that name.[17]

There was little time to dwell on the difficulties, however, for on 22 August 1915 No. 3 CSH began accepting patients. Although minor actions continued to take place at Gallipoli, for the next six months it was disease that ravaged the Allied troops fighting there and after August 1915 Lemnos only handled medical cases. Those requiring surgery were sent to Malta or England, where there was less danger of infection setting in. In contrast to the huge numbers of wounded on the Western Front, the nurses found themselves dealing with a range of illnesses largely resulting from the climate and primitive conditions of the Dardanelles campaign. Nursing Sister Katherine Wilson's first duty was on a ward filled with patients suffering from malaria or amoebic dysentery, a disease that has troubled soldiers for centuries. No. 1 CSH also began admitting patients with similar problems, and despite their limited facilities the Canadian hospitals soon saw what a difference proper nursing care among "friendly Allies" could make to men who were "critically ill with fevers" or "worn out, pessimistic."[18] They began to recover after a few days of rest and treatment but unfortunately the medical staff succumbed one by one to dysentery until at No. 1 CSH, only three out of thirty-five nurses were fit enough to be on duty.[19]

As the battle against heat, lack of water, disease, flies and mosquitoes continued – the latter proving such a menace that additional netting had to be requested from Egypt – the first few weeks on Lemnos were gruelling. Yet despite all the problems, the men being treated considered themselves more fortunate than those fighting the Germans. "The Turks fought like gentlemen" was a comment often made, nor did the patients complain about their sufferings, for as one was heard to say, "It's worth living or dying for, is this old Empire of ours."[20]

The decision not to treat surgical patients at Lemnos proved fortuitous, as by early September the dysentery problem had worsened. There were hundreds of cases in the wards and a total of ninety-five Canadian medical personnel developed "acute enteritis mainly of the amoebic variety."[21] At No. 1 CSH, Florence Hunter was one of the nurses who contracted the illness. She put on a brave face, simply stating in her diary that she was "feeling rather ill with dysentery."[22] The situation was the same at other hospitals on the island and ten Canadian nurses were seconded to help at No. 2 Australian Stationary Hospital (ASH), where only a small number of staff had escaped the disease. The Canadian women did their best while trying to establish the whereabouts of the nearest British Red Cross headquarters. Medical supplies were badly needed, but it was clear that in their remote location it would be weeks before anything was likely to arrive.

With many nurses sick and some having to be invalided back to England, life was hard enough at No. 1 CSH but it was even worse at No. 3 CSH, which happened to be situated on the site of a former military camp and was declared insanitary. The unit's matron, Jessie Jaggard, who had helped to establish the Moore Barracks hospital at Shorncliffe, set an example to her nurses by not dwelling on the challenges, reminding them instead that they were part of the forces striving for final victory. Among those who contracted dysentery was Nursing Sister Frances Munro from Montreal, who sadly died of the disease on 7 September 1915. Jessie Jaggard herself then fell victim and Katherine Wilson described how "our very much loved Matron Jaggard has taken ill." As someone who always put the welfare of her nurses and patients above her own, she was unable to combat the disease and died on 15 September 1915 at the age of forty-two. Katherine paid tribute to her matron as "a fine, unselfish woman" who would forever "remain in the hearts of those who were privileged to serve under her."[23]

Frances Munro and Jessie Jaggard were buried at a Greek cemetery in the nearby village of Portianos. It was a barren spot with no grass or flowers growing, and the graves had to be outlined with stones. Laura Holland was struck by the terrible "loneliness of it all," and Helen Fowlds of No. 1 CSH felt much the same way.[24] She described it as "such a desolate place for a woman to be buried," with "everything so different from what it would have been at home."[25] The deaths cast a sense of gloom over everyone, all the more so given the fact that the tragedy of Lemnos had not been anticipated. Of the nurses from Britain, Canada, Australia and New Zealand who cared for the soldiers of the Gallipoli campaign, the two Canadians were the only ones who died on active service. As Mabel Clint remarked, their graves on Lemnos became "a corner that is forever Canada."[26]

At the height of the dysentery epidemic patient deaths were so numerous that according to one account, "a burial party stayed at the cemetery all day, and fifty graves were dug every night." Mabel Clint likened the situation to "the Great Plague of London," which had killed thousands in Britain's capital several centuries earlier. After the high standards of nursing in France, she admitted that it "made us feel helpless, bewildered and disgusted."[27] Faced with so many problems in trying to treat men who were dying at such a rate, the nurses felt demoralized and Helen Fowlds could not help envying those colleagues who had been accepted for temporary service aboard hospital

Laid to rest far from home. Matron Jessie Jaggard and Nursing Sister Frances Munro of No. 3 CSH died during a dysentery epidemic at Lemnos. They were buried in the local graveyard at Portianos, and this photograph, taken by Nursing Sister Helen Fowlds, shows their graves. (Helen Fowlds Marryat Papers, Trent University Archives)

ships bringing casualties from Gallipoli. For the time being at least, they could escape Lemnos and its troubles.

As the worst of the dysentery epidemic passed, thoughts turned to improving conditions on Lemnos. As Mess Sister* for her hospital, Laura Holland tried to obtain better food supplies to supplement the sour local bread, hard tack (a type of long-lasting biscuit made from flour, water and sometimes salt) and spasmodic allocations of meat and vegetables. Oil stoves were needed since the temperature at night could drop sharply, and with no means of boiling water or sterilizing anything bonfires had to be built over which an army dixie† could be suspended.

Constance Bruce described life on Lemnos in an often humorous account of her time there. She managed to find uplifting moments and enjoyed the peace and the beautiful "yellow and orange glow of the Aegean sunrise" before the sound of reveille heralded the start of another day.[28] After coming off duty, she looked forward to tea at 4.30 P.M. in the nurses' mess tent, which was "a picture of cosiness" with "pink candleshades" and an improvised fireplace made out of "rock and tin."[29] When it came to night duty, Constance described how it was "an adventure" to make her rounds armed only with

---

* In addition to their traditional work, nursing sisters could be allocated other duties. As examples, Home Sisters took care of housekeeping and shopping needs, while Mess Sisters undertook the procurement of food and other necessary provisions.

† A dixie is a large cast iron pot with a fitted lid.

lanterns or torches. She mentioned how she could often make out "flashes of light on the eastern sky" which she assumed were "reflections of gun fire on the Peninsula," and which sounded surprisingly near when the wind was blowing in the right direction.[30] Katherine Wilson also saw "star shells over the trenches of Gallipoli, and contemplated the fact that "beneath the beauty of the night men were at war, deliberately trying to kill one another."[31]

There being few newspapers and only fragmentary information about the war, the arrival of mail at Lemnos was a boost to morale. In such an isolated situation it often felt as if those posted there had been forgotten, but as Katherine Wilson later wrote, "We were not discouraged, we had faith in the pioneering spirit" of all the medical units on the island. Although there were days when life seemed "almost unbearable," a sense of humour, coupled with the fact that "we were all young, earnest, unafraid, taking things in our stride," helped the Canadian nurses to cope.[32] Little by little things began to improve, aided by better food supplies purchased from incoming ships even though, according to Anne E. Ross, they "had no orders to sell us supplies." As a result, items such as fruit, biscuits, ginger ale and even butter began to appear, and "we have all been having a treat," commented a delighted Laura Holland.[33]

With the approach of the autumn equinox the formerly hot weather became unsettled, bringing high winds and driving rain which caused flooding and general disruption. On one occasion Katherine Wilson watched as in her ward "slippers and bed pan basins went floating merrily away" beneath the rolled-up sides of the marquees, and the nurses and orderlies were reduced to wading around in raincoats and rubber boots, much like their colleagues in France.[34] Mildred Forbes described how the wild conditions "brought our tent down over our heads!" and she and a colleague were "two pitiful objects staggering out into the dark, stormy night, leaving our 'home' in what seemed to be ruins."[35] Although the patients themselves were kept dry, the tarpaulins covering the ground inside the tented wards became slippery and "many a time I nearly landed on my head," recorded another nursing colleague.[36]

As the bad weather continued, the patients were moved to new wooden huts which offered better shelter for the coming winter. When news of conditions on Lemnos finally reached Canada in October 1915, the government cabled the London authorities "to inspect the hospitals and redress disabilities."[37] Following a visit by the Assistant Director of Medical Services, things began to improve and the nurses rejoiced that the "heat and flies were over, water supplies adequate, latrines properly constructed," and they themselves had canvas collapsible huts with floors and portable coal-oil stoves.[38]

Social life on Lemnos. After several grim months combatting primitive conditions and disease, the Canadian medical staff posted to Lemnos welcomed some light relief. This snapshot shows Nursing Sister Florence Hunter (right) and her friend Nursing Sister Beatrice Blewett in improvised costumes as they prepare to attend a Hallow'een party on 31 October 1915. (Canadian War Museum, George Metcalf Archival Collection, Acc 20070103-015)

When boxes of gifts and supplies arrived courtesy of the Canadian Red Cross Society, the hospitals at Lemnos were grateful. Despite their ordeal the staff were able to appreciate such gestures and to recognize the positive aspects of their remote location. Katherine Wilson spoke of good colleagues, recreational activities, and social opportunities such as an invitation to dine with the officers of "HMS *George*",* anchored in Mudros harbour, where they enjoyed the luxury of a four-course menu with "Iced Figs," "Lindon Haddock" and a choice of beef or mutton for the main dish.[39] Among those who made the most of outdoor pastimes was Florence Hunter, who enjoyed riding, tennis, and exploring the tracks and trails that crossed the island.

Social gatherings became more frequent and the sisters' mess at No. 1 CSH proved to be popular. The remoteness of Lemnos made it easier to socialize without the strict rules normally enforced, and visitors to the mess were frequent. Given that army personnel were likely to be ordered to Gallipoli before long, these occasions could have a bittersweet quality, and one officer told his favourite nurse that he hoped "we shall meet some day in England,

---

* Probably the cruiser HMS *St. George*.

after the war, if I am lucky." But of all those who visited the Canadian nurses it seems none were more welcome than the officers of the Royal Navy, both those stationed at Mudros and others whose ships stopped at Lemnos. These young men were "the first to make life worth living on the island," wrote Constance Bruce, and she was far from alone in appreciating their presence, their invitations to take tea on board ship and their offer of a proper bath![40]

Cumulatively, such occasions and gestures had a beneficial effect on the morale of the Canadian nurses and did them "heaps of good," reported Constance. The gallant naval officers also sent regular baskets containing "cocoa, oatmeal, butter and bread," which helped to prevent "the climate, infection and the filthy surroundings on the Island from taking more toll than they did."[41] When a certain naval sub-lieutenant set his sights on a particularly "sweet and shy" Canadian nurse, who gradually overcame her reticence, he was able to sail for Egypt with "a joyful heart," proving that even on primitive Lemnos love could blossom.[42]

As winter approached the senior medical officer of No. 1 CSH decided to commandeer a newly-built hut hospital erected on higher ground which was intended for a British medical unit. The Canadians were permitted to use it and were better able to care for their patients as temperatures dropped. The last two months of the year were marked by some special events: a Hallowe'en fancy dress masquerade with improvised costumes; a band concert given by New Zealand troops; and a visit by Field Marshal Lord Kitchener, Britain's Secretary of State for War, who arrived to "decide on future plans."[43] As the autumn rain turned to snow and sleet, a "freak of climate we never would have expected," said Katherine Wilson, the latter days of the Gallipoli campaign produced many tragic cases of men who, after the earlier heat and dysentery, were now suffering from conditions such as frostbite and gangrene.[44] With the limited facilities and treatment available at a time before the discovery of antibiotics, nursing such patients remained "a heart-rending" job on occasions. Mabel Clint tried to remind herself that "we were lending whatever comfort was in our power."[45]

By now the nurses themselves were feeling the effects of the past few months and exhibited problems such as weight loss, general debility, anemia and other troubles that led to some of them being found "medically unfit."[46] There were also those who fell ill with more serious ailments, and Florence Hunter recorded in her diary during November 1915 that she was "just recovering from jaundice & feel rather rotten."[47] She was sent on leave to recuperate while most of the medical staff on Lemnos began to prepare for Christmas. They were determined to make the best of things even with a lack of traditional decorations, and thanks to a shipment of food brought from Malta by the Royal Navy there was a festive atmosphere at the two Canadian hospitals. As part of the seasonal celebrations special events were organized, including tea in the form of "sandwiches, shortbread, sweet biscuits and fruit cake" that was served to 160 guests.[48] To the British and ANZAC troops who had recently arrived from the Dardanelles, the kindness they experienced at the end of 1915 was of immediate benefit, and one of the nurses at No. 1 CSH felt nothing but admiration for "these princes among men" who laughed and joked lightheartedly in spite of their suffering.[49]

Having not met with the success they hoped for at Gallipoli, the Allied War Committee decided to bring the campaign to an end and to evacuate the troops still serving there. It was anticipated that during the withdrawal there could be as many as 25,000 casualties and the hospitals on Lemnos were ordered to increase their capacity. The arrival of a further twenty-three Canadian nurses boosted staffing levels but in the end, amid conditions of secrecy, the evacuation from Gallipoli was completed in January 1916 with almost no casualties. The total number of Allied dead or wounded during the campaign was around 189,000, of which some 56,700 died, and Helen Fowlds expressed her feelings of "sadness connected with Anzac and Suvla – such loss of life, such glorious bravery and now it is all over and in vain."[50]

The Allied medical units were ordered to begin packing up in preparation for departure, and on 28 January 1916 the staff of No. 1 and No. 3 CSH boarded the hospital ship *Dover Castle* for Egypt. They enjoyed a pleasant five-day voyage during which Florence Hunter, always able to appreciate good company, noted that there were "some charming officers on board."[51] On 2 February 1916, the day of their arrival at Alexandria, the Canadian medical staff went by train to Cairo for sightseeing, shopping and comforts that they had not enjoyed for months. No. 3 CSH was subsequently ordered to France, while No. 1 CSH left a few weeks later for Salonika in Greece.

What were the thoughts of those who had served on Lemnos? Writing about it later Mabel Clint could not remember hearing one nurse say she was sorry to have worked there despite everything they had endured, and some, like Katherine Wilson, felt it had been "a wonderful experience in many ways."[52] Laura Holland's opinion was that "we may land in a worse place than Lemnos (perhaps!)," but she was still "mighty thankful to feel we have had this experience & are off the island none the worse for it."[53] Constance Bruce looked back on Lemnos as "a chapter, unique in its joys and sorrows," and she wrote a poem of which the following verse appeared to sum up an experience she would never forget.

We were sick and we were lonely,
We were 'fed up' with no food,
We were dirty, we were dusty,
        We were sad;

But we stuck it out together,
And we tried to be polite,
And be thankful for the things
        We never had ...[54]

The Canadian "bluebirds" of Lemnos were "surely tried," wrote their Matron-in-Chief, Margaret Macdonald, in her official report, "yet of such soldierly material were they constituted, that complaint was rare."[55] The value of their work is amply illustrated in the following quote taken from a letter written in September 1916 by Sir Alfred Keogh, Director-General of British Army Medical Services, to Major-General G. Carleton Jones in Ottawa: "I called upon you for assistance. You gave me ... Hospitals. As events proved, these saved the situation ... I shall always be indebted to you for the help you gave me at a time when I was very pressed."[56]

In 1916 when volunteer nurse Vera Brittain stopped at Lemnos on her way to Malta, she visited the cemetery at Portianos. She had heard about the Canadian nurses buried there and made a point of visiting the graves of Matron Jessie Jaggard and Nursing Sister Frances Munro. Vera was deeply affected by her visit and left with the certainty that she would never again visualize Lemnos without thinking of the Canadian women who had done their duty for no reward other than being remembered in "the hearts of humble men they saved." She subsequently wrote a poem which she entitled "The Sisters' Graves at Lemnos," and in the following verse she paid her own tribute to Jessie Jaggard, Frances Munro and all their colleagues:

Seldom they enter into song or story;
Poets praise the soldier's might and deeds of War,
But few recall the Sisters, and the glory
Of women dead beneath a distant star.[57]

Vera gave her poem the Latin subtitle of *"Fidelis ad extremum"* or "Faithful to the end." Those words surely exemplify all the medical staff and the men they cared for during that arduous summer, autumn and early winter of 1915-1916 on faraway Lemnos. Distant it may have been, but they have not been forgotten and on 17 April 2015 Robert Peck, Canada's ambassador to the Hellenic Republic, unveiled a new memorial plaque at Portianos Commonwealth War Graves Commission Cemetery. Not only does it honour the memory of Jessie Jaggard and Frances Munro, but it also stands as an eloquent reminder of the medical work accomplished on the island by those "without whose dedication many more servicemen would have died."[58]

"NURSE OF THE MEDITERRANEAN": MALTA

During the First World War the British colony of Malta, an island fifty miles south of Italy and nearly 186 miles east of Tunisia, was one of the Royal Navy's principal bases in the Mediterranean. It also served as a medical treatment and recovery centre for sick and wounded soldiers posted to the eastern Mediterranean theatre of war, as a transfer point for men evacuated from Gallipoli, and as a respite posting for nursing and medical staff who themselves needed rest or recovery time from illness. Hospital personnel travelling by ship often stopped at Malta en route to other destinations and some Canadian nurses served at the island's hospitals, usually on a short-term basis. Malta's several roles meant it became a gathering place for people of various nationalities, lending the island a cosmopolitan ambience.

At its peak in January 1916 Malta housed some thirty hospitals staffed by over 900 nurses and 300 medical officers. The first patients were admitted there in March 1915 and thousands followed, with hospital staff working at a frantic pace to treat incoming casualties. Even though facilities on the Greek islands of Lemnos and Imbros were in constant use once they were established, Malta continued to handle wounded from the Dardanelles campaign and according to Australian Private O. Waller, they were well cared for. On arrival, "ladies were waiting at the landing stage and gave us drink, cigarettes, matches, biscuits, chocolates, grapes, etc.," said Waller. He described how "on certain days ladies visit the wards, bring papers of every description and other comforts too numerous to mention." As for the nurses, Private Waller found them "a very nice obliging lot they cannot do enough for us."[59]

Medical care on Malta extended well beyond emergency treatment to encompass rest, remedial care and volunteer-run social facilities for those not fully fit to return to active service. Tea rooms were set up in the town of Sliema, where popular weekly concerts were also held, and in the autumn of 1915 a former gymnasium in the capital, Valletta, was equipped with a library, bar, billiard table and a fully working stage. A convalescent home for nursing sisters was housed in what looked like a "barren, rambling house" according to Laura Holland, who visited it in August 1916. She and her colleague Mildred Forbes were on their way back to England and the sisters' home provided them with overnight accommodation. They were apparently "left to shift for ourselves," said Laura, who slept in a seven-bed dormitory with "absolutely no comforts," not even "a nail to hang one's clothes on." Regardless of the "general air of discomfort," she came to like the place and accepted that wartime arrangements, even if imperfect, were often the best available.[60]

Canadian nurse Edna Moore of Alliston, Ontario, worked at the island's St. Patrick's Hospital while awaiting orders to proceed to her next posting, while Torontonian Laura Gamble also completed a short posting there in November 1915. St. Patrick's was about four miles from Valletta on terraced land in the centre of Malta and was an encampment which Laura described as having "very comfortable Indian tents" that could accommodate fourteen patients in each.[61] The hospital's overall capacity was 1,000 beds and Laura worked under the direction of a Maltese medical officer to care for men from Suvla Bay, Gallipoli. As she helped to nurse them back to health, she came to appreciate the kind of suffering they had undergone.

Some nurses were posted to St. George's Hospital, which, according to VAD Vera Brittain, stood "on a lovely peninsula of grey rock and red sand almost encircled by the sea."[62] After England she was captivated by the warmth and light, the tropical shrubs and the hospital garden bright with "pastel-blue plumbago and pink geranium."[63] According to Private Sidney Scowcroft, who spent time there as a patient, St. George's was "one of the most up-to-date" medical facilities on the island."[64] Off duty, those working at the hospital found there were opportunities to enjoy walks, tennis parties and other social events. The difference between the "stiffness and starchiness" of the nurses in Britain and the more relaxed atmosphere of somewhere like Malta was also noticeable, so much so that "the freedom here is quite remarkable," commented Vera Brittain.[65] The Canadian sisters would undoubtedly have felt more comfortable in the less formal atmosphere and Louise Peat from Toronto, who served with the QAIMNS, spent a year there from 1916-1917 before transferring to the CAMC.[66]

Most nurses did their sightseeing in groups, as it was considered unsafe for them to travel in the region by themselves. Mabel Lucas from Toronto decided the island was an exciting "international place," but admitted that she "wouldn't dare walk alone."[67] Nevertheless, her fascination with the character, history and architecture of Malta overcame her reservations and others felt the same. Nursing Sister Elsie Collis and several of her colleagues from No. 5 CGH stopped there on the way to Greece and managed to visit local landmarks, markets, gardens and a church with paintings by an Italian master.[68]

Among Canadian nurses who recorded their impressions of Malta, Luella Denton found it an "easy and pleasant assignment," and Laura Gamble felt

Malta. The island became a British colony in 1814. The harbour at Valletta made it an important base for the Royal Navy. During the war hospitals at Malta treated wounded men from the Gallipoli campaign and other fronts in the region until enemy attacks on Allied shipping led to medical units being transferred to the Greek mainland in 1917. This post-war photograph shows the harbour and its surroundings, which Canadian nurses would have seen on their arrival. (Library of Congress)

similarly, commenting favourably on the island and its "wonderfully quaint" scenery.[69] Constance Bruce enthused about the landscape and in particular, her first glimpse of Valletta as she approached it by ship. "Very beautiful it looked," she wrote, describing "its lacy spires gleaming in the early morning sun, like a miniature model of a city, carved in white stone, floating upon the surface of the blue Mediterranean."[70] Laura Holland's brief visit left her feeling that it was a place with "much of the charm of the East, with but few of its drawbacks." Commenting on the "streets so immaculate, the people so polite & attentive, & the view at every turn glorious," such was her enjoyment of Malta that she was determined to return if ever she had the chance.[71]

As the war went on, the Mediterranean became a hunting ground for German submarines and a number of Allied warships and merchant vessels were sunk without warning in Maltese and Greek waters. After two Allied hospital ships were lost in April 1917, it was decided that the sea journey to Malta was becoming too dangerous and many of the island's hospitals were closed down in favour of new facilities on the Greek mainland. During its most active period the island acquired the apt title of "Nurse of the Mediterranean," and Canadian medical staff who spent time there certainly knew it as such. From their accounts, there is a sense that whether they were working or in transit, Malta had a unique place in their Mediterranean experience.

CHAPTER 5

"Quite different to the work we had in France"

Medical Service in Greece, the Balkans and the Middle East

O little Mother of the Island Race!
O Mother-Mistress of the distant seas!
We heard your call, and proudly take our place
Now by your side, no longer at your knees![1]

"A THOUSAND TIMES MORE COMFORTABLE THAN LEMNOS": SALONIKA
The war front that saw Allied troops in and around the Greek port of Sal-onika eventually extended from the Albanian Adriatic coast to northeastern Greece. In 1914 Austria-Hungary declared war on Serbia, which in turn de-clared war on Germany. The two Central Powers were joined by Bulgaria on 21 September 1915 and on 7 October they launched an attack on Serbia. Bul-garian units rapidly overran weaker Serbian forces, preventing them from withdrawing to the Greek border.

The Allies had promised but failed to send troops to help Serbia and when its situation became desperate, France and Britain despatched a small exped-itionary force. It arrived too late to prevent the fall of Serbia and had to re-treat in the face of massive Bulgarian opposition. By mid-December 1915 the Allies had pulled back to Greece and began to consolidate and reinforce their numbers around Salonika, the nearest port to Serbia that was situated on a gulf of the Aegean Sea. Although Greece was officially neutral in the war, Salonika became an enormous entrenched camp where Allied forces were joined by remnants of the Serbian army that had managed a difficult retreat through the mountains of Albania. By the end of 1916 the number of troops at Salonika had swelled to some 160,000.

Hospitals were needed to serve this large force, and Canada contributed three medical units as part of her agreed assistance to the Royal Army Med-ical Corps.[2] The Canadians were aware of developments in that area of the war zone and medical officer Dr. H. C. L. Lindsay recalled that, "at the ex-

86

act moment when we learned our destination the enemy had pushed back some of our divisions, and the poor Serbians were being rapidly forced from their country." That knowledge plus the challenges of disease and climate that awaited them, meant that the Canadians knew their "outlook, therefore, was not bright." But, as Dr. Lindsay admitted, "we were soldiers enough to go where we were ordered with every intention to do our best for the stricken people."[3]

No. 4 Canadian General Hospital was sent to Salonika in November 1915 and set up as a tented unit some four miles north of the city centre. It was joined by No. 5 CGH from Victoria, B.C., which had crossed from Canada a couple of months earlier and was allocated a campsite east of Salonika. For No. 5's nurses under their matron, Jean Matheson, it was the end of a journey of more than 5,900 miles that had started when they marched through the streets of their island capital and ended with their dramatic arrival at Salonika harbour, where their ship narrowly missed being bombed during an air attack. The final Canadian unit, No. 1 CSH, would arrive later after concluding its service at Lemnos.

Sisters Ruby Peterkin and May Bastedo, both from Toronto, joined No. 4 CGH in November 1915. Ruby had come straight from France and May was fresh from service on a hospital ship. May Bastedo found Salonika "very dusty & such a dirty place. Such smells."[4] Ruby Peterkin observed that it was cold with "a vicious wind I have never known." She resorted to extra sweaters and a raincoat, plus "I am wearing puttees," * she announced, preferring them to long socks.[5] When the rain turned to snow and sleet the nurses piled on additional layers of undergarments beneath their uniforms, and those on night duty slept in the beds vacated by day nurses so they could benefit from the warmth. Decent food was "very hard to get and prices appalling," so when friends from home sent boxes of supplies the Canadian nurses were grateful. Ruby Peterkin soon decided that she needed "heaps of things" for "we cannot buy a single, solitary thing" apart from items available through the military commissary. "What wouldn't we give for a day on Yonge Street," she added wistfully.[6]

No. 4 CGH was situated on a hill with a good view over the surrounding area. It thus witnessed much of the local activity: the arrival of No. 29 British General Hospital as a new neighbour; the passage of the train that brought supplies to Allied troops at Salonika on the last stage of a long over-

---

* Puttees consisted of strips of fabric wrapped around the lower leg to cover it from the knee to the ankle. They were intended to prevent water, dirt etc. from soaking into pants or boots and, by reinforcing the lower legs and feet, to reduce sprains.

Donkey riding. In 1916, while serving with No. 4 CGH at Salonika, Nursing Sister Ruby Peterkin decided to give the local transport a try. Here, in the company of a local woman who appears to be hand-spinning yarn, she is mounted on her donkey and ready to go. (Library and Archives Canada, PA-149876)

land supply route avoiding enemy-held territory; and the general road traffic with despatch riders, wagons and motor cars carrying military personnel. Because of the nature of military operations there were often quiet interludes at the hospitals, but when activity at the front intensified the noise of "guns firing back to the hills" brought concern that the medical personnel and patients might have to evacuate. As the year drew to a close and the build-up of Allied troops continued, May Bastedo noted that there were British and French soldiers in defensive positions on the outskirts of Salonika and military "camps everywhere, even to the top of the mountains."[7]

After a relatively peaceful Christmas things soon livened up, and on 29 December 1915 the nurses were startled by explosions. As May Bastedo explained, "We took [them] to be guns at first," but she later discovered it was an Austrian air raid. "Ten or twelve bombs in all" were dropped near the hospitals and "one was not 200 y[ard]s from the tents," wrote May.[8] Salonika itself suffered numerous casualties but after Allied ships in the harbour opened fire and French pilots gave chase, the enemy airplanes flew off. Undaunted, the staff of No. 4 CGH went ahead with their plans for a masquerade ball on New Year's Eve and the medical staff continued shopping and sightseeing in the city when they could. The fortifications and remains of bygone civilizations proved to be a treasure trove of history, and Dr. Lindsay of No. 5 CGH found that "nothing astonished me more than the ancient bath house" that was "so old that Egyptian hieroglyphics were still discernible on the stones."[9] As for the shops, prices were found to be exorbitant but, even so, it meant "a great deal to feel things *can* be got," observed one nurse who appreciated what Salonika had to offer.[10]

On 7 January 1916 another airplane was spotted, this time German, and one of its bombs fell in front of No. 4 CGH, where it fortunately failed to explode. Had it done so, "the casualties would have been many," reported Nursing Sister Laura Gamble, who described how she and her colleagues were "more or less terrified." Her account describes how after a shell "fell through our mess tent" and did some damage, bomb-proof dugouts were constructed for use by the nurses. This was a timely precaution in view of the enemy's reappearance on the night of 1 February.[11] A German Zeppelin airship proved to be the culprit and it returned on 27 March accompanied by ten enemy planes, which "dropped bombs all about." Laura Gamble recounted how an incendiary bomb fell on a French ordnance and ammunition column, causing "a fierce explosion & big fire," with "a good many injured and killed" and a considerable amount of damage.[12]

The final Canadian unit, No. 1 CSH, reached Salonika in March 1916 after its service at Lemnos, and took over a New Zealand tented hospital at Lembet camp, which stood "on a slight rise overlooking a long valley" three miles northeast of the city.[13] On first seeing the local terrain, Nursing Sister Mildred Forbes decided it was "very attractive," and she was struck by the snow-capped mountains in the distance, the most prominent of which was Mount Olympus, the highest peak in Greece.[14] Her friend and colleague Laura Holland was much taken with her first sighting of Salonika from the sea, describing the "mass of softly tinted square buildings closely clustered together" on a hillside which were "topped by a most picturesque citadel or fort," around which ran an ancient city wall. There were "numerous minarets" visible, and in contrast to all the "soft pastel colors," darker cypress trees could be seen here and there in the background.[15] Following nearly five centuries of Ottoman rule the picturesque old city, known today as Thessaloniki, had been annexed to Greece in 1913 after the Second Balkan War and its mixed population of Turkish-speaking Muslims, Greek and Bulgarian Christians, and Sephardic Jews made it "multicultural *avant la lettre*."[16]

Among No. 1 CSH's nurses who had transferred to Salonika were Constance Bruce, Helen Fowlds, Laura Gamble and Florence Hunter. Florence was now the hospital's assistant matron and Laura Holland felt she would do the job well, describing her as "a pretty attractive girl with a great deal of tact, & so a good one to have in the office."[17] The nurses from Lemnos found the hospital facilities "the most comfortable" they had seen in a long time, and Helen Fowlds felt "awfully fortunate" after her previous posting.[18] She decided that as a unit, "we are vastly improved … We all know each other's weak points and indulge in the plainest of home truths as if we were one big family."[19]

Things were seldom quiet for long, and on the night of 6 May 1916 German Zeppelin LZ 85 arrived over Salonika. It was quite a spectacle, according to Laura Holland, who watched "the magnificent search lights all focused on the one object, & every shot from the anti-aircraft guns illuminating the sky."[20] A shell fired from the harbour by the British battleship HMS *Agamemnon* brought down the airship, which crashed on some marshes outside the city. Most of the crew survived and were captured, and the bulk of the wreckage was put on display. Staff from the hospitals were able to acquire souvenirs, including "pieces of the frame."[21] It was an event the Canadians would not forget and Sister Emily Edwardes of No. 5 CGH had her photograph taken while she was standing on top of the wreck.

As 1916 wore on, the Greek authorities came under pressure to maintain the country's neutrality in the war. After the government in Athens buckled to German pressure and surrendered a vital fortress, tensions mounted, and

A grounded Zeppelin. When a German Zeppelin was shot down in May 1916 just outside Salonika, it created quite a stir among all those living and stationed around the city. Here, Nursing Sister Emily Edwardes can be seen standing on top of the wreck, the remains of which provided many visitors with interesting souvenirs. (City of Vancouver Archives, Port N16)

on 3 June, the day the Greeks celebrated the birthday of their king, Constantine I, political disturbances were expected. Laura Holland happened to be in Salonika and described how in the midst of a demonstration, "the French calmly walked in & took possession of the town, which is now under martial law. No resistance was shown & the whole affair was settled quite quickly."[22]

Greek soldiers waited at the harbour for a ship to take them "dear knows where, but anyway out of Salonika," said Laura, whilst on every street corner "a French soldier stood with bayonet drawn," and guards were posted at the more important buildings.[23] On 6 June the Allies "closed all Greek harbours," wrote Laura Gamble, and she and her colleagues were forbidden to leave their hospital premises. Some weeks later a Bulgarian invasion of Macedonia began, and with the Athens government refusing to support or condone any firm action, the surrender of their territory outraged many Greeks. On 31 August Laura Gamble wrote in her diary that "Macedonia has declared itself a republic," with demonstrations on the streets.[24]

It was an eventful summer, but news of the Somme offensive on the Western Front overshadowed local events and some of the nurses felt they should be helping out in France. There was, however, much work to be done where they were and No. 4 CGH moved to a new premises on the east side of Salonika, where it increased its bed capacity to 1,540. As elsewhere in that part of the world, the majority of patients were suffering from diseases endemic to the region: enteritis, dysentery, malaria and typhoid. Climatic conditions fluctuated between bitter cold winter weather with strong winds off the Macedonian plain and intense summer heat with temperatures as high as 107 degrees Fahrenheit.[25] There were the usual insects, particularly flies and mosquitoes, which emerged during the summer months to plague staff and patients alike. Surgical cases were few and Constance Bruce recalled the first one at No. 1 CSH – a man with a shrapnel wound in the foot who became the subject of intense excitement.[26]

On 22 July 1916 Laura Gamble described the hospital wards as "v[ery] busy, 1300 p[atient]s," most of whom had dysentery, malaria."[27] With so many serious medical cases and a number of nurses falling ill with malaria, those who had so far escaped it lined up for their daily dose of quinine as a deterrent, and started to wear mosquito veils, elbow-length gloves and boots. Despite such precautions, two thirds of the staff of No. 1 CSH caught the disease.[28] Such conditions were trying, especially for those who had lived through Lemnos. "We are all peevish and cross," wrote Helen Fowlds, while Mildred Forbes admitted to "getting sick of roughing it, not that we are not a thousand times more comfortable than in Lemnos." Laura Holland also felt "fed up" at times, but she recognized that she and her colleagues were nevertheless "mighty lucky to be where we are."[29]

Fortunately, the Canadian nurses could find diversions from disease, air attacks, intense heat and all the rest. There were professional lectures, committee meetings to attend and a variety of outings and events that took place away from the hospital wards. Laura Holland's letters mentioned a camp concert, a boat trip and a picnic; a "most interesting" exhibition of paintings by French military personnel in aid of the Red Cross; and how she escaped the heat one afternoon by finding a shady tea garden in the city, "where there was a beautiful breeze blowing off the sea."[30] Ruby Peterkin hoped for a chance to dance at some function or other, for "we have not danced since we joined the Army," she said, reluctant to think of "such excellent opportunities going to waste."[31]

The Canadian medical staff were hosted by the military of the different nationalities based in the vicinity of Salonika. Invitations arrived for the nurses to visit naval vessels or, when things were quiet, to join army officers for tea in their entrenched encampments above the city. The sociable Ruby Peterkin, who had been enjoying the company of a young lieutenant in the Army Service Corps, was among those asked aboard a British submarine, the *E.11*. The sub was famous for its exploits, which included the destruction of a dozen Turkish ships in the Sea of Marmara between 20 May and 8 June 1915. Her captain, Lieutenant-Commander Martin Nasmith, was awarded the Victoria Cross, and so excited was Ruby to meet him and his crew that she declared, "It is worth coming to the war just to have been on the *E.11*."[32]

Off duty, the medical staff also enjoyed getting together at cafés in Salonika such as Flocca Frères and the Café Roma, both of which were always "crowded at the tea hour."[33] Another well-known rendezvous was the White Tower, an old Venetian fort with a restaurant and beer garden illuminated at night by electric lights in the surrounding trees. It offered dinner and vaudeville entertainment with an "orchestra and gabbling waiters scurrying to and fro" and was popular with the Allied troops as the "centre of gaiety for the whole city."[34]

Constance Bruce provided a lively commentary on the diverse, international nature of life at Salonika. In addition to the Serbs, who Laura Holland thought were "good looking, well-built & the cleanest & best" among the troops she saw, Constance mentioned Turkish prisoners of war, Albanians, uniformed Greeks, "rather reserved and dignified looking" Italians, steady British soldiers striding by with their "get-there-or-die" expression and the French with their "immaculate officers always hurrying along as though

Breakfast at the White Tower. At this popular place in Salonika, Canadian nurses are seen during the summer of 1916 enjoying breakfast outdoors complete with fine china and white linen tablecloth. (Canadian War Museum, George Metcalf Archival Collection, Acc 19830499-003)

bound on urgent business." She also left a description of the Russian camp, where "every evening at dusk, the men were lined up" for a daily religious service, and how it was "thrilling to hear their voices coming on the wind."[35]

The Russians proved to be generous hosts, inviting the Canadians to join them for supper along with other Allied guests. To Constance Bruce they were "these splendid troops, singing as they marched among the mountains," and she praised them as "fine, sturdy-looking men."[36] One officer, Lieutenant George [Georgi] Kolenko, became enamoured of Florence Hunter, the assistant matron of No. 1 CSH, and when he heard she was being sent to England to recover from malaria, he wrote her a note lamenting her departure. "What shall I become here without you?" he lamented, reminding her that "here in this far and poor Macedonia there is a very warm heart that is beating only for his dearest Florence Hunter."[37]

The accumulation of Allied forces at Salonika created opportunities for international friendship and shared camaraderie. Among the lasting impressions of their time there, few Canadian nurses would forget the disease and the air raids, but neither would they forget a city full of the history of earlier civilizations, nor the happy gatherings of different nationalities set against a background of a "gorgeous sunset over Mount Olympus" and the sound of "the strains of the National Anthem" coming from the direction of the harbour.[38] Salonika, described by one medical officer as "the most cosmopolitan place for its size in the whole world," would live on in the memories of those who served there.[39]

"IF WE FOREIGN DOCTORS WERE NOT THERE... IT WOULD HAVE BEEN A CATASTROPHE": SERBIA

To the north of Greece lay the Kingdom of Serbia. Its capitulation to the Central Powers in the autumn of 1915 was another disaster in a year that had already brought great suffering to its people. Some months earlier the country had been the centre of the worst typhus epidemic in world history, and only with the aid of the Red Cross and a great deal of foreign assistance was it brought under control.

The Balkans was a region where life was harsh. The mountainous areas were isolated and many communities had primitive housing which lacked basic sanitation and electricity. In such conditions fleas and lice were common, and diseases which were easily treatable with proper resources and facilities could lead to death. The onset of typhus and relapsing fever in Serbia began at the end of 1914 and was quickly spread by lice, which were highly infectious. A British surgeon, Dr. James Johnston Abraham, was a member of the first British Red Cross mission to Serbia in 1915 and he found that the country's medical services were almost nonexistent. Widespread overcrowding and insanitary conditions were an ideal breeding ground for typhus, for which there was little preventive treatment available at the time.

At the first hospital he visited, Dr. Abraham found 600 patients and only one Russian woman doctor. There were no indoor sanitary arrangements, no running water and no operating theatre. The situation was much the same elsewhere, and when Abraham saw his first case of typhus, it "filled me with horror," he wrote, because he knew that a high percentage of people would catch it. Having at first tried to cover it up, the country's military and civil authorities had to admit the extent of the typhus epidemic. It was an old enemy that had been the "scourge of the Middle Ages," had helped "to annihilate Napoleon's army in the retreat from Moscow" and had "practically finished the Crimean War."[40]

As thousands of soldiers became ill, the disease spread to the civilian population and "people died unattended in their homes. They died in the trains fleeing south. The died in the streets of the towns," recorded James Abraham. The Serbian authorities called for international help and the British surgeon warned that all who volunteered for medical work in Serbia would face "very rough campaigning," such that only those in first-class physical health would

The typhus epidemic. In 1915 Serbia was the centre of one of the worst outbreaks of typhus in history. Here, a patient is being helped out of a wagon at a field hospital. (Library of Congress)

Ox cart ambulance. The number of sick people during the Serbian typhus epidemic led the Red Cross to use whatever means of transport were available. In this photograph its symbol can be seen on an ox cart bringing patients for treatment. (Library of Congress)

be selected.[41] Among the doctors who volunteered at the Red Cross recruiting centre in London were Montreal physicians Dr. Albiny Paquette and Dr. Irma LeVasseur. They embarked on a ship for the French port of Marseilles, arriving there on 15 June 1915, and another vessel transported them to Salonika, where French doctors and Red Cross officials briefed them, making it abundantly clear that with medical facilities in Serbia so limited and conditions so filthy, there would be a risk of "extreme contamination."[42]

It was a crisis calling for the highest level of courage and dedication, both of which Irma LeVasseur clearly had. Born into a family of artists in Quebec City, she had decided that her future lay not in art but in medicine. French-Canadian universities did not admit women medical students, so Irma went to the United States. In 1900 she qualified at the University of Saint-Paul, Minnesota, before completing her residency and undertaking further training in Europe, but she still had to petition the provincial Legislative Assembly of Quebec to be allowed to practise medicine in her home province. Her interest in setting up a facility in Montreal for sick children resulted in 1907 in the founding of the *Centre Hospitalier Universitaire Sainte-Justine*, the largest mother and child hospital in Canada. When war broke out in 1914 Irma LeVasseur was working at St. Mark's Hospital, New York, where she was also researching the causes of childhood disease at the city's health unit.[43] She had begun to find true career fulfilment but when the call came for medical help in Serbia, she answered it.

France had established a medical mission in the Serbian city of Kraguyevatz, and it was here that Irma LeVasseur began working alongside other French and Québecois medical staff, including Dr. Albiny Paquette. Paquette, who later served as a medical officer in France and Britain until the end of the war, wrote about his colleague's service during the worst of the epidemic:

> Irma LeVasseur is based at Kraguyevatc [sic] and proceeds to immunise the population at a rate of a thousand a day. She has as helpers four Austrian prisoners of war who act as her orderlies. She is setting up a makeshift hospital in the town, and patients without beds sleep on the floor. Medicines are rare, the boat that was bringing them sank in the Aegean Sea. She is overwhelmed by an impossible situation, working under daily bombardment, and has to cross large pits where the dead are piled up in their hundreds. She is a woman of action and extraordinary energy.[44]

Albiny Paquette was full of admiration for Irma's ability to survive in the midst of "so much horror and privation," but she was not the only Canadian woman who went to help the Serbs. News of their plight moved Ella

A woman of courage. Irma Le-Vasseur, a doctor from Quebec who was practising medicine in the United States at the outbreak of war in 1914, volunteered to join one of the international medical teams working in Serbia in 1915 to combat the typhus epidemic. She displayed great fortitude, staying on to set up additional medical facilities and to help Serbian women, and was imprisoned for a time by the Austro-Hungarian army. (Public domain)

Lawrence, a nurse from Winnipeg, to join the Serbian Red Cross. She was on her way to help when her ship, the *Lusitania*, was torpedoed off the south coast of Ireland by a German submarine on 7 May 1915 (see Chapter 8). Sadly, Ella was not among the survivors.[45]

Another Canadian physician, Dr Catherine Travis, went to Serbia that year. She was a native of Saint John, New Brunswick and like Irma LeVasseur, had qualified as a doctor in the United States, at Johns Hopkins University, Baltimore. In 1914 she was working as a physician in Connecticut and decided to join an American Red Cross team to provide both medical and humanitarian help to the Serbs. Catherine hoped to set up a hospital for babies, no easy task given that superstition was rife among the Serbian population and a source of interference in the treatment of patients, especially the young. With the help of colleagues, the woman doctor from New Brunswick succeeded in opening a centre to treat infants in the midst of the typhus epidemic. "Your heart would be wrung with pity," she said, as she faced suffering and tragedy on a daily basis.[46]

When enemy troops overran Serbia in the autumn of 1915, the skills of international medical units were especially needed, among them the Scottish Women's Hospitals (SWH) which had been operating three units to cope with typhus, surgical cases and general diseases, and the First Serbian-English Field Hospital run by British suffragist Mabel St. Clair Stobart.[47] She, her colleagues and others, including Catherine Travis, retreated with the Serbian army through the autumn and early winter of 1915. During their chaotic and often dangerous journey they found themselves in the midst of the "throng-

So many refugees. When German and Austro-Hungarian troops invaded Serbia in October 1915, people fled. As town after town fell to enemy soldiers, the local inhabitants moved out. Here a large number of them are gathered with their carts and possessions in the main square of Prokuplje, a community in the path of the invading army. (Library of Congress, No. 2014646269)

ing, the pressing, the hurrying" of endless numbers of refugees on the roads, and a continuous stream of "horribly smashed" troops needing attention day and night.[48] To Dr. Elsie Inglis, the medical director of the SWH, it felt as if they were all "at the very centre of the storm" and she described it as "anything but pleasant" to be with a "beaten and retreating army."[49] She and other medical staff had to treat disease, deal with accidents, and suffer through total exhaustion, bombing raids, cold weather and attacks by bandits.

Personal accounts provide further insights into the ordeal they underwent. On her return to Britain an SWH nurse was interviewed by Canadian journalist Beatrice Nasmyth. She described the bitter cold weather, the hunger endured, the harshness of the terrain that had to be crossed, frostbite that had affected her foot, and the fact that on one occasion "the head of the German Red Cross" had told her and her colleagues they were "prisoners."[50] To Beatrice, the woman's "old wicker basket, her battered granite mug, and her frost-bite" represented "a finer heroism and a brave and loyal spirit untouched by hardship and peril."[51] Tens of thousands died during the retreat, and the personnel of the SWH were among the medical units which survived that arduous time. Dr. Catherine Travis was also fortunate to be among the survivors, and when she left Serbia to return to England she had to travel by a circuitous route to avoid German and Austro-Hungarian troop lines. Crossing part of the war zone via Russia and Scandinavia was not easy and brought concern over "monetary depreciation and shortage, harsh baggage searches at national borders, black-outs, Zeppelin raids, destruction and neglect."[52]

As for Dr. Irma LeVasseur, she decided to remain in Serbia despite the difficult conditions. She was intent on making a difference to the quality of medical care and succeeded in turning an abandoned factory and a run-down school into emergency medical clinics. Repeatedly resisting orders from the occupying military forces to abandon her sick and elderly patients, she has since been described as "indomitable."[53] Irma's determination to continue her work led eventually to her incarceration in a women's prison run by the Austro-Hungarian army. There she found herself among mainly Serb women who were separated from their husbands and children, and her presence both as a doctor and as someone who believed strongly in the importance of educating women for their role as wives and mothers, was undoubtedly a source of strength. "We are now beginning to understand the importance of the housewife," Irma had stated at a lecture she gave before the war, and she fully approved of preparing women to be both educators and nurturers "with dignity." As she saw it, "a mother owes herself to her children" and their future, something that was still very uncertain in 1915.[54]

Dr. Albiny Paquette recalled that after he left Serbia he did not see Irma LeVasseur again and wondered how she had managed to get out of the country. It transpired that she left beleaguered Serbia a year later than many of her medical colleagues, when she and her fellow women prisoners were led by Austrian soldiers to Montenegro. A ship took them to safety in England or France, but Irma still felt no calling to return to Canada. She went to work for the Red Cross and continued her overseas service at a French military hospital.

Early in 1916 Catherine Travis returned to New Brunswick but she had decided that "I really want to go back to Europe." She did go back, not to work but en route to China where she chose to serve as a medical missionary. Irma LeVasseur, meanwhile, remained in France until 1922, helping many who needed care in the aftermath of the war. Both women had been part of a vital international mission to Serbia, and as fellow physician Albiny Paquette later emphasized, "If we foreign doctors had not been there to serve the population it would have been a catastrophe."[55]

"ALL NOISE AND CONFUSION ... AND OH! WHAT HEAT!": EGYPT

At the outbreak of war in 1914, Britain declared Egypt to be a protectorate. Britain had had trading and commercial interests in that country for more than a century, and the Suez Canal was of strategic importance. With the declaration of hostilities martial law was imposed, the Egyptian legislative assembly was suspended, and a new ruler, Husayn Kamil, was appointed as sultan. The Suez Canal was closed to all but Allied and neutral shipping and a sizeable British force was maintained in the country throughout the war to protect it, forming a substantial presence with other soldiers of the British Empire serving in the region. The Egyptian capital, Cairo, was a busy centre of commerce and the port city of Alexandria acted as a staging post for military movements. Both cities, in addition to being popular destinations for those on leave, also housed Allied hospitals.

When Canadian nurses arrived in Egypt on their way to or from postings, for most of them it was their first visit to a land more exotic than any they had seen before. Sailing into Alexandria harbour, they found it crowded with British and Allied warships and transports, cattle boats, hospital ships, feluccas and rafts.* Nursing Sister Katherine Wilson's first impression was "all noise and confusion, with natives slinking around in all directions, dirt, flies, and OH! what heat!"[56] Fellow nurse, Constance Bruce, was fascinated by those same "dusky natives in their unique dress" who were so different from the more familiar uniformed soldiers on board a nearby British troop transport bound for Gallipoli with its full compliment of men and a military band playing on deck.[57]

Ashore, the nurses were fascinated by Alexandria's busy streets and the "oriental confusion" of its bazaars. They noticed other features such as the crowded buildings "bleached by the sun" and the "elaborate minarets with domes."[58] It was a new cultural experience in which constant activity, sand, dust, intense heat and a blazing sun were all part of daily life. Helen Fowlds told her mother, "I loved the East ... there is something about it that fascinates one," and she was particularly taken with the native quarter of the city, which "alone was worth the whole journey."[59] For Laura Holland, the chance to visit Cairo after leaving Lemnos in 1916 was not to be missed. She liked the "wonderful picturesqueness" of all she saw and found some favourite locations, including Groppi's, a popular teashop where there were "luscious cakes & candies, & good tea & coffee."[60] Despite the heat Laura went shop-

---

* A felucca was a traditional wooden sailing boat used in the eastern Mediterranean and other protected waters such as the River Nile. It was propelled by oars or triangular-shaped lateen sails.

Staging post. After travelling through the Mediterranean by ship, Canadian nurses arrived at the Egyptian port of Alexandria and had a few days to explore what for most of them was a totally new continent and culture. Here a number of the nurses are waiting to reboard their ship for Lemnos in August 1915. (Helen Marryat Papers, Trent University Archives)

ping, finding a "semi-silk sweater" for herself and a French hairdresser where she was able to enjoy the luxury of "a good shampoo."[61] Despite its dirtier, seamier side, it seemed there were unexpected rewards in Cairo for sight-seers and shoppers alike.

No. 5 CSH was sent there in August 1915, and its personnel travelled from Alexandria by train along the banks of the River Nile. The new medical facility was housed at the Abbasieh cavalry barracks on the outskirts of the city. Mary McNaughton from Port Hope, Ontario, was on the hospital staff and seemed excited to be spending time in Egypt. She wrote to her local newspaper in Canada confirming she was "glad we are going to be left here," in spite of the heat and insects that included "flies, also mosquitoes, fleas, scorpions and little red ants that bite like mad." To people back home Mary knew it would "not sound very nice," but "the doctors say that the buildings (formerly barracks) are very large and airy. We expect to go any day now."[62]

While the new hospital accommodation was being prepared, the Canadian nursing sisters and their matron, Bertha Willoughby from Lyndhurst, Ontario, were assigned to other local medical units. One of these was the Citadel Military Hospital, housed in a medieval Islamic fortifications erected by Saladin, the famous first sultan of Egypt and Syria and leader of a 12th-century Muslim military campaign against the Crusader states in the Levant. As one of Cairo's famous landmarks it was likely to be an experience that no Canadian nurse would forget, and an inducement to delve further into the country's history.[63]

At Abbasieh No. 5 CSH, which was enlarged to become No. 7 CGH in January 1916, chiefly handled sick and wounded men from Gallipoli but it also took patients from among the Allied troops in the region. In addition to the more familiar medical conditions encountered, there was occasionally something more unusual and, as one historian pointed out, "What Canadian nursing sister could have expected to find herself dressing a camel bite?"[64] Mary McNaughton's first spell of night duty involved her in the care of ninety-four patients. Most were suffering from fairly minor problems and were "able to be up during the day and look after themselves," but she also had "a few surgical cases." Morning dressings at the end of her shift were, she decided, "the hardest work of the night" and overall she found her duties "quite different to the work we had in France," where she had served at No. 1 CGH, Étaples. Despite the drawbacks, Mary McNaughton was one Canadian who was "glad we had the chance to come to this part of the world."[65]

Mary and her fellow nurses could travel into central Cairo by street car. During their off-duty hours they became "tireless sightseers," visiting the Sphinx, the Pyramids and other ancient sites such as Heliopolis, the famed ancient Egyptian "City of the Sun." Mary also enjoyed "a sail on the Nile at sunset" and the chance to sample local food that included "cooked cucumbers, ripe figs (they are delicious), ripe dates etc." Another nurse at the hospital, Elsie Collis from Victoria, was also very taken with Egypt and in December 1915 she accepted a temporary posting with an Australian auxiliary hospital housed in a former hotel close to the Pyramids. In company with other members of the hospital staff, she made several memorable moonlit expeditions into the desert, which she described as "magic."[66]

At Alexandria, Allied medical units included British and Indian field ambulances, Australian, New Zealand, Indian and British hospitals, and some privately-run facilities such as Convalescent Hospital No. 6, established in the face of official opposition by Margherita, Lady Howard de Walden.[67] The wife of an English officer, she and others like her, including the Dowager Countess of Carnarvon, who during the Gallipoli campaign took on the post of Coordinator of Hospital Ships at Alexandria, garnered admiration for their extraordinary efforts and sheer "pluck."[68]

Of the British hospitals, No. 19 BGH handled mainly colonial non-

A very famous landmark. Few nurses wanted to miss the chance of visiting one of the most famous landmarks in the world. Here Nursing Sisters Laura Holland and Mildred Forbes (seated on the right) are seen at the Great Pyramid in January 1916 during a period of leave in Egypt following their departure from Lemnos. (Helen Marryat Papers, Trent University Archives)

commissioned officers and men. It was in a large building constructed in the Arab style with decorative arches, crenellated battlements and a minaret tower. Accommodation for the nursing staff was in the nearby New Khedival Hotel, a rather grand and ornate building. Life at No. 19 BGH was described by Voluntary Aid Detachment nursing assistant Mary "May" Bird (see Chapter 9), a music teacher from Bracebridge, Ontario. She was fortunate to be able to cope with the environment, the work and the climate, and to enjoy her outdoor activities and sightseeing in much the same way as the nurses quoted above.

The facilities to be found in Alexandria, Cairo and surroundings seem to have been appreciated by all the Canadian medical personnel who spent time there. Whether riding on a camel, lunching at Cairo's stylish Shepheard's Hotel, "full of English officers," hunting for items in shops that seemed better stocked than those in London, enjoying "the tiny cups of Turkish coffee," or being "awfully comfortable" in the elegant surroundings of the Semiramis Hotel, a symbol of the golden age of travel with its hanging gardens overlooking the Nile, Canadian nurses made the most of such opportunities.[69] Despite the arid terrain, the high temperatures and the annual sandstorms – "we have been living in and on sand and we go about the hospital armed with duster, brush and drinks," was how one of them described it – there was an undeniably large slice of adventure that came with a visit or a posting to the land of the pharaohs.[70]

Nursing Sister Mabel Clint spent longer in the country than most of the Canadians after being diagnosed with phlebitis following her return from Lemnos in 1916. She was admitted to the Anglo-American Hospital at Gezira, an island on the Nile in central Cairo, where she remained for some three months. Laura Holland felt sorry for her colleague, who she knew had not been in the best of health for some time. "Poor girl," she wrote, "she is far from young – intensely interested in her work & being of an active disposition, is going to find it difficult."[71]

Mabel was cared for by nurses from Australia and New Zealand, and found them "excellent professionally." During her time in hospital she experienced "many kindnesses" from English and other colonial nurses, and from Americans. Some of the latter ran a mission school at Heliopolis, while others had escaped from Turkey in a British ship and were happy to "adopt a Canadian derelict," recalled Mabel.[72] When she was fit enough she walked down the "avenue of great scarlet flowers" that fronted the hospital and enjoyed the proximity of the Nile, which provided some relief from temperatures that even in the month of May reached 100 degrees Fahrenheit by 6 A.M.

During her recuperation Mabel recorded several memorable occasions, one of which was a visit to the place "where Moses was found, this being the garden of Pharaoh's daughter."[73] Another was watching "that entrancing spectacle, sunset over the desert from the citadel" in Cairo. Mabel was also able to gain a deeper appreciation of the fact that "Egypt was again linked with the momentous events on a world-wide scale, and the upheaval brought uniformed men and women flocking to her ancient cities, and ships thronging the Canal."[74] Sitting on the terrace of Shepheard's Hotel watching the "pictorial review of the British Empire that passed every few minutes," the procession of "brass hats and crossed swords" of military personnel from far and wide left Mabel Clint with a feeling that Egypt would "never again see the like."[75] In the midst of a modern world war, such a striking land of desert and ancient civilizations left an indelible impression.

"BADLY OFF AS WE WERE … WE ALL DID OUR BEST": MESOPOTAMIA

After the Ottoman Empire entered the First World War on 29 October 1914, Britain had to open a military front in the province of Mesopotamia, part of present-day Iraq, to protect the oil interests that were vital to the war effort. British and Indian troops were sent to the Persian Gulf and made rapid progress inland against weak Ottoman resistance. As they headed up the Tigris

River and advanced to within some 120 miles of Baghdad, Mesopotamia's major city, by the end of September 1915 medical services were necessary to support them. Meeting a Canadian nurse in such surroundings and at such a time seemed an unlikely prospect, but the diary of a Canadian pilot on operations there during 1918 confirms her presence.

After Ottoman military leaders hastily assembled an air force by enlisting German airmen into their army, Britain sent three squadrons of the Royal Flying Corps (RFC) to Mesopotamia to maintain aerial superiority. One of many Canadians who served with the RFC was Lieutenant Harold Price from Toronto. In common with all First World War pilots he faced the challenges of flying the early airplanes, which, as one historian has described, involved a "hazardous relationship between muscle and mechanism" to keep airborne and stay alive.[76] In addition, all those posted to Mesopotamia encountered difficulties that included extremes of temperature, sandstorms, high winds and regular flooding, flies, mosquitoes and other vermin, and primitive, insanitary conditions. There were high levels of sickness and death, compounded by the difficulties of evacuating wounded men who could spend anything up to two weeks travelling by river to reach a hospital.

Nurses working in such an inhospitable area had to contend with all of this. British nurse Ida Jefferson, posted to a desert hospital inland from Basra, found the worst drawback was "the terrible heat," which was sometimes as much as "125 degrees [Fahrenheit] in the shade." She listed other problems that included rats, jackals, a limited diet with no fresh food, and a shortage of staff, often due to illness from "malarial and sandfly fevers." She and the other medical staff persevered, and "badly off as we were," she said, "we all did our best and tried to be cheery and bright." On the positive side, there were "lovely evening river picnics" along the Shat-el-Arab waterway and "magnificent change of tints in the sky" at sunrise and sunset.[77] It was, without doubt, a very demanding life for a Western woman, but Ida Jefferson and those like her at hospitals in Mesopotamia kept going.

On 1 February 1918, Lieutenant Harold Price and a fellow pilot, Lieutenant Durward, paid a social visit to No. 32 British General Hospital at Amara, a town southeast of Baghdad on the tip of the marshlands that lay between the Tigris and Euphrates rivers. They announced their presence by flying over the hospital and dropping "a message on No. 32 BGH" for the nurses, which apparently "found its way into the Sisters Mess" almost as soon as it touched the ground. Having left their planes at a nearby airfield, Price and Durward had to cross some water to get to the hospital. On the opposite bank, "half a dozen sisters were sitting waiting for us," said Price, clearly enjoying the moment.[78]

After being offered tea, the young pilots were introduced to "at least twenty sisters, amongst whom was a Canadian girl from Winnipeg, and a genuine Canadian she was too, the most energetic there," wrote Price. Known as "Bunny" to one and all, she was serving with the QAIMNS and seemed to take an upbeat approach to being in that part of the war zone. Harold Price decided that of all the girls, "Bunny" was definitely "the best sport." He and Lieutenant Durward invited some of the nurses "down to the hangars" at the airfield, and took them to the officers' mess where "a good time was had by all."[79] Two days later, before they flew north to their base at Samarra, the Canadian airmen, in a spirit of fun, "dropped a silk stocking on No. 32 … complete with messages" for the girls at the hospital. After a farewell flypast, they "crawled up to 3,000 [feet]" and headed back to base.[80]

To survive the rigours of life in such a tough location, the Canadian nurse from Winnipeg required the kind of cheerful, "have-a-go" outlook that was evident to Harold Price. British nurse Ida Jefferson described how "the good fellowship" among her colleagues was "amazing," and it meant so much that everyone was "persevering and making the best of things" while they waited for better times. Life in Canada, with its vast distances and extremes of climate, had, since the early pioneering days, tended to produce people with a practical, positive and self-sufficient approach to life. It would undoubtedly have served "Bunny" well amid the "intense number of drawbacks" to living and working in wartime Mesopotamia.[81]

CHAPTER 6

Caregiving in "the realm of politics and diplomacy"

MEDICAL SERVICE IN RUSSIA

Out of the West they come,
Into the East they go,
And ever the throbbing battle-drum
Beats on against the foe.[1]

A "GIFT TO OUR RUSSIAN ALLIES": A NEW HOSPITAL COMES INTO BEING
Russia entered the First World War in 1914 as an ally of France and Great Britain, but with the disadvantage that neither her economy nor her industrial base were able to compete with the other developed European nations. Many among the population were still living as peasants, and the Russian work force had become progressively more discontented with low wages and poor employment conditions. With the outbreak of war the people set aside their grievances to unite behind their ruler, Czar Nicholas II, but Russia was moving towards a crisis. As one observer commented, "Those who had eyes to see knew that the long-drawn drama of the Tsardom* was swiftly approaching its climax."[2]

The country's war effort began badly and deficiencies in training, supplies, equipment and military leadership became evident. The Russian army under Grand Duke Nikolai Nikolaevich, a first cousin of the czar, advanced rapidly and met little opposition until it crossed the German frontier to invade East Prussia. As supplies and ammunition ran out it faltered, and German forces steadily pushed it back towards Warsaw. In the south the Russians successfully invaded Galicia and defeated troops of Germany's ally, Austria-Hungary, but it was not long before the Austrians were on the march once more and inflicting heavy casualties.

The Russian military leadership came under re-evaluation and Czar Nicholas received a disturbing communication from General Alexei Bru-

---

* The Russian word "czar" translates as ruler or emperor. There are various transliterations of this term from the Russian (cyrillic) alphabet, including "tsar."

The czar and his family. Czar Nicholas II ruled Russia from 1894 until his forced abdication in 1917. He is seen here with his wife, Czarina Alexandra, their daughters,
Olga, Tatiana, Anastasia and Marie, and their son, Alexei. Following the so-called
"February Revolution" of 1917, the former monarch and his family were taken to
the Ural mountains and placed under house arrest. On the night of 16-17 July 1918
at Yekaterinburg, they were shot and killed by Bolsheviks. (Library of Congress)

silov, commander of the 8th Army, that his men had no rifles and were
forced to "wait patiently until their comrades fell" so that they could pick
up weapons. "The army is drowning in its own blood," concluded Brusilov,
and on 5 September 1915 Grand Duke Nikolai was replaced as commander-in-chief of the Russian forces by the czar himself.[3] As the Russians retreated, they were joined by civilians fleeing the German advance "from the
plains of Lithuania, the ports of the Baltic, and the mountains of Galicia."[4]
Military medical services had been overwhelmed early on, and with great
numbers of wounded and refugees seeking safety, shelter and medical assistance, both Moscow and Petrograd* – at that time the Russian capital and
known today as St. Petersburg – doubled in population. By the end of 1915
there were, according to one study, more than a thousand hospitals in and
around Moscow alone.[5]

---

* The city, known as St. Petersburg until the First World War broke out, changed its name because of
its German origins.

News of the scale of Russian casualties reached Britain, and the situation created an opportunity to give humanitarian assistance that could also benefit political relations. Britain was sensitive to the fact that a sizeable number of Russia's citizens, including the czarina, Alexandra Feodorovna, were of German heritage, and that valuable mineral and oil resources were to be found near the border with Germany. Concern that Russia might break with France and Britain and ally herself with the Central Powers meant that any gesture that could help keep her within the Allied entente was given special consideration. In 1915 such a gesture came in the form of a proposal for a hospital unit to be sent to Petrograd.

The idea, described as the British Empire's "gift to our Russian allies," was put forward by Lady Muriel Paget, a British humanitarian relief worker and philanthropist who before the war had led a conventional upper-class life.[6] Having grown tired of what she described as the "busy idleness" that was often the lot of women at her social level, she was determined "to do good for mankind." When she learned via a British volunteer of thousands of "famously brave and stoic" Russian soldiers suffering and dying in far greater numbers than those on the Western Front, she decided to take action.[7]

Muriel Paget's determination as "an entrepreneur and organizing genius" led to widespread support for her idea to mount a hospital project.[8] The British government and its embassy in Petrograd promoted it, and the British Red Cross, the Order of Saint John of Jerusalem, the British establishment and its Russian equivalent, also gave it their blessing.[9] The Anglo-Russian Hospital, as it would be known, was funded by public subscription and a list of prestigious donors was headed by King George V, Queen Mary and the Russian czarina. Municipalities also contributed along with the British Dominions, of which Canada sent the sum of £10,000 (the equivalent of £1,034,766 or C$1,801,556 today). The hospital's committee, under the patronage of Queen Alexandra, included the British Prime Minister Herbert Asquith, the Foreign Secretary Sir Edward Grey and other dignitaries.

As Honorary Organizing Secretary, Lady Paget put her talents to work and the fact that the Anglo-Russian Hospital came into being at all was due in no small measure to her energy and dedication. She continued to be deeply affected not only by accounts of the slaughter on the Russian front, but also by the dire situation of the wounded. When British war worker Sarah Macnaughtan arrived in Russia with a group of helpers delivering ambulances, she was told there were twenty-five thousand amputation cases in Petrograd alone. At a time before penicillin and antibiotics were available, amputation was often the only resort to prevent infection spreading and leading to death.

What Sarah Macnaughtan saw so moved her that she wrote, "This war is the crucifixion of the youth of the world."[10]

Muriel Paget began to assemble a team to help her run the Anglo-Russian Hospital and quickly identified someone she described as "the perfect person in every way." She was referring to Lady Sybil Grey, the daughter of Earl Grey, governor general of Canada from 1904 to 1911.[11] Lady Sybil, who had trained as Voluntary Aid Detachment nursing assistant (see Chapter 9), was running a convalescent hospital at Howick Hall, her family home on the northeast coast of England. Her VAD training had provided "rudimentary experience of wounds, surgery and nursing care," but Sybil Grey possessed other attributes including a background that enabled her to mix with people at all levels of society and an ability to handle situations with tact and sensitivity.[12] She spoke fluent French (the preferred language of the Russian court), had strength of character and displayed "imperturbable common-sense." In the words of her brother-in-law, Sybil's "charm, her warm human sympathies," and above all, her selfless "devotion to duty," made her an ideal candidate to help in the establishment and administration of the new hospital.[13]

The question of medical and nursing staff for Petrograd then arose. Given the nature of the mission it was decided that appointments would be made on the basis of personal recommendation. Letters were duly despatched and on 26 September 1915 at No. 3 CGH, Sophie Hoerner wrote to her mother to announce not only her own promotion, explaining that "I am to be Assistant Matron" of the hospital, but also that "one of our sisters [is] going to Russia." The nurse in question was "Miss Cotton" who was to "represent the Can[adian]. Allied Hospitals."[14]

Nursing Sister Dorothy Cotton, from Quebec City, had been recommended by Matron-in-Chief Margaret Macdonald. She was twenty-nine years of age and a member of a distinguished family with a strong military tradition. Her late father, Major-General William H. Cotton, had been Inspector-General of Militia before his death in 1914, and an elder brother had died in the South African War. Dorothy, a nursing graduate of Montreal's Royal Victoria Hospital, was appointed a sister with the Canadian Active Militia in 1914, and when No. 3 CGH was raised in Montreal she enlisted with that unit. Confirmation of her posting to Russia came through only a matter of months after her arrival in France.

Dorothy was not the only member of her family to serve overseas during the war. Two younger brothers, Charles and Ross, volunteered early, as did her brother-in-law Alexander Rosamond, who was married to Dorothy's elder sister, Mary. In happier times Alex had been the president and man-

Lady Sybil Grey. One of the organizers of the Anglo-Russian Hospital, Sybil Grey was a daughter of Albert, 4th Earl Grey, governor general of Canada from 1904 to 1911. She became a good friend of Dorothy Cotton during their time in Russia, and is seen here on her father's left, with her sister, Lady Evelyn, to his right and members of the vice-regal entourage to the rear. (Library and Archives Canada C-050179)

aging director of the Rosamond Woolen Company, a family concern in Almonte, Ontario. It was one of the leading textile manufacturers in Canada and when war broke out, Alex was in England on business. He decided to volunteer as a private soldier with the Royal Fusiliers but became an officer and transferred to the newly-formed Princess Patricia's Canadian Light Infantry.[15]

By the spring of 1915 the "Princess Pats," as they were familiarly known, were in Flanders and Mary Rosamond decided to move to England with her four daughters and sister, Elsie, so that she could be closer to her relatives overseas. The family arrived at the end of October 1915 and Mary soon found a property at Sandgate, near Folkestone in Kent. Before she went to view the Manor House, as it was called, she was able to meet both her sister Dorothy, who was on embarkation leave for Russia, and her husband, Alex, who had managed to get a few days' leave from France. The reunion took place on 31

Three devoted sisters. This photograph shows Nursing Sister Dorothy Cotton (left) with her sisters Mary (centre), whose husband, Alex, was serving on the Western Front with the Princess Patricia's Canadian Light Infantry, and Elsie (right). (Photograph courtesy of Anne and Barry Roxburgh)

October 1915 and was recorded by Mary Rosamond's eldest daughter, Kathleen. In a postcard to her grandmother, she reported that "Daddy and Aunt Doss* were at the station to meet us," and that she and her younger siblings were going to be staying at a hotel, "while mother goes & fixes up the house at Folkestone."[16]

By this time Lady Sybil Grey was on her way to Petrograd with an advance party that included Dr. Andrew Fleming, the future Commandant of the Anglo-Russian Hospital, and a young Anglo-Russian translator, Countess Olga Poutiatine.[17] On 2 November the rest of the hospital's medical staff left England from the east coast port of Immingham. Their ship, the SS *Calypso*, would take them to the Russian port of Archangel on the Dvina River, close to the White Sea. By now the Baltic Sea was part of the war zone, Germany having mounted a major but unsuccessful attack on the Gulf of Riga.[18] This meant that Allied sea traffic had to take the long route around the north coast of Norway and enter Russian waters from the Arctic.

As the only passengers on board the *Calypso*, the medical personnel consisted of twenty nursing sisters and their matron, Sophia Irvine Robertson, plus ten VAD workers, three British doctors and four orderlies. Dorothy Cotton was one of several nurses from the Dominions and the first Canadian to

---

* "Doss" was the name by which Dorothy Cotton was known to her family.

represent her country at the new Anglo-Russian Hospital. All the medical staff were briefed to be prepared not only for cold weather but also for the fact that there would be no patients to treat for some time while the hospital was being made ready.

Despite stormy conditions the *Calypso* made good progress and, on 7 November 1915, entered the Arctic Ocean. According to Dorothy Cotton there were "no ships to be seen – nothing but grey rolling seas and grey leaden sky, whilst the Northern Lights lit up the heavens at night." On 11 November the captain told his passengers that they were "at our 'Farthest North,'" and Dorothy recorded that "it was practically dark all day as the sun!!! rose at 11.20 A.M. and set at 12.40 A.M." Most of the time the only daylight was "a subdued twilight."[19] The ship was given an escort of British minesweepers to guide it through dangerous waters which "extended to the entrance of the White Sea, a distance of nearly a hundred miles." They went ahead, clearing a passage and anchoring beside the *Calypso* every day at dusk.[20]

The senior officers of the minesweepers were delighted to spend time with the medical staff on the *Calypso*, and as Dorothy Cotton wrote, "One can imagine the joy of these men meeting a British ship" having seen "no one for three months." After some good meals, and armed with "all our old newspapers and magazines!" and as many woollen items as the nurses could find, the naval officers went away happy.[21] However, mines and other wartime hazards did not always appear on cue, and after their escorts had departed and the *Calypso* was beyond the supposed danger zone, there was "much excitement" when, as Dorothy described,

> we had a narrow escape from striking a floating mine. Fortunately it was sighted by one of the officers on the look-out. The boat swerved so suddenly from its course that it was with the greatest difficulty that anyone was able to remain standing. Those who were on deck saw the mine float past not more than forty yards from the ship, looking like a huge, but menacing, football.[22]

By 18 November 1915 the SS *Calypso* was approaching Archangel and the scene ashore – sleighs on the move, lumber mills and huge piles of wood – reminded Sister Cotton of places she knew in Quebec. She never forgot her first glimpse of the town with the "rounded and exotic shaped domes of the Russian churches painted in bright blues, and the glistening of the gilded spires and crosses."[23] After docking, the medical team was greeted formally on behalf of the Russian government by an officer sent to accompany them to Petrograd. On 21 November an icebreaker, which to Dorothy's delight was flying the Canadian flag, took her and her colleagues upriver to the nearest railway station, where they began the final stage of their journey. The following three days on a train with "no blankets or linens for the berths, no dining car" and only one tap supplying water, sounded uncomfortable, but despite the inconveniences the weary travellers arrived in Petrograd at 4.15 A.M. on 24 November 1915. Waiting to greet them were Lady Sybil Grey, Dr. Andrew Fleming, several nurses and some Russian officers.[24]

Petrograd was already snow-covered, and it transpired that the *Calypso* was the last ship to navigate the Dvina River before winter. The nurses were taken to a former monastery being used as a rest home for Russian Red Cross sisters, where, in accordance with local custom, they were presented with "cake and a little salt," which they accepted to show "we appreciated their kind welcome." The newcomers spent their first night in Russia in "one enormous room, the Russians at one end and we at another," wrote Dorothy to her mother. There was little privacy, but by now everyone was accustomed to taking things as they found them, and "we have all made the best of it," she added. Breakfast included rye bread that was "villainous" in Dorothy's estimation and tasted "like weak liquorice of some sort." There then followed some "small raw smoked fish, all slithering about the plate," and "some sort of boiled turnips, I think, with a white sauce."[25] Better accommodation for the nurses was soon arranged at a former men's club in the centre of Petrograd, and all was well after they found a place where they could enjoy the luxury of a hot bath.

While the medical staff were making their way to Petrograd, Lady Sybil Grey had managed to find suitable premises for the new hospital. By now, the city was one vast medical "camp" with many of the larger houses given over to the treatment of the wounded, while hundreds of volunteers made dressings and clothing for the army. Lady Sybil had to keep in mind the political importance of the Anglo-Russian Hospital and the need for accommodation that would convey the right image. She settled on the former palace of Grand Duke Dimitri Pavlovich, a first cousin of the czar. It stood on Petrograd's principal thoroughfare, the Nevsky Prospekt, adjacent to a canal, and was an impressive Neo-Baroque building where sumptuous banquets and lavish parties for Russian high society had been held in the past. Lady Sybil was offered one floor of the palace which could accommodate 200 beds, but it would require a considerable amount of conversion work to make it suitable for use as a hospital. There being "nothing better" available, she decided to accept the offer, knowing full well that "beggars cannot be choosers, and this is War not Peace."[26]

Site of the Anglo-Russian Hospital. This view, taken some twenty years before the First World War, shows the imposing building used to house the Anglo-Russian Hospital from 1916 to 1918. Formerly a palace belonging to a member of the Russian royal family, it is today known as the Beloselsky-Belozersky Palace. (Library of Congress, 2014646337)

It was soon clear that the necessary conversion work would take time to complete. The priceless parquet floors and engraved plaster walls needed to be covered, and the space required partitioning and re-equipping. Fortunately, Sybil Grey had help from personnel of the Russian Red Cross, whose large headquarters in Petrograd administered over 500 hospitals and convalescent homes of its own.[27] Together, they addressed various matters that included the problem of language, the fact that facilities in the palace were rather basic, and how to achieve the optimal layout for wards, an operating theatre, dressing rooms, a laboratory and X-ray department, offices, a kitchen, a dispensary and storage space.[28] On 20 October 1915 Lady Sybil was invited to meet the czarina, Alexandra Feodorovna, who had agreed to be a patron of the new facility and understood what was involved in such an enterprise, having turned a large part of the Imperial Winter Palace into her own hospital. According to Sybil's description, the czarina had a "beautiful face full of sympathy and charm" and was "very, very easy to get on with."[29]

While things were taking shape at the Dimitri Palace, the nurses were at something of a loose end but invitations began to arrive, one of which involved a visit to the British Colony hospital, a small unit run by Lady Georgina Buchanan, wife of the British ambassador, Sir George Buchanan. Approaches also came from other members of the British community in Petrograd, and from some of the Russian hospitals. Dorothy Cotton noticed how in terms of nursing practices, training and standards, the Russian units differed from Canadian hospitals. Among other things, they provided an area for patients to do work which would later be defined as occupational therapy. Whatever the differences, the local hospitals seemed to "have all the modern equipment they could want" and the patients looked "clean and happy."[30]

During their first weeks in Russia the medical staff of the Anglo-Russian Hospital became more familiar with the life and culture of Petrograd, home of the famous Mariinsky Ballet, which was also known as the Imperial Russian Ballet. Despite the cold weather they explored the picturesque city with its Winter Palace and famous Hermitage Museum. Many of the museum's treasures had been taken away on account of the war, but the czar had forbidden the removal of the paintings, which were his personal property, "for fear it should cause panic."[31] The nurses enjoyed browsing in the city's commercial area, which struck Dorothy Cotton as "all very cosmopolitan," and she made a point of sampling tea at the elegant Grand Hotel d'Europe, whose terrace offered fine views over the centre of Petrograd.[32] At Gatchina, a town some twenty-eight miles distant and the site of a palace where the czar had spent his boyhood, Dorothy visited a large Polish refugee camp housing around 1,000 men, women and children.

Extra hands were needed at the Winter Palace, and the nurses of the Anglo-Russian Hospital were invited to "help the people who are working for the Russian Red Cross."[33] An area of the magnificent building had been allocated to the preparation of medical supplies, and Dorothy Cotton found herself among Russian society ladies in a huge room furnished with "work tables and a couple of [sewing] machines – Singer by the way – and two big looms … all the work looks as if it were turned out of a factory." Dorothy enjoyed her daily visits there, confirming in a letter to her sister Elsie that the "idea of rolling bandages and so on for the Russians appeals to me tremendously."[34]

The presence of troops and refugees in and around the city was a constant reminder of the war, but otherwise "we hear very little news here and never see a paper," reported Dorothy. It seemed as if people in Petrograd were "trying to hide the evidence of war" by putting on a cheerful face, behind which lay a dread that the Germans might ever invade the city.[35] According to one well-connected British resident who had "taken other steps" to keep himself informed, the situation at the Russian front had been going from "worse to worst." There were "heart-rending accounts of the Russians burning their own villages" rather than have them fall into enemy hands, of "ripe, un-reaped corn ablaze" and of "the despairing sorrow of the country people poor things!" Despite the sense of foreboding there was, according to the Russian government's Council of Ministers, no cause for alarm since "the Germans cannot reach Petrograd this winter."[36]

December heralded the festive season and the much anticipated Russian Christmas. Sybil Grey, who by now had realized how much Petrograd "re-minded me of Ottawa – deep snow and park and pines and firs so like Rock-cliffe," decided to host a party at the city's English Club. It was a lively affair, with a balalaika orchestra playing "Russian music full of airs and dancing," and Dorothy Cotton was among those invited.[37] "Being 'Canada,'" she ex-plained to a friend, "I always come in for everything that is going on," and she was pleased to make some new friends who included Francis Lindley, counsellor at the British Embassy, and his wife, Etheldreda.[38]

The highlight of Dorothy's Christmas came on Boxing Day evening, when she attended a performance of the Imperial Russian Ballet, which she re-garded as "the chance of a lifetime." She enthused about the dancing and thought the "colourings and scenery and dresses were too wonderful, much more so than anything I have seen." The year ended in style when, on New Year's Eve, Francis and Etheldreda Lindley invited Dorothy to a party at their home where everyone was plied with "supper, vodka and caviar, truly Rus-sian."[39]

"LINKING HANDS WITH RUSSIA IN THE CAUSE OF MERCY":
THE ANGLO-RUSSIAN HOSPITAL, 1916

Early in January 1916 the nurses of the Anglo-Russian Hospital helped to set up the wards and prepare for the official opening. The equipment and stores had arrived and by 25 January Dorothy Cotton reported to her mother that everything was nearly ready. At the inaugural ceremony priests of the Rus-sian Orthodox church would be present, for as Dorothy explained, "all of our hospital has to be blessed before we can take the soldiers." She had been told she would have charge of a seventy-bed ward, the largest in the hospital, with help from two nursing sisters, a VAD volunteer and *sanitars* (the name given to Russian hospital orderlies), the latter usually being men from convalescent hospitals who had recovered sufficiently to undertake such work.[40]

On 1 February 1916 the hospital was blessed and the next day at 2.30 P.M. everyone assembled for the formal opening. The wards were immaculate and the staff were smartly turned out with the doctors in their khaki dress uniform, the majority of the nursing sisters "all in white," and the VADs in their dark blue dresses and "white aprons with a red cross in the front of their bibs." Matron Sophia Irvine Robertson donned her QAIMNS uniform and Dorothy Cotton appeared in her CAMC uniform, for she was "still under the Canadian contingent."[41] The gathering, replete with choirboys, personnel from the British embassy, Russian Red Cross officials and the "High Priest in his gorgeous robe of cloth of gold and mitre thickly jewelled with diamonds and emeralds," awaited the arrival of members of the Russian royal family.[42]

Any function involving royalty was carried out with due protocol, and there were "no half measures about it!"[43] Making a striking entrance were the czar's mother, the Dowager Empress Marie Feodorovna, who was to perform the opening, accompanied by two of her granddaughters, the Grand Duchesses Olga and Tatiana, and other members of the royal family. The czarina, who had not been well, decided at short notice that she would also attend, resulting in a "great deal of work" on the part of Lady Sybil Grey and her staff. By the time the royal party arrived she was satisfied that "the palace really looked quite charming" with "pots of tulips and 'groves of palm trees', thoughtfully loaned by the Russian Red Cross."[44] Lady Sybil, meeting the Russian empress for the second time, found her "most gracious," and all present were impressed by the charm, ease of manner and extraordinary savoir-faire of the Dowager Empress.[45]

Dorothy Cotton observed that the young Grand Duchesses were dressed alike in "plain terra cotta coloured suits with ermine toques with white osprey [feathers] on one side, huge ermine muffs, soft white blouses, rather open at the neck, black velvet bands around their throats, diamond earrings." In addition, one wore "a string of pearls, the other a diamond pendant," and both were "perfect ducks, so bright and natural."[46] Publicity and visibility were part of the hospital's political agenda but unbeknown to those present that day, the occasion would mark the last gathering of Russian royalty to be seen in public.

Because Dorothy's ward had formerly housed a chapel, it was chosen as the location for the religious aspect of the day's events. She described how "the medical and nursing staff were drawn up at one side" with the priests and the choir to their right, while the officers and officials stretched from "wall to wall, a gallant array all in their different coloured uniforms and wearing numerous orders and medals." After the service the Dowager Empress and czarina toured the hospital preceded by the priests, who "blessed every room and its occupants."[47] Nursing Sister Cotton was presented to the Dowager Empress and described her as "very nice. She looked quite like

Grand opening in St. Petersburg. One of several group photographs taken at the official opening of the Anglo-Russian Hospital, this shows Czarina Alexandra Feodorova with the hospital staff. She is seated in the centre of the second row with Lady Muriel Paget to her right, Lady Sybil Grey to her left and the British ambassador, Sir George Buchanan, fourth from her left. Nursing Sister Dorothy Cotton is standing in the third row, fifth from the right. (Library and Archives Canada, PA-157352)

Queen Alexandra," which was understandable given that the two were sisters. When the royal party departed it brought to an end what Dorothy regarded as "a most successful and brilliant function."[48] The British press gave the event prominent coverage, emphasizing the "political entente" between the two countries. In the *Daily Graphic* newspaper, a photograph of the Russian royal family and hospital staff carried the headline "Linking hands with Russia in the cause of mercy."[49]

The first convoy of patients arrived on 4 February 1916 and Dorothy Cotton's ward took fifty, most of whom had been in recent actions at Riga and Dvinsk.[50] She was kept busy nursing shrapnel wounds and at first thought the condition of her patients was "not as good as that of our own Tommies." After several weeks, however, she was pleased to note that "they have improved wonderfully." To everyone's enjoyment, the czar sent balalaika players from his body guard to provide entertainment.[51]

As the winter months passed, people began to look forward to the spring and Easter. Petrograd shoppers searched for gifts, food and decorations, and Dorothy Cotton was fascinated to find that "everything has a tiny egg tied to it." As she browsed in the stores she also discovered "wonderful artificial flowers, or little stuffed birds; or chenille devils, balloons ... and all sorts of things."[52] Among the Russian Easter customs, candles were lit and at the Anglo-Russian Hospital a service was held in the chapel on Good Friday. Dorothy sent her family some Russian Easter gifts and attended an Orthodox church service, listening at midnight as "the church bells all over the city began to ring," marking the start of Easter Day.[53]

Soon "Sister Buttons," as Dorothy was known around the hospital, had more news to pass on to her family.[54] The Russian high command, to help take pressure off the besieged French city of Verdun, had opened an offensive near Vilna and thousands of wounded soldiers were arriving from great distances.[55] There was need of small, mobile medical units that could be set up nearer the source of casualties, and the Anglo-Russian Hospital decided to help. "There is a Field Hospital promised now," wrote Dorothy to her mother, "and the Matron said she would send me amongst the first."[56] It was a compliment to Dorothy that Matron Irvine Robertson, who had served in the Balkans and knew the rigours of such work, had decided that her Canadian nursing sister should serve with the mobile hospital when the time came.

On 29 April 1916 Czarina Alexandra Feodorovna paid another visit to the hospital, this time accompanied by all four of her daughters. The Grand Duchesses Olga, Tatiana, Maria and Anastasia toured the wards with their mother and "gave each patient a little ikon to wear around his neck." Dorothy Cotton was presented to the Empress and found her "very gracious" and affable, a woman who "must have been lovely" in her youth. The royal party was entertained to tea and it included numerous ladies-in-waiting and a Cossack bodyguard, who always accompanied the czarina and served as an escort to her son, Alexei, heir to the Romanov throne.[57]

The new field hospital was due to leave Petrograd in early June and as the weeks passed and the waterways became free of ice, stores and supplies arrived from Archangel. Dorothy's place on the staff of the mobile unit was confirmed, and before her new posting began, she used some of her leave entitlement to visit Moscow. On arrival she found her hotel balcony, where she enjoyed leisurely breakfasts, provided a splendid outlook. "What a joy and luxury this is to me" after "such a scramble ... for the last five months," she declared. Exploring the "old original city" on foot, she enthused about it in a postcard to her sister, Mary, remarking that "the place is full of beautiful gilded turrets and spires – some dark copper, others the most beautiful bright gold – How is it I am such a lucky person."[58] At the same time it was impossible not to be affected by the plight of the many refugees she saw. Their stories affected her deeply and Dorothy wrote in her diary, "it brings forcibly before one all the horrors of war much more even than seeing the maimed and wounded soldiers."[59]

By the time she returned to Petrograd, plans for the field hospital were nearly complete. Sybil Grey felt it would be useful for her to accompany the unit for the first few weeks it was in operation, and as the day of departure drew near an open-air service was held to mark the Anglo-Russian Hospital's first mobile facility intended for the war front. In the presence of Sir George and Lady Georgina Buchanan and a grand duchess, Russian Orthodox priests blessed the enterprise, its medical team, ancillary staff, transport and equipment.

On 10 June 1916 the field hospital set off from Petrograd in a "very long and imposing looking train." According to Dorothy Cotton, in addition to Matron Irvine Robertson and Lady Sybil Grey, the staff comprised "four English sisters including myself, and three Russian sisters, one of whom looked after the housekeeping." There were also "two English and one Australian doctor and one English dentist," two Russian VADs, four Russian Red Cross officials and 125 *sanitars*. Accompanying them would be twenty ambulances, a large number of ponies and two-wheeled carts, plus "a dog cart, and wagonette for the Staff."[60]

The journey provided a chance to relax and observe the scenery, which according to Sybil Grey changed from "very flat and rather uninteresting" to "more attractive, rather hilly with lots of lakes and pine trees."[61] At one point, "the booming of the big guns was distinctly heard," and when the train arrived at Polotsk in what is now Belarus, Sybil Grey went to negotiate with Russian army commanders close to the front line about where to set up the hospital.[62] Orders came to proceed to Varapaeva, a small town where the unit would be attached to the Guards regiment of the Russian 2nd Army. With the prospect of going to the war front came the realization that the hospital staff would soon be caring for Russian soldiers "at the heart of the fighting."[63]

At Varapaeva, wet weather transformed the ground into a sea of mud and the nights were surprisingly cold for early summer in Russia. The unit camped at the top of a hill close to a pine forest, where it remained while Sybil Grey, on the advice of a senior Russian medical officer, went ahead to Volki, a place where the Anglo-Russian Hospital field hospital would be able to use its ambulances to bring in casualties. While there, she learned that the

Guards regiment was being sent to Maladzyechna in the Minsk region of Belarus, "where the heaviest fighting is expected to take place," and that the Anglo-Russian field hospital would soon be following suit.[64]

Back at Varapaeva, a Russian officer brought news that the Canadian troops on the Western Front had again been "attacking, doing splendidly, regaining the ground previously lost, with few losses to themselves and heavy damage to the enemy," said Dorothy Cotton. "This must have been the fighting of June 14th," Dorothy told her sister, Elsie – a reference to the fact that on that day Canadian troops had re-taken positions near Ypres that had been lost earlier. It was an unexpected bonus as far as Dorothy was concerned, that "even in this out of the way Russian village, the gallantry of our men was being talked of."[65]

While awaiting orders to proceed to Maladzyechna, some of the field hospital staff went on a picnic in the nearby pine forest, which Sybil Grey described as "a great success – buttered eggs, potatoes. We watched a lovely sunset and played some foolish games." Dorothy partnered her for one of the games, the two women clearly enjoying each other's company and a friendship that had grown from their shared knowledge of Canada.[66] Soon afterwards on 27 June 1916 a large delivery of mail caught up with the Anglo-Russian field hospital, and it brought Dorothy the tragic news that both her brothers, Captain Ross Cotton of the 3rd Canadian Infantry Brigade and Lieutenant Charles Cotton, serving with 2nd Brigade, Canadian Field Artillery, had been killed in action on the Western Front. Ross, aged twenty-three, died on 2 June while leading a bombing detachment and Charles, aged twenty-five, died on 13 June. The two young officers had been in action during the Battle of Mount Sorrel and had met their end in the fighting that their sister, Dorothy, had heard about in her remote Russian posting. She must have thought of her last communication with Ross – a postcard she had sent him on 12 June 1916 saying "hope to see you in England."[67]

It was the painful duty of Dorothy's brother-in-law, Alex Rosamond, to leave his regiment at Steenvoorde, Belgium, and cross to England to break the news to his wife and sister-in-law. Alex's commanding officer, Lieutenant-Colonel Agar Adamson, wrote to his wife that "two sons of poor old General Cotton were killed, one of our officers, Rosamond, married to one of the girls … got the news in advance and he is very cut up."[68] From Sandgate Elsie Cotton wrote a moving letter to Dorothy in which she voiced her grief over the death of their brothers and how life now felt "so bleak and hopeless." "I know how heartbroken you are about those two darling boys," Elsie told Dorothy. "Everyone is talking about Charlie and Ross and saying that no two brothers have done better in the war and how sad it is that they should both go down in the same battle."[69]

Dorothy Cotton was granted permission to return to England to be with her family. As Lady Sybil Grey recorded, Dorothy made the decision to go "as it makes such a difference to her mother," who was at Sandgate with her other two daughters. Dorothy was obliged to vacate her post with the field hospital and Sybil Grey admired her handling of the situation, describing her as "marvellously plucky, I don't think I have ever seen anybody pluckier." After having "a long talk" with Dorothy the night before she left, Sybil concluded that "she really is quite wonderful."[70]

The day after Dorothy's departure the Anglo-Russian field hospital set off for Maladzyechna, a journey that for Sybil Grey brought drama and a narrow escape. On 1 July, while watching hand grenade practice by Russian troops from the shelter of a supposedly bombproof dug-out, she was hit in the face by a small piece of grenade shell. The fragment entered her cheek above her mouth and lodged in her skull, but fortunately it did not do more extensive damage. Lady Sybil was quickly and quietly taken back to Petrograd for an operation, and before long was able to reassure her parents of her recovery and the fact that her wound would "eventually show only a very small scar."[71]

Meanwhile, the Anglo-Russian field hospital moved on towards Lutsk in northwestern Ukraine, where it began its real work. Lady Muriel Paget visited it for a month and proved that she was made of stern stuff. At the end of July 1916 the field hospital was caught in the middle of a four-day battle along the banks of the River Stokhod, where it handled 538 wounded and carried out seventy-four operations. Lady Muriel wrote to her husband about seeing hundreds of untended casualties "still in the first agony of their fresh wounds," and a "continuous stream of mangled human beings." She described how a bomb fell on the field hospital compound early one morning, killing patients in an adjacent unit and peppering the tents with shrapnel. An air raid over Lutsk inflicted further casualties and deaths, and Muriel Paget admitted she had never seen "such a heart rending sight as the outside of the hospital that night." Dr. Andrew Fleming and Dr. W. Douglas Harmer, the Anglo-Russian Hospital's senior medical officers, worked for four days and nights in arduous conditions, but they and their colleagues had the satisfaction of knowing that "our hospitals were really wanted at the front."[72]

Back in England, Dorothy Cotton was temporarily attached to Moore Barracks Hospital, Shorncliffe, a few miles from where her sisters were living. At the Anglo-Russian Hospital her duties were taken over by two other Canadian nurses seconded from France, Edith Hegan of Saint John, New Brunswick, who had been with No. 2 CGH, and Gertrude Squire of Norwood, Ontario, who came from No. 1 CSH at Wimereux.[73] Dorothy's presence in Petrograd was clearly missed, however, and one of her Russian nursing colleagues, Syra Timasheff, wrote to tell her that "the two Canadian sisters are now on night duty ... They remind me of you." "I wish you were still here," added Syra, who proceeded to tell Dorothy that "the time I worked under you, was my happiest and brightest."[74]

"IT IS NOT OFTEN THAT ONE CAN WATCH THE DEATH OF A MONARCHY AND THE BIRTH OF A NEW REPUBLIC": EVENTS IN PETROGRAD, 1917-1918

Towards the end of 1916 Dorothy Cotton was invited to return to Petrograd. She had been able to spend several months with her family in England, but during that time tragedy struck again. Lieutenant Alex Rosamond was in action with his regiment, the "Princess Pats," during the Somme battles that lasted from July to November 1916. On 15 September the regiment's commanding officer, Lieutenant-Colonel Agar Adamson, wrote to his wife that at Courcelette, "the whole Division attacked after a 12-hour, most awful Artillery preparation. The Batt[alio]n gained their objective but have suffered very severely." He listed Alex Rosamond among the officers who had been wounded but he was still trying to get definitive information about casualties. The following day Colonel Adamson had to revise his casualty list and confided to his wife, "I fear poor Rosamond is dead not wounded."[75] Mary Rosamond and her sisters, Elsie and Dorothy, had now suffered three losses in the space of as many months.

Lieutenant Alexander Rosamond. Husband of Dorothy Cotton's sister Mary, and father to four young daughters, Alex was killed at Courcelette, France, during fierce fighting on 15 September 1916. He and all who died there are commemorated in the following verse of a poem by Canadian officer Captain Theodore Roberts: "September the Fifteenth. That was a day of glory, / With blood, with life, they captured the fortress town; / While far away, in the dear land they died for, / In frosty coverts the red leaves fluttered down." (Photograph courtesy of Anne and Barry Roxburgh)

During Dorothy's absence from Petrograd new staff had been arriving at the Anglo-Russian Hospital. Among them was a British VAD, Dorothy Seymour, who was struck by the "really lovely" interior of the hospital building and thought the nurses were "a very nice lot and we are awfully well treated by them."[76] As the weeks went by, she described how there was "no day without some excitement, sometimes sheer rumour, sometimes only too true," even though the average person in the street appeared to take "very little interest" in the ongoing conflict.[77]

On the home front in Russia, social tensions and unrest were worsening and the war was having a considerable impact on the country's morale and economy. Not only were Russian casualties greater than those sustained by any nation in any previous war, but daily life was beset by widespread food shortages, misery and discontent. As public support for the conflict began to wane people became receptive to propaganda and anti-war rhetoric, much of it spread by the Bolsheviks, members of what was known at the time as the Russian Social Democratic Labour Party. Founded by Vladimir Ilych Lenin and Alexander Bogdanov, it consisted mainly of people who regarded themselves as leaders of the revolutionary working class in Russia. In addition, moderates were joining the more radical political elements to call for the overthrow of Czar Nicholas II, many of whose subjects had lost faith in his ability to lead them. The situation was combustible, and it was only a matter of time before it would escalate into open revolt.

On 20 January 1917 Dorothy Cotton returned to Petrograd with another Canadian nurse, Mabel Lindsay of Ottawa, who had served in England at No. 16 CGH and with an American medical unit near Paris. They arrived in time to witness what came to be known as the "February Revolution."* Dorothy's replacements, Edith Hegan and Gertrude Squire, were still serving at the hospital and both Edith and Dorothy documented what they witnessed over the next few weeks.

By mid-February 1917 more than 100,000 Russian workers were on strike and before the end of that month the Duma, the Russian parliament, criticized the government for its failure to deal with the food shortages. As tensions mounted, Dorothy Cotton and the other Canadian nurses used a free afternoon on 1 March to visit Tsarskoye Selo, about fifteen miles south of Petrograd. It was the site of the Catherine Palace, a residence of the Imperial family and a late baroque masterpiece with extravagant interiors which Dor-

---

* In this chapter, all dates are shown in accordance with the Gregorian calendar, which the Russians later adopted on 4 January 1918.

A country in revolution. Street scenes like this in Petrograd during the so-called "February Revolution" were typical of what the nurses working at the Anglo-Russian Hospital witnessed during March 1917 in the days leading up to the abdication of Czar Nicholas II and the advent of Russia as a republic. (Library of Congress)

othy found "awfully interesting." When the women returned to Petrograd in the evening, "at the corner of the street we live on and the Nevsky, we saw a regiment of Cossacks," wrote Dorothy. By now the nurses were accustomed to seeing troops in and around the city but they learned that in their absence "there had been rioting."[78]

Next day there was "no excitement" except that the "long queues of people waiting for bread seemed longer and noisier than usual." At noon Dorothy was preparing to leave the hospital when she was told that "a crowd was coming down the Nevsky ... and that the Cossacks were out." Knowing they were the czar's mounted troops, she decided to delay her departure and wisely so, for soon a mass of people "hurled past and the Cossacks riding in the opposite direction rode right into them and scattered them." The following day crowds again gathered and "surged up and down the Nevsky, which is all guarded with soldiers," while "whole companies of Cossacks" were positioned at certain street corners to keep order.[79] On 4 March the government introduced food rationing, which instead of easing the situation led to panic buying, especially in cities where supplies had reached a critically low level.

As events unfolded, it was clear that the situation was becoming "much more serious," with many people milling around and the sound of "shooting several times." The nurses were "brought over to the hospital by motor" and remained in the building. They watched from the windows as a crowd in the Nevsky Prospekt "started to form across the street" but suddenly "every one ran wildly in all directions, most of them falling flat and crawling along on their stomachs." It was apparent that "the soldiers had fired on the people" and that they were "placed across the Nevsky higher up and it was quick rifle fire." The hospital being close by, "a few of the wounded were brought in here," said Dorothy Cotton in her account, after which "nothing more happened near us except the crowd surged." When soldiers began patrolling the streets later in the day, everyone dispersed and "hardly a soul" was to be seen.[80]

Four days later on 8 March, large crowds again gathered on the streets of Petrograd for International Women's Day* and were joined by striking workers and political agitators. Nursing Sister Edith Hegan could see hungry demonstrators clamouring for food and they joined a mass of people in the city centre. By 10 March the number of people on strike had reached 200,000 and there were sporadic violent clashes with the police. Edith's account of this phase of events also documented the fact that as angry bands roamed freely, police stations were destroyed and on one occasion a drunken mob, all of whom were "armed with a rifle or a revolver" which they "let off at intervals," forced their way into the building where the VAD nursing assistants were living. This gave Dorothy Seymour "one or two scary moments," and she likened it to a "shilling shocker night."[81]

Czar Nicholas II ordered the permanent dissolution of the Duma on 11 March 1917, and the situation remained volatile. As Edith Hegan explained, "Several times we had to stop while on the way to the hospital" because of the sound of heavy gunfire. She and her colleagues were anxious to get to safety and were concerned "lest the shots might strike some of our already badly injured patients." The upper windows of the Anglo-Russian Hospital provided an excellent vantage point from which to observe events, especially given the fact that, "it is not often that one can watch the death of a monarchy and the birth of a new republic."[82]

---

* After the Socialist Party of America organized a Woman's Day in New York City on 28 February 1909, it was proposed that an event be held annually. It became known as International Women's Day, which is celebrated around the world every year on 8 March.

A guard was posted outside the main door of the hospital and as Dorothy Cotton went on duty at 8 A.M. on 12 March, all remained quiet. Clusters of soldiers were to be seen on the Nevsky Prospekt, this time infantrymen, and there were fewer people about than normal. With rumours of the army in revolt, the nurses were despatched to their living quarters just as "thousands of people" once again emerged onto the streets. Everything was "absolutely quiet and still – an uncanny stillness in the air," as it emerged that two garrisons of soldiers in Petrograd had mutinied and shot their officers rather than continue to obey orders to fire on civilians. When regiment after regiment of the Petrograd garrison defected to join the demonstrators, the Imperial government was forced to resign and a provisional government was formed. On 15 March 1917, Czar Nicholas II abdicated the throne in favour of his brother Michael, whose refusal of the crown brought to an end the Romanov dynasty in Russia.

After the czar's abdication, "all Imperial signs or coats of arms over the shops or anywhere" were "taken down and burned." Soldiers "with fixed bayonets" demanded that the Russian flag be removed from outside the Anglo-Russian Hospital, and everyone seemed to be "wearing [a] red rosette or ribbon," while red flags flew "from the Winter Palace and the Dowager Empress's."[83] The hospital staff were left in a state of unease as the revolution progressed, and in the interests of safety they slept in the building. During further street fighting between police and rioters, machine guns were positioned at various points, one of which was thought to be on the roof of the hospital. Two bullets "came through one ward," wrote Dorothy Cotton, describing how one passed through a window while the other lodged in a cornice of the ceiling. After the hospital was searched one night at midnight by "the people" who "demanded that we at once hung out a Red Cross flag," Dorothy recorded that despite the tension, she and her colleagues "sat up all night," because they did not want to "miss anything."[84]

Throughout this time the staff of the Anglo-Russian Hospital had been treating casualties from the events taking place in Petrograd. There had been "very little trouble" with the patients and orderlies at the hospital, but even so it was "hard to settle down to anything." "I cannot tell you how it affects us," Dorothy Cotton told her sister. What she had witnessed was still "all so hard to understand," for events had moved quickly during those "most thrilling days."[85] However, by the time she completed her account of events, Dorothy was able to confirm that "now one understands what they were about."[86]

Observers of the momentous days that led to the end of Romanov rule could not help noticing how quickly the general situation returned to relative

Watching history being made. In two scenes from Dorothy Cotton's photo collection, soldiers with bayonets mounted take up a position in the street and nurses and a patient at the Anglo-Russian Hospital watch what is taking place outside their window as the February Revolution of 1917 unfolds. Members of the medical staff recorded events during that momentous time, but the full extent of what was happening did not become clear until later. (Library and Archives Canada, Dorothy Cotton fonds, PA-157327 and PA-157356)

calm and order. As far as Dorothy Cotton was concerned, "the Revolution has really been wonderful, so well managed ... quick, clean, and very tidy, little dirty work although we hear new and awful stories almost every day."[87] Dorothy Seymour, the British VAD, agreed that it had been "a most wonderfully organized thing." The transfer of power meant that "nothing is working yet," but it was soon noticeable that "the price of butter and many things has gone down tremendously" in the shops, where soldiers ensured that people were "attended to and not over charged."[88]

For the population of Petrograd, memories would remain of the seizure of the military arsenal; of Cossacks on the streets and regiments mutinying; of motor lorries and vehicles "distributing ammunition to every one, even small boys"; and newspapers that kept appearing with the latest information.[89] Most conspicuous was the colour "'Red' about everywhere," wrote Dorothy Seymour, describing it as visible evidence that "the people had won the day." On 20 March 1917, in the final act of what had been an unforgettable drama, the former czar and his family were placed under house arrest.[90]

The inevitable changes that came with the new republic began to affect the Anglo-Russian Hospital. As an example it was soon noticeable when the orderlies, instead of taking orders, formed their own committee to decide where and when they would work.[91] Dorothy Cotton, disillusioned at the decline in discipline, later summed up the work of the Anglo-Russian Hospital in three distinct phases. She referred to the first

> during the Czar's regime, when we had prestige from being under the pa-tronage of the Royal family and had only wounded soldiers as patients; the second during the revolution, with patients of all classes and in all walks of life and of both sexes … Thirdly, during the Bolshevik régime, when the patients held council to decide if they would allow one another to be operated upon after the M.O's had given their order. This time we had no patronage or prestige from any party.[92]

The third phase came about after leftist revolutionaries, led by Bolshevik party leader Vladimir Lenin, launched a nearly bloodless coup in the autumn of 1917 against the provisional government. The new regime began making peace with Germany, a move that brought to an end Russia's involvement in the First World War. The Anglo-Russian Hospital continued in operation until January 1918, when conditions were deemed too disorganized and un-safe for it to continue. It had lost its status politically and the majority of the medical staff were sent back to England, leaving the Russian Red Cross in charge.

The work of the Anglo-Russian Hospital was commemorated in 1996 when a plaque was unveiled in the entrance of the Dimitri Palace, St. Peters-burg, known today as the Beloselsky-Belozersky Palace. On 30 January 2016, to mark the 100th anniversary of the opening of the hospital and its "great symbolic significance" in helping to keep Russia "from becoming allied with Germany during the First World War," an event was held in the presence of Sir Laurence Bristow, British ambassador to the Russian Federation, and des-cendants of the medical team who worked there from 1916 to 1918.[93] All who served at the Anglo-Russian Hospital were, at a critical time, able to extend "caregiving into the realm of politics and diplomacy."[94] In doing so against the backdrop of a turbulent and changing Russia they witnessed history be-ing made, and the four Canadian nurses who went to Petrograd could look back on their service as part of their country's contribution to a unique mis-sion.

"The courage displayed by the nursing staff matched that of the greatest heroes of the war"

Medical Service at Sea

O sacred Freedom, in life's holy war,
We pay thy cost however great it be,
Through ruined cities all the earth should scar
And ships go down at sea![1]

"THE MOST DANGEROUS PART IS STILL TO BE GONE THROUGH":
THE OCEAN AS A WAR ZONE

The ships of Britain's Royal Navy were superior in numbers to those of the German surface fleet and, given the global extent of the Empire, they operated on most of the world's oceans. Both Britain and Germany relied on imports of food and other commodities, including raw materials, to supply their war industries and both nations set out to blockade the other's movements at sea. Surface vessels of the *Kaiserliche Marine*, the Imperial German Navy, were restricted mainly to the southeastern bight of the North Sea, bordered to the south by Germany and the Netherlands and to the east by Germany and Denmark. Elsewhere, the Germans increasingly used *Unterseeboote* (submarines), commonly referred to as U-boats.

The idea of a submarine sinking a ship carrying passengers, military or civilian, had been explored before the war by the writer Arthur Conan Doyle, who realized that this underwater vessel was going to change the nature of naval warfare. He was one of a few far-sighted individuals who foresaw its use offensively, and by the spring of 1916 the U-boat was recognized in Berlin as "the most effective of all naval weapons."[2] From 1914 to 1918 Germany waged submarine campaigns against Allied trade routes and shipping mainly in the seas surrounding the British Isles and France, and in the Mediterranean.

In April 1915 the *Kaiserliche Marine* sent its first U-boats to the Mediterranean in response to the Allied campaign in the Dardanelles, but found that anti-submarine netting and booms in the straits restricted movement.

Nevertheless, the Germans were intent on attacking Allied trade in the Mediterranean and deployed submarine flotillas that began menacing Allied shipping there in October 1915, sinking eighteen ships that month alone. Closer to home the German admiralty had issued a statement earlier that year that put its British counterpart on high alert. The main text was worded as follows:

> All the waters surrounding Great Britain and Ireland, including the whole of the English Channel, are hereby declared to be a war zone. From February 18 onwards every enemy merchant vessel found within this war zone will be destroyed without it always being possible to avoid danger to the crews and passengers.
>
> Neutral ships will also be exposed to danger in the war zone as, in view of the misuse of neutral flags ordered on January 31 by the British government, and owing to unforeseen incidents to which naval warfare is liable, it is impossible to avoid attacks being made on neutral ships in mistake for those of the enemy.[3]

By the end of June 1915 the Germans were deploying mine-laying submarines in the Mediterranean, and in April 1916 the U-boat *U-73* laid a minefield along the northeast coast of Malta. Soon afterwards it claimed several victims, including the British battleship HMS *Russell*, which sank in just twenty-five minutes. On 23 November 1916, while His Majesty's Hospital Ship (HMHS) *Braemar Castle* was taking casualties from Salonika to Malta, it hit a mine and among the medical staff on board was Canadian nurse Emily Edwardes, who was at Salonika with No. 5 CGH. She described how she was sitting on deck reading a book when suddenly, around 11 A.M., there was "a frightful bang" amidships. Everyone hurried to the lifeboats and life rafts, and with the ship's wireless radio destroyed in the blast its whistle sounded "a terrible prolonged noise" that eventually brought two minesweepers alongside. As Emily Edwardes later recalled, the vessel's coal bunkers "had cushioned the explosion," which still "did great damage," and a total of "five lives, all wounded soldiers" were lost. One further death occurred after everyone had been evacuated "in the small boats." Fortunately the ship did not sink and the survivors were taken ashore on the Greek island of Syros.[4]

Whether mines or submarines, the threat they posed only added to the precariousness of life, as the Canadian nurses posted to Lemnos discovered when they stopped at Alexandria in August 1915. In the harbour their ship, HMHS *Asturias*, docked next to a British transport vessel, the RMT *Royal Edward*, bound for Gallipoli with troop reinforcements and members of the

Royal Army Medical Corps. Many of the officers joined the Canadian nurses for tea and enjoyed the opportunity for some pleasant socializing. The Canadians watched the *Royal Edward* weigh anchor a day later on 13 August 1915 and an impressive sight it was as it steamed out of Alexandria. Nursing Sister Katherine Wilson recorded what happened subsequently. "Five hours later," said her account, the ship "went to the bottom of the Mediterranean, sunk with all on board, by a German submarine."[5] The U-boat in question was *UB-14*, captained by *Oberleutnant zur See* Heino von Heimburg, and the British vessel went down very quickly about six nautical miles off the Aegean island of Kandelioussa.

For many nurses from North America, medical service overseas involved crossing the Atlantic during the periods of unrestricted German submarine warfare (February-September 1915 and February 1917-November 1918). Troopships heading to Britain were normally given escorts as they approached the seas around the British Isles, and accounts by Canadians describe the precautions necessary in case of enemy attack. Katherine Wilson remembered her voyage from Halifax to Liverpool in May 1915 aboard the RMS *Hesperian*. It was soon after the tragic sinking of the passenger liner RMS *Lusitania* (see Chapter 8) and there was understandable tension. Apart from the *Hesperian*'s painted camouflage markings, inside the vessel the port-holes were "draped with black cloth that was drawn at night" so that no lights would be visible. Other strict rules were enforced: there was no lighting of matches or smoking cigarettes on deck, no whistles could be blown and "white handkerchiefs were forbidden." The Canadian nurses had to wear "a Red Cross on our uniforms" at all times, even though it was clear that they were members of the CAMC. After dark, when even the smallest light could be visible and noise could be picked up by a submarine, personnel had to be in their cabins or "in the lounge area" so that, "shrouded in darkness and silence, masked with paint and low to the water," a ship was made as inconspicuous as possible.[6]

After the Germans resumed their campaign of unrestricted submarine warfare in February 1917, the danger at sea intensified. Between then and the end of the war nine hospital ships were sunk in British and French waters and German U-boats were responsible for the loss of 6,235,878 tons of Allied and neutral shipping in 1917 alone. Canadian nurses Ella Mae Bongard and Hannah Lister, both of whom enlisted with the USANC, the nursing service of the American Expeditionary Forces, described their Atlantic crossings that year. Hannah left the United States on 7 August 1917 and had to observe rules similar to those described by Katherine Wilson.

Lights out and all women in their staterooms at 8 P.M. No light colored clothing was allowed lest the keen eyes of the Boche submarine commanders spot us. It was terrifying to undress in absolute darkness and then to lie in the dark, wondering just what you would do first if the ship were attacked.

On the tenth day of Hannah's crossing an order was given "that no-one should undress at night and that all should arise at 3.30 A.M. and be on deck at 4 A.M. That was the hardest order I think was ever given us," she decided. There were clearly concerns about the possible location and presence of enemy submarines and finally, on 20 August 1917, the ship's warning signal for an attack was given, which was "six blasts of the whistle and the firing of a gun." The nurses made their way to the lifeboats and watched what was afterwards reported to be the first real battle with German submarines since the United States had entered the war. "The firing lasted one hour and twenty minutes," Hannah recorded, adding that "on the whole the nurses were quite thrilled."[7]

Both Hannah and Ella Mae Bongard arrived safely in Britain. After a rough crossing in October 1917, Ella Mae was relieved to see destroyers waiting to escort her convoy as it approached the British Isles. "Our nine ships are still intact but the most dangerous part is still to be gone through," she wrote in her diary. "Tonight we are sleeping with part of our clothes on and the men leave all theirs on they say." Next day she noted that "we are in the most dangerous part of the danger zone but no one seems afraid. I don't realize it at all & we carry our life preservers as a matter of course. A submarine was sighted and we all turned about like a streak & turned a big circle. Quite thrilling for a few moments."[8]

In the hazardous waters around Britain, enemy activity was a constant worry. Crossing the English Channel remained risky despite the best efforts to patrol it, and six British hospital ships were lost there between 1915 and 1918.[9] When No. 3 CSH returned from Lemnos to France in early 1916, a transport vessel ferried the medical staff from Southampton to Boulogne under cover of darkness. As usual, the ship was blacked out and in the windy, rainy conditions the nurses felt that "even the swish of our rubber raincoats made eerie noises as we walked about." They were told that a British hospital ship which made the crossing regularly to bring wounded men back to England, had quite recently "been sunk … by a German submarine" and also that "the wharfinger* at Le Havre had been arrested as a German spy."[10]

---

* A wharfinger is the owner or keeper of a wharf.

Precautions were stepped up in 1917 and when Nursing Sister Beatrice Kilbourn of No. 2 CGH crossed from England to France in February of that year, she travelled with soldiers returning from leave. Since U-boats had been spotted in the area, everyone was issued with life belts and ordered to remain absolutely silent. British patrol boats busily searched for enemy activity and mines, but the two-hour Channel crossing was completed uneventfully. As far as Beatrice was concerned, the most important thing was the fact that "I was ... on my way to do the work I had dreamed of doing for so long."[11]

"NEVER BEFORE IN THE HISTORY OF THE WORLD WERE WOMEN SO SITUATED": WORKING ON A HOSPITAL SHIP

Sea transport formed a necessary part of general military operations from the outbreak of war in 1914, both for the movement of troops, war materiel and supplies, and for the evacuation and treatment of wounded men. As casualties mounted the Allied military forces pressed civilian ships into service. Hospital ships during the First World War were operated by the military or naval forces of the warring nations in or near the war zones. As an example, New Zealand had two steamers, the *Maheno* and the *Marama*, which in peacetime had carried passengers across the Tasman Sea for the Union Steamship Company. They became His Majesty's New Zealand Hospital Ships (HMNZHS) Nos. 1 and 2 and were used during the Gallipoli campaign to take thousands of men to hospitals in Malta, Alexandria and the Greek islands of Lemnos and Imbros. When the campaign ended in January 1916, the two ships transported New Zealand casualties from the Western Front to their homeland. Britain had over ninety hospital ships that operated during the war and five of these, the *Araguaya*, *Essequibo*, *Llandovery Castle*, *Letitia* and *Neuralia*, were offered to Canada.

Providing medical facilities at sea required a remarkable level of logistics. To convert a vessel to a hospital ship involved removing staterooms and setting up wards with "beds hanging from the ceiling" in a way that no matter how rough the sea, "the beds would hang practically level."[12] They were fitted with a means of making effective disinfectant through the electrolysis of sea water. The war diaries of British hospital ships reveal the challenges they could face: severe weather, difficult climatic conditions, staff sickness while coping with a full complement of wounded, outbreaks of disease on board, problems with food supplies, and very testing situations when transporting patients directly from a battlefield such as Gallipoli.

At the Dardanelles hospital ships operated within a war zone that encompassed action on land and at sea. A number of Canadian nurses were involved in the evacuation of casualties, and for most of them it was their first experience of such work. Nursing Sister May Bastedo was posted temporarily to HMHS *Kildonan Castle* and went to Gallipoli in late October and early November 1915. As her ship drew nearer to Suvla Bay, she recorded how "guns boomed all night. We are now off the Peninsula, a slip of sand with big hills behind. Guns everywhere – we can see the flash, and smoke and hear the sound of them. We are waiting for patients. No one hurries in the army, we may be here two days." May later heard and saw "a big bombardment from a gun boat off one bow and a gun boat around the point off the stern. Sound stiff at first but got used to it ... Who'd ever think I'd see a modern bombardment ... Took on board about fifty patients."[13]

Having safely evacuated its cargo of wounded, the *Kildonan Castle* was ordered to return to Suvla Bay on 10 November 1915. "We were there two days," wrote May Bastedo to her mother,

> and of course the fighting and bombarding didn't stop. In fact one gunboat on our bow fired the big guns across us on to the hills. We could hear the shells whizz through the air and see them burst and hit. Then another ship behind the point started ... You know how I love guns – well I had nervous prostration fairly. At night it was quite a sight.[14]

Another nurse on board the *Kildonan Castle* was Laura Gamble, and her diary described how she "got a splendid view of 'Chocolate Hill' and of the trenches – dug-outs – maxims and large guns. They were firing too from the sea – and we saw the huge shells exploding – shrapnel, anti-air-craft and the booming of the big guns kept us all somewhat nervous."[15] The situation was serious enough to warrant the comment in a medical publication that "surely never before in the history of the world were women so situated. In the midst of a battle fleet in action!"[16]

Once casualties had been loaded aboard a hospital ship, they were assessed and treated in conditions that could be extremely arduous. A Canadian medical officer, Lieutenant N. King Wilson, described how on one occasion there were at least a thousand patients aboard his ship, leaving him overwhelmed and "utterly lost amongst the multitude" needing his care. Each medical officer had a nursing sister to help him and they worked "hour and hour on end, all day and all night," often in "dark, hot, and ill ventilated" conditions. Wilson described how despite the best efforts, the operating room became "a veritable stinking, bloody shambles" and "the whole voyage was a nightmare."[17]

HMCHS *Llandovery Castle*. Originally built in 1914 for the Union Castle Line, the *Llandovery Castle* was one of five Canadian hospital ships to serve in the First World War. Requisitioned in 1916, she worked in the Mediterranean and on the transatlantic route transporting wounded and recuperating patients home to Canada. On 27 June 1918 she was torpedoed by the German submarine *U-86*, resulting in the loss of 234 doctors, nurses, members of the CAMC, orderlies and seamen. The incident came to be regarded as one of the worst atrocities of the war. (Nova Scotia Archives)

"THE LAST I SAW OF THE NURSING SISTERS": THE FINAL VOYAGE OF HIS MAJESTY'S CANADIAN HOSPITAL SHIP *LLANDOVERY CASTLE*

Hospital ships were protected under the Hague Convention X of 1907, the second of two international peace conferences convened at The Hague in the Netherlands. According to Convention X, such ships had to be clearly marked and lit and were obliged to give medical assistance to the wounded of all nationalities. They were not to be used for any military purpose and were prohibited from interfering with, or hampering, enemy combatant vessels. If violations of any of these legal regulations were suspected by belligerent nations, a hospital ship could be searched and if found to have contravened any of the aforementioned restrictions, it had to be warned and allowed a reasonable period time to comply. Failure to do so entitled a belligerent to capture it or take other means to enforce compliance. A non-complying hospital ship could only be fired upon if capturing it or diverting it was not a feasible option; if there was no other available means of exercising control; and if its violation was serious enough to warrant its classification as a military objective. In all other circumstances, any attack upon a hospital ship was deemed to be a war crime.[18]

Although German U-boat commanders had been instructed that "hospital ships are to be spared; they may only be attacked when they are obviously used for the transport of troops from England to France," as the U-boat campaign against Allied shipping intensified it also became more brutal.[19] In the view of certain members of the German high command, hospital ships of the Allies were in violation of the above-mentioned restrictions anyway, and German submarine captains tried to use as partial justification for their actions the fact that one of their own hospital ships, the *Ophelia*, had been taken as a prize of war in October 1914 after a naval battle off Texel on the Dutch coast.

It was an action that resulted in a British victory and the *Ophelia* was supposedly sent out to pick up survivors. British intelligence, however, ordered the vessel to be seized because it suspected that the German ship was sending coded wireless transmissions even though secret codes or their use were forbidden on hospital ships. *Amiral* Carl Scheer, commander of the II Battle Squadron of the German High Seas Fleet, was one senior naval officer who saw the incident as reason enough to "consider ourselves released from our obligations." He believed there was now "far more justification" to take action "against hospital ships which, under cover of the Red Cross flag, were patently used for the transport of troops."[20]

Medical personnel working at sea were aware that they were facing an enemy who played fast and loose with the rules of war. Whether in British waters or the Mediterranean, nurses on hospital ships were at risk, yet it was one thing to be evacuating troops from an active theatre of war such as Gallipoli, "in the midst of a battle fleet in action" with explosions "so terrific that one marvels to find oneself alive," as one nurse described it, and quite another to be proceeding peacefully and still be in danger from enemy attack.[21] Many people refused to believe that any country "would stoop so low as to fire on the Red Cross," whose symbol was prominently displayed on hospital ships, but as one nurse observed, "How little did we reckon with our enemy's want of honour."[22]

On 26 July 1916 the *Llandovery Castle*, one of the vessels leased to the Canadian forces, was commissioned as a hospital ship. Before the war the ship had been in service with the Union Castle Line and she replaced HMCHS *Letitia*, which had run aground in fog at Halifax harbour the previous year. After conversion for medical use, the *Llandovery Castle* offered space for 662 beds and was staffed by 102 medical personnel under the command of Lieutenant-Colonel Thomas H. MacDonald from Port Hawkesbury, Nova Scotia. The ship's duties took her to different theatres of the war including the eastern Mediterranean, whence she transported the nursing sisters of No. 4 CGH after the unit left Greece in August 1917.[23]

In June 1918 the *Llandovery Castle* set off from Liverpool to Canada with a full complement of wounded and convalescent soldiers. Among them was Private T. H. Potts of the 158th Battalion CEF, who was going home after losing a limb. He wrote about the voyage, describing the ship's rousing send-off by the people of Liverpool, and how the "bruised and battered" men in transit were treated to a "delicious" supper with the "first taste of real bread" in some time. When the captain alerted his passengers by sounding "the submarine signal," everyone thought that a "fatal blow had been struck" by the enemy, but soon discovered it was a boat drill. "How can we crippled, maimed, and bed-fast patients get up to the boat station in time?" wondered Private Potts, but he was impressed at how efficiently the orderlies organized the movement of patients by stretcher. "That night," said Potts, "we slept with our life-belts very close to hand."[24]

Fortunately for that particular contingent of troops, the remainder of the voyage to Canada passed without incident and once they were clear of the danger zone "the boys sang and danced to their hearts' content" with concerts, card and deck games, and even the creation of their own souvenir newspaper to mark the trip. "Of course," said Potts, "none of the passengers ever thought that 'Fritzie' would try to sink a hospital ship, travelling unprotected, all lights burning, and three big Red Crosses all illuminated, on each side."[25]

After arriving safely at Halifax on 17 June 1918, where many of its patients spoke in the highest terms of the treatment they had received, the *Llandovery Castle* prepared for its return journey to Liverpool. Favourable comments were not surprising given the professionalism and experience of the medical staff on board. Their commanding officer, Lieutenant-Colonel MacDonald, had served in Britain and France, first with a stationary hospital and later as medical officer to the 4th Canadian Labour Battalion, where he worked for many months in a forward sector of the Western Front. He had taken up his present posting some three months earlier on 19 March 1918.

The fourteen Canadian nurses serving on the *Llandovery Castle* were mostly mature women who collectively had seen a great deal of service. They came from towns and cities across the Dominion, from Victoria, British Columbia, to Souris, Prince Edward Island. Five of them had been overseas for nearly four years, having been members of the first contingent of nurses that left Canada in October 1914. A further five sisters had served at casualty clearing stations close to the front line in France and Belgium and all but two had been posted to base hospitals in France. In addition, several had spent time in the eastern Mediterranean and all had worked, even if briefly, at CAMC or Red Cross hospitals in England. Six of the nurses, including their acting matron, Margaret Fraser, also had prior experience of working on British hospital ships.

The rigours of medical work could take their toll on nurses in various ways, though a hospital ship was generally regarded as an easier posting. Of the *Llandovery Castle*'s nursing staff, two had earlier suffered nervous exhaustion caused in one instance by "the strain of constant duty for part of the time in a casualty clearing station" and in the other by months of night duty in the eastern Mediterranean. Another woman had been serving on HMCHS *Letitia* when she went aground in 1917, and Matron Fraser had spent no less than two years with No. 2 Canadian CCS on the Western Front, worrying for much of that time about the safety of her two brothers. The elder, Alistair, had already been badly wounded and not long before joining the *Llandovery Castle* Margaret Fraser learned that her younger brother, James, a lieutenant with the 16th CEF Battalion, had been killed in action on 4 March 1918.[26]

Among her subordinates, Sister Rena McLean from Souris, P.E.I., nicknamed "Bird," had nursed gas cases after the Second Battle of Ypres and been awarded the Royal Red Cross Second Class. She was described as "an attractive, fun-loving woman, kind and caring." She wrote to her family on 15 June 1918 as the *Llandovery Castle* was approaching Halifax, explaining that "this trip more than half our patients are amputation cases," and they "would make you heartsick only they are so cheerful and happy themselves." With what proved to be uncanny foresight she added, "This may be my last trip over and if it is, that means that I don't get home until dear knows when."[27] Nursing Sister Margaret Fortescue of Montreal, slender and attractive, had been with No. 3 CGH near Boulogne where the workload and climate had resulted in severe bouts of bronchitis. For her, time at sea meant lighter duties and the benefits of ozone and fresh air. Nursing Sister Carola Douglas of Swan River, Manitoba, had already spent a good deal of time on the ocean as the daughter of a sea captain and engineer. The adventurous Carola was well travelled by the time the war had started and had hurried back from Australia to enlist with the CAMC.

Nursing Sister Mae Belle Sampson from Toronto was "a pretty young woman with short bobbed fair hair and a shy smile."[28] By 1918 Mae Belle had nursed in France and the eastern Mediterranean and had been mentioned in despatches.[29] After being hospitalized with diphtheria in 1917, she was assigned to the *Llandovery Castle* on the recommendation of a medical board. Mary McKenzie, known as "Nan" to her friends, had wanted to be a nurse since her teenage years in Toronto. Before the *Llandovery Castle* left Halifax on its return journey to Britain, Nan promised her mother that she would visit her when the ship next returned to Canada. Sister Alexina Dussault from Montreal was a militia nurse who had been overseas since 1914. Her war service included time at a stationary hospital and a casualty clearing station in France. Sister Anna Stamers of Saint John, New Brunswick, had experienced enemy air attacks over her hospital at Étaples, while Sister Minnie Follette from Wards Brook, Nova Scotia, was the nurse who had been on HMCHS *Letitia* when the ship went aground at Halifax. These and the remaining members of the team constituted a dedicated group, whose only concern was for the men under their care.

The *Llandovery Castle* began its return journey to Britain and by the evening of Thursday 26 June 1918 had reached the southern end of the Western Approaches, a roughly rectangular area of the Atlantic Ocean to the west of Ireland and extending to the extremities of the British coastline – Land's End in the south west and the Orkney Islands in the north. The vessel was 116 miles from land and within the danger zone of German submarine activity, but as described by Private Potts it was clearly identified as a hospital ship. It carried no patients, only its crew of 164 men, eighty orderlies and medical officers and the fourteen nurses. As it grew dark the *Llandovery Castle* steamed quietly through the waters of the war zone, her crew watchful for any enemy activity. Unfortunately she was sighted by *U-86*, a U-boat captained by *Oberleutnant zur See* Helmut Patzig.

Major Thomas Lyon, one of the medical officers, left an account of what followed. "At 9.30 P.M. the night was clear," he said, and

> all lights were burning, with the large Red Cross signal prominently displayed amidships. Most of the medical personnel had not yet retired. Without previous warning or sight of any submarine the ship was struck just abaft the engines at No. 4 hold.
>
> There was a terrific explosion, badly wrecking the afterpart of the ship. Immediately all lights went out. The signal to stop and reverse the engines was without response, all engine room-crew evidently being killed or wounded. Consequently the ship forged forward, but was gradually forced down by the head.[30]

The *Llandovery Castle* had received a direct hit from a torpedo fired by the German submarine, which lodged in the aft end of the engine room and made it impossible to reverse the engines so as to slow down or stop the ship. Just as Major Lyon had described, it began to sink.

With the vessel's Marconi wireless wrecked, a distress signal could not be sent and as the *Llandovery Castle* started to list badly, Major Lyon explained how Lieutenant-Colonel MacDonald assembled all his medical personnel in an orderly manner at the boat stations. The evacuation began but it was dangerous work made worse by the "extreme slopes of the deck by this time, and the continued forward movement of the ship." All those who survived the explosion attempted to reach the lifeboats, two of which were already swamped with water and had broken away, and everyone was soon climbing aboard those which remained. Major Lyon, one of the last people to leave the ship, got into a lifeboat carrying the commanding officer, Captain E. A. Sylvester, and his officers. They were only some thirty to forty feet away from the *Llandovery Castle* when the stern went under, the boilers blew up and the bow stood up in the air. Then the ship disappeared in the increasing swell of the Western Approaches.[31]

Sergeant Arthur Knight from London, Ontario, another member of the medical staff, found himself in the same lifeboat as all the nursing sisters. He described the difficulty he and the boat's eight-man crew had in getting free from the ropes holding their lifeboat to the side of the ship. The boat kept smashing against the hull and repeated efforts to cut it free were to no avail. Finally the ropes snapped, allowing the lifeboat to drift away "towards the stern of the ship," said Knight. Hardly had this happened, when he saw that "suddenly the poop deck seemed to break away and sank. The suction drew us quickly into the vacuum, the boat tipped over sideways and every occupant went under."[32]

The sergeant's account made special mention of how bravely the nursing sisters faced the situation – one in which they were powerless against the force of the water. With exemplary courage they behaved "unflinchingly and calmly," said Knight, who estimated that "we were together in the boat about eight minutes." During that time "there was not a cry for help or any outward evidence of fear" shown by the women. Throughout their ordeal, Knight only heard one remark when the matron, Nursing Sister Margaret Fraser,

> turned to me as we drifted helplessly towards the stern of the ship and asked: "Sergeant, do you think there is any hope for us?" I replied, "No", seeing myself our helplessness without oars and the sinking condition of

the stern of the ship. A few seconds later we were drawn into the whirlpool of the submerged afterdeck, and the last I saw of the nursing sisters was as they were thrown over the side of the boat. All were wearing lifebelts, and of the fourteen two were in their nightdress, the others in uniform. It was doubtful if any of them came to the surface again.[33]

Knight himself went under and re-surfaced three times before he managed to cling to a piece of wreckage and was picked up by Captain Sylvester's boat. He paid tribute to the nurses and the tragic way in which their lives ended, for "these sisters had endured the hazards of the shelled areas in France, splendidly contributing to the efficiency of our Medical Service. How magnificently they faced the final ordeal on that awful evening," he said.[34]

The *Llandovery Castle* sank in just ten minutes but the horrors of 26 June 1918 were far from over. Seeing the lifeboats and men in the water, *U-86*'s captain, *Oberleutnant* Patzig, ordered his submarine to surface and to move towards them. It was quickly apparent that the German vessel intended to run down the survivors and leave nobody alive. The crew turned their machine guns on the Canadians and in the two hours that followed appalling scenes took place as the submarine attempted to erase all evidence of its actions with a "savagery and callousness" that baffled description and understanding.[35]

Major Thomas Lyon, whose lifeboat had been picking up men from the water, was shot at and, together with Captain Sylvester and two of his officers, Lyon was ordered at gunpoint to go aboard *U-86*. *Oberleutnant* Patzig apparently showed no particular surprise when informed that he had torpedoed a hospital ship and charged it with transporting eight American pilots. He accused Major Lyon of being one of them, and after denying the accusation, the medical officer was taken to the vessel's conning tower and questioned in a "coolly polite" manner about how much ammunition the ship had been carrying. "I replied that it was purely a hospital ship and that we had never carried ammunition at any time," responded Lyon. "I was then ordered back to the lifeboat" and "we pushed off. We had only gone about fifty yards when they headed for us again and asked for me."[36]

After Lyon was once more interrogated and released, another crew member, Private G. R. Hickman, was taken to Patzig and questioned before being deposited in Captain Sylvester's lifeboat. Major Lyon then reported that all of a sudden "we saw the submarine coming at us at full speed. There was no doubt of their intention to ram us. She missed us by less than two feet. Had we been stationary we certainly would have been submerged".

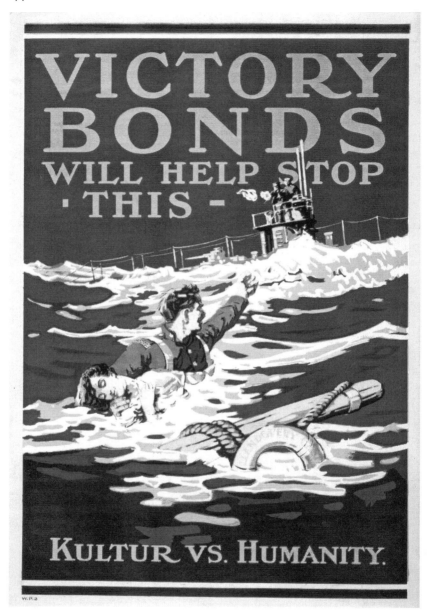

"Kultur vs. Humanity." The sinking of the *Llandovery Castle*, which caused international outrage, led to a flurry of anti-German propaganda. This poster, promoting the sale of Victory Bonds, features the central figure of a drowned woman against a background of the ship's destruction. The reference to *"Kultur"* (culture) contrasts inhumane German beliefs and attitudes with those of other nations. It was a theme that featured prominently in Allied propaganda during the war. (Library of Congress)

Lyon and his comrades redoubled their efforts to get away and were "distant probably half a mile when we heard shell fire," he said. "I can recall at least twelve shots presumably in the area where the lifeboats and survivors were supposed to be. One shell came very close to our own boat."[37] Sergeant Knight was clearly able to recall that while he was in the water, which was starting to develop a heavy swell, he witnessed a boat being shelled by *U-86*. In his opinion at least thirty shells were fired by the submarine in the vicinity of the lifeboats and the surrounding wreckage.[38] The U-boat was still searching out the survivors of the *Llandovery Castle* more than an hour and a half after she had sunk.

Only the twenty-four people in the captain's lifeboat managed to survive the attack, including six of the medical staff. In addition to the nurses, their commanding officer, Lieutenant-Colonel Howard MacDonald, was also lost, and all those who did not survive that night were officially reported "missing presumed drowned."[39] From 11 P.M. on the night of 26 June until 9.30 A.M. on the morning of 28 June the one surviving lifeboat headed for the Irish coast, covering around seventy miles by alternately sailing or rowing. Those on board were finally rescued by the British destroyer HMS *Lysander* and taken to Queenstown before being moved to Plymouth on 30 June 1918.

After the Secretary of the Admiralty announced the loss of the *Llandovery Castle* on 1 July 1918, newspapers gave it detailed coverage the following day. The London *Times* went to press at 12.01 A.M. on 2 July with the headline "Hospital Ship outrage off the Fastnet."[40] In Canada, the *Halifax Chronicle Herald* chose the banner headline, "Canadian Hospital Ship Sunk and Hundreds Missing," while the Toronto *Star* highlighted "The Last Victim of Hun Ferocity." The *Star* also mentioned that six hundred seamen and stewards at Liverpool had passed a resolution "strongly protesting against the latest crime of sinking the hospital ship Llandovery Castle without warning."[41]

At base hospitals and casualty clearing stations in France, where most of the dead nurses had worked, the news was received with great sadness. Nursing Sister Mildred Forbes wrote to a friend, "Wasn't it *awful* about those fourteen girls on the Hospital ship? I knew most of them & it haunts me at night."[42] Only a few weeks earlier Assistant Matron Sophie Hoerner of No. 3 CGH had been granted leave in Canada and had worked her passage home on the ill-fated *Llandovery Castle*.[43] Now, in addition to grief at the death of skilled and dedicated medical staff whose only desire was to save lives, there was a determination among Canadians that their sacrifice should not be in vain. Wartime Victory Bonds posters were printed, one of which showed a Canadian soldier floating in the ocean and holding a drowned woman, while

raising his fist at a nearby German submarine. With the slogan "Kultur ver-
sus Humanity," it was a reference to the sinking of the *Llandovery Castle* and
a few weeks later, the tragedy was still fresh in the minds of Canadian troops
as they prepared for a major offensive on the Western Front. In the early
hours of 8 August 1918, as the men of the 3rd Canadian Infantry Division
waited for the signal to attack, their commanding officer, General George
Tuxford, gave the order that the battle cry should be "Llandovery Castle" and
that this cry should be "the last to ring in the ears of the Hun as the bayonet
was driven home."[44]

The very worst aspect of that dreadful June evening was, as Major Thomas
Lyon emphasized, that "the submarine made no attempt to rescue any one,
but on the contrary did everything in its power to destroy every trace of the
ship and its personnel and crew."[45] Sergeant Knight also described the per-
sistent efforts of the submarine to erase all evidence of its crime by cruising
numerous times in a zig-zag fashion through the area where the survivors
were, and the testimonies heard at the subsequent formal enquiry into the
sinking only served to add weight to the evidence of "wanton destruction" on
the part of the German captain and his crew.[46] The official British report stated that the regulations covering hospital ships "were being observed in both
spirit and the letter" and it was clear that "there were no grounds whatever
for mistaking the ship for anything other than what she was," a ship "immune
by every law of war and peace from attack or molestation." The report further
stated that it was "unnecessary to assert" that the accusation on the part of
the German U-boat commander that the *Llandovery Castle* had American
pilots or munitions of war on board was "pure fiction."[47]

The story of the *Llandovery Castle* was publicized as First World War
propaganda in Britain, Canada and the USA during the remaining few
months of the conflict. When hostilities ended, a committee of lawyers was
convened to examine the subject of war crimes and a commission was set
up for the same purpose, attended by representatives of all the Allied countries. Immediately after the Treaty of Versailles came into force in January
1920 a list of people wanted by the Allies was submitted to Germany, including the names of the captain of *U-86, Oberleutnant zur See* Helmut Patzig,
his first officer, *Leutnant* Ludwig Dithmar, and second officer, *Leutnant* John
Boldt. Dithmar and Boldt were arrested in Germany for complicity in the
act of firing on the lifeboats of HMCHS *Llandovery Castle* and were taken
to Leipzig, where they were put on trial. Patzig, however, evaded arrest and
was thought to have returned to Danzig, his birthplace, which was a free city
not under German jurisdiction. At the invitation of the German authorities

"Something to Remember after the War." This cartoon by American W.A. Rogers, who worked for a variety of publications including *Harper's Weekly*, the *New York Herald* and the *Washington Post*, was completed in 1917. By the middle of that year, no fewer than sixteen Allied hospital ships had been sunk by German U-boats or mines, and the cartoon drew attention to the fact that flying the flag of a hospital ship and caring for those in need was no protection from such attacks. (Library of Congress)

the British government sent a mission to Leipzig to supply evidence against Patzig.

During the hearing it was stated that the German Naval Command had given orders that hospital ships "were only to be sunk within the limits of a certain barred area" and that this was a long way from where the *Llandovery Castle* was attacked. "Patzig knew this and … was aware that he was acting against orders," said the report of proceedings, which also reiterated the fact that the submarine captain was of the opinion, based on various sources of information, that Allied hospital ships were being used to transport supplies, combatants and munitions.[48] Assuming this to be true for the *Llandovery Castle*, Patzig had decided to torpedo the ship.

Although the German court could find no conclusive evidence that *U-86* had been intent on ramming the lifeboat containing Major Lyon, Captain Sylvester and the other occupants, it did accept, based on an expert examination of the number of shots fired by *U-86*'s large gun, that the firing was

Margaret Fraser. Nova Scotian Margaret Marjory Fraser, born in 1885, enlisted in the CAMC in 1914. At that time her father was the lieutenant governor of the province. Margaret was posted to No. 2 Canadian Stationary Hospital, France, and in 1916 she served with No. 1 and No. 2 Canadian Casualty Clearing Stations on the Western Front. During 1917 she was posted to hospitals in England, and that same year undertook periods of service on two other hospital ships, HMCHS *Letitia* and *Araguaya*. Her leadership qualities led to her appointment as acting matron of the *Llandovery Castle* in March 1918. (Public domain)

directed at boats which "by their very proximity would form an excellent target."[49] In addition, evidence given by members of the U-boat's crew "made it abundantly clear" that the firing from *U-86* was directed against the "unhappy men and women in the life-boats." The German court concluded that the lifeboats had been "fired on in order to sink them."[50]

Both Dithmar and Boldt refused to give evidence at the trial, maintaining that they had given their word to their captain that they would disclose no information concerning the *Llandovery Castle*. This led the court to conclude that "events which deserve punishment did take place," and that if the promise of secrecy had only referred to the act of torpedoing the ship, Patzig could have found a way to release his subordinates from that promise.[51] Also significant was the fact that Patzig endeavoured to conceal all the events that took place after the torpedoing and made no entry at all in his ship's log, even going so far as to mark on his navigation chart incorrect details about the route taken by *U-86* in relation to the sinking. It could be assumed, therefore, that Patzig had taken that step so that "official inquiries could not connect him with it." As a result, the German Admiralty had no knowledge of the fate of the *Llandovery Castle* and denied that the events of 26 June 1918 had ever taken place when the British protested to Berlin.[52]

Oberleutnant Patzig's conduct was the subject of severe censure by the state attorney who prosecuted at the trial. He described it as "cowardice" and

Rena McLean. Born in 1879 at Souris, P.E.I., Rena was the daughter of a businessman and Conservative politician. She trained as a nurse at Newport, Rhode Island, and was working in the United States when war broke out. After enlisting in the CAMC in 1914, she was posted to No. 2 Canadian Stationary Hospital and helped to establish the unit at Le Touquet. She later served in England and Salonika, and undertook a short posting to another hospital ship, the *Araguaya*. Rena was assigned to the *Llandovery Castle* in March 1918, and plaques in her memory can be found in her home province at Souris and Charlottetown. (© Imperial War Museum)

"colossal meanness," and was convinced that all the while Patzig remained out of reach of the German authorities, he knew that two of his crew were being held responsible for the crime that had been committed. "It would be natural and his duty for him to appear to tell the truth," said the German attorney. "If Patzig believes that he, and not the accused officers, is guilty, he should come before the court."[53]

As the trial in Leipzig moved towards its end, the court concluded that "the act of Patzig is homicide" but found it to be manslaughter rather than murder. It also found that whilst the principal guilt rested with him, his subordinate officers, Dithmar and Boldt, should have refused to obey Patzig's orders even though doing so would have been extremely unusual. "The killing of defenceless shipwrecked people" was "an act in the highest degree contrary to ethical principles," said the German court, and both men were sentenced to four years in prison. Dithmar was ordered to be dismissed from the Imperial German Navy and Boldt, who had by then retired from the service, was barred from wearing an officer's uniform again.[54]

The case became famous on account of Patzig's avoidance of prosecution and the fact that Dithmar and Boldt subsequently escaped from imprisonment with help from an organization associated with the militant right wing in Germany. Despite police investigations and generous rewards, they remained at large. At a later Court of Appeal they were acquitted on the

Alexina Dussault. Born in 1882, Alexina Dussault was a trained nurse from Quebec who joined the CAMC in September 1914. She served on Salisbury Plain, later joining No. 2 Canadian Stationary Hospital. In 1916 she was posted to No. 2 Canadian Casualty Clearing Station, where she remained until May 1917. She then began work on board the hospital ships *Letitia* and *Araguaya*. In March 1918, Alexina transferred to the *Llandovery Castle*. (© Imperial War Museum)

Minnie Follette. From Wards Brook, Nova Scotia, Minnie Follette was born in 1884. She enlisted in the CAMC in 1914 and served at a Canadian casualty clearing station and at hospitals in England and France. In March 1916 she was found to be suffering from nervous exhaustion and received treatment in England. She returned to duty and worked at a hospital in France until March 1917, when she was hospitalized with bronchitis. Following her recovery, she served on HMCHS Letitia and at No. 16 Canadian General Hospital in England before joining the *Llandovery Castle*. (© Imperial War Museum)

grounds that *Oberleutnant* Patzig was solely responsible for the crime that was committed.[55]

The sinking of the *Llandovery Castle* came to be regarded internationally as one of the major atrocities of the First World War. Within the tragedy were moving stories of dedicated men and women who fulfilled their duty to the last. The loss of all the nurses was a source of great grief, but also pride.

IN MEMORIAM

Christina Campbell of Victoria, B.C., aged 30. Joined the Canadian Expeditionary Force (CEF) on 16 September 1915. Served in France, Salonika and England.

Carola Josephine Douglas of Swan River, Manitoba, aged 30. Joined the CEF on 2 March 1915. Served in France, Salonika and England.

Alexina Dussault of Montreal, aged 36. Joined the CEF on 25 September 1914. Served in France, England, and on transport duty with two other hospital ships.

Minnie Asenath Follette of Wards Brook, Nova Scotia, aged 33. Joined the CAMC on 21 September 1914. Served in France and England.

Margaret Jane Fortescue of Montreal, aged 40. Joined the CAMC on 13 April 1915. Served in France.

Margaret Marjory Fraser of Moose Jaw, Saskatchewan, aged 33. Acting Matron. Joined the CAMC on 28 September 1914. Served in France, England, and on transport duty with two other hospital ships.

Minnie Katherine Gallaher of Ottawa, aged 37. Joined the CAMC on 2 September 1915. Served in France and England.

Jessie Mabel McDiarmid of Ashton, Ontario, aged 37. Joined the CAMC on 16 September 1915. Served in France and England.

Mary Agnes McKenzie of Toronto, aged 38. Joined the CEF on 31 January 1916. Served in England.

Rena McLean of Souris, P.E.I., aged 38. Joined the CAMC on 28 September 1914. Served in France, Salonika, England, and on transport duty with another hospital ship.

Mae Belle Sampson of Duntroon, Ontario, aged 28. Joined
the CAMC on 24 September 1914. Served in France.

Gladys Irene Sare of Montreal, aged 29. Joined the CAMC on
26 January 1916. Served in England, France and on transport
duty with another hospital ship.

Anna Irene Stamers of Saint John, New Brunswick, aged 30. Joined
the CAMC on 3 June 1915. Served in France, England and Egypt.

Jean Templeman of Ottawa, aged 33. Joined the CAMC on
3 June 1915. Served in France, England, and Egypt.[56]

On 26 and 27 June 2018, to mark the centenary of the tragedy, a new opera
was performed in Toronto. Entitled "The Llandovery Castle," it was the work
of Canadian composer Stephanie Martin and librettist Paul Ciufo, who wrote
it as an act of remembrance. In his words,

The sinking of the *Llandovery Castle* has been inexplicably all but forgotten by everyone except historians, and the incredible contributions and
bravery of nurses throughout the war have also largely been overlooked.
It is a privilege to help shine a light on this significant story and these remarkable women.[57]

With very much the same feelings the author, in this chapter, has sought
to tell their story and honour their memory. In one tribute to the lost of the
First World War, the belief has been voiced that "As long as we remember,
the brave live forever." The example of the nurses who went down with the
Llandovery Castle continues to be a moving reminder of "the deep debt of
gratitude Canada owes to the nursing service."[58] In the words of Canadian
poet S. Morgan-Powell,

They died that we might live. They fought their fight
And passed – beyond all sorrow and all pain.
But love shall keep their memories ever bright.
Above the graves where their dead selves have lain
Flowers shall grow and greet the noonday sun
In bloom of beauty.[59]

* * * * *

According to the records of Matron-in-Chief Margaret Macdonald, 2,504
Canadian nurses served with the overseas military forces of Canada during
the First World War, a further 313 went overseas with the Imperial nursing

Carola Douglas. Nursing Sister Carola Douglas, born in 1887, was the daughter of an engineer who worked in South America and gave his children an adventurous upbringing. She began her nursing career in Philadelphia but continued to enjoy overseas travel and was on a trip to Australia when war broke out in 1914. Returning to Canada, she enlisted in the CAMC and subsequently worked at No. 2 Canadian General Hospital in France. In 1916 she was posted to Salonika, where she remained until 1917 when she was found to be suffering from debility. Sent to England for recuperation, she served for a short period at No. 16 Canadian General Hospital before being posted to the *Llandovery Castle*. (© Imperial War Museum)

Christina Campbell. Born in Scotland in 1877, Christina was a trained nurse who moved to Canada with her brother. She joined the CAMC in 1915 and served at Salonika until 1916, when she was found to be suffering from nervous exhaustion. After a period of rest and recuperation, she worked at hospitals in England until March 1918, when she joined the *Llandovery Castle*. (Library and Archives Canada, MIKAN 3523169)

services, and 437 undertook home service.[60] She later paid tribute to them, emphasizing that their

> arduous duties were carried out under most trying conditions ... their devotion was a wonderful inspiration. In periods of gravest danger they were superb ... During enemy bombardment in France and England, and at the sinking of the hospital ship, *Llandovery Castle*, the courage displayed by the nursing staff matched that of the greatest heroes of the war.[61]

A beautiful Nursing Sisters memorial on Parliament Hill in Ottawa stands in permanent tribute to their achievements and legacy. Funded by nurses and nursing associations across Canada and unveiled in 1926, the text reads: "Led by the spirit of humanity across the seas woman by her tender ministrations to those in need has given to the world the example of an heroic service embracing three centuries of Canadian history."[62]

The bravery, selflessness and high sense of duty demonstrated by Canada's nurses during the First World War remains a source of pride and inspiration to their profession, their country and the wider world.

CHAPTER 8

"If only you knew what a comfort you are to us, dear Madame"

CIVILIAN VOLUNTEER WORK

To bring home near to those whose homes are far;
This Our Crusade,
To follow War's dark way
Smoothing his dreadful footprints as we may![1]

"ALL DURING THE VOYAGE WE WERE TALKING OF SUBMARINES":
CIVILIAN TRAVEL TO EUROPE AND THE SINKING OF THE *LUSITANIA*
When Canada's men began volunteering for overseas service in August 1914, their wives, mothers, sisters and daughters rallied behind them. It was the start of what was to be a huge effort on the home front, and an endorsement of the opinion that war "summons women to the colours."[2] As the men of the First Canadian Contingent completed their training at Valcartier and departed for Britain, some of their womenfolk were making plans to head in the same direction. They ranged from wealthy society ladies to those of more modest means who could apply to the Canadian Patriotic Fund – a privately funded organization established to give social and financial assistance to soldiers' families – for help to purchase a second-class ticket for the trans-Atlantic crossing. Although the Admiralty requisitioned passenger liners for military use, Allied and neutral shipping lines continued to offer scheduled crossings which, subject to the risks of war, continued during the autumn of 1914 and into 1915.

Wartime regulations were in operation and new arrivals to Britain were subject to stringent checks, as Mabel Adamson, wife of Captain Agar Adamson of the Princess Patricia's Canadian Light Infantry, discovered in late October 1914. She and her fellow travellers were not allowed to disembark from their ship until they had been "cross-questioned as to their nationality, business, etc.," and in addition, "all foreigners have to have passports."[3] Canadians, who were classed as British subjects at that time, normally passed through these formalities without difficulty but the era of "free and easy travel" was over and within a year passports would be mandatory.[4]

155

Sea travel to Europe became a great deal more dangerous in February 1915 when the German government issued its declaration of unrestricted submarine warfare. Liners, whether or not they were suspected of carrying military personnel or war supplies, became targets for attack by German U-boats. Thereafter, those civilians who made the crossing to Europe from Canada or the USA did so at their own risk. Since the biggest ships travelling at maximum speed could easily outrun a submarine, and it was generally thought that a civilized nation would not fire on a vessel carrying civilians, people continued to book their passage.

On 1 May 1915 the RMS *Lusitania*, one of the great ships of the Cunard Line and billed as "the Fastest and Largest Steamer now in Atlantic Service," left New York bound for Liverpool.[5] Of her 1,960 passengers, many of whom were American or British, there were some 360 people whose declared country of residence was Canada.[6] They included women from across the nation, among whom were society ladies such as Lady Marguerite Allan, wife of Montreal businessman and philanthropist Sir Montagu Allan, who was travelling with two of her daughters, and Frances Stephens, widow of a Montreal businessman who was travelling to meet her son on medical leave from the Western Front. Also on board were Mary Ryerson of Toronto, wife of Dr. George Sterling Ryerson, founder of the Canadian Red Cross Society, and her daughter Laura. Mrs. Ryerson had recently lost her son, Captain George S. Ryerson, killed during the Second Battle of Ypres, and planned to see another son, Lieutenant Arthur Ryerson, who had been wounded in the same action but had survived.[7]

Margaret Gwyer, wife of the Reverend Herbert Gwyer of Saskatoon, had been married for just two weeks when she and her husband boarded the *Lusitania*. Annie Palmer of Toronto and her three young children were going to spend time with their family in England, as were Christina Stewart, also from Toronto, and Dorothy Braithwaite of Montreal. Another Torontonian, Bertha Prescott, hoped to meet her husband in Devon, where he was recovering from wounds, while Gertrude Adams from Edmonton was taking her young daughter to live with relatives in Britain so that she could see more of her husband, Albert, a stretcher bearer with the 4th Battalion, Central Ontario Regiment. Lorna Pavey from Fort Qu'Appelle, Saskatchewan, and Ethel Lines of Toronto planned to volunteer with the Canadian Red Cross, while Ella Lawrence from Winnipeg, mentioned in chapter 5, was making her way to the Balkans, having offered her services to the Serbian Red Cross during the country's typhus epidemic.[8] Everyone was aware of the recently published German warning that travellers sailing in the war zone did so at their own risk, and Sarah Lohden, who had her eleven-year-old daughter with her, remembered that "during the voyage we were all talking of submarines. It seemed people could do nothing but discuss the possibility of attack. I had a presentiment that we would be struck."[9]

By 7 May the *Lusitania* was within the war zone eleven miles to the south of the Old Head of Kinsale, a landmark on the coast of southern Ireland. In the early afternoon and in calm conditions she was torpedoed without warning by the German submarine *U-20*, captained by *Kapitänleutnant* Walter Schweiger. The ship went down in only eighteen minutes and a total of 1,193 people perished in the water, with another four dying from the effects of shock and trauma. Of those Canadians mentioned above, Marguerite Allan was injured but was rescued. However, she had to endure the loss of her daughters, Anna and Gwen, who both drowned. Frances Stephens, her grandson and members of her staff also drowned, as did Mary Ryerson, Dorothy Braithwaite and Ella Lawrence. Annie Palmer, Margaret Gwyer, Ethel Lines, Lorna Pavey, Sarah Lohden and her daughter Rose were among the survivors, most of whom had dramatic stories to recount.[10]

Margaret Gwyer's escape was remarkable. Having not managed to get into a lifeboat she was still on the main deck as the water rose to cover it. She began

Lady Allan and her daughters. Marguerite Allan (1860-1957) was the wife of banker and ship owner Sir Montagu Allan, and was one of Montreal's most prominent society hostesses. In 1914 she raised funds to establish a hospital in England for Canadian troops and travelled to the UK in 1915 aboard the *Lusitania* with two of her four children. After the ship was torpedoed and sank, she survived but her daughters, Anna and Gwen, seen here with their mother, were lost. (Courtesy of the McCord Museum, Notman Archives, Montreal) to swim but a moment later, caught by a rush of water, she was sucked "head first" into the top of one of the ship's funnels. As "horrified onlookers" in the lifeboats watched her disappear, her husband among them, they believed her to be lost but "in another instant they were amazed to see her shoot out from the top of the funnel just before it went under." Covered in soot, she was picked up, scarcely able to believe what had happened to her.[11]

Many people spent time in the water and in lifeboats before they were rescued. Gertrude Adams witnessed the death of her two-year-old daughter "through drowning and exposure," and Lady Marguerite Allan described how she held her daughters' hands "up to the last moment, but the suction of the sinking ship separated them."[12] While afloat on a raft for two hours, Lady Allan was struck in the back by a lifeboat and later discovered she had broken her collar bone. Those aboard the raft managed to keep it afloat until they were picked up by a freighter. "I shall never forget those two hours of drifting," Lady Allan recalled. "At times we were surrounded by bodies of the dead," and "always we could hear the dying shrieks of men and women in the water." She and the others on her raft "joined in '[It's a Long Way to] Tipperary' and other songs. We sang to keep up heart," she later told a newspaper reporter.[13]

These and other accounts bear witness to the ordeal of the people aboard the *Lusitania* that day, and its sinking sent shock waves around the world. Anti-German feeling was widespread and voluble, and among the many who condemned the attack, Canadian journalist Mary MacLeod Moore described how "there is only one topic now in England and in Ireland and that is the crime of murder committed by the Germans in sinking the Lusitania." As she told her readers, "the deliberate murder of hundreds of innocent women and children and non-combatants, men over military age, or neutrals," was "something that cries to heaven for retribution."[14] Coming as it did in the wake of some of the worst fighting of the Second Battle of Ypres, it was a double blow for Canadians, but as Archdeacon Henry Cody of St Paul's Anglican Church in Toronto told his congregation, "This policy of frightfulness is designed to inspire terror, but it will only deepen the grim determination of every Briton to fight through until this hideous, war-god of militarism and brute-force is shattered forever."[15] Anyone who went overseas after 7 May 1915 was mindful of the threat posed by a ruthless enemy.

Once travellers reached Britain and were cleared to proceed to their destination, they saw evidence of the country's war effort in action on the home front. From early in the war British women answered the call for "work, work, work," and began to take on volunteer duties and vacant jobs in towns and cities around the country.[16] There seemed to be an understanding that every responsible person would play their part, and with the men having gone to fight, women were shouldering responsibilities in areas that were new to them. They were to be found in shipyards and factories; on public transport as ticket collectors, bus conductresses, porters and dining car attendants; in banks and the civil service; as postmen, gas fitters and garbage collectors; and as volunteers for the Women's Police Service, an organization sanctioned by the Commissioner of Police on the understanding that it remained "resolutely unofficial."[17] In hitherto male preserves they took the initiative and set an example. Seeing British women in action was undoubtedly an impetus for others to find ways in which they, too, could contribute to the war effort.

A journalist, writing for *Punch* magazine in 1915, described how he was witnessing "a *tide* of women: 'She is everywhere superseding men' on the home front and at the same time earning more money, having more independence, and enjoying a new sense of freedom and self expression."[18] Not all were in favour of such marked changes even if they were driven by necessity, but newspaper magnate Lord Northcliffe, who believed that women had not previously been given their "opportunity in most parts of the Empire," now recognized that a tremendous reservoir of untapped energy had become available when it was most needed.[19]

"CAPABLE, DEVOTED WOMEN WHO HAVE HELPED TO MAINTAIN THE FINE REPUTATION WON FOR CANADA BY HER FIGHTING MEN": WAR WORK IN BRITAIN

London, as Britain's capital and nerve centre of its war effort, was where many charitable and war-related organizations were established to support the Imperial and Allied forces. As in Canada, voluntary work was replacing leisure time and newspapers were full of information about meetings, lectures, bazaars, first aid classes and appeals for help with everything from packing parcels for soldiers to making bandages and preparing other essential supplies. In addition, for those willing to take on more responsible work as organizers, fund-raisers or charity workers, there were plenty of openings. The independent and capable ladies who pursued this type of war work were often from wealthy or privileged backgrounds, had a genuine desire to help and care for others and were able to use their advantages to achieve their aims. Projects soon sprang up that utilized skills such as being able to drive a motor vehicle, a knowledge of French or the ability to motivate and lead others.

Canadians with specific experience soon found an outlet for their talents, as in the case of Grace Ferris from Edmonton, wife of Captain William Ferris, a medical officer with the No. 1 Canadian CCS in France. She began training women in bookkeeping at the Westminster Technical Institute in London and proved so capable that she later accepted a senior position with the Navy and Army Canteen Board.[20] Lillian Amy, the wife of Lacey Amy, a Canadian novelist and the editor of the *Medicine Hat Times*, took on the work of welfare supervisor with a company in west London and became responsible for the well-being of its staff. Her work was acknowledged when she became one of the first Canadian women to be made a Member of the Order of the British Empire.[21]

Someone whose contribution endured far beyond the war effort was Canadian writer, editor and activist Margaret "Madge" Watt of Metchosin in British Columbia. When war broke out in 1914 the widowed Mrs. Watt took her two sons to Britain to complete their education and saw how, as the men went to fight, their wives, mothers and daughters were left to run farms and other rural enterprises. In 1914 the lives of many country women were still rather narrow – they worked their fingers to the bone doing outdoor work and often had to manage large families on little income. When war came it brought change to the countryside, and for the first time in recent memory home-grown food was suddenly profitable and greatly needed. Women managing rural enterprises could now make a proper living, and when food shortages became a concern for the British government, county committees were formed to identify those willing to work the land.

As a strong believer in the idea of women working together and fulfilling their potential to do good, Madge Watt recognized the importance of encouraging them to increase agricultural production at such a critical time. The Women's Institute was already active in Canada and Mrs. Watt introduced the concept to Britain. Starting in 1914, she helped to set up the first 100 branches of a British Women's Institute (WI) and, ably assisted by a friend, Josephine Tyrell Godman, she began to train organizers who would help to increase the contribution of farming and rural communities to the country's wartime needs. The new WI branches promoted education, cookery lectures, egg collection and marketing, jam making, gardening advice and confidence-enhancing ways to help women become involved. In 1918 Madge also founded the first WI school to train leaders and administrators, with an emphasis on the fact that "the home is the beginning of all the country will be." From those efforts, the WI grew into a national institution in Britain that continues to this day.[22]

Lady Emily Perley. Emily Perley (1866-1948) was the second wife of Sir George Perley, a businessman, politician and diplomat who served as Canada's high commissioner to Great Britain throughout the First World War, and Minister of Overseas Military Forces from 1916 onwards. Energetic and resourceful, Lady Perley was a tireless worker who mobilized Canadian women in England for the war effort and was prominent in a number of charitable organizations. She and her husband remained overseas until 1922, when Sir George was recalled to Canada. (Library and Archives Canada, MIKAN 3544531)

Canadians seeking ways to be part of their nation's war effort overseas found that London was the centre of a thriving community headed by the High Commissioner, Sir George Perley. Politician, diplomat, businessman and philanthropist, Sir George held the post of Minister without Portfolio in Canada's Conservative government and was later appointed Minister of Overseas Forces from October 1916 to October 1917.[23] Accompanied by his wife, Emily, he had only just taken up his posting to London when war broke out and the Perleys quickly became known as a busy, sociable couple who entertained regularly at their elegant apartment on Park Lane. A few days after Canada's declaration of war, a meeting was convened for expatriate Canadians and what resulted was the formation of the Canadian War Contingent Association (CWCA), which, at the request of the British War Office, would work under the leadership of Sir George Perley for "the comfort of Canadian soldiers in camps and in the trenches" and "in such other ways as might be possible."[24]

Emily Perley entered into this new effort enthusiastically and earned respect as "an indefatigable war worker."[25] Taking on the chairmanship of the CWCA Ladies Committee, she had close contact with Lady Eleanor McLaren Brown, the wife of the European manager of the Canadian Pacific Railway, who was appointed honorary secretary. The two women wasted no time in getting down to business and "worked steadily and faithfully for the soldiers."[26] Eleanor McLaren Brown later recalled how the association

Comforts for the troops. The Canadian Field Comforts Commission established a base in England near Folkestone, Kent, where it distributed a wide variety of articles to Canadian troops in the field. Supervised by Mary Plummer, who is seen in this photograph seated at centre among the crates, with her assistant, Joan Arnoldi (standing at left), and members of her staff, the organization did valuable work throughout the war years. (Library and Archives Canada, PA-005197)

"received and distributed literally to the four corners of the earth vast supplies of field comforts." "Month by month and year by year" she described how she "counted and sorted and checked" incoming items, constantly marvelling at the quantity that continued to arrive at the CWCA office.[27]

Another similar enterprise but smaller in scale was the Canadian Field Comforts Commission (CFCC), an agency appointed by the Canadian government. Its personnel were among the first to arrive in Britain and under the leadership of Mary Plummer of Ottawa, aided by Joan Arnoldi of Toronto, it began its work on Salisbury Plain with the First Canadian Contingent. Later relocating to Shorncliffe, Kent, the commission used money and donations from Canada to put together "Soldiers' Comfort Boxes" containing such things as candies, books, tobacco, soap, notepaper, toothbrushes, pipes, candles and the like. As Mary Plummer later wrote, she and her helpers believed themselves fortunate to "have had the privilege of working for our men" and to "have known and admired and loved them." To bring some cheer to the grim life of the trenches and to be a link between the soldiers and their families in Canada, was reward enough.[28]

Both at home and overseas, an extraordinary contribution to the well-being of serving Canadians was made by the Imperial Order Daughters of the Empire (IODE). Founded in 1900 by Margaret Polson Murray of Montreal to support Canadian troops fighting in the South African War, by 1914 it had become a federation of some 24,000 women in chapters across the country who, according to one recent study, displayed "a congenial combination of female imperialism, patriotism and maternalism that circulated among middle- and upper-middle class English Canadians of the period."[29] Its aims were patriotic and included a commitment to "supply and foster a bond of union amongst the Daughters of the Empire," and to efficiently provide "prompt and united action" by women and children of the British Empire "when such action is desired."[30]

Under its motto of "One Flag, One Throne, One Empire," and the vice-presidency of Mary Gooderham of Toronto, the wife of a prominent businessman and philanthropist, the IODE swung into action. It began by calling an emergency conference with representatives from all national women's societies, and by raising money for a fully equipped hospital ship.[31] What followed was a range of essential projects that included recreation and reading rooms for military camps; temperance canteens; Christmas boxes for the soldiers; ambulances and transport trucks; a vast range of essential supplies for troops and medical units; food and clothing for Canadian prisoners of war; and veterans' homes for disabled men. It also undertook bigger plans including the provision of a hospital in London, four convalescent homes and twelve soldiers' and sailors' clubs.[32]

Mary Gooderham went to London with her husband, Alfred, after the couple decided to donate almost all the equipment for the IODE Hospital for Officers erected in Hyde Park Place. Mrs. Gooderham made several visits to the new facility and personally oversaw fund-raising for X-ray machines and an operating theatre. To accomplish all their proposals, IODE members worked with great commitment both in Canada and Britain and raised an impressive total of more than C\$3 million (C\$68,300,000 today).[33] They cooperated closely with the Canadian Red Cross Society (CRCS), whose efforts are described later in this chapter, to meet the need for medical supplies and equipment, and they enabled women to contribute "by caring for the sick and wounded through the gift of their time, talents and money."[34] The story of the Imperial Order Daughters of the Empire during the First World War has been described as a "long record of splendid achievement."[35]

Numerous other charitable concerns were keen to attract helpers and raise funds. With much of the fighting on the Western Front taking place in France, Paul Cambon, the French ambassador to Britain, saw the need for an agency to coordinate the assistance being offered to the French Red Cross and called into being a London committee, or *Comité Britannique*. With offices in the Knightsbridge district and a large depot in Paris, incoming gifts and parcels could be processed. Statistics for 1916 confirmed more than 2,000 personnel, including Canadians, were employed by the *Comité*. Not only did they carry out "every kind of work," but they also proved to be people who were "embarrassed" by any expression of thanks.[36] At home in Canada some 200,000 articles were sent to France via the French-Canadian section of the CRCS. In 1917 a special Canadian "France's Day" appeal was further proof that people at home were working as hard as ever in support of those overseas.

Flag days became a meaningful part of the war effort, whereby the British public could purchase a flag to wear in aid of many different causes. These included: Russian Day for wounded Russian soldiers; France's Day, mentioned above, which raised money for the French Red Cross; YMCA Flag Day to help fund facilities for the soldiers; Mesopotamia Flag Day for efforts in that theatre; Soldiers' and Sailors' Flag Day; and Alexandra Rose Day, which benefited London hospitals. These events flourished, not just because they drew attention to the many good causes vying for public support, but also because they were occasions when women flag sellers could dress up, make their presence felt on the streets and possibly see their names in newspapers which gave coverage to these voluntary efforts.[37]

Among other organizations seeking helpers was the Women's Volunteer Reserve (WVR), which set out to train "a body of girls who, expert, disciplined, and efficient, could do much to stem panic in the event of a German raid by sky or sea."[38] They cooked, cleaned, learned first aid, drove vehicles and acted as motor cycle messengers wherever required. Another body, the Women's Emergency Corps, was set up by suffrage campaigners who were determined that women's work should be regarded as no less vital for victory than the efforts of men. The skills of their volunteers were matched to different requirements, which grew in number as the war progressed, as did the demand for those willing to help with a variety of fund-raising projects. In May 1917, according to *Strand Magazine*, a review entitled "Hello Canada" was scheduled to open at His Majesty's Theatre in London's Haymarket. With a virtually all-Canadian cast, the proceeds would be donated to St. Dunstan's Fund for Blind Soldiers. Performers included Muriel Dunsmuir, daughter of

Canadian industrialist and politician James Dunsmuir, and Martha Allan, the eldest and only surviving daughter of Lady Marguerite Allan. Martha, who had studied theatre in Paris, appeared in the show wearing the costume of "a Canadian cowboy."[39]

One charitable organization which was never short of support was the Canadian Red Cross Society. Beginning its war effort in 1914 as a small operation based in Toronto, it expanded rapidly to become a leading humanitarian agency. With branches across the nation and all CRCS work overseas made possible by its nationwide operations at home, women's involvement proved crucial to its success. Mary Gooderham and Adelaide Plumptre, the wife of the rector of St. James' Anglican Cathedral in Toronto, became associate members of the CRCS executive committee and Mrs. Plumptre, an Oxford-educated former teacher with great energy and managerial skills, was appointed superintendent of CRCS supplies. She created a rationalized outwork production system never before seen in Canada, and one which efficiently procured and processed all manner of items from rolled bandages to food for hospitals, and a range of useful supplies for the troops.

CRCS fund-raising activities at local and national level continued on the home front throughout the war years and brought in a total of more than C$9 million (almost C$205 million today). The money raised supported many important initiatives that included the provision of a motor ambulance convoy, the setting up and running of an information bureau, and the establishment of five CRCS hospitals. It also paid for special wards and equipment, canteens, recreation huts, rehabilitation workshops and nurses quarters at most Canadian hospitals in England and France, as well as rest homes for Canadian nurses at Margate, London and Boulogne. Also to be found on both sides of the English Channel were CRCS offices and storage facilities, and all the society's activities were aided by Canadian women volunteers, who could be selected for clerical or administrative work, fund raising, hospital visiting, help at soldiers' clubs or hospitality centres, and so on.

A London office for the CRCS was opened in September 1914, headed by a commissioner who was assisted by a war committee. It worked closely with the British Red Cross Society, its parent organization, and benefited from the latter's experience, greater size, budget and proximity to the war front. Integral to the organization's mission to care for the sick and wounded during the conflict, its operations prioritized the welfare of troops, prisoners of war and their families, and the procurement and distribution of a wide range of supplies and necessities.[40] "Our Red Cross work is Imperial," said the commissioner, Charles A. Hodgetts, but when the Belgian Red Cross was forced to disband during German occupation of its territory, the CRCS extended its remit by donating money and supplies to the "The Belgian Red Cross Behind the Lines."[41] CRCS efforts continued throughout the war on both sides of the Atlantic, and a prediction made by Adelaide Plumptre that Canadians would not lose interest in the Red Cross "until they lost interest in their own wounded and captured boys" proved true.[42] It was work that embodied the service of the nation and evidence of how much Canadians cared about their fighting men.

Some Canadian women chose work which brought them into direct contact with troops and their families. After the *Lusitania* disaster and the tragic loss of her daughters, Lady Marguerite Allan devoted herself to setting up and overseeing a convalescent home for Canadian officers at Sidmouth, a pleasant town on the Devon coast. Those with driving qualifications could apply to work for groups like the Motor Transport Volunteers, who offered general chauffeuring duties under the slogan "Give Tommy a Lift." Even busy journalists found time to be of service, Beatrice Nasmyth choosing to work at one of many soldiers' and sailors' railway buffets scattered across the country. Wearing a white apron and a blue armband, she served coffee, bread and butter and cake to men who dashed off passing trains to purchase the snacks. With an average of twenty trains passing during each of her four-hour shifts, she was kept busy. Mary MacLeod Moore volunteered with the Soldiers' and Sailors' Families Association, which helped families suffering financial difficulty by distributing money, food, clothing, coal and other essential items.[43] Throughout the conflict Mary maintained a strong interest in civilian welfare in Britain and the realities of wartime living. Her newspaper and magazine columns examined topics such as economizing, maintaining morale, the war effort of British women and the fact that many of those engaged in war-related work were "tasting the joys of an independent income to be spent or saved as one chooses for the first time."[44]

Officers' wives devoted time to assisting the soldiers and families of their husbands' regiments. At Folkestone on the south east coast, a lively Canadian "colony" existed during the war amid a certain rivalry, and one visiting soldier remarked that "everybody hates everybody else like the very devil" and "all the good wives think their husbands ought to be brigadier generals."[45] However, those same wives put their talents to use by running a club for the troops which offered accommodation, meals and other assistance. Martha Black, whose husband, Captain George Black, was one of more than 200 men from the Yukon serving in France, undertook more than the usual range of duties. She administered funds raised by the territory to support its troops, sent them supplies, did "their shopping when so requested" and made sure that all regimental families received their entitlements.[46]

Commanding officers' wives were expected to fulfill particular duties in respect of their husbands' regiments, all the more so when they were on active service. Henrica Belson, who was married to Lieutenant-Colonel Berkeley Belson, commanding officer of the 81st Battalion CEF from the Niagara region, urged the unit's ladies through its official newspaper, *The Record*, to "do their bit" both at home and overseas. By supporting the men at the front in whatever way they could, they would be ensuring that "the same unity and 'esprit de corps' will exist among the women as among the men of the 81st."[47]

Lady Evelyn Farquhar and Mabel Adamson, whose husbands commanded the PPCLI at different times during the war, certainly did their duty to the regiment with an impressive level of commitment. Evelyn's husband, Lieutenant-Colonel Francis Farquhar, died of wounds in March 1915 but she subsequently continued to work on matters regimental from the townhouse she rented in Mayfair. Mabel Adamson, who was determined from the start of hostilities to do "something of significance for the war effort," managed to combine war work in Belgium (described later in this chapter) with keeping a caring eye on the affairs of the PPCLI during her husband's period of command from 1916 to 1918.[48] She stood ready to help whenever required and found herself visiting men in hospital, driving those on leave in England and checking on wives and families. Mabel also dealt with many requests from her husband, Lieutenant-Colonel Agar Adamson, for "extras" to make his life in the trenches more bearable. As someone who clearly appreciated the finer things of life, Colonel Adamson's diverse requirements included real clotted cream, silk underwear, smelling salts, a dozen tins of oysters from Selfridges, "slippers felt with thick soles" and "excellent cigarettes." In addition, he sought practical items such as batteries, rubber gloves, a periscope and mosquito netting. With the comfort of the men in mind, Mabel sent the regiment "a set of portable baths and a stove for heating water."[49]

The number of Canadian women in Britain grew over time and by 1917, according to the *Canadian Annual Review*, there were "about 30,000" of them, mainly "relatives of soldiers, but including others who had drifted to England in one of the curious contrasts of wartime, for social reasons, for pleasure, for curiosity or similar motives."[50] Among the latter, those who proved they were "unable or unwilling to do war-work" or "work of any kind which would be helpful to the community," were "gradually sifted out by the Canadian authorities," and the *Review* mentioned that some of them "were brought home and no more were allowed to go from Canada."[51] For the women who remained in Britain, the risk of air attacks grew more pronounced. By 1917 the Germans had developed airplanes capable of reaching mainland Britain from German-held territory in Belgium, and that year enemy bombers made eight mass daylight raids that resulted in 1,364 civilians killed or wounded.

On 25 May 1917, after a squadron of the new German Gotha airplanes had to abort an attack on London, they looked for secondary targets on the Kent coast and dropped bombs in and around Hythe. The German pilots then headed for Folkestone, where they bombed Shorncliffe military camp and the town centre on a day when people were queueing outside a greengrocer's store to buy potatoes from a newly-arrived consignment. When the air attack began, a Canadian sergeant in the vicinity recalled how "the whole of the street seemed to explode. There was smoke and flames all over, but worst of all were the screams of the wounded and dying... we watched those swine in the sky."[52]

At her home in north Kent, housewife Ethel Bilbrough heard about the attacks from her cousin, who happened to be the vicar of Hythe parish church. She regarded the Folkestone bombing as "the worst raid that we in England have experienced yet," with people "killed outright amidst the debris of the shops: poor old women, helpless children, babies in arms." Following that "awful scene," and the realization that helpless civilians had been "ruthlessly mutilated – killed and wounded," there was outrage at the ninety-seven deaths suffered and widespread concern at the likelihood of further attacks.[53]

The biggest loss of life occurred some three weeks later on 13 June 1917 when a school in east London was hit and 162 people, many of whom were children, were killed. At the time British land and coastal defence was shared between the army and navy, who were still working on an effective system to prevent these incursions from the air. Enemy raids continued into 1918 and the "horrible sound of engines overhead" only added to the growing strain of life in wartime Britain. However, the resolve shared by British, Canadian and other Allied residents was not easily weakened. Architect Sir Edwin Lutyens demonstrated a typically pragmatic approach to the German air menace when he advised his London staff "not to cower like idiots" but to carry on as normal because they would either "see it coming and can engineer your safety or you are caught unawares – and then nothing but chance can save you."[54]

"WOMEN OF GREAT ABILITY WHO DEVOTED THEMSELVES BODY AND SOUL TO THE WORK": VOLUNTEERING IN FRANCE

Canadian women seeking to undertake war work in France knew they would be taking the home front to the troops and that they would be much closer to the harrowing face of combat. They might well encounter exhausted men, bereaved family members, harassed medical staff, enemy air attacks, shelling in areas behind the front line and a range of other challenges. Those responsible for selecting suitable staff for France looked not only for "good character" and "honesty, enthusiasm, integrity and good manners," but also the ability to handle the situations they would be likely to face.[55]

One volunteer, Katherine Wallis of Peterborough, Ontario, was among Canadian women working under the auspices of the *Société de Secours aux Blessés Militaires* (Association for Aid to Military Wounded), one of three constituent organizations of the French Red Cross that welcomed volunteers during the war. She was sent to a new hospital in Paris, funded in part by money raised through the Montreal newspaper *La Presse*. The French government had made a "superb effort" to provide a *Service de Santé*, a health service that would care for the wounded, but it was unable to equip all the medical units hastily created to handle the huge numbers of casualties.[56] Offers of assistance were gratefully received, and funds from Canada went to help with war relief, aid to displaced citizens and medical assistance. Katherine Wallis and another Canadian, Mrs. Gordon Monro of Toronto, were both volunteers with the *Société de Secours* for three years and received awards for their work in France.

At a French hospital near Paris was Lucile Jones, wife of Major Stanley Jones of the PPCLI. She volunteered with *l'Union des Femmes de France* (Union of Women of France) and was based at Champigny-sur-Marne in the southeastern suburbs of the capital. After the Battle of Mount Sorrel in June 1916, Lucile received a telegram telling her that her husband was missing in action. She took compassionate leave and went to London "for a week trying everything to get news." Pursuing her enquiries through the CRCS and determined that "I shall not give up hope," Lucille finally learned that her husband had died of wounds on 8 June 1916 as a prisoner-of-war at Moorseele, Belgium.[57] Despite her loss Lucile Jones resolved to continue her hospital work, knowing how much it was needed.

Canadian women also worked at American Red Cross hospitals, while others signed up with an organization entitled the French War Emergency Fund (FWEF), which had its headquarters in London under the patronage of the Duke of Connaught, former governor general of Canada. A committee met regularly to allocate resources, and Canadian Mrs. W. M. Dobell was appointed its honorary secretary. Those who gave their time to the fund could take on clerical duties, driving, facilities management or liaison work. For the latter, volunteers had to speak excellent French and be qualified to drive a motor vehicle. Their task was to visit French hospitals, determine and prioritize needs, submit their reports to London, and be on hand to collect and deliver supplies when they arrived in France. Theirs was a worthwhile and valuable role.[58]

The FWEF also set up some fifty canteens at stations, barracks and troop rest camps, where women served "free refreshments to the tired soldiers" on their way to or from the trenches.[59] The bulk of canteen work was undertaken by British and Canadian volunteers, some of whom also made financial contributions from their own pockets. Several women from Quebec, the Maritimes and Ottawa served at canteens behind the lines and one, Jane Whitman of Nova Scotia, had arrived in France soon after the outbreak of war to help with the provision of comforts for French troops passing through Paris.[60] The FWEF canteens proved to be very successful and were followed by the establishment of *foyers* or recreation rooms for the *poilus*,* where they could read, smoke, write letters, play card games and relax. One woman who helped at these facilities said she felt happy "that we had given so much joy to the poor French soldiers … any little attention we show them they make much of."[61]

Would-be volunteers, or those seeking the assistance of the CRCS in France, only had to step off a boat or a train at Boulogne to find its offices in the Hotel Christol, which stood beside the harbour. It proved to be "a little oasis for Canadians," where they could be sure of a cheery greeting and the help they needed.[62] Also in Boulogne was a hotel which the CRCS converted into a rest home for Canadian nurses. It became their "nearest link with Canada to be found in France" and was under the management of Ethel Gordon-Brown of Ottawa, who transformed it into a real "home-from-home" with "the prettiest chintzes and freshest curtains, good china and restful furniture, and the willing service of a staff of charming Canadian girls."[63]

Warehouse space and lorries were provided to the CRCS by the French government, enabling it to send a wide variety of supplies to Canadian hospitals in France and to some 300 French medical units. Whether delivering socks, pyjamas, blankets, medical equipment, food or comforts, the efficient CRCS distribution system, in which many willing hands were involved, meant that the organization could respond quickly to sudden or urgent demands. Hospital matrons expressed their appreciation of this valuable assistance, one Canadian among them remarking that "without the Red

---

* The term "poilu" referred to a French infantry soldier, and was much in use during the First World War.

Cross stores we would often-times not know where to turn." She also wished "the women at home, who are so busy making all these Red Cross supplies, could realize fully how much their work means to us."[64] Matron Katherine MacLatchy of No. 3 CGH also paid tribute to their efforts, declaring that the "devotion of our noble women at home will never be forgotten," and one French hospital superintendent admitted, "I wept when I saw the piles of sheets" that had been sent to him. "I did not know that Canada loved France like that," he added, much moved.[65]

The dedication of women working for the CRCS never faltered, even in 1918 when enemy air attacks put operations under severe pressure. The Boulogne office had orders to evacuate immediately if the German advance should make it necessary, but "there was not one application for anyone to be transferred to England."[66]

For those who enjoyed working with the troops, an important arm of CRCS war work in France was the management of its recreation huts, which provided a comfortable space for men who were convalescent or resting behind the front line. The Canadian women who helped to run these huts were responsible not only for the comforts and amenities provided, but also for staging entertainment, talks and other events. Jessie Dennison and Margaret Strathy from Montreal were among those who took on this work and were sent to France by Lady Julia Drummond of the CRCS Information Bureau, whose work is covered in Chapter 10. According to another Canadian who knew the two women, they were attached to No. 1 Canadian General Hospital, where the introduction of a recreation hut proved to be a "splendid success."[67] They and others like them were praised by one British visitor for being "helpful and energetic" and for undertaking their work with "tact and devotion."[68] In general, the work being done in the recreation huts was described as "invaluable." Not only did these facilities provide "comfortable and homelike" surroundings for the soldiers; they helped to keep them free from drunkenness by "supplying wholesome recreation and music as a counter-attraction to the numerous estaminets" that were often found within reach of the camps.[69]

Relief work was another important aspect of aid to the French people. The Manitoba War Relief Fund, based in Paris, had a team of helpers working under Ida Lyall, who was appointed as official representative. Also in the French capital was an operation to help refugees from eleven devastated French villages. With the official sanction of the government and under the management of Marguerite Gault, wife of Major Hamilton Gault of the PPCLI, over thirty refugee women were employed in workrooms which pro-

Marguerite Gault. The daughter of the Honourable G. W. Stephens of Montreal, in 1904 Marguerite married wealthy businessman and industrialist Andrew Hamilton Gault. The couple were prominent members of Montreal high society before the First World War. In 1914 Andrew raised a new regiment, the Princess Patricia's Canadian Light Infantry, whose cap badge bore the insignia of a single white daisy in honour of his wife's name. Marguerite undertook volunteer work in France during the conflict, which took its toll on her marriage. She and her husband divorced, and both later remarried. (Courtesy of the McCord Museum, Notman Archives, Montreal)

vided them with income, friendship and support now that their own communities no longer existed.

On an individual or independent basis Canadian women accomplished valuable work in France, and their efforts merited inclusion in a history of Canada's participation in the First World War that was written soon after the conflict. As examples Lily Martin, an Irishwoman who had settled in Canada, saw a need for a comfortable English-speaking "refuge" in Paris where Allied soldiers on leave could go for tea, coffee and a relaxing break. She called it "A Corner of Blighty" and took on Canadian women to run it and act as guides for soldiers who did not know the city well.[70] A Miss Kerr of Toronto spent time as a voluntary driver before being allocated the task of inspecting hospitals in the French interior, and an Ethel Foster donated her time to various charitable undertakings, including the *Ouvroir pour les Blessés* (Workshop for the Wounded), which made special apparatus for disabled soldiers. The organization's president, Louise Noufflard, later wrote that Ethel "rendered us the greatest possible service."[71]

Among other individual or collective efforts by Canadian women, Mrs. J. F. W. Ross, Mrs. H. Burnham and a Miss Tate opened a convalescent home for officers using funds secured through voluntary donations, a grant from the CRCS and a military billet and ration allowance for each patient. The facility, near the Channel coast resort of Trouville, was housed in the summer residence of French aristocrat Baron Henri de Rothschild, and the staff of ten Canadian women, a professional nurse and a masseuse, worked under a superintendent.[72] At the other end of the country the South of France Relief Association was formed by an energetic Canadian, Mrs. Wilfred Drew, with financial assistance from across Canada. At her office in Cannes she recruited voluntary workers to help in French hospitals, and Mrs. Drew's staff included "women of great ability who devoted themselves body and soul to the work," often undergoing further training and frequently taking charge of medical units. Some of them worked under shell fire and one, Katherine Weller, was awarded the *Médaille de la Reconnaissance Française*.[73]

Canadian journalist Elizabeth Montizambert also found a way to involve herself in voluntary work. In July 1915 she joined members of the Paris Press Syndicate, a union of writers and journalists which funded a box car attached to a hospital train. The car, equipped with counter, stove, urns for coffee and soup and gifts for French troops, enabled Elizabeth and her colleagues to distribute these items where they were needed. She described how the train brought her "nearer the front than ever, so near that the firing of the canon makes the window of our box car shake."[74] It took her to an evacuation hospital where she witnessed the loading and unloading of patients and the condition of wounded and sick French soldiers, who were very grateful for any attention. In addition to spending days travelling back and forth across France, Elizabeth also joined another voluntary group that provided food and refreshments to French troops at Amboise in the Loire Valley. While working there she heard about their experiences and encountered a Frenchman who had emigrated to Canada and returned to fight with his countrymen. "I am very pleased to see so many Canadian ladies holding canteens," he told her. "It shows there is as much heart in Canada as in any other country. I wish you would express my best admiration to the Canadian ladies who are with you."[75]

He may well have met some of the French-Canadian women working in France during the war years. Among them were Madame Paul Watel, founder of a hospital for French soldiers, and a Madame Bergas, who directed a casualty hospital. The Mesdemoiselles Davignon and de Longueuil of Montreal did canteen and hospital work, with the latter training French nurses and organizing visits to French soldiers suffering from tuberculosis. Madame Marie Louise Chase-Casgrain, wife of the postmaster-general of Canada, directed refugee work and collected money in Canada for French relief efforts. For her services, she too was awarded the *Médaille de la Reconnaissance Française* by the French government.[76]

One of the most remarkable Canadian women in France was undoubtedly Julia Henshaw from Vancouver. The wife of a well-connected investment broker, Mrs. Henshaw was a multi-talented and adventurous person who before the war had made a name for herself as a writer, botanist, literary and theatre critic, founding member of several clubs and an intrepid traveller. She held the distinction of being the first woman to cross the Rockies by motor car, and Canada's Minister of Militia, Sir Sam Hughes, commissioned her as a lieutenant in the Canadian militia with "vague duties concerning recruiting and promoting the war effort in general." Julia Henshaw was sent to France in December 1915 to complete "a tour of inspection of the war zone" and to distribute gifts to Canadian troops. After completing her mission, she gave a series of lectures across Canada describing what she had seen and urging women to support the war effort. Her presentations were described as "vivid and compelling," and her audiences left "with awakened consciences as to their duty along the line of financial aid."[77]

Julia Henshaw returned to France in March 1918 and joined the French Red Cross as director of an ambulance unit. Her work began just as the Germans launched their massive spring offensive that year, and she helped to coordinate a *Service de Blessés et de Réfugiés* (Service for the Wounded and Refugees), working with the army and the medical services. Much of this work was completed under shell-fire and Julia's fearlessness won her the French *Croix de Guerre*. Her citation described her skill and calm approach in the face of danger, and she was certainly living proof that courage could also be found "in a softer package."[78]

"Devotion and courage worthy of the highest praise." Julia Henshaw (1869-1937) was born in England and studied in France and Germany before moving to Canada, where she married and settled in British Columbia. She travelled to France in 1915 and returned to Canada to give speeches about her visit and in favour of conscription. In 1918 she worked on the Western Front with the French Red Cross. Her leadership and exceptional courage in evacuating troops and civilians under shell fire and aerial bombardment earned her the *Croix de Guerre*. (City of Vancouver Archives)

Whether involved in something on a grander scale or, like Emma Morrison, wife of a Canadian officer who gave help and support to friends and fellow Canadians from her base in Paris, all such efforts were valued. When Emma decided to send "a chocolate and coconut cake" to her husband's unit at the front, the men were delighted at this simple but welcome gesture.[79] Canadian women in France, whatever their part in the war effort, frequently witnessed the truth in the old saying, "It's the thought that counts."

"THE FUND SEEMS TO BE CARRYING ON QUITE DECENTLY":
HELPING THE BELGIANS

When German troops invaded Belgium on 4 August 1914 to bypass a strong system of defensive fortresses along its eastern border, civilians fled. The tide of refugees grew as the Germans torched towns, took hostages and beat or shot civilians. The city of Liège was attacked and fell on 7 August, and the city of Louvain suffered similarly towards the end of that month. Many public buildings were destroyed including the library of the University of Louvain with its collection of ancient manuscripts. The German army had been ordered to live off the territories it occupied, resulting in looting and seizure of food supplies. There was widespread shock and sympathy for the Belgian people, and those who escaped to Britain had gruesome stories to tell.

Voluntary assistance was greatly needed, among the first of which was a British mobile ambulance unit under the direction of Dr. Hector Munro, which spent four years based at Pervyse, Belgium. Aided by several spirited volunteer women, Dr. Munro's unit worked amid badly wounded soldiers, traumatized refugees, destruction, confusion and danger. Funded by donations, the staff remained there despite enemy shelling, convinced that being near the action helped them to save more lives. It was their belief that "we must exert ourselves almost to breaking point in order to see the work carried through."[80]

Such courage and dedication inspired others, and the plight of the Belgian people was widely publicized. Appeals were launched to help them and individual cases were described in newspapers and magazines. A letter appeared in the Catholic publication *The Tablet* about the Sisters of Charity of St Vincent de Paul, Belgian nuns who had escaped from German captivity "bringing nothing away with them except their parrot," which they dared not leave to its fate. Others had fled with them, including a number of elderly people "some of whom they had to bring away in wheelbarrows." All were "in dire distress," and their "poverty and want" created an urgent need for clothing, particularly items suitable for children because in many cases the nuns had "their village pupils still with them." Donations were to be sent to a Mrs. Innes-Taylor of the Belgian Canal Boat Fund, which was working for the "Relief of the Civil Population behind the firing lines."[81]

The idea for the Belgian Canal Boat Fund came about when Mabel Adamson, the wife of Lieutenant-Colonel Agar Adamson of the PPCLI, met Kathryn Innes-Taylor, a singer from Toronto whose husband was also serving on the Western Front. The women shared an interest in the plight of the Belgian civilian population still living in the part of their country that remained in Allied hands. This amounted to a narrow strip of territory about thirty miles long and ten miles wide that ran inland from the English Channel coast to the beleaguered city of Ypres. Not far behind the front line, people there faced the threat of enemy artillery fire and the danger of losing their homes, livelihood and even their lives. A shortage of food, medical necessities, clothing and other basic items added to their difficulties, and Adamson and Innes-Taylor came up with the idea of buying a barge and distributing supplies to local residents via the waterways that crossed the area. Military constraints were a hurdle to be overcome, but it was not long before Mabel and Kathryn found the means to accomplish their goal.[82]

Providing relief in a dangerous region of the war zone was not for the faint-hearted, but the two Canadian women were up to the task. Mabel, from one of Toronto's most wealthy and powerful families, was talented, capable, financially secure, worldly and well connected. In addition, her willingness to provide a sizeable donation meant she was ideally placed to become the London-based president and treasurer of the Belgian Canal Boat Fund. Kathryn Innes-Taylor, whom Mabel liked and described as "a most enthusiastic person," was married to Captain Ranolf Innes-Taylor of the Canadian Mounted Rifles. Personable and committed, Kathryn spoke excellent French and volunteered to be the project's organizer in Belgium. Mabel found suitable offices in London's Duke Street and set about recruiting an executive committee. She also decided to take French lessons, as she and Kathryn planned to rotate their positions.

Despite meeting "everywhere with entrenched male chauvinism," Mabel pressed on.[83] On 30 March 1915 she and Kathryn, having secured the necessary visas, set off for France to meet officials of the Belgian government in exile. After putting forward their ideas for the Belgian Canal Boat Fund and spending an entire day conversing in French, Mabel admitted that "another hour would have given me paralysis."[84] It was all to the good, however, and the two Canadians left with a letter from the Belgian minister of the interior that allowed them to proceed with their plans.

Helping the Belgians. Mabel Cawthra Adamson (1871-1943) was the wife of Lieu-tenant-Colonel Agar Adamson, who commanded the Princess Patricia's Canadian Light Infantry during the war. A talented and well-travelled woman from a promin-ent Toronto family, Mrs. Adamson helped to set up and run the Belgian Canal Boat Fund, which provided help to refugees and citizens of that country. She is seen here in the company of two Allied soldiers. (Toronto Public Library, S259_Box 6_File 13 Photo)

There were still obstacles to surmount, including a refusal by the British military authorities to allow a relief ship to bring supplies into the war zone. However, help came from an American businessman, Herbert C. Hoover, later to become president of his country. Hoover was the chairman of the London-based American Commission for Belgian Relief, and since the United States was a neutral country he was able to negotiate agreements to allow the passage of food, clothing and medical supplies through the Allied naval blockade in force, and across the German front line. While delighted to have Hoover's help, Mabel Adamson worried about what might happen if ever "Germany and the [United] States go to war."[85]

Hoping that day would be long in coming, Mabel Adamson and Kathryn Innes-Taylor established their Belgian base on the outskirts of Furnes, a medieval gem of a town only twenty miles from Ypres. A nurse who worked

Promoting a worthy cause. To publicize the Belgian Canal Boat Fund, Mabel Adamson commissioned a poster. Created by British illustrator John Hassall, who was known for this kind of work, it was produced as a lithograph and shows a despairing mother and her two children. The poster asked the public to send donations for the relief of "the civilian population behind the firing lines" in Belgium, and raised awareness of the needs of many families still living in that part of the war zone. (Library of Congress)

at a military hospital near Furnes described it as "a quaint little town" which for a time was also the headquarters of the Belgian army. The old market square was filled with "every sort of war vehicle, officers occupied the inns and soldiers swarmed everywhere." With its proximity to the Ypres Salient, Furnes "suffered constantly both from enemy aeroplanes and long distance guns," and the above-mentioned nurse described how "we were never out of hearing of the constant boom of and thunder of artillery."[86] She also mentioned one period of activity at the front when "the sky was afire with the battle going on to the east of us," only a few miles away.[87]

Despite the proximity of the war front the Belgian Canal Boat Fund proceeded with its mission, feeding and clothing local schoolchildren, distributing food and garments to hundreds of refugees and establishing a medical clinic. By April 1915 Mabel Adamson had commissioned an eye-catching poster for publicity and fund-raising purposes. It was displayed on billboards and at underground stations around London, where it had considerable impact. There was reason to feel optimistic about the direction in which the project was heading and Mabel was encouraged. Never one to "stay at home and keep house" or fritter away her time, she concentrated on her work for the Belgians and by September 1915 she was able to report that

> we now have 250 children at Furnes and 120 at Chateau les Vieux, absolutely depending on us and we are bound to feed them until next Spring anyway. I hope with our present funds to be able to do it, but we shall have to be very economical."[88]

As requests for help continued to arrive at her London office, Mabel concentrated on maintaining stocks of necessary items, especially since Furnes itself was suffering damage and before long was "more or less a wreck."[89] By October 1915 the once "beautiful little city" looked "like a fairy town of ruined houses and battered walls." It was not unusual to have someone issue a warning to "clear out of here just as fast as you can! They've been shelling this place hard every half hour or so, and the next lot is about due."[90] With families living at subsistence level, and some of them "eating out of one dish without any plates at all," needs were urgent. Thanks to the help of Herbert Hoover, all Mabel Adamson's Canadian supplies were reaching their destination and with the approach of winter, which in her view was "the test of wants," the Belgian Canal Boat Fund was able to meet the demand for basic items, boots, stockings and warm garments.[91]

Things were going well enough that Mabel was able to inform her mother that she had "heard from an entirely outside source, namely through Lady Dorothy Fielding, that our depot at Furnes is doing splendid work and wonder of wonders, the personnel is popular."[92] When Mabel's husband, Lieutenant-Colonel Agar Adamson, visited her at Furnes early in 1916, he found her in good spirits, and Esther McNeil, another of Mabel's volunteers in Belgium, reported that "the Fund seems to be carrying on quite decently" with sufficient consignments of clothing, both ready-made and in pieces that could easily be made up, and parcels going to Belgians who had fled to France.[93]

Letters sent to the Belgian Canal Boat Fund's offices in London and Furnes expressed gratitude for the help. As an example, a nun in charge of a group of Belgian refugee children sheltering at a chateau in Normandy wrote after receiving two trunks of clothing. "Thank you, dear Benefactress," she said, "in the name of these unfortunate little Belgians" living "so far from our own dear country." She gave her assurance that "we do not forget you and pray daily to God to bless you," adding appreciatively, "if only you knew what a comfort you are to us, dear Madame."[94]

While managing the affairs of the fund and fulfilling her duties as wife of the commanding officer of the "Princess Pats," Mabel Adamson took her turn at working in Belgium. She soldiered on through the summer of 1916, taking time off for "appendicitis or something" and hampered by a serious eye condition, but her determination carried her though. She also found the time to meet her husband in Paris, where they had "great fun wandering about together."[95] By the spring of 1917 Mabel was spending much of her time in Belgium, but life was becoming dangerous at Furnes. German air raids were a source of concern and the fund's wooden huts, whilst suitable for the relief work being carried out, were no protection against German aircraft.

It was not long before two of Mabel's women workers were wounded "by a bomb from an aeroplane" and at the beginning of July 1917, Furnes was shelled continually for twenty-four hours. Thereafter, bombing or shelling continued every few days with the result that Mabel Adamson and her staff transferred to an abandoned school so that they and the many refugees arriving to join them had somewhere safer. They also opened a dispensary where people could go for urgent medical treatment from a Belgian military doctor, and provided an ambulance to take the sick or wounded to local hospitals. Many civilians were "so terrified" that they were afraid to return after the worst of the bombardment was over.[96]

Through much of that autumn, the Third Battle of Ypres overshadowed life in the region. Civilians suffered accordingly, and in December 1917 Mabel Adamson sent out a request for further funding. "As the distress in Belgium becomes greater," said her appeal, "we are more in need now of funds or supplies in kind – food or clothing – than we have ever been."[97] With generous help from the Toronto Women's Patriotic League and individual subscribers in England, Canada and around the British Empire, Mabel Adamson, Kathryn Innes-Taylor and their helpers continued their aid to the Belgians, individually and collectively, through the following year and after the Armistice of November 1918.

The efforts of Canada's civilian women who undertook volunteer war work far from home speak for themselves. Censorship meant that fellow Canadians knew comparatively little about what they accomplished, but those who witnessed it paid tribute to all the "capable, devoted women who have helped to maintain the fine reputation won for Canada by her fighting men."[98] It was a tribute they both earned and deserved.

CHAPTER 9

It was enough to have had "the privilege of being of service"

Volunteers in Uniform

We do not boast: but we are proud this day
That we have stood the stern and sudden test;
We too have done a little in the fray,
And we have given of our little best.[1]

"THE GIRL BEHIND THE MAN BEHIND THE GUN": PUTTING ON A UNIFORM

In 1914 the sight of women doing voluntary work in a variety of uniforms gave rise to a good deal of comment. After the elegant clothing that had characterized the Edwardian era, the sudden appearance of purposeful ladies in new roles and attire evoked strong reactions. In some quarters it came across as a "signal, invested with hierarchy and significance," while elsewhere it was seen as "aping the men."[2] As time went by, convention was set aside as the war gave rise to new norms and expectations. Opinions shifted, especially after female volunteers returned from the war zone with accounts of their work and experiences.

To those women who offered their services in this way, donning a uniform for voluntary work was a noticeable sign of their commitment to play their part in the greater war effort. There was no intention of taking up arms. Rather, it enabled them to contribute with visible affiliation to recognized causes. What they wore varied from the less formal attire of an organization like the Women's Volunteer Reserve, whose members sported skirts and jackets that were seen as "practical and sensible," to the regulation uniforms for those who joined the new Women's Royal Naval Service (WRNS). Its ratings were issued caps and long frock coats, while officers wore a felt tricorne hat, a fairly long skirt and a well-cut navy blue jacket with a double row of gold buttons.[3] As one of their number explained, to see women wearing the uniform of "that most conservative of institutions" gave her "quite a lump in one's throat, it was so splendid and unexpected."[4]

AN "ARDENT BAND OF LADIES:" THE VOLUNTARY AID DETACHMENT
AND SERVICE IN BRITAIN

After the onset of hostilities, the Canadian government established a National Relief Committee to coordinate voluntary medical assistance, bringing together the Department of Militia and Defence (DMD), the Canadian
Red Cross Society and the St. John Ambulance organization. The DMD was
responsible for identifying the type of assistance needed, while the huge and
well-coordinated volunteer programme mounted by the CRCS focused on
services, funds, supplies and materials. Part of that programme involved
training and supervising Voluntary Aid Detachment (VAD) workers.

A VAD system had been founded in 1909 to provide field nursing services
in Britain and other countries of the empire, and Canada's VAD was organized largely through the Red Cross and the Order of St. John of Jerusalem.
Before 1914 VAD service was intended for home duty and it seemed unlikely
that Canadian women would have an opportunity to volunteer for overseas
work. However, the declaration of war brought many changes, among them
opportunities to be part of "an organized auxiliary" support network.[5] Young
women interested in pursuing this path tended to come from "good" families with "Imperialist traditions" of service and an understanding of what
that stood for.[6] In civilian life they might be found working in fields such
as teaching, nursing and social work, but they demonstrated that they were
ready to join the war effort even if it meant setting aside their employment.

Having a military or medical connection was considered an ideal background for someone interested in becoming a VAD nursing assistant, but
there were other options. A recruitment poster advertised for "nursing members, cooks, kitchen-maids, clerks, house-maids, ward-maids, laundresses,
motor-drivers, etc." Applicants had to be ready to "give a ready and willing
obedience to the orders of all superior officers and never question or hesi-
tate to obey an order."[7] Once accepted, they had to be prepared to work in a
variety of settings from hospitals to hostels, convalescent homes, draughty
religious buildings, ambulance trains and other facilities.[8]

England was normally the first port of call for potential Canadian VADs
seeking to work overseas. Those especially anxious to get started could proceed to London independently and apply directly at Devonshire House, the
organization's headquarters. Since women who chose this route had to fi-
nance their own travel and training and subsidize their basic living costs,
money was a deciding factor. Daisy Johnson of Regina, Saskatchewan, was a
case in point, setting aside her job as secretary to the provincial deputy minister of education to join the VAD.[9] Another was Sophie Smethurst of Sas-

Wartime recruitment. Advertising became a major force in western economies in the late 19th century, primarily in newspapers and magazines. During the war it was used to promote such causes as selling war bonds and to aid recruitment. Here workers are invited to apply for a variety of Voluntary Aid Detachment posts. The VAD nursing assistants shown look smart in their uniforms. On the left is a British Red Cross VAD, while the woman on the right wears the plain apron and embroidered armband of a St. John Ambulance VAD. (Public domain)

katoon, who paid her way to Britain armed with her "First Aid and Home Nursing Certificates." She hoped to join the CAMC nursing service but was prevented from doing so by its strict regulations and was concerned that the money she had saved for her return passage to Canada would be used up on living costs. In the end, Sophie volunteered as a VAD with the British Red Cross Society and was soon among kindred spirits as keen as she was to do their patriotic duty.[10]

The minimum age limit for UK-based VAD service was twenty-one, and after completing the formalities and obtaining their uniforms, recruits were initiated into their work. Many women had no particular vocational qualifications but compensated by having "impeccable social credentials."[11] Canadian VADs soon discovered they were among "the most glamorous of all the uniformed women in London" as they walked the streets in their long coats and broad-brimmed hats.[12] According to Canadian Bessie Hall, she wore beneath her outdoor clothing a "grey dress" with a black armband emblazoned with a Maltese Cross, a "white apron with bib, stiff linen collar, stiff cuffs, white belt and the cap." Bessie, who was proud of her uniform, described it as the "Mecca of my existence!"[13] Although she and her fellow recruits were mostly unaccustomed to the long hours and hardships of manual work under discipline, they professed themselves "ready to go anywhere" when the need came, in order to be "of use to our soldiers."[14]

That use was not long in coming, and in October 1914 Katherine Furse, founder and first commandant of the Joint Women's VAD Committee, took volunteers to France, where they opened a rest station for soldiers in "three trucks and two second-class coaches on a siding" at the Gare Centrale in Boulogne.[15] As a result of fighting at Ypres that autumn, wounded men started to arrive at the rest station on 27 October and the VADs were faced with "a great crowd of supposedly walking wounded." In the midst of hundreds of men, they handed out tea and cocoa and gave help to a few trained nurses who were treating those who needed it. As Katherine Furse recorded, her volunteers proved to be "the heroes of the hour" and were subsequently offered whatever they needed to continue their work.[16]

With medical care a priority, most Canadian VAD nursing applicants were recruited through the "St. John Ambulance-Anglo-imperialist framework."[17] The idea of untrained personnel in a professional nursing environment met with resistance, particularly on the part of the CAMC. Matron-in-Chief Margaret Macdonald perceived a "tremendous risk" in accepting unqualified volunteers into her service, fearing they might "undermine the efficiency and status" of the regular staff.[18] Not only that, but the idea of taking on such workers when those in authority were intent on promoting a "modern professional image of Canadian nursing" meant that maintaining "a visible distance" between volunteers and qualified nurses was regarded as essential.[19]

Even though a VAD nursing programme was introduced at the University of Toronto in November 1916, with half the study time allocated to practical work "such as bandaging and taking temperatures, etc.," few Canadian VADs who opted for nursing work believed their knowledge in any way equated to that of the trained personnel they worked with.[20] In the Imperial nursing service they had the same standing as junior nurses or probationers, and there were times when the overbearing approach of some British nursing staff provoked reactions. Violet Wilson, the daughter of Edmonton's first medical director, worked as a VAD nursing assistant in a London hospital where the matron seemed to be biased against women from the colonies and complained that they had "no sense of discipline." Violet and her colleagues "had to take a good deal" from the English nursing sisters and she did not mince words, telling them that "I'd come to help wait on the men, not the Nurses, and I said it very loudly!"[21] Jean Sears, who had worked in a Toronto hospital before 1914, encountered a similar problem and told a ward sister, "I haven't come 3000 miles to work voluntarily to be spoken to like that by anybody."[22] Jane Walters from southern Ontario also admitted that "the discipline in a British military hospital was something!" There were nurses that she "couldn't bear," but she nevertheless felt that her experience broadened her outlook because "you did things you never thought you were going to do … It was a wonderful character builder."[23]

Such experiences could be discouraging, but VADs were needed and Frances Cluett, a teacher from Belleoram in Newfoundland, was one volunteer who immersed herself in her work at a British hospital. Her duties included changing dressings, giving blanket baths, taking temperatures and checking stocks of essential supplies. "We are allowed to speak but little to the patients" she said, "and to tell you the truth we scarcely have time to speak to ourselves sometimes."[24] Torontonian Leah McCarthy was a VAD who worked at a hospital in Kent. She described how, "when the casualties from ships came in, we got them" as it were, "directly from the front line dressing stations." She and her colleagues regularly saw patients in a very serious condition and she referred to the limited treatment they could offer. Many of the "terrific" wounds she observed had to be cleaned and dressed with little more than "saline solution" and a mixture of "phenal, camphor, and alcohol." Nevertheless, the saline could be "extraordinarily effective," said Leah in the knowledge that the patients "got no injections or anything at all" at a time before antibiotics. Leah McCarthy reported that at her hospital there was "no evidence of friction between Sisters and VAD workers," proving that not all British nurses disapproved of colonial volunteers.[25] Frances Cluett also managed to get along well with her British colleagues, undoubtedly helped by the fact that she was described as a woman of "self confidence, courage, determination, humour, strong faith, devotion to service," with a "calm and pragmatic" temperament.[26]

In addition to working at military hospitals, VAD nursing assistants were taken on by a variety of independent units and convalescent homes. Two Ottawa women, Winnifred Lewis and Mrs. S.H. Fleming, opened the Clarence House Convalescent Hospital at Roehampton, Surrey, which handled mainly amputation cases and was staffed by nurses and VADs from Canada. Another establishment was the Perkins Bull Hospital for convalescent Canadian officers at Wimbledon in south-west London. This was launched in June 1916 by lawyer, businessman and philanthropist William Perkins Bull, KC, and his wife, Maria. Their daughter Dorothy worked there as a VAD and met some of her parents' famous visitors, among whom was the movie star Douglas Fairbanks.

Lady Ridley's Hospital for Officers in London's fashionable Carlton House Terrace also had VADs on its staff who grew accustomed to a procession of VIP visitors. Society hostess Rosamond Ridley was one among a number of titled ladies who opened and managed their own hospitals during the war, and she used part of her London town house for the purpose. As someone blessed with a knack for "accomplishing the impossible with ease and grace," Rosamond supervised the conversion of her drawing room and Long Gallery, full of impressive paintings, into wards. The addition of extra space took the total number of beds to sixty, with an operating theatre on the ground floor. The hospital held the status of an acute and convalescent unit and handled patients who had inhaled poison gas, lost limbs and suffered other life-changing injuries, as well as some with shell shock who were tended in a quiet, separate area.[27] It was obvious when the convalescent officers were feeling better because things became somewhat boisterous on occasions, causing the nursing sister in charge to become "furious." However, "all blew over though in the end."[28]

Lady Ridley's staff included Isabel Bell-Irving from Vancouver, who was the eldest daughter of Henry Ogle Bell-Irving, a Scot who had made his fortune setting up the Anglo-British Columbia Packing Company. Henry, an ardent Imperialist, believed that "a man is the maker of his own fortune" and

Duty to King and Country. The Bell-Irving family of Vancouver served with distinction during the First World War. Taken in 1917, this photograph shows VAD Isabel Bell-Irving, who worked as a volunteer nursing assistant in London, with her six brothers (from left to right): Roderick, Henry, Aeneas, Richard (seated), Malcolm and Duncan. (City of Vancouver Archives)

had high expectations of his large family. Isabel was close to her father and by 1914 had accompanied him to Europe on a number of occasions.[29] When two of her six brothers were wounded in the war and taken to Lady Ridley's Hospital, Isabel visited them. She decided to volunteer as a VAD and soon learned that the hospital had acquired a reputation for being "by far the most fashionable" of its kind. Among the many visitors was Queen Alexandra, who graced the wards with her presence "quite often," wrote Isabel. "She is kindness itself," she continued, but because the queen was Danish and spoke with a heavy accent, "the men can't understand her."[30] Members of the extensive Bell-Irving clan appeared regularly, with the result that, according to Isabel, the hospital was known as "The B-I town house."[31] With a park nearby for walks, and concerts in the evenings, it was a lively place on occasions where humour clearly helped to make light of the seriousness of injuries. One patient, a Captain Taylor who was a double amputee, told Isabel Bell-Irving to "cheer up … I've always wanted to be a shorty."[32]

No matter what a VAD undertook, it was clear that the test of a good worker lay in adapting "quickly and quietly" to an established routine, and in providing efficient and reliable help.[33]

"I SHALL NEVER FORGET IT AS LONG AS I LIVE ... SUCH SIGHTS":
VADS IN FRANCE

Canadian VAD nursing assistants served an average probationary period of six months in British hospitals under the auspices of the BRCS, after which they could apply to work in France or further afield. Among them were some who merited speedy promotion; Frances Cluett and Alice Wynne-Roberts, who had worked in a Toronto bank before the war, acquired the status of "senior VAD." Frances was offered the chance to work in France after only five months' probation – an indication of her competence and the need for additional help. By 1916 a shortage of trained nursing personnel prompted a request from London for additional VADs to serve in British military hospitals, and volunteers between the ages of twenty-three and thirty-eight with a minimum of three months' hospital experience were henceforth considered for medical service overseas.[34] Alice Wynne-Roberts described how she had been moved from "the eternal cleaning or supervising of cleaning" to helping with surgical dressings and "applying fomentations," packing gauze into large wounds or applying bandages. She found it "rather a change from banking anyway," and it was not long before she too was on her way to the Western Front.[35]

Although the BRCS had sent additional nursing staff and some VADs to De Panne in Belgium early in the war, most nursing opportunities occurred in France. Frances Cluett joined No. 10 British General Hospital near Rouen, where she worked a 12-hour shift from 8 P.M. to 8 A.M. Her responsibilities were spread across five wards and she found that "night duty is no laughing matter." Even if she felt tired, Frances knew that "sleep must be sacrificed on all accounts" because of the vital necessity to "look out for all sorts of things, such as amputation bleedings, deaths, drinks, etc."[36] On her twenty-second birthday Frances wrote to her mother describing her work: "I had to help with some dressings today. Oh mother! I shall never forget it as long as I live ... such sights ... You can read about war, and the wounded, but when you are brought face to face with it, I tell you it is heart rending."[37] Relief came through her interest in photography, painting and gardening, and in maintaining regular contact with Newfoundland servicemen, who were never far from her thoughts.

By the autumn of 1917 the risk of air raids over the Allied base hospitals in northern France was increasing, but it was not enemy action that shocked Frances Cluett so much as the suffering of the patients she was helping to look after. Doreen Gery, another Canadian VAD, was soundly reprimanded for barely being able to face the sight of a man's exposed intestines. "You're no good to me if you can't do the work," the ward sister barked at her. That same ward sister, however, was impressed a few weeks later when she saw that Doreen, who had made a great effort, was now able to deal with the wounds of mortally ill men.[38]

In an environment in which even trained nurses were often distressed at the suffering of their patients, the work remained challenging. A positive outlook helped a great deal, as VAD Mary "May" Bird, from Bracebridge, Ontario, discovered. She worked for a while with a unit of the Scottish Women's Hospitals at Asnières-sur-Oise among an army of women uniformed in "workmanlike greys and blues with a gay touch of tartan on collar and hat-band."[39] May was a buoyant character who fitted the "Very Adaptable Dames" interpretation of the VAD acronym. She was delighted to find that her superior was "a very sporting soul with regard to the work at hand" and also "very loyal" and good to her staff. There was little that bothered May Bird, apart from the fact that night duty was "ghastly hard on stockings – every morning I darn up the damage of the night's wear."[40]

Canadian VADs also served with medical units of other nations in France, and Neuilly, near Paris, was the location of the American Ambulance hospital, maintained through private subscription. Its fifteen VADs, who had a high level of responsibility, included Canadians Rosalind Cotter, Beatrice Page and Rachel Webb. Rachel worked at Neuilly for sixteen months before being seconded to help at several French hospitals during the German spring offensive of 1918 – at times under enemy shelling. The value of these VADs was "enhanced by the fact" that "practically all of them" spoke good French.[41] With duty as their priority, they were expected to maintain a professional distance, even though there were many opportunities to form relationships with troops, patients and medical officers, the latter having the appeal of being educated young men from similar social circles. VAD Jean Sears phrased it well when she said, "We had ideals in those days," and she admitted that to be "thrown in with men … from all over the world, it took some doing … not to have your head turned."[42]

Women engaged in non-medical VAD service in France, be it driving, domestic, administrative or clerical duties, found that much was expected of them too. The hours were "often long and the labour hard," but the work was worthwhile and rewarding. VADs at recreation huts attached to Canadian hospitals provided the men with some of the "happiest reminders of home and of a woman's care." As hostesses and organizers they helped to maintain a friendly, homely environment with "music and laughter and fun."[43] Another important aspect of VAD work was tracking down men missing in action, and Canadian Gertrude Arnold was one of the "searchers" who tried to find "clues of missing men" and helped to update information held by the CRCS. While carrying out her research, some of which involved talking to hospitalized patients, Gertrude could also help them with things like letter writing or gentle exercise.[44]

VADs who took on domestic work in France were also in demand. Those who volunteered at hospitals and rest homes had to work flexible hours, attend to the particular requirements of patients and help maintain standards of cleanliness, hygiene and catering. Canadian Olive Dent worked at a medical unit near Rouen and listed her domestic and housekeeping duties. "We planned the menus," she said, and "laid the tables, carved, served out the different meals, cooked certain dishes, did the shopping, dusted," and managed the staff accommodation. This involved preparing rooms for new arrivals, keeping an eye on any staff member who was not well and overseeing the general "smooth running of affairs."[45] Violet Wilson, who spent time at a convalescent home for Canadian officers at Deauville, recalled that her work was more domestic than medical, and with plentiful nutritious food available many of the patients made rapid recoveries.[46]

VAD truck drivers did essential work distributing cases of supplies to French hospitals. They had to be familiar not just with their vehicles but with every part of the Allied lines of communication. Motor transport was proving indispensable and the armies came to depend upon it. Through the French Red Cross, women could also take on transport duty for one of its three separate arms: *La Société de Secours aux Blessés Militaires, l'Association des Dames Françaises* or *l'Union des Femmes de France.* The volunteer drivers wore a khaki uniform with blue flashes on the collar and cuffs which had been agreed jointly by the British and French war offices.[47]

The Canadian Red Cross Society maintained motor ambulance convoys at Étaples and Paris, which ferried sick and wounded men between stations and hospitals and triaged casualties requiring specialized or urgent treatment. The need for ambulance convoys was confirmed once it became clear that they could play an important role in the evacuation of casualties. By late October 1914 there were 120 ambulances of the Red Cross and the Order of St. John available for use, and over the following year Canada sent more than sixty-five to the war zone. They were among the most modern of their type and each bore the name of a Canadian town or city. The ambulances were not only a reminder of Canadian generosity, but also symbols of the nation's desire to reach out and care for its troops.

Driving an ambulance was seen as "arguably the most glamorous VAD role," but women drivers had their fair share of challenges in breakdowns, bad weather, air raids, night driving in difficult conditions and other unpredictable situations.⁴⁸ Canadian VADs who volunteered for this work had to persist with their applications and prove they were up to the task, leading one would-be applicant from Edmonton to take a motor mechanics' course and work in a garage before going overseas. Applicants from Canada included Honor Heward of Montreal, Elsie Chatwin from Regina and Grace MacPherson of Vancouver, whose only desire was to get behind the wheel in the war zone.⁴⁹

In early August 1916 Grace arrived in London and went to VAD headquarters at Devonshire House to offer her services. To her dismay she discovered that she had "by one day missed … a job in France" and was "simply broken-hearted about it."⁵⁰ She decided to wait for another vacancy and meanwhile took a clerical job with the Canadian Pay and Records Office. Grace made the most of her time in the British capital and her diary mentions shopping for clothes, dining at well-known and popular restaurants, seeing shows and making new friends. She also took first aid courses and visited the Canadian camp at Shorncliffe, where she found "the boys are as lovely as ever."⁵¹

On 28 March 1917 Grace's patience was rewarded when "my marching orders did actually come," she wrote with relief.⁵² She purchased her new uniform, which consisted of a blue peaked gabardine cap, blue serge jacket and matching gored skirt, white blouse, black tie, long double breasted blue coat, white gloves, and black boots or shoes. She was one of twenty women chosen to join a CRCS ambulance convoy based with No. 7 Canadian General Hospital at Étaples. It was the largest Red Cross convoy in France, and from April 1917 Grace became one of a handful of Canadian girls doing such work. "It was glorious to think that at last I was actually driving an ambulance. It was a 2½ year dream hatched out," she recorded, "and means more to me than anything has meant yet."⁵³

Despite having realized her ambition, Grace MacPherson found her first few months in France "utterly miserable," and had it not been for other Canadians she met, she admitted that she "could not possibly have remained." Her independent, outgoing manner did not always fit easily with the more conservative British approach, and she found herself among those who did not "stand in high favor with the commandant and four section leaders."⁵⁴ Fortunately, she found a friend in Armine Gosling, the daughter of the mayor of St. Johns, Newfoundland, and together they made efforts to fit in. Grace managed to break the ice with some of the other British drivers, admitting later that she came to "value their friendship very highly." All the girls held the rank of "honorary lieutenant" but as VADs there was "not the salary, nor

Driver MacPherson. Grace MacPherson of Vancouver volunteered for overseas service as a VAD and went to France as an ambulance driver in April 1917. Based at Étaples, she left lively and informative accounts of her work. Grace was singled out for a series of publicity photographs and this shot shows her adding water to the radiator of her Canadian-made McLaughlin vehicle. (Canadian War Museum, George Metcalf Archival Collection, Acc 19920085-359)

do we get any gratuity," Grace explained. Strict regulations included only being permitted to dine with a brother, father or husband if they happened to be visiting, and dancing was prohibited on pain of dismissal.[55]

Women ambulance drivers were expected to take on day and night duty, which changed every two weeks. Work averaged one convoy and one evacuation per day, but at busy times they could be driving at any time and taking turns for emergency duty, which meant being dressed and ready to move at a moment's notice. Grace MacPherson soon memorized the routes she had to drive, and between runs she was responsible for maintaining her vehicle. This included changing, pumping and repairing tires, and carrying out regular checks. There were daily and periodic inspections by the commandant, who had rigid rules and on occasion decided that the spirited MacPherson was not taking her work seriously enough or accepting the discipline. After being reprimanded a number of times over various minor infractions, she decided it was "a bit thick when one considers that I've come only 7,000 miles for the express purpose of driving."[56]

As she transported wounded soldiers, Grace learned how to handle them and to "drive as carefully as one possibly can" in all weather conditions and situations. She described summer thunderstorms, a week when the water supply was cut, and on one occasion driving in an area where there were "thousands of troops and 30 or more transports on the road and I was the only girl." It suddenly felt, she said, as if she were truly "in the War Zone." Another time, when "all kinds of guns" fired at an enemy aircraft overhead, "it was quite thrilling" wrote Grace, thankful that none of the bombs fell near her vehicle.[57] On 12 April 1917, soon after the Canadians had been in action at Vimy Ridge, Grace noted that "for the first time we have men *direct* from the line."[58]

A few weeks later on 8 June 1917, Grace MacPherson and her ambulance were photographed by the *Illustrated War News* for an article about women in the war effort. "They wanted me as representing Canada – Canadian girls," said Grace, recounting how she had to pose at the wheel of her ambulance, then "in my overalls with sleeves rolled up," and finally, "jacking up a tyre."[59] The ambulance drivers took part in a military sports day at Camiers near Boulogne, and after helping her team win a relay race Grace was delighted to receive "a gorgeous pair of black silk hose" and an "exquisite bottle of Corlys Lilas perfume in a lovely box."[60]

The passing weeks brought further challenges: five trainloads of wounded to be transported, making it "the busiest day we have ever had"; a large number of badly gassed soldiers "with their eyes bound up"; German air raids on three consecutive nights when "lights had to be out"; the ordeal of the Third Battle of Ypres and the knowledge that the Canadians were very "badly cut up but gained their objectives."[61] There was also the time Grace was given a ride in one of the new tanks, and days when she had to complete her work in freezing temperatures such that "I was too cold to sleep." A period of leave in London brought a welcome break and the fun of falling "madly in love with a boy at the next table" of a restaurant but she was soon back in France, where the hospitals were "expecting a gigantic drive from [the] Hun."

During the German spring offensive of 1918, the ambulance convoy at Étaples was "frightfully busy." Grace MacPherson's diary recorded "Huns advancing in hundreds of thousands. Everyone anxious but not depressed." During this "most strenuous time," the drivers were working around the clock and during a three-week period "we carried over forty-eight thousand patients." On 27 March 1918 she noted that "30 of us carried 2,500 cases between 8.15 [P.M.] and 7 A.M." and there was "not one puncture all night!"[62] The pace remained hectic, and her last diary entry was on 20 May 1918, the day of a major German air raid that resulted in "appalling damage and loss of life." Seeing bombs "dropping on every side," Grace and her fellow drivers had "no protection whatever and were ordered to remain in our huts." Thankfully the ambulances survived and nobody was hit by shrapnel, "which was falling like hail all about us." During a lull in the bombing thirty of the drivers were ordered out and saw "ghastly, gruesome sights indeed," wrote Grace, but all of them felt better being on the move rather than "sitting idle in our huts."

After Grace MacPherson had finished her service in France, she decided that her worst experience was not the air attacks or the pressure of work, but being hauled up in front of the commandant for some misdemeanour or other. "All the girls were terrified of our O[fficer].C[ommanding]," she admitted, alluding to the fact that she herself was "picked on very generously indeed."[63] Nevertheless, the plucky Grace completed some eighteen eventful months as a driver before returning to England in the autumn of 1918.

"SUNBURNT AND FRECKLED … BUT WHO CARES": VADS FURTHER AFIELD

Ambulance drivers like Grace MacPherson needed a level-headed approach to their work in whatever conditions the war generated. Some worked further afield, and Jessie McLachlin of Ottawa drove in Serbia, where fighting and disease created tough conditions for nurses and voluntary workers that "challenged their finer sensibilities" as well as their well-being. Yet such considerations, according to VAD Jane Walters, did not figure in the equation. As she stated, "You didn't think about the costs to yourself, you just did what was needed."[64] By 1918, with qualified British nurses in diminishing supply, capable VADs were given more responsibility and autonomy. Muriel Wainwright from Ottawa was sent to Italy and seconded to the staff of a new military hospital on the Mediterranean coast. In one year and under pressing conditions, Muriel achieved a level of seniority that normally took twice as long.[65]

Some VADs were offered the chance to work in Egypt and accounts include tales of having to pitch a mess tent in a hurricane-like storm; dressing for the heat with white cotton clothing and a sun helmet; and fending off flies while preparing food in hospital kitchens. Canadian Mary Gordon worked there for two years and on 14 January 1918, was mentioned in despatches for "valuable service to the sick and wounded."[66] Just ahead of her was Mary "May" Bird, who left her work in France and joined No. 19 British General Hospital at Alexandria in 1915. She arrived there in October to find "very, very hot" days, overcrowded conditions on the wards and the ever-present insect problem.[67] Convoys of sick and wounded Allied troops arrived mainly after dark, and May found it "heart rending"

> to look along the long rows of beds and think how horrible is the toll of this endless war. Ours is an enteric section of two wards – sixty patients in all … we have some extremely bad cases, but some of our "impossibles" have pulled through the most critical stage … The dysentery cases are innumerable, and are still being brought in in great numbers.[68]

May was fortunate to work with a nursing sister who was "perfectly sweet" and far more accommodating than some of her colleagues. "She has the patience of a Saint – and a huge sense of humour," May noted, adding that, "she treats me quite as a human and not in the least like a know-nothing – which in truth I am." Having acknowledged how much she owed to the trained nurses she worked with, May paid particular attention to learning and mastering her duties. Although dedicated to her work, she was aware of the need for a life away from the hospital and resolved to "accomplish a bit more in the numerous branches of work and pleasure."[69] Free time was used for sailing, swimming, sightseeing and picnics in the company of nurses and officers – welcome opportunities to "get away from the town, the patients and all things hospital." Dress regulations were strict even during the hot season, but May described a small and welcome degree of relaxation.

> We are allowed a street dress of a slightly less conventional design and I had a great fight constructing mine. It has a regulation hemstitched white collar and cuffs, black V.A.D. crest, buttons and black belt & in the correct shade. Got a small panama hat to wear with it – and there you have me complete.[70]

When a precious week of leave came her way, May Bird chose to spend it in Cairo. Three of her VAD co-workers proved to be "perfect bricks" and agreed to cover her duties, prompting her to comment jokingly that "you can see how much they must want to get rid of the domineering 'Canada.'" Her fear was that "by the time I get back from Cairo the patients and staff will have decided that they can very well manage without me."[71] When her leave ended, the lively Canadian had fulfilled her wish to visit the Pyramids and ride on a camel, relishing every new experience. May Bird was someone who coped well with the work and the climate, reassuring her family that, "the hot weather is not affecting my health in the slightest. I am as well and flourishing as ever – and night duty is proving quite agreeable." Before long she described herself as "sunburnt and freckled … but who cares."[72]

At the Great Pyramid. VAD Mary "May" Bird from Bracebridge, Ontario, served in France and Egypt. She made the most of her free time to explore her surroundings and here she and two colleagues have undertaken a camel ride to one of the most famous ancient sites in the world. Mary is probably the figure on the right. (Canadian War Museum, George Metcalf Archival Collection, Acc 20060079-004)

"PART OF A NATIONAL COMMUNITY": CANADA'S IMPERIAL VAD

In response to an urgent request from the Joint Women's VAD Committee for further colonial support, an independent organization known as the Canadian Imperial Voluntary Aid Detachment was founded in 1918. Lady Emily Perley, wife of Canada's high commissioner in London, agreed to become its commandant and more than 180 Canadian women had enrolled by the time the war ended. Most of them were already working overseas but there were also new recruits, and "36 VADs just over from Canada" arrived in London in time to meet Queen Mary when she visited the headquarters of the new organization on 25 July 1918. Everyone was "lined up in the hall" and the girls were "thrilled at seeing the Queen" in person.[73]

Some of the new "Imperials" were chosen to staff a CRCS rest house for Allied nursing staff that opened in Boulogne that year. Thirteen of them were on duty when Dame Maud McCarthy, head of the QAIMNS in France, visited the facility and complimented the "charming" Canadians who were helping to run it.[74] It was a tribute not only to the women concerned, but also to Emily Perley, who as leader was described by one of her staff as "the most delightful and charming person I have met in my travels" and "a mother to all Canadian girls overseas."[75]

After a relaxation in CAMC rules was announced in April 1918, more than twenty Canadian Imperial VADs were allowed to work in CAMC hospitals in a non-nursing capacity. Others took up work at CRCS hostels in England and France, at the CRCS London headquarters and at St. Dunstan's Hostel for Blinded Soldiers and Sailors, where VAD Elsie Thorne, from Cobalt, Ontario, was on the staff for some time. All the girls volunteering with the new VAD service were recognizable by their "Canada-R" shoulder badge, which was worn with their regular uniform and by which they could now be identified as "part of a national community."[76]

"THE HELPING HAND AND THE CHEERY WELCOME": VOLUNTEERING WITH THE YMCA

The Young Men's Christian Association (YMCA) worked from the start of the conflict to provide canteens and recreation tents, club houses, rest rooms and, wherever possible, a range of other options including religious services, for soldiers training in Canada and Britain. With generous support from the public, who realized the value in having decent places of recreation for young men, the YMCA's "Red Triangle" badge became well known. In London a "Beaver Hut" was established not far from Charing Cross Station with dormitories, a restaurant, theatre, billiards room, barber shop, showers and meals. These facilities were supervised by Helen Fitz-Randolph from Saint John, New Brunswick, assisted by Gladys Aitken, who had been living in Britain with her husband, Canadian millionaire Max Aitken (later Lord Beaverbrook), since before the war.

The YMCA also maintained a kit stores in the city, a separate hut for officers, a leave department that provided information on hospitality and travel possibilities, and recreation grounds where men could play a variety of sports.[77] In addition to a club at Shorncliffe, officers' facilities were also opened at Seaford, Bramshott, Witley and Rhyl. Help was always welcomed at Canadian YMCA centres throughout the country, and some 600 volunteers kept them running. It can safely be said that no Canadian soldier reached Europe without being aware of the organization's presence.

YMCA operations in France meant there was a network of venues for the troops where they could obtain refreshments or attend concerts, sports and athletics meetings.[78] In Paris the organization took over the Hotel d'Iéna, a first-class establishment with "silken hangings, beautifully carved furniture and every modern luxury." It became a stopover for Canadian troops, and among the staff Mrs. J. C. Mowrer from Regina helped to organize "a series of excursions and entertainment" for soldiers on leave.[79] Canadian women were volunteer helpers at YMCA facilities in France and were still handing out drinks and snacks to French refugees after the fighting had ended.

Typical of those who gave their time to the "Y" were Edith Morris of Toronto and Eileen Kellett from Cobourg, the wife of a serving soldier. She spent five months working at a canteen, while Edith Morris worked for the YMCA in a clerical capacity from 1917 until after the end of the war. She was based at Étaples and Abbeville, but later transferred to the Franco-American YMCA, where she helped at the *Foyer des Soldats* (Soldiers' Home). All those who worked with the "Y" had memorable experiences: evenings when the huts resounded with laughter and voices of soldiers glad to escape the grim reality of the trenches; the tired, strained faces of men lining up for hot drinks on their way back from the front line; and for those at Étaples, where there was a sports field beside the local cemetery, the memory of games that were stopped every time the Last Post sounded and "thousands

"Help Us Help Our Boys." This poster, issued jointly by the American YMCA and YWCA, shows a volunteer helper wearing the organization's smart grey uniform and velour hat. Canadian women served in Britain and France with the YMCA, including its Franco-American branch, and did valuable work. (Library and Archives Canada, e010696642-v8)

of men sitting on the slopes" of the sports park "stood up in dead silence" out of respect.[80]

The "Y" Red Triangle sign stood for "the helping hand and the cheery welcome – the one place where men could escape from the "soulless machinery of war and relax as in the house of a friend."[81] Those women who worked for the YMCA and wore a grey uniform and panama or velour hat, were the kindly face of Canada where it was most needed.

"SOMETHING USEFUL IN THE SERVICE OF THE EMPIRE": THE FIRST AID NURSING YEOMANRY

During the First World War the First Aid Nursing Yeomanry (FANY) carried out a great deal of valuable work for the French, Belgian and British armies. It was founded in 1909, and in addition to a thorough training in first aid and the treatment of casualties, its members were also drilled in horsemanship, signalling and camp work with the idea that they would "ride onto the battlefield to attend to the wounded who might otherwise have been left to a slow death."[82]

All FANY members were volunteers, and under the direction of two determined and distinguished women, Lilian Franklin and Grace Ashley-Smith, the corps overcame hostility on the part of the public and succeeded in gaining support from parts of the military establishment. When war broke out the FANY offered its services to the British War Office, whose leading lights believed that the Western Front was no place for women. They did, however, give permission for them to cross the Channel and help the Belgians during the autumn of 1914, enabling a group of members to set off with their first motor ambulance. They more than proved their worth, and fund raising made it possible to buy more vehicles. The FANY also maintained a hospital for Belgian wounded from October 1914 to October 1916, and its Belgian ambulance convoy assisted the French at times of particular emergency. Collecting civilian and military casualties under bombardment won FANY members praise for their "phenomenal courage" as they coped, month after month, with the carnage that resulted from the fighting.[83]

In 1915 representatives from the organization went to the War Office to suggest that it should employ women drivers for ambulance work on British bases in the war zone. The offer was not considered "practical" and until the end of that year most female ambulance units were part of the Red Cross. Finally, with effect from 1 January 1916, the FANY won its battle to become the first women's ambulance convoy to work for the British army. That year alone its drivers transported some 80,000 wounded, and in October 1916 they were asked to take on "Service of Bombardment," which meant being ready to work during air raids or naval attacks.

FANY volunteers had to buy their own uniform, which consisted of a khaki tunic with four pockets, special buttons, badges and a Red Cross circle on each sleeve. A long khaki skirt, shirt, tie, brown shoes or boots and khaki puttees completed the ensemble, with the addition of a long coat for wear in open-cab ambulances. FANYs were trusted not to bring the name of the corps into disrepute and to maintain their hard-won image. Experienced ambulance drivers gave talks and lectures to the public in an effort to publicize their work and attract donations to cover ongoing costs.[84]

Among Canadians who joined the FANY was Katie Snyder of Calgary, who arrived in England in 1916 "with one thought in mind," which was to do "something useful in the service of the Empire." She had experience of driving a motor vehicle and secured a place at the British School of Motoring, where she was the only Canadian training with some 200 women. Having learned "the art of driving, mechanics and repairs," she began work as a volunteer ambulance driver transporting patients and convalescent soldiers in London and undertaking staff work. Katie was then sent to France, where she joined the organization's ambulance convoy at St. Omer. There were "fifty of us altogether," she recalled, discovering that she and Evelyn Gordon-Brown from Ottawa were the only Canadians at that depot. "From this point," said Katie, "we did considerable driving, our area extending from Calais at the coast to Abbeville on the Somme."[85]

One aspect of the job involved meeting barges using the canal systems to evacuate patients. Moving seriously wounded men by water minimized the jolting experienced with road travel or hospital trains, and drivers went to great lengths to circumvent uneven surfaces on the routes they had to take. FANY ambulance drivers in France, especially those based at Calais, experienced air raids, shelling, accidents and the general wear and tear of working in the war zone. What they had to contend with on occasion is clear from an account left by Muriel Thompson, a British woman who later took command of one of the FANY ambulance convoys. On 25 April 1916 she had to meet "railway trucks full of burnt and blown up men. We took the fifteen worst … They were mad with pain."[86]

During the German spring 1918 offensive, the St. Omer convoy worked round the clock, transporting the wounded from casualty clearing stations to ambulance trains. After the strain of that kind of service, Katie Snyder was prescribed a period of rest, and while she was a patient at No. 10 British Stationary Hospital at St. Omer, she had what she described as her "most

A FANY ambulance. The First Aid Nursing Yeomanry , founded in 1909, carried out valuable work for the French, Belgian and British armies. As part of their duties, volunteers collected wounded soldiers and civilians and this photograph shows Belgian troops helping to push an ambulance out of the mud while the FANY driver hangs onto the wheel. Canadian women with the organization were among those given awards for their bravery. (First Aid Nursing Yeomanry Archive)

thrilling experience." During a German air raid on 26 May 1918 three bombs struck the hospital, killing patients in a room adjacent to hers. She had a narrow escape when "the bed I had vacated was demolished by a falling wall."[87] With the main staircase "blown to pieces" and in "utter darkness," Katie and others negotiated their way through debris and damage to escape down a staircase. When she returned to her camp at St. Omer, it too had been badly damaged by German bombing but fortunately the ambulances had been moved before the raid. As Katie admitted, "the adventure went rather hard with me for I was quite done up." She was given a period of leave before being repatriated to Canada and later admitted that "one of the things that I learned overseas was why the boys never liked air raids. The reason is still vivid in my memory."[88]

FANY members received countless citations for bravery, having faced shell fire, entered recently gassed areas and suffered through air raids with no thoughts of their own safety to complete their vital work.

"WE TOO HAVE DONE A LITTLE IN THE FRAY": THE WOMEN'S SERVICES

A history of Canadians in the First World War refers to Canadian women serving in the ranks of the British Army Corps of Clerks, part of the Royal Army Service Corps, and the WRNS, where they could undertake shore-based work in trade categories that included: household worker; motor driver; signals; storekeeper, porter or messenger; postwoman; telegraphist; and technical worker. Officers and ratings were classed as either "mobile" or "immobile," meaning that a woman was either willing to move or travel wherever required in Britain, or that she wished to stay at or near to her place of residence. Those in the latter category were usually to be found in London or near naval bases such as Chatham, Portsmouth or Plymouth, and over 5,000 women served with the WRNS during the period 1917-1919.[89]

Canadians are also mentioned as serving with the Women's Army Auxiliary Corps (WAAC), which was renamed the Queen Mary's Army Auxiliary Corps (QMAAC) in 1918 after the queen became its patron. It was formed to free up men for active service and its members, who by the end of the war numbered more than 50,000 volunteers, undertook mainly "feminine" roles such as administration, store work and catering. Initially confined to service in Britain, their work was later expanded to France, and Ethel Norman was one Canadian who served with the organization as a driver based at Calais.

Members of the WAAC and Women's Royal Naval Service worked at air stations belonging to the Royal Flying Corps and the Royal Naval Air Service (RNAS). These two services merged in 1918 to form the Royal Air Force and a new organization, the Women's Royal Air Force (WRAF), was formed on 1 April 1918, absorbing 2,000 WAAC and WRNS members to take on trades such as clerks and storewomen, household, technical, and non-technical. The WRAF was keen to provide training in the latter categories, although most of its members chose to work in an administrative or secretarial capacity. Pay was related to skills and experience, and shorthand typists received the highest remuneration. One popular ladies' magazine marvelled at the possibility that women might decide to become "aero-engine fitters, riggers, acetylene welders, magneto repairers, and so on."[90] With about 15,500 women in the new service by 1 August 1918, the idea of the "Girl behind the Man behind the Gun" was now becoming a reality.[91]

Among the awards received by Canadian women volunteers in uniform, eight were mentioned in despatches for reasons that included "valuable service in the field" and gallantry during air raids in France. FANY Evelyn Gordon-Brown won the Military Medal when an Allied ammunition dump in France was set on fire and destroyed by the Germans. She, together with other women ambulance drivers, arrived at the scene and, "in spite of the danger from explosions, succeeded in removing all the wounded." Another Canadian FANY volunteer, Jessie McLachlin, was decorated by the French government for "devotion to duty."[92] One contemporary account described them and their colleagues as "splendid" and "a legend of the war."[93]

* * * * *

After months, or indeed years, far from home in conditions that could be arduous and at times dangerous, Canada's women volunteers more than proved their worth. The war effort of the organizations they worked for was recognized, and, as an example, women serving with the VAD attended a special service of thanksgiving and commemoration at London's St. Paul's Cathedral in the spring of 1918. Among the tributes given was one by Lady Rosamond Ridley, who confirmed that it was "largely owing to the devoted band of V.A.D.'s" that her hospital "achieved such a standard of efficiency and comfort" and "was able to bring such a great measure of relief and happiness to those who suffered so much."[94]

The Canadian YMCA mustered more than 3,000 volunteers for wartime service, and over 2,000 Canadian VADs worked in various capacities. Of the latter, more than 500 were nursing assistants who served in hospitals overseas and fifteen were ambulance drivers. Seven Canadian VADs are confirmed as having died from illness or infection during their war work.[95] Despite all the challenges and the darker days that at times cast a shadow over their work, there were those who would doubtless have agreed with Sybil Johnson from Newfoundland. She ended her final day overseas with the comment, "I'm most glad I came."[96] Among others who commented on their contribution to the war effort, VAD Jean Sears decided that for her, it was enough to have had "the privilege of being of service."[97] All who benefited from that service rendered by many willing volunteers had reason to be grateful.

CHAPTER 10

WOMEN WITH A MISSION (1)

"A splendid courageous devotion"

LADY GRACE JULIA DRUMMOND, "MOTHER" TO THE CANADIAN FORCES

The Mothering Heart of Empire
Is beating to fife and drum;
The measured march of a million feet
Tell where the soldiers come.
And the women stand as the men sweep by,
And cheer them on their way'
The Mothering Heart of Empire
Is proud of its sons today.[1]

"AN ARDENT SUPPORTER OF THE BRITISH EMPIRE": JULIA DRUMMOND AND HER LIFE BEFORE 1914

In September 1916 Canadian officer Georges Vanier wrote that "in this war a woman's lot is the most terrible. She has neither the excitement nor the glory, but only the awful suspense."[2] As true as this was for many wives and mothers at home in Canada, there were some whose longing to be nearer their menfolk "in their time of trial" and to improve their well-being became the driving force behind their choice of war work. One such woman stood on the shore at Quebec City in September 1914, and as she watched the First Canadian Contingent departing she could already visualize the possibility that someone might "mother" all those "who were destined to suffer in the Great War."

Lady Grace Julia Drummond, a well-known figure in Montreal society, was respected for her commitment to her community as well as to her country and the British Empire. Soon after Canada declared war on 5 August 1914 she told a meeting of the Montreal Local Council of Women that the moment for action had come, and that they should no longer "waste money on balls and dinners and fashionable luncheons." Instead, she urged them to buy essential items "for those who need them, not luxuries for yourselves," and to consider how they could contribute to the war effort in the weeks and months that lay ahead.[3] At the same time, she pondered how she, already much involved in charitable and benevolent work, could best be of service.[4]

Pre-war life for this doyenne of the city's exclusive "Square Mile" – home to some of the wealthiest families in Canada – had been busy, eventful and privileged. Born in 1860 to Scottish parents and widowed at a young age, she met Sir George Alexander Drummond, a senator and prominent business-man who sat on the board of a number of major national companies. When the couple decided to wed in 1884, Julia, as she was generally known, became part of a thriving family headed by her successful and prosperous husband, whose properties included a magnificent home on Montreal's Sherbrooke Street.[5]

With a network of business, political and social connections in Canada and abroad, the Drummonds were an impressive couple. They were commit-ted to improving the lives of those less fortunate, and among their philan-thropic projects Montreal's Home for Incurables was founded by Sir George in 1894. At his side, Lady Julia became known as a woman "closely con-nected with various benevolent undertakings" who did "much for the public good."[6] When the Drummonds visited London in 1900, Julia was presented to Queen Victoria, and a subsequent meeting in Canada with the future King Edward VII and Queen Alexandra led to George and Julia Drummond re-ceiving an invitation to Edward's Coronation in 1902.[7]

Well read, articulate and an accomplished public speaker, Julia Drum-mond firmly believed that women should play a distinctive part in society and was horrified to read that in the opinion of one commentator, they were "incapable of further intellectual development after the age of twenty-five."[8] She made her own views clear when she addressed the inaugural meeting of the Canadian Women's Club in December 1907, telling the select audience that "women were made to be the cement of society and came into the world to create relations among mankind."[9] Julia took the view that they had a sig-nificant contribution to make, and backed up her words by helping to found the Victorian Order of Nurses. She also decided to take an active interest in the burgeoning women's suffrage movement.

The marriage of Sir George and Lady Julia Drummond produced two children, one of whom died in infancy. Their surviving son, Guy, was twenty-seven years of age when war broke out and newly married to Mary Braithwaite, daughter of the assistant director of the Bank of Montreal. The young couple had not long returned from a European honeymoon, and as men began vol-unteering for the Canadian Expeditionary Force, Guy Drummond resolved to be among them. He was commissioned in the Royal Highlanders of Canada (The Black Watch), a Montreal-based regiment that formed part of the 13th CEF Battalion. Other young men from Square Mile families also volunteered, including Percival Molson of the famous brewing family and Hugh Allan, whose father ran the well-known shipping line of that name. They shared Guy Drummond's belief that it was not possible to enjoy advantages in life without assuming the corresponding obligations to family, community and nation.[10]

Sir George Drummond having died in 1910, Lady Julia was a widow, and as she watched her son and many other young men preparing to leave Canada for the war in September 1914, her thoughts were not of "the perils" that awaited them, but the knowledge that they did not want the fight to be over "before they had a chance to prove their mettle and bring honour to their country's name."[11] Deciding that her own participation in the war effort lay overseas, she set off for London with her daughter-in-law, Mary, in early November 1914.

On arrival Julia made her way to Brown's Hotel, Mayfair, where she had reserved a suite of rooms. This was a popular establishment which had first opened its doors in 1837 and attracted many famous names, including writers Arthur Conan Doyle, J.M. Barrie and Rudyard Kipling. The first telephone call in Europe had been made from Brown's by Alexander Graham Bell, and during the First World War it hosted European royalty, including Queen Elisabeth of the Belgians. The hotel was not far from the residence of Canada's High Commissioner Sir George Perley and his wife, Lady Emily, and Julia Drummond soon became prominent among Canadians in the British capital.

News from the Western Front and visits to Guy Drummond and his regiment on Salisbury Plain, where the First Canadian Contingent was training, helped Julia to focus on how the lives of Canadian troops could be made more comfortable. The Canadian Red Cross Society, in which she was already actively involved, had established a headquarters in London to coordinate its war work in Britain and France, and it was here that Julia hoped to find a role.

She recognized that when a man was far from familiar surroundings, work, family and friends, it was natural that he would wish to know somebody was interested in him and his well-being. With this in mind, she formulated a proposal to set up and run an information bureau as part of CRCS overseas operations. Behind it lay her dearest wish "to bring some measure of comfort to our soldiers in hospital, some ease of mind to those who

Lady Grace Julia Drummond
(1860-1942) from Montreal set up and ran the Information Bureau of the Canadian Red Cross Society from 1915 to 1919. Based in London, it provided a range of invaluable services to those serving overseas with the Canadian forces and to their families. Seen here in a passport photograph taken in 1915, this dedicated and selfless woman received well-deserved recognition for her wartime work. (McCord Museum Archives, PO15_C1_190206.P2)

loved them across the sea."[12] As a central resource, the bureau would be responsible for a range of important tasks such as attempting to trace troops missing in action, maintaining files on Canadian prisoners of war with the assistance of the International Committee of the Red Cross, arranging volunteer visitors for convalescent Canadian soldiers in Britain, and informing families in Canada about the status and condition of their wounded, sick, missing or captured loved ones. This important work was to be undertaken in co-operation with the British Red Cross Society as parent organization of the CRCS.

Having presented the idea of the new bureau and her willingness to contribute funds for it, Julia Drummond waited while the plan was formally considered. Even though the women's movement had been making headway, it seemed that amid the "bustle of war" the notion of "womanly schemes" still did not easily attract serious attention.[13] The delay meant that Julia could spend the first Christmas of the war with her son, Guy, and his wife, Mary. She also met other Canadians in London, among whom were Mary's older sister, Marjory, and her husband, Captain Trumbull Warren, an officer in the 48th Highlanders and a close friend of Guy's. The two men were on leave from their training in Wiltshire and were among many servicemen and their families making the most of the time they had together.

"AN INVALUABLE LINK BETWEEN THE PEOPLE OF CANADA AND THEIR SOLDIER SONS OVERSEAS": THE CANADIAN RED CROSS SOCIETY INFORMATION BUREAU

In the New Year came news of the official authorization of Julia Drummond's information bureau. Even better was that Colonel Charles Hodgetts, chief commissioner of the CRCS in London, gave her "a free hand to organize and direct it and left the way open for the widest expansion of the work."[14] Iona Carr, who became Julia's assistant, described how on 11 February 1915, the day after the First Canadian Contingent left Britain for France, three ladies

> were put in possession of a couple of rooms in the Canadian Red Cross Society's head-quarters in London, at that date 14 Cockspur Street. They were Lady Drummond as head and director, Miss Erika Bovey and Miss Ermine Taylor, and the alliance was known as the Information Department (later known as Bureau).[15]

Cockspur Street was a thoroughfare that linked Trafalgar Square to Pall Mall, where a number of London's renowned clubs were located. For some time before 1914 Cockspur Street had been a centre for the international travel industry and a place where people from all over the world came to plan

Home of the Canadian Red Cross Information Bureau. For much of the First World War, the Canadian Red Cross Society's Information Bureau was housed on one of the upper floors of this building at 14 Cockspur Street in central London. Formerly the premises of a German shipping line, it was handsomely appointed throughout. This modern view shows the original shop front still in place. (Photograph by Dianne Graves)

travel arrangements. Railways, shipping lines, travel agents, map retailers and luggage rooms where trunks could be delivered and stored – all were to be found along Cockspur Street.

The building where the CRCS had its offices had previously housed the German-owned Hamburg-Amerika shipping line or *Hamburg-Amerika Packetfahrt-Aktiengesellschaft* (HAPAG), next door to which stood the London office of the Grand Trunk Railway Company of Canada.[16] In its heyday the public had passed through the Hamburg-Amerika's imposing doorway into a spacious shipping hall intended to reflect the company's prestigious image. By the time Julia Drummond arrived the British government had commandeered German offices in London and at 14 Cockspur Street the Hamburg-Amerika signs had been removed. The ground floor of the building was now an army recruiting centre with huge enlistment posters in the windows that told passers-by, "Men of the Empire, Your King and Country Need You Today!" Above street level were four floors of office space and the CRCS was located in rooms that retained mahogany panelling, elegant columns and plasterwork, and ornate fittings.

The staff of the Information Bureau were chosen for their "ability and devotion" as well as their accuracy, tact, sensitivity and sympathy.[17] Erika Bovey of Montreal, aided later by Dinah Meredith, a relative of Canadian physician Sir William Osler, was appointed to run a busy section that dealt with the recording of casualties. They handled enquiries in person or by telephone, reports to relatives, officer hospitality and the appointment of hospital visitors. Other departments were responsible for services such as forwarding Red Cross parcels to the troops, supplying Canadian newspapers and "drives and entertainments for Officers and men in hospital." Under the leadership of Julia Drummond, who inspired confidence and respect, it was not long before the CRCS Information Bureau was in full swing.[18]

As the pace of the work gathered speed, Julia learned that both her daughter-in-law, Mary, and Mary's sister, Marjory, were pregnant. Their husbands, Lieutenant Guy Drummond and Captain Trum Warren, were now in France with their battalions, and following an inspection on 11 April 1915 by General Sir Horace Smith-Dorrien, General Officer Commanding the Second British Army, the Canadians were informed that they were soon to "take over from the French in the Ypres salient, a most important part of the line."[19] They set off for Belgium, where the fighting of the previous autumn had resulted in a salient or bulge in the Allied front which protected the medieval city of Ypres in Flanders. Guy Drummond's unit, being part of the 13th Battalion CEF, was tasked with taking over a section of the line northeast of the city, little realiz-

Striking sisters. Mary Braithwaite (seated) and her sister, Dorothy, were daughters of a senior executive of the Bank of Montreal. In the spring of 1914 Mary married Guy Drummond, and after he volunteered for overseas service she followed him to England. Dorothy Braithwaite went to join her sister in May 1915 but was lost at sea when her ship, the liner *Lusitania*, was torpedoed and sunk by a German U-boat. (McCord Museum Archives, M2004.160.126_1 90206-P1)

ing it was about to be involved in the creation of "a glorious page in Canadian history."[20]

On 21 April 1915, apart from unusually heavy shelling during the afternoon, "nothing had indicated that behind the German lines a blow was being prepared such as had never fallen in civilized warfare."[21] Early the following day, 22 April 1915, Guy Drummond wrote to his mother with the sad news that his friend Trum Warren had been killed by artillery fire two days earlier. "Dearest mother," he began, "of course I came to the war knowing that its bitterest trial would be the loss of my friends or relatives, but I had not expected such a sudden or heavy loss as that of Trum Warren the day before yesterday."[22]

Asking his mother to pass on to Marjory Warren information about where Trum had been buried, Guy completed his letter. A few hours later the Germans launched a major attack against the Ypres Salient, unleashing a new weapon, poison gas, in contravention of the Hague Conventions of 1899 and 1907. Allied intelligence had been aware of the German intention to use gas for some weeks but senior commanders refused to believe their enemy would resort to anything so dreadful. Meteorological conditions were favourable on 22 April and around 4 P.M. that day, after a tremendous artillery bombardment of Allied positions, the Germans released 160 tons of chlorine gas which was carried on a light breeze towards the French-occupied trenches to the left of the Canadians. Few of the troops understood what was happening until they found themselves inhaling the gas which, in addition to causing a "burning sensation in the eyes, nose and throat," quickly resulted in severe breathing difficulties.[23]

As it drifted over the French lines there was panic as men collapsed or retreated at the sight of German troops advancing in gas masks. According to Colonel J. A. Currie of the 48th Highlanders, who had last seen and spoken to Guy Drummond that morning, as the French colonial troops came "streaming across the field tearing through his company of Montreal Highlanders," Guy and another officer "tried to rally these men." Currie then described how "Drummond fell, together with his comrade, each a victim to a German bullet," and paid the following tribute to the young officer:

> No braver lad, no more ardent Highlander ever donned the tartan of the Black Watch than Lieutenant Guy Drummond. When he fell Canada lost a valuable and useful citizen. His training, education and charm of manner, coupled with his intense patriotism, marked him for a great career.[24]

In the letter to his mother written a matter of hours before he was killed, Guy told her, "Words are no good, are they?" and he echoed Georges Vanier's sentiments when he added, "Indeed and truly it's much harder for you women at home," whether that home was in Canada or London.[25] A telegram to Julia Drummond at Brown's Hotel gave further details of Guy's demise, which had occurred while he "was placing men for cover. Shot in neck killed instantaneously."[26] Julia had only just written to Guy about the ongoing battle and the

A life of promise cut short. Guy Melfort Drummond (1887-1915), seen here with his men, was the only surviving son of the Sir George Drummond and his wife, Grace Julia. A graduate of McGill University who had enjoyed a privileged upbringing and had a bright future ahead of him, he was killed on 23 April 1915 at the beginning of the Second Battle of Ypres. (McCord Museum Archives, M2004.160.135-P 1.1)

part being played by Canadian troops. "What can one say to-day with a heart full to breaking from grief and pride," she told him. "God have you in His keeping what e'er befall! No-one speaks of any but the Canadians."²⁷ Despite her distress and that of her daughter-in-law, Julia Drummond set an example by appearing for work the day after receiving the news of her son's death. She continued to bear her sorrow privately and immersed herself in the multitude of tasks that filled her time. To her it was "truth and honour" together with "sacrifice and service" that "alone give dignity to life and significance to death," and she acted on those beliefs.²⁸

By the time the Second Battle of Ypres came to an end in mid-May 1915, more than 6,000 of Canada's troops had been killed, wounded or posted missing. Canadians everywhere reeled from the impact, for until then casualties had been light. Journalist Mary MacLeod Moore wrote in *Saturday Night* that "day after day one reads with pride the comments and the appreciation" for the men who had fought and "died so gallantly" and proved "their splendid courage, their endurance, their enterprise."²⁹ A service of commemoration was held at St. Paul's Cathedral on 10 May 1915 for those who had lost their lives during the battle and on the torpedoed passenger liner *Lusitania*. Julia Drummond was among the congregation who heard the Bishop of London, Arthur F. Winnington-Ingram, pay tribute to her country's troops and how "the manhood of Canada was tested and came out as pure and unadulterated gold." The heroic stand of the Canadians at Second Ypres, he said, meant that "they will live in history forever."³⁰

By late May 1915 the atmosphere in London was tense, with "quite a sensational sense of strain," heightened by more frequent German air raids.³¹ British housewife Ethel Bilbrough, who lived south of the city, commented, "There's no more playing at things. Life is real and life is earnest, and I doubt if it will ever seem quite the same again."³² The sight of wounded soldiers was becoming so commonplace in the British capital that they passed almost unnoticed, and news of the losses and the suffering of the troops during the Second Battle of Ypres was still proving hard for many people to digest. Canada's "baptism of fire" had affected everyone deeply, as had the news of the *Lusitania* tragedy.

Captain Talbot Papineau of the Princess Patricia's Canadian Light Infantry was still recovering from the Second Battle of Ypres when he arrived in London in the last week of May. As a friend of Guy Drummond, Papineau had lunched with him "only a few days" before Guy's death and the young officer went straight to Brown's Hotel to see "poor Lady Drummond and Mary Braithwaite (Guy's wife)." He soon discovered their situation was worse than he had appreciated, for Mary's younger sister, Dorothy Braithwaite, had been among the passengers who had perished on the *Lusitania*.[33] It was therefore little wonder that Captain Papineau felt he was in the midst of "a veritable roundelay"* of death.[34]

During this difficult time the work of Julia Drummond and her team continued unabated as they dealt with many enquiries resulting from the recent fighting and weathered "unpleasantly frequent" air attacks plus rumours that London had "spies in its midst."[35] A new member of staff, Evelyn Rivers Bulkeley, joined the bureau to head a section concerned with the care of some 1,500 Canadian prisoners-of-war taken by the Germans in the Second Battle of Ypres and subsequent actions.[36] Under the Geneva Convention the CRCS was responsible for the well-being of troops held by the enemy, and twice a month it supplied food parcels and other items such as clothing and blankets. Within the limits of censorship and other wartime restrictions, the new department would be a source of support for imprisoned men and their families.

News of the bureau's effectiveness reached no less a personage than Queen Mary, wife of King George V, and she made a point of visiting the CRCS offices with her daughter, Princess Mary. The royal visitors showed "a keen interest" and Julia Drummond was invited to tea at Buckingham Palace so that the queen "might hear more." She took with her a written account of the bureau and its work, and the queen's favourable reaction was clear from a note she wrote to one of her ladies-in-waiting. "I have read all the papers with much interest," she said. "What a splendid organisation."[37]

Day after day Julia channelled her "sympathy and her many advantages" into helping Canadian troops on active service. Her staff said they knew when their leader was "out to conquer" because she arrived at the office in the morning with the "light of battle" in her eyes.[38] It all hinged on Julia's "absorbing wish" to "bring to the fighting men of Canada … some sense of personal interest and sympathy, of individual thought and care." She understood that while soldiers in wartime had to be regarded as "units of an army" to preserve its discipline and cohesiveness, those same men deserved every consideration.[39] One of Julia's assistants later marvelled at how the Information Bureau "comprised so wide a field" of services and was, at the same time, "so simple, for all it sought was the privilege of being a friend to every fighting Canadian, and to his people."[40]

---

* A circle dance that originated in medieval times.

To meet the demands placed upon them, Julia and her team were working harder than ever. Correspondence had to be answered in timely fashion, an enquiries team continued to trace missing men and bereaved families back home were given as many details as possible concerning loved ones. The newspapers section managed to provide local papers from even the remoter parts of Canada, and the entertainments department was kept busy arranging outings for wounded men sufficiently mobile to enjoy a concert, tea party or visits to places of historic or scenic interest. In the parcels section packages were prepared with supplies and comforts to meet the needs of soldiers, and Canadian prisoners-of-war were among those who received them. For those men undergoing medical treatment in Britain, CRCS visitors were kept busy going to "some hospital to see a lonely Nursing Sister or some wounded boy" whose mother and father had contacted the bureau seeking information.[41]

Journalist Mary MacLeod Moore was invited to become a CRCS hospital visitor in 1916 and regularly spent time with wounded Canadians, whom she described as "such splendid dears." She also went to see exchanged prisoners-of-war who had been taken captive by the enemy and who were "quite matter of fact about the way the Germans neglected their wounds and left it to chance that they recovered." Hearing such accounts from men who were "so moderate and reasonable," Mary told a former newspaper colleague that if he heard tales about "the German neglect and cruelty being exaggerated, just refer them to me for facts!"[42]

As the guiding light of all this activity, Julia Drummond herself had few spare moments that she could "count on as her own," wrote one of her staff. Nobody who asked to see her "was ever denied an interview if it was possible to arrange it," and she would always find time to help anyone who came to the office, whether "a private soldier worried by some personal or domestic difficulty" or "a harassed wife or mother whose agitation would protract an interview long beyond reasonable limits." Visitors were never made to feel they were imposing and they usually left "comforted and encouraged." It was no wonder that there were many evenings "when the light burned late" at 14 Cockspur Street.[43]

In what little free time she allowed herself, Julia met and entertained friends and maintained her membership of several favourite London clubs – the Royal Colonial Institute, the Overseas Club and the Ladies Empire Club. The birth of her grandson in October 1915, named after his father, provided her with a new source of happiness. Occasionally she found herself the subject of gossip, as was the case when one Canadian officer serving in France wrote to his wife that, "I hear Lady Drummond is to marry the Bishop of London." In reality Dr. Arthur Winnington-Ingram was a lifelong bachelor and Julia's heart and mind were firmly invested in her work, but the wartime rumour mill seemed to alight constantly on new topics for speculation.[44]

As the war ground on, the CRCS Information Bureau, as "an invaluable link between the people of Canada and their soldier sons overseas," was reckoned to be "in the front rank" of war work.[45] The organization continued to expand its remit and to maintain its welcoming human touch, as one young Canadian pilot discovered when he visited the CRCS offices in Cockspur Street. He was delighted to find "two Canadian girls there. I nearly fell on their necks, it was so darn good to hear real English spoken after the jolly, rotten, beastly, rawther stuff you hear here."[46] Whenever Canadian troops needed help, even if only in the form of a friendly face from home, the CRCS remained "a reservoir ... in time of need."[47]

That need extended to large numbers of soldiers on leave who milled around the streets of London and were exposed to the dangerous temptations of big city life. Grace Morris from Pembroke, Ontario, saw the problem for herself. She travelled to Britain in 1916 to meet her brother Ramsey, recovering from a wound, and as the two of them walked around the capital, Grace noticed how the streets seemed to be "awash with eager females anxious to comfort lonely soldiers." Even though she found herself acting as "a sort of bodyguard" to her brother, she had to admit that London was "a very exciting place to be."[48] At the time prostitution on its streets was rife, causing one senior member of the Women's Police Reserve to describe the Strand, the well-known street that passed Charing Cross Station, as "a veritable Devil's Playground" where "scenes of indescribable disorder prevailed."[49]

Leave in Britain was something a great many men looked forward to. For British troops it meant going home, and doubtless many shared the view of one officer who said it had been worth "doing months and months of trenches to get that buoyant, electrical sensation" that overcame him on seeing the familiar English countryside.[50] Troops on leave were given a travel pass to go anywhere in Britain, but the majority chose to spend their time in London, which had much to offer. Canadian officers were well catered for, often staying in hotels or one of the well-known clubs. However, things were different for the average soldier whom one historian described as being "inarticulate and shy." When given a furlough "from field, hospital or camp into a strange world," his mood was often said to be "bitter" as he compared "his own misery with civil ease."[51]

Many were the enquiries received by the CRCS Information Bureau from commanding officers of Canadian units and matrons of hospitals who were concerned about finding accommodation for the men "where they could feel themselves at home." Some Canadian troops were lucky, as in the case of Andrew Baird, who went on leave with a friend. As he wrote, "We spent our first evening in London out at a nice home, the invitation for which we got at the Y.M.C.A.," but there were others who did not fare so well and felt a long way from the comforts of family and friends. George V. Bell of Baring, Saskatchewan, remembered when he finally got leave and arrived in London. He saw "crowds on the platform. Men climb off trains, women and children embrace them. A lump comes to my throat and my eyes are misty. How much it means to them. I am alone."[52]

Hotels could be expensive and crowded, while private lodgings were often far from ideal. Julia Drummond was troubled about this predicament and on more than one occasion "emergency provision" for soldiers was arranged "through her representation" at Brown's Hotel. The men would otherwise "have slept or sat, as they said, on the Embankment," which ran along part of the north shore of the River Thames.[53] It was easy for soldiers to find themselves sleeping rough or getting into bad company – something that was particularly regrettable given that with the high death toll on the Western Front there was always the thought, "Will I get another leave?"[54] The temptation to "live for the moment" in such uncertain times could bring unpleasant consequences, and venereal disease was much more common among troops from overseas than those from Britain. In the Canadian army during the war 66,083 cases were recorded – an average of 158 per thousand men.[55]

"ONE OF THE MOST VALUABLE INSTITUTIONS YET PROMOTED BY PRIVATE ENTERPRISE": THE MAPLE LEAF CLUB

Julia Drummond knew there was an urgent need to provide a decent and affordable place to stay where men could have a bath, wash, change their clothes and take care of personal matters such as banking. "Nothing succeeds in leadership so much as a strong personality," wrote Iona Carr, knowing that her boss would find a way to solve this problem.[56] Julia came up with the idea of a "Maple Leaf Club," and estimated that $5,000 would be needed to establish it. She cabled a relative in Montreal informing him of the "crying need" for funding, and following Canadian newspaper coverage of her appeal for help, a total of $8,500 was received in donations.[57]

Several offers of accommodation for the new club soon came from British friends and acquaintances. The best in terms of size and location was a house

The first Maple Leaf Club. This photo shows No. 11 Charles Street, generously offered by British society hostess Margaret Greville for use as the premises of the first Maple Leaf Club. It initially offered sixty beds and a range of other facilities that enabled men to feel "at home" in comfortable accommodation while on leave. (Photograph by Dianne Graves)

in Charles Street that belonged to society hostess Margaret Greville. Widow of the Honourable Ronald Greville, Margaret had secured a place among the elite of London society and King Edward VII himself had complimented her on possessing a "positive genius for hospitality."[58] She had vacated her house at 11 Charles Street in 1913 when she moved to another family property, and offered it to Julia Drummond. Her offer was accepted and from "first to last" Mrs. Greville proved to be someone who took "an untiring personal interest in the work."[59]

As word of the new project spread, Julia Drummond received messages of encouragement, among them one from Rudyard Kipling on one of his periodic visits to Brown's Hotel. They arranged to meet and Kipling expressed his support for the "Maple Leaf Club," having met Canadian soldiers who said "they actually dreaded their leave, for they had nowhere to spend it." Julia told him the project "could make no better start than under the patronage of Earl Grey, Lord Milner and himself."[60] She was well acquainted with former governor general Earl Grey, who was happy to become a patron of the new venture, knowing it would be "safe in your hands." Rudyard Kipling and his wife, Carrie, became "warm supporters of the movement" and Mrs. Kipling consented to take on the position of chairman of the project's committee.[61]

The formal opening of the first Maple Leaf Club was carried out by Canadian Prime Minister Sir Robert Borden on 4 August 1915. He told Julia Drummond that "the splendid work which you and other Canadian ladies are doing in many spheres of activity for the solace of our Canadian troops, is

Grand opening. In August 1915 the first Maple Leaf Club was officially opened in London. The event was attended by Canadian Prime Minister Sir Robert Borden, writer Rudyard Kipling and his wife, and other dignitaries. Here Sir Robert (front, right) is accompanied by Lady Julia Drummond and behind them can be seen Lady Emily Perley, wife of Canada's high commissioner, Sir George Perley. (Library and Archives Canada, PA-005668)

appreciated most deeply by all Canadian people." Everyone who attended the inauguration of what was the first residential club for overseas troops celebrated the fact that the Canadian soldier was about to discover "how many there were who really did care for him" and were ready to help him return to duty "with a new heart."[62]

The Maple Leaf Club became a part of a broader Imperial organization created in late 1915 and known as the King George and Queen Mary Clubs, which catered to soldiers of the British Empire. Margaret Greville was among the patrons and was delighted when her premises at 11 Charles Street received a visit from Queen Mary, who much approved of the spacious, comfortable accommodation and described it as "very nice and informal. I shook hands with all the officers before leaving."[63]

The men serving on the Western Front soon heard that the King George and Queen Mary Clubs offered a comfortable place to stay at reasonable cost, and Canadians knew that their Maple Leaf Club was a place where they could find "not only good food and a warm bed but a hot bath, a change of underclothing, a dressing gown and easy slippers," all for a daily charge of three shillings and sixpence or thirty cents in Canadian currency at that time.[64] A lounge with easy chairs, a billiard room and a recreation room with a supply of books were among the amenities, and the newsletter of 1st Canadian Infantry Brigade informed its readers that "the club is always full up. That in itself is a good testimonial."[65] Such was the popularity of the facilities at 11 Charles Street that the demand for accommodation began to outstrip supply and the original sixty beds had to be nearly doubled in number.

Comments by the men who experienced Maple Leaf Club hospitality were generally favourable and particularly so if they discovered their waitress at table on occasions was none other than Princess Patricia, daughter of the Club's Honorary Patron, the Duke of Connaught. She volunteered her time when she could, and visitors to the club not only enjoyed excellent meals but also described how it was an "unalloyed pleasure just to get into bed and feel the sheets and pyjamas." Often there was a "look of utter bliss" on the faces of troops arriving from the Western Front when they realized the degree of comfort they could look forward to. Andrew Munro of Toronto came straight from the trenches covered in "mud from head to foot, unashamed and dirty, some sight believe me," but after taking a bath at the club he felt "like a new man." Another soldier wrote to the club expressing his "thankfulness that comes from knowing that somebody cares enough about us to provide such quarters. It keeps us from feeling we are absolutely alone when we get to London."[66]

Comments like these would have gladdened Julia Drummond's heart, and they were substantiated by those of a mother in Canada who wrote that "my boy is only 23 and young enough to be very lonesome ... I must write and express my gratitude for the kind welcome he received."[67] The Canadian military authorities added their praise, describing the Maple Leaf Club as "one of the most valuable institutions yet promoted by private enterprise, giving men ... proper accommodation and ensuring their safety from harpies who infest the arrival station."[68]

Julia Drummond made regular visits to the club premises and was sometimes photographed with the men staying there. Eventually it became necessary to expand beyond the building at 11 Charles Street and she sent another cable to Canada asking if a further $25,000 could be raised to provide more "King George and Queen Mary Maple Leaf Clubs" as "an urgent necessity."[69] It was now the summer of 1916 and her request reached the desk of the Premier of Ontario, Sir William Hearst. As someone who had two sons serving overseas, Hearst felt it was the duty of his province to support the war effort. He attached the greatest importance to the welfare of the soldiers and argued that "too much praise cannot be given to Lady Drummond and her excellent Voluntary Committee."[70] Thanks to provincial funding, contributions from various chapters of the IODE and donations from the Canadian public, five new Maple Leaf Club buildings with bed space for 350-400 men were opened in December 1916 by the Duke of Connaught, who reminded everyone that "in this sad war there is a very human side." Julia Drummond told those in attendance that "the men were indebted" for the new premises, and her remarks were enthusiastically received.[71]

While the Maple Leaf Clubs occupied much of Julia's time, the Information Bureau and its staff remained as busy as ever. It had earned the trust and appreciation of people back in Canada but Julia Drummond "deprecated praise for work that was so great a privilege," believing instead that it actually "eased the strain of the war as nothing else could." In keeping pace with her daily schedule, she said that she "always regretted that in the rush of work it was impossible to keep a register, even of visitors from Canada who came and went." Those who passed through her office ranged from grateful individuals and families to distinguished supporters such as Princess Patricia and Lady Emily Perley. They were so numerous that, as Julia confessed, when trying to list them she "could begin but not finish!"[72]

Throughout 1917, with huge numbers of casualties on the Western Front and increasing air attacks, Julia and her team were in great demand. In June she found time to visit CRCS war workers in France, and Canadian ambulance driver Grace MacPherson noted in her diary that "Lady Drummond, Head of the C[anadian]. R[ed]. [Cross] S[ociety] in London" was among those who came to her convoy headquarters at Étaples. In the later summer Julia went on leave to Canada, the first time she had done so in nearly three years, and when she returned to her desk in London she continued to focus on meeting the needs of the troops. Ongoing support from the Ontario government together with private donations, campaign drives and contributions from corporations, made it possible to acquire several more Maple Leaf Club buildings just before the darkest days of 1918, when German progress on the Western Front seemed unstoppable. "Never has there been a more anxious or critical time in the whole war," wrote British housewife Ethel Bilbrough, no doubt expressing what many people were thinking.[73] Throughout the year, as the Allies succeeded in tipping the balance of the conflict in their favour, the CRCS Information Bureau continued to serve Canadian troops and their families, and when the fighting ended in November 1918, Julia Drummond and her staff paused to join the crowds celebrating on the streets of London.

The humanitarian work of organizations such as the CRCS continued after the Armistice was signed. There were large numbers of troops to be repatriated, and as the Canadians were moved from the Western Front to Britain before their return to Canada, numbers swelled. London was soon overrun with soldiers and Maple Leaf huts were set up to provide meals and recreation during the day. Additional overnight accommodation was made available and the Maple Leaf Clubs stayed open until 15 August 1919, following which a small staff was retained to close facilities and wind down operations. At the CRCS Information Bureau, Julia Drummond remained at her desk until the very last day.[74]

Officials of the CRCS met to officially recognize Julia's achievements, and on behalf of Canadian soldiers overseas they presented her with an engraved silver salver. Her mission had been completed but it would not be forgotten, and she received well-deserved acknowledgment of her war work. A letter from the office of British Prime Minister David Lloyd George thanked her and her staff for what they had done and praised their inspiring and "earnest spirit of duty and devotion which animates all who have thus consecrated their voluntary services to the nation."[75]

Lady Grace Julia Drummond was awarded the British Red Cross Medal, the French *Médaille de Reconnaissance* and the Serbian Red Cross Medal.[76] The title of Lady of Justice, Order of St. John of Jerusalem, was conferred upon her, and Prime Minister Sir Robert Borden supported a proposal that she be awarded the Order of the British Empire in recognition of her major role in charitable work.[77] In 1921 she received an honorary doctorate of law from McGill University.

As a woman of dedication and the highest sense of duty, Julia Drummond accomplished so much. At no time did she consider withdrawing from war service after the death of her son, choosing instead to do all she could for the sons of other mothers. Within the framework of the Canadian Red Cross Society, the Information Bureau contributed significantly to the experience and confidence gained by the organization during the First World War, and Julia fulfilled the wish she had carried with her since the day in September 1914 when she watched the First Canadian Contingent sail from Quebec City. After the war she issued a public statement of thanks for the "generous appreciation" she had received, and paid her own tribute to the "unsurpassed devotion" of all who had helped her.[78]

Julia's personal records of the war years are sparse, mainly because, as she admitted, "while we worked at the Bureau there was little time to transmit to paper the happenings of a single hour or day." She therefore valued the fact that her assistant, Iona Carr, decided to write the story of the CRCS Information Bureau, which, as Julia herself said, would otherwise "have remained untold and been forgotten."[79] She contributed her own foreword to the book and hoped that the publication would "convey to another generation something of the glory and the suffering, the striving and the sacrifice ... which set forever apart the greatest and most terrible years the world has seen."[80] Julia sought no gratitude for "our bit of work to which we had given our heart and soul," believing instead that "thanks were due from us" to the many Canadians who had helped and supported her and her colleagues.[81] In her words, "if some of us more than others were able to devote all our time and strength" to a particular project, then "that was a greater privilege." As far as she was concerned, "the tasks that can be wrought in silence are henceforth best."[82]

Julia Drummond's legacy of service to her country and to Canadian and Allied troops was evident in the thousands of soldiers and their families who benefited from her efforts. In later years she finally had an opportunity to reflect on what she had achieved – on the idea that had consumed her, the drive that had made it a reality and the fact that she "never let the vision go" until the task was completed. "It was impossible," wrote Iona Carr, not to feel that much of Julia's "ideal was attained." As for the lady herself, it was her opinion that the experience in its entirety could only be felt by those who had been part of it, for as she said, "We know, who worked together through those years of splendour and of pain, we know that never did we come into such close touch with reality as in those years, and the mark and the memory of them are forever ours."[83]

The value of what Lady Julia Drummond accomplished is a testament to an exceptional woman. A sense of the high regard in which she was held is perhaps best expressed by Earl Grey, who told her in a letter,

> You have given the whole Empire a great example not only in the way in which you carried the heavy burden of your heart's sacrifice, but in the way in which you have inspired all who have come within your reach, with a glorified sense of Duty to the Empire and with a splendid, courageous Devotion to truth, loyalty and service. I feel you have ennobled all womankind.[84]

CHAPTER 11

WOMEN WITH A MISSION (2)

"Bringing laughter, hope and healing"

LENA ASHWELL AND "CONCERTS AT THE FRONT"

It's easy to fight when everything's right,
And you're mad with the thrill and the glory;
It's easy to cheer when victory's near,
And wallow in fields that are gory.
It's a different song when everything's wrong,
When you're feeling infernally mortal;
When it's ten against one, and hope there is none,
Buck up, little soldier, and chortle;
Carry on! Carry on![1]

"SHE WILL … ACHIEVE JUST AS HIGH AS SHE WORKS": LENA ASHWELL'S PATH TO SUCCESS

The image of men in uniform, stretched out on the ground and singing in the warmth of a summer evening, is one that offers a pleasant contrast to those commonly associated with life for soldiers during the war years. Thanks to the tireless efforts of one woman who ensured that Allied troops were able to enjoy professional entertainment in various forms, it became a reality. Through her efforts they experienced not only relief from the worst of life in the trenches but also benefits, especially through music, which she described as "one of the greatest healing and comforting elements in the world."[2]

The main inspiration and driving force behind an organization that staged concerts, recitals, plays and other amusements for those serving on the Western Front and further afield was a woman who had grown up in rural Ontario. Lena Pocock, born in September 1872, was the daughter of Charles Ashwell Pocock, an officer in the Royal Navy who had retired and taken his wife and six children to live in Canada. Lena was young at the time and described how her "early days were spent in a pretty little wooden house in a place called Brockville," east of Kingston on the north shore of the St. Lawrence River. Lena regarded it as a place of "great beauty, but also great discomfort," for there was "no water laid on in the house, no drainage, no gas nor electric light, no modern conveniences whatsoever."[3] Compensations came, however, in the form of "a river to swim in, a canoe to sail or paddle" and "a forest to wander in." It was a "strenuous, healthy, invigorating and inspiring life in the Canadian backwoods" that had given her an appreciation of the grandeur of nature and of Canada's distinctive seasons. As a girl she was fascinated by the changes they wrought, especially on the St. Lawrence, which metamorphosed from a "sunlit summer river one half of the year" to being "frozen over" and "tossed with tempest the other."[4]

When she was not busy helping with the domestic chores, Lena began to show an interest in acting and remembered how she

> always longed to play Lady Macbeth from very early days when as a child in Canada, I sat on the granite rocks under the great pine trees in a forty-two acre pine wood on the banks of the St. Lawrence River, and recited plays to the wild columbines.[5]

After the Pococks moved to Toronto, Lena attended the Bishop Strachan School, where she proved to be an excellent student who was "always reading Shakespeare" and had a penchant for poetry and recitation, which became a "perfect passion."[6] Lena Pocock's early years in Canada were undoubtedly influential in shaping her personality, her remarkable drive and the independence of thought that characterized much of what she later achieved.

After Lena's mother tragically died in a carriage accident, her distraught husband took Lena and her two sisters to Lausanne in Switzerland, where they continued their education and Lena studied music at the local *conservatoire*. She went to London against her father's wishes with the intention of embarking on a career as an opera singer and was offered a place at the Royal Academy of Music. Recitation and the theatre, however, continued to attract her and the talented Miss Pocock was selected to perform in front of the celebrated actress Ellen Terry, who was impressed with her performance.[7] Miss Terry decided that Lena was "incomparably better than any one" else and that her future lay not in the concert hall but on the stage. "Her life must be given to it," said the actress, "and then she will … achieve just as high as she works."[8]

Lena followed this advice. In the late Victorian era London was a flourishing centre for the theatre, where she was able to learn stagecraft and gain experience. She made her acting debut in 1891 and soon acquired more substantial roles with favourable reviews. In 1895 Lena understudied Ellen Terry in the play "King Arthur," which also starred the great Victorian actor Sir Henry Irving, who gave her a leading role in his production of Richard III the following year. Her success led to press interviews, including one with an

Lena Ashwell (1872 –1957) was a prominent actress, theatre manager and suffragist, and the first woman to arrange large-scale entertainment for serving troops during the First World War. Having spent her formative years in Canada, she moved to Britain to pursue a successful career on the stage and from 1914 to 1919 was the driving force behind Concerts at the Front, an organization that staged hundreds of musical and theatrical performances for troops on the Western Front and in other theatres of war. In 1917 she received the Order of the British Empire, an award established that year by King George V for outstanding public service, contributions to the arts and sciences and charitable work. (Public domain)

Ottawa newspaper which proudly proclaimed that "Miss Ashwell has been heralded as a Canadian." The change of surname was Lena's choice, having decided to use one of her father's first names as her *nom de scène.*[9]

By the early years of the twentieth century, Lena Ashwell was achieving widespread recognition for the emotional intensity and realism she brought to every role. It was a period in her life she described as a "golden time," but away from the theatre it brought challenges in the form of a short, unhappy marriage to another actor, Arthur Playfair, and the "break up of all my illusions and day dreams" after her father became ill and died in 1898.[10] With encouragement from friends and colleagues Lena continued to pursue her career in Britain, playing varied and challenging parts and undertaking poetry recitals that enabled her to build a wide repertoire and a useful range of contacts. She also became increasingly interested in the growing women's movement and in the working conditions and status of theatre staff.[11]

By 1906 Lena Ashwell had become one of the most famous and best loved thespians in the country and was lauded as "a great actress."[12] She accepted an invitation to tour "throughout America" in the autumn of 1906 from Broadway theatre producer and impresario Charles Frohman. Reporters clamoured to interview her and discovered that in addition to speaking about her acting "with the utmost earnestness," she was also "a woman with an active interest in current affairs."[13] The tour ended prematurely when Lena became ill from exhaustion. During her lengthy convalescence she had time to consider another step in her career, that of becoming an actor-manager. Having worked with men who had made a great success of it – Henry Irving and Herbert Beerbohm Tree among others – Lena saw the advantages of being able to stage plays that interested her.[14] This was an unusual undertaking for a woman, but after she put her toe in the water by briefly taking charge of the Savoy Theatre, she secured financial backing to lease and run the Kingsway Theatre, starting in 1907.

Every step in Lena Ashwell's life from that point onwards seemed to be preparing her for the work that she would take on a few years later. In 1908 she married again, this time to Henry Simson, an eminent Scottish obstetrician with whom she found "complete happiness."[15] Her marriage provided her with stability and motivation as a performer, theatre manager and promoter, and also underpinned her efforts on behalf of causes dear to her heart. In 1909 she joined forces with a group of actresses among whom were some of the great names of the day – Edith Craig, Lily Langtry, Ellen Terry and Sybil Thorndike – to set up the Actresses Franchise League (AFL) with the aim of working for women's enfranchisement by educational means.

All this time the famous leading lady had kept in close touch with her family, and in particular her brother Roger, who had remained in Canada with another sister married to a Canadian engineer. Roger Pocock enjoyed the open air life and had worked on the construction of the Canadian Pacific Railway before joining the North West Mounted Police. Like his sister Lena, he was an independent, pioneering individual who saw active service in the Riel Rebellion of 1885, and despite being invalided out with frostbite he found the life of an outdoorsman and adventurer suited him. Roger shared Lena's energy and zeal and was always ready to try something new, whether driving horses to the Klondike, serving in a unit of scouts which fought in the South African War, or reporting on the effects of the Russo-Japanese war in 1905 for the *Illustrated Mail*.[16]

The last few years before the First World War were busy for his actress sister professionally and personally. Charles Frohman invited Lena to be a leading name in his new theatre company in London and she also made her debut in vaudeville, which gave her an appreciation of its "variety, modernity and ability to bring 'all classes of the community together.'"[17] Off stage she continued to support the women's suffrage movement, undertaking many commitments for the Actor's Benevolent Fund and the AFL. The year 1913 saw her performing, giving interviews and initiating projects such as a cooperative scheme for women, aimed at having theatrical agencies run by females from start to finish.[18] She spoke on working conditions for women in the theatre and lectured widely, advocating that "sex need be no bar in any direction."[19] With her name often in the news, whether for a review of her latest stage performance or her other activities, it was little wonder that Lena Ashwell was regarded as a public figure of note.

"THESE CONCERT-PARTIES HAVE ACTUALLY SAVED LIVES": THE LAUNCH OF "CONCERTS AT THE FRONT"

When war was declared in August 1914, Lena became chairman of the War Distress Fund, formed to provide immediate help for members of her profession, and was a founder member of the Women's Emergency Corps, a service organization set up to train women doctors, nurses and motorcycle messengers, and which held a register of skilled personnel for use by any authority requiring a particular service. More significantly, Lena was one of the first to suggest that "artists be gainfully employed to boost troop morale by providing entertainment."[20] She understood the value of the arts and saw culture as essential to well-being, especially in the testing conditions of war. At her instigation the AFL launched Women's Theatre Camps Entertainments, by means of which members performed at military camps and hospitals around Britain. "The closer we women come to the realities of war," wrote Elizabeth Robins, another actress and feminist, "the better we understand the function of the theatre in such times as these."[21]

It was gratifying to Lena Ashwell and those who shared her vision to see how entertainment could take its place in the war effort. She was convinced that soldiers far from home, family and normal interests needed something to lift their spirits and provide distractions from their military service and the tough conditions they faced. Canadian soldiers arriving in Britain with the First Canadian Contingent in October 1914 were no exception, and after some of them resorted to alcohol with unfortunate consequences, the authorities looked for other ways to keep them occupied. As a result, the Canadians on Salisbury Plain were treated to concert parties from London three times a week, "and they are top notch too," commented Private Jack Stickney of Edmonton.[22] However, with the entertainment of Canadian troops assigned to the Canadian Expeditionary Force and the cost of providing professional performers increasing as the number of troops increased, soldiers were encouraged to form their own entertainment groups.

Men with talent got together to stage comic routines, skits, songs and plays. The most famous was Gitz Rice of Nova Scotia, who had enlisted in the Canadian Field Artillery and whose song "Dear Old Pal of Mine" became an enormous hit and remained popular throughout the war. There were comed-

ians, jugglers, Charlie Chaplin impersonators and drag artists, the latter having been standard in British music hall for many years and a tradition in military theatricals. Such a routine was central to one famous Canadian group
called "the Dumbells," a regimental comedy ensemble whose "ladies" wore
whatever feminine attire they could beg or borrow. The Dumbells cheered
up their colleagues and were in demand for shows staged at brigade, division
and corps level.[23]

The bawdy, risqué nature of such entertainment, whilst invariably appreciated by the men, concerned someone like Lena Ashwell, who envisaged
offering something more refined and uplifting. She wanted to bring culture,
in the form of concert performances and dramatic productions, to the Empire forces serving on the Western Front, and went to the War Office with
the suggestion that every military camp should have its own theatre where
professional actors and musicians could perform for the soldiers. "I tried
very hard to get the entertainment of troops put on national lines, and was
interviewed several times," she later confirmed, but "there was little interest
shown" for "we were still considered of no more use than a billiard-marker,
or a golf professional."[24] The War Office pundits did not share Lena's views on
the importance of entertaining the average fighting man, who, in the opinion
of senior officers, was perfectly capable of amusing himself.

Understandably, "very sad and disheartened," Lena found help and inspiration in the person of Lady Corisande Rodney, who on "one never-to-be-for-
gotten day" came calling on behalf of the Women's Auxiliary Committee of
the YMCA.[25] Corisande Rodney had just returned from France, where the
"Y" was offering support and wholesome pursuits for the soldiers. Its huts
and tents at many locations behind the lines, where men could go for "reading, writing, recreation" and relaxation, provided a useful service.[26] Lena
Ashwell recognized that for the men from larger towns and cities "where
civilization means opportunities for amusements," what the huts offered was
limited, and it was "occurring to an unpleasantly surprised Army that modern warfare was unexpectedly dull."[27]

Corisande Rodney and the YMCA Women's Auxiliary Committee,
which was chaired by Princess Helena Victoria of Schleswig-Holstein, a
grand-daughter of Queen Victoria, suggested that the organization's huts
"might welcome the diversion of a concert." To her delight, Lena Ashwell
was asked whether it "was possible for a concert party to go to Havre."[28] The
port of Le Havre, on the coast of Normandy, was a base for the British Expeditionary Force and Lena responded "with enthusiasm."[29] The combined
weight of Princess Helena Victoria and her committee convinced the War

Princess Helena Victoria (1870-1948). Helena Victoria of Schleswig-Holstein was a granddaughter of Queen Victoria. Born in Britain, she did not marry but followed her mother's example by doing charitable work with a number of organizations, including the YMCA. During the First World War she founded its Women's Auxiliary Division and obtained permission from Lord Kitchener, British Secretary of State for War, to arrange entertainment for the troops on the Western Front in the form of "Concerts at the Front." (Public domain)

Office that such a scheme should be launched on an experimental basis. It marked the beginning of what came to be known as the "Concerts at the Front" scheme, in which musicians and entertainers performed for Allied troops on the Western Front and later, in the eastern Mediterranean and Middle East. Its organizer, by her own admission, liked "to get on in whatever I take up," and Lena Ashwell threw herself into the new enterprise with characteristic zest and commitment.[30]

Since the YMCA was involved, it was necessary to overcome the initial doubts of its senior personnel. As a Christian organization concerned with modesty and probity, they were apprehensive as to "what unknown terrors they were letting loose on themselves."[31] It was also made clear to Lena and her colleagues that self-promotion would not be permitted among the musicians, actors and other artistes taking part in concert parties, and that their inclusion would depend not only on a guarantee of suitability from Lena herself, but also upon their being "known" to Princess Helena Victoria, who was, in effect, responsible for their conduct.

Cartoonist Ada L. Ward remembered having to perform in front of Her Highness before being approved to join a concert party. "I assure you it was something of an ordeal to face a real live princess," she said, well aware that "they only engaged the very best."[32] Such vetting procedures rested, according to Lena Ashwell, on the fact that "there is a great prejudice among a section of the nation against artists, especially actors," who were regarded as "a class of terribly wicked people who drink champagne all day long, and lie on sofas, receiving bouquets from rows of admirers." She felt sure there were those who "expected us to land in France in tights, with peroxide hair, and altogether to be a difficult thing for a religious organization to camouflage." Lena wanted to right this misconception and felt that one of the good things that resulted from the war was "the breaking down of barriers due to mis- understanding." To that end, the "co-operation of the actors and musicians with the Y.M.C.A." could be regarded as important progress.[33]

With clear guidelines and royal patronage, the Concerts at the Front project was launched as a "tentative" experiment.[34] During January 1915 Theodore Flint, accompanist and musical director, went ahead to work with the YMCA in France and oversee the arrangements, including accommo- dation and transport. A timely donation covered the expenses for the first group of performers, who made up "a real concert party with a programme of really good music."[35] On 15 February 1915 four singers, an instrumental- ist and an entertainer crossed to Normandy. They were conscious that their performances were "an experiment in every way," and that given the hidden hazard of German submarines, "there was a preliminary risk that the concert party might never arrive." However, the real anxiety for the performers was not the danger at sea but "whether the music would really please the audi- ence or bore them." Happily, that worry was dispelled when, after the first item of the first concert on 18 February 1915, "the thunderous applause of the soldier-audience crammed into the hut at Havre swept away all doubt."[36]

The power of the musicians and entertainers to connect with their audi- ence was evident to all at that first concert, and to cries of "More!" the per- formers continued on their way. Over the next two weeks they staged thirty- eight performances, which were well received, and Theodore Flint's reports were encouraging. The members of the touring party were, he said, "so ob- liging and charming and don't mind a bit how much they sing or what they do," and the "roars and yells" of the delighted audiences were "simply thrill- ing."[37] Lena put together a second concert party that crossed to France in March 1915, and the two groups worked different routes. One went between Le Havre and Rouen, which was a major supply and logistics centre with base hospitals, and the other between Dieppe and Boulogne, where there were more hospitals and a considerable military presence.

Lena herself went to France with a third concert party group that same month and gave recitations at eighteen venues. The first concert she attended was held in a new YMCA cinema hut in the Harfleur Valley near Le Havre, where she had to use duckboards to cross ankle-deep mud. Among the per- formers that evening was singer-songwriter Ivor Novello, who performed his new song, "Keep the Home Fires Burning." Lena watched the audience in the crowded, smoke-filled hut as they listened to what became one of the most

Ivor Novello (1893-1951) was a Welsh composer, actor and one of the best-known entertainers in Britain during the first half of the twentieth century. As a songwriter, his first major success came in 1914 with "Keep the Home Fires Burning," which became one of the most popular songs of the war. He performed in France with Concerts at the Front during 1915 before enlisting with the Royal Naval Air Service. After the war his musical career flourished; he wrote the scores for musicals and revues and was so successful as an actor that by the late 1920s he was the most popular male star in British films. (Library of Congress)

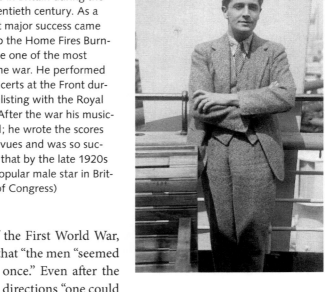

famous songs of the First World War, and she noticed that "the men "seemed to drink it in at once." Even after the concert, from all directions "one could hear the refrain of the chorus."[38] What Lena had observed was that soldiers liked any song that was "simple and beautiful." They had a tendency to "love and adopt at once music that is new to them" and their favourite songs quickly became "word perfect" as they marched back to camp singing them.[39]

Another of Lena's star performers was soprano Elsie Griffin, who had been a chocolate packer at the Fry's factory in Bristol. Her voice came to the attention of lyricist Frederic Weatherly, who, impressed with the beauty of her rendition of his compositions, wrote two songs with her in mind that became famous: "Danny Boy" and "Roses of Picardy." At the age of nineteen, Elsie was selected for Concerts at the Front and her career began as she toured in France popularizing Weatherly's songs.[40]

Now that Lena's concert groups were clearly in demand, Theodore Flint set about organizing a schedule of three or so performances a day for the coming year. With a hospital concert every afternoon and two productions each evening, troops and medical units could look forward to entertainment once a month. The programmes included solos, string quartets, operatic arias, recitations of poetry and prose and popular songs. There might also be a story teller or a comedian, whose humour was, "of course, almost indispensable."[41] Shows were scheduled to last an hour and a half, but as Lena Ashwell explained, "Our audiences altered that arrangement for us … by encoring everybody and everything over and over again."[42] The performers were driven to their venues in YMCA motor vehicles, which sometimes entailed a fifty-mile round trip "in an open car, after having given three concerts." In addition, if "a tyre punctures or the road is missed," a weary concert party might well "get back again at 3 A.M."[43]

Managing everything was hard work for Lena Ashwell and the staff of her London office. It included selecting performers, watching over the welfare of those employed, publicizing the scheme and finding ways to cover the costs involved. Lena, who placed great store by publicity, spoke at meetings around Britain, wrote newspaper and magazine articles, and pursued major fund-raising initiatives. She arranged her first major event at the London Coliseum on 25 March 1915 in the presence of Queen Mary, and her efforts to attract support for Concerts at the Front included a series of lectures between 1915 and 1919 that raised close to £100,000 (worth some C$2,520,000 today). Combining these responsibilities with her career was a tall order, encompassing rehearsals for her stage performances, public appearances for various war charities and other obligations in support of women's organizations. As Lena affirmed, "of course one's heart was in war work," for "it is such a splendid thing that artists should be of use in wartime."[44]

In early May 1915 when she heard about the loss of the *Lusitania* Lena was distressed to learn that among the 1,195 victims who died was impresario Charles Frohman, with whom she had worked before the war. Frohman had been travelling to Britain with another actress, Rita Jolivet, who was to take part in several Italian films now that the era of the silent movie had arrived. Before leaving New York Frohman had talked with the *Lusitania*'s captain, William Turner, who had "no concern" about the German warning of unrestricted submarine warfare in the waters around the British Isles. He apparently thought the idea that his ship could be caught and torpedoed by an enemy U-boat was "the best joke I've heard in many days." When the *Lusitania* went down, Turner was among the survivors, and after learning that Charles Frohman was one of those lost, "tears filled his eyes" and he was overcome with emotion.[45]

A few weeks later Lena Ashwell made another visit to France, where she took part in a series of concerts at base hospitals and depots. In the drier, warmer weather, beds could be moved outside and she long remembered the sight of a "crowded stand filled with boys in blue" and the rows of beds and tents with their flaps fastened back, making it possible for the men to enjoy the concert across "the great distance of silent listeners."[46] Whether performing indoors or outdoors "to an audience stretched at ease upon the grass just as far as it can hear," Lena gained a lasting impression of the wonderful spirit of the soldiers and medical staff, and the benefits that music brought to patients. It "seemed to break the spell that the horrors and the deafening noise of modern artillery warfare lay on the nerves of so many of the men," she said, and was convinced that the "good it does is permanent."[47]

This impression was borne out by the many comments she received in person and by letter. To hear from a soldier that he and his comrades "agreed that we would go back to the trenches and fight all the better for the happy remembrance of the concert-party" was rewarding.[48] As Concerts at the Front continued, the performers themselves wrote about how privileged they felt to be involved. One woman made it clear that "the work may be tiring, but for sheer inspiration and love of one's job it is hard indeed to beat."[49] Ada L. Ward approached her work "determined that whatever happened the boys would have a good time if I and others could give it to them." Seeing the condition of some of the wounded men only made her more intent on meeting that objective. "God knows," she said, "they have given their best to us, and it is a privilege to be able to do anything that might make them forget for a little time the agony they have gone through."[50] Ada decided that "If you are chosen to go to France you can look on yourself as hall marked because you will speedily find that Tommy understands music … You will find he is a fine critic. We were, therefore, on our mettle, and gave the best we could."[51]

There were nurses among the hospital audiences who, being subject to the same discipline as the troops, were "never allowed out in the evenings at all except to come to the concert we give them once a month," said Lena Ashwell. She remarked on the "pretty sight" of the nursing sisters in their uniforms and "their happiness over the very simple pleasure" that the touring parties gave them.[52] Sister Clare Gass of No. 3 CGH noted in her diary for 8 August 1915, "Princess Victoria Concert party entertained at the YMCA this evening. Such good voices & attractive personalities." She attended two more concerts on 18 October and 16 November 1915, mentioning in particular "a wonderful young girl violinist & such a clever funny ventriloquist."[53] In a military environment where life consisted of hard work, discipline and little else, a concert was "an event looked forward to for weeks beforehand and talked of for weeks afterwards."[54]

In August 1915 Princess Helena Victoria, as chair of the YMCA Women's Auxiliary Committee, made an eight-day visit to France accompanied by a delegation that included Corisande Rodney. In addition to visiting YMCA and military facilities, hospitals, bakeries, stores and an ambulance train, their itinerary included two Concerts at the Front performances at Boulogne on 16 and 17 August. They were held at the "Queen Mary huts (YMCA)" and were well received, the princess describing the first performance as "an excellent entertainment." The second concert also impressed her and she noted that "there must have been at least two thousand men present."[55] With so many in attendance it was important to have performers who could strike up a rapport with them, and a young cellist, Daisy Godfrey, admitted that she was chosen because, "so they said, I managed to get on happy terms with a big audience of men."[56]

By the autumn of 1915 men at base camps in France were able to enjoy a new addition to the Concerts at the Front repertoire – one-act plays. These productions were often staged without "curtains, footlights, dressing rooms or furniture" but "what did it matter when we had audiences who thronged to the halls … and laughed and cheered as audiences have never done before!" wrote playwright Gertrude Jennings.[57] Behind the scenes Lena Ashwell continued to keep things running while urging women on the home front to "make themselves efficient" for some kind of war work. She also returned to her role as actress-manager at the Kingsway Theatre, employing a largely all-female team for stage management, lighting, props, electrics, scene shifting and orchestra. She was, said one newspaper, "a tower of strength to all organizations with which she is connected."[58]

There were now no fewer than fifteen concert parties working on the Western Front, with more ready to be called into service. Life for the performing artists was not just a matter of being driven from one engagement to the next. They found themselves at times in unlikely venues where they had to improvise props and set up a makeshift stage in "wharves, at the docks, on the railways, in convents, monasteries" and even "in greenhouses."[59] The work involved long hours, travel delays, bad weather and, on occasion, performing to the sound of artillery fire. At one show rats were discovered among the audience "in a dark barn in the middle of nowhere," while at other times gas masks were issued as a precaution. Such eventualities were part of life for spectators and performers alike.[60]

Whatever the challenges, the enthusiasm and gratitude of audiences made everything worthwhile. Ada L. Ward discovered this for herself when she was invited to a hospital where the patients were men with serious facial disfigurements. Despite being deeply affected by their suffering, Ada was able to make them smile, and "the laughter in their eyes" was testimony to what "those dear boys" could endure. "It was a wonderful thing to me" she said, concluding that "the courage and example of our boys nerve us to do things that at the beginning of the war we could never have done."[61]

Open air concerts. The soldiers relished the chance to enjoy open air concerts, and this photograph shows troops at a performance by Concerts at the Front actors and musicians. The staging of such events was entirely dependent on local facilities, which seemed to matter little to audiences, who usually entered fully into the spirit of things. (Press photo reproduced in *Stage Year Book*, 1919)

After a year of managing Concerts at the Front and the administrative and fund-raising work that underpinned it, Lena Ashwell received official acknowledgment of her project by the War Office in 1916. The YMCA promoted its musical and theatrical performances and used them to open new huts in France, thus making it possible for more touring groups to go to the Western Front and for repertory companies to perform in the base areas. Lena now turned her thoughts to Allied bases in the eastern Mediterranean, and "we began arrangements for sending artists to Malta and Egypt, with the possibility of Salonica," she recorded.[62] On 28 February 1916 the *Daily Malta Chronicle* reported on the "first appearance of the 'Malta Concert Party,'" which took place at Valletta, the capital. Although it was a formal occasion attended by the island's governor, the concert received the same enthusiastic reaction as in France. Performances followed in Italy and Egypt, where a touring group remained for two years.

Given the expansion of the programme, Lena Ashwell was once again very much concerned with fund-raising, appealing to one British audience to "give me all you have got, and then more" for "the sake of the boys at the

THE LENA ASHWELL CONCERT PARTY Y. M. C. A. MALTA 1916

Malta concert party. In 1916 the first Concerts at the Front group performed at Malta, which at the time was a centre for hospitals that cared for troops serving in the eastern Mediterranean theatre of war. The artists, shown outside the local YMCA, gave concerts that proved as popular there as they did in other areas of the war zone. (Postcard, public domain)

front."[63] Casting her net wide, Lena enlisted help from an old school friend in Canada whose sons were serving overseas. She returned to France in June and August 1916, where hospital wards were full of patients from the fighting of that summer. Many of them were simply too ill to attend a concert, so the kindly entertainers went into the wards and "sang softly without any accompaniment to those well enough to listen," bringing them enjoyment "through the time that is usually so awful."[64] Lena continued to believe wholeheartedly in the power of music to ease physical and mental suffering and received confirmation from medical staff and military chaplains that "music does what nothing else can do" to help a patient's recovery.[65]

Lena's summer 1916 visit to France was memorable for several reasons, not the least of which was the fulfilment of her childhood dream to play the role of Lady Macbeth. She acted in scenes from the "Scottish play," as it is known in the profession, at theatres and army bases in Rouen and Le Havre, and admitted that she had never imagined herself doing so in front of "thousands and thousands of men" who were far from homes and loved ones "in the midst of the greatest war that has ever been known."[66] Such memorable moments occurred farther afield too, as when the Egyptian concert party played to audiences of several thousand men. Shows were held in Cairo and in the open air, where the performers found that the atmosphere was so clear that every word could be heard across the vast, silent concourse of men gathered under the stars to enjoy a "glimpse of home" in the desert.[67]

In France, meanwhile, where Concerts at the Front had now given almost 2,000 performances, permission was granted to send a group to the forward trench lines. Given the risks and conditions, it was specified that performers must be men over military age and medically unfit for active service. Nine "firing line" parties were thus created for France and Belgium, and it was not work for the faint-hearted. One performer described a lengthy heavy bombardment and how between concerts he and his fellow musicians had walked up a hill and had "a wonderful view of the line. The nearest we have been to the front line is a mile or a little over." Another reported on a performance outdoors close to the trenches, with airplanes flying overhead and German shells "bursting all round. But I stuck it out, and got a huge encore, which came off in a torrent of shrieking shell-fire," he confirmed. Instead of feeling fear, the gentleman in question described the experience as "absolutely ripping."[68]

Among Lena Ashwell's many fans in France was one of the sons of her friend in Canada. The young man was a company commander who wrote to her while he was recovering from wounds. "We had one of your concert parties last night," he told her, "and, Lena dearest, it was wonderful, such a treat as we seldom get out here... Music means more than can be realized." For him it came as "a beautiful thought from home," and he was certain that every man in the audience "left feeling that life really was worth living and the war worth winning."[69]

In a written account of her work during the First World War, Lena referred a good deal to the Canadians, "because when one is brought up in a country, all the memories of one's childhood link up with the later events and make a deep impression on one's mind."[70] As she travelled with one of her concert parties she saw almost a thousand Canadians "in the very pink of training and fully equipped" on parade at Rouelles in the Harfleur Valley. "They were just being despatched up the line," wrote Lena, who watched as they were given a "tremendously inspiring farewell speech" from their colonel, followed by prayers and a short address by their padre. Headed by a piper, they formed up in preparation for their departure, and Lena did not forget them. As she later reflected, "There are one or two faces I still see; I

expect I shall always see them, as they marched away down the valley." Another memory was the time when Lena gave a solo recital to an audience of
Canadians at the same location. There was considerable excitement at her
appearance, especially for men who could claim her as one of their own, and
she described how moved she was when, at the end of the performance, the
commanding officer "spoke kindly of me, and of the concerts."[71]

Quite apart from the pleasure of listening to Shakespeare or classical
music, the troops continued to enjoy the latest popular songs. Those training or recuperating in Canada were treated to entertainment such as that
given at Camp Sewell, Manitoba, where an all-female group called "The
Khaki Girls of Winnipeg" wrote and sang their own tribute, entitled "Boys
Our Hearts Are With You."[72] Whether they were songs from home or other
hits such as "When Irish Eyes Are Smiling," "When the Boys Come Home"
or "Pack Up Your Troubles," the emotion generated in a hut or tent filled with
men who wondered whether they would survive the front line resulted in "a
whole massed audience singing as their last experience before going up to
the blood and horror." Lena Ashwell witnessed it many times and could find
no words to express the "aching sympathy" she felt, knowing that many of
the men would not return.[73]

In the last few weeks of 1916 the Concerts at the Front repertory companies staged their first performances in France. They consisted of professional
actors and actresses supplemented by troops working at base camps who
"just came along and did their best." Their programme included Shakespeare,
plays from London's West End and popular one-act plays. For many soldiers,
watching a play was a new experience but "once they caught the habit, they
were enthusiastic and earnest playgoers." Soldier-performers grew in number and it was regarded as "a great distinction to be numbered amongst the
players."[74] In due course, more of these companies were established at Rouen,
Dieppe, Étaples, and Calais.

A few months later, playwright and suffragist Cicely Hamilton, who was
a close friend of Canadian journalist Elizabeth Montizambert, joined Concerts at the Front to direct plays "in the shadow of the front lines."[75] Cicely had been doing administrative work at the Scottish Women's Hospital
in Royaumont and undertook her new assignment from a house at Abbeville, on the River Somme. Elizabeth "prayed that her friend would remain
safe" as she ventured into the war zone and it seems her prayers were answered.[76] Cicely was fortunately absent with one of her touring plays when
a bomb hit her office, completely demolishing it.[77] The plays continued, and
when Lena Ashwell made her next visit to France she received special thanks

from the Canadian YMCA for "the entertainment given," often in difficult conditions.[78]

By 1917 many people were wondering how much longer the war would last. German air raids over Britain and the north French coast made life hazardous, and having suffered more than one raid herself, Lena described it as "a terrible experience."[79] The touring concert parties who played that year in Calais and Boulogne "must be included amongst the 'firing line' experiences," she wrote, explaining how, at the end of one performance in which she herself took part,

> all the lights were turned off and the warning siren sounded. Then it began, and continued for four hours, such a bombing and firing as none of us had ever heard before, and the knowledge that we were entirely surrounded by ammunition dumps and poison-gas shells did not help.[80]

That evening, as she and the other performers attempted to eat a meal, "shrapnel was falling all around us. Shells were shrieking, bombs were dropping continually with deafening explosions, and the sound of the guns at the Front was drowned by the noise of the guns" closest to them.[81]

Lena's "firing line" concert parties were having to endure "difficult, often appalling" conditions close to the battle front, and with fewer and fewer eligible men available it was not possible to continue sending parties to that area of the war zone after March 1917. Lena decided instead to recruit solo artists such as story-tellers, ventriloquists and magicians, who could work more easily in limited spaces like dug-outs or tents. In April 1917, as news broke of America's entry into the war and Canada's victory at Vimy Ridge, the Concerts at the Front staff were preparing more fund-raising events in Britain, namely a review and a charity matinée performed by a group of society women. Both involved prominent people, with celebrated society beauty Lady Diana Manners performing in the matinée, while composer Edward Elgar wrote some new ballet music for the review and artist Augustus John illustrated the programme.[82] Lena also used testimonials such as that of the British Commander-in-Chief, Field Marshal Sir Douglas Haig, that her concerts were "a source of endless pleasure and relaxation for many thousands of soldiers."[83]

During further visits to France, Lena wrote movingly about "the great losses and pain suffered by so many," but maintained her belief that although "The tears might blind one's eyes," these "signs of sorrow must not be seen, for we were there to help."[84] She spent time at Boulogne with her brother Roger, who, too old for front line service, was on leave from his duties as a platoon commander in the Canadian Labour Corps.[85] By now the Germans had resumed unrestricted submarine warfare, and crossing the English Channel once again put lives in danger. Undeterred, Lena Ashwell continued her work in France and London, where her latest idea of staging light musical entertainment for the people of the city was soon drawing capacity audiences.

On 27 August 1917 work stopped briefly when she received news that she was among the first twelve women to receive the Order of the British Empire in recognition of their achievements. The front page of the *Daily Graphic* newspaper published details, praising Lena for her remarkable success with Concerts at the Front.[86] Inspired by the award, she gave speeches that autumn which highlighted the idea of women playing a strong role in the world after the war and reminding them that "we know we are a strength behind the armies."[87] The year ended with the passing in December 1917 of the Representation of the People Bill in the British Houses of Parliament, which included the vote for women.

In January 1918 the British Army gave permission for mixed concert parties to perform in certain areas of the Western Front, while in the eastern Mediterranean additional Concerts at the Front groups were planned for Palestine. Lena Ashwell spent much of February 1918 in France, where she worked and endured the usual damp winter conditions. Typical was her description of plays being staged in "a hangar inches deep in mud" and how one actress, wearing a long dress, had to leap "from plank to plank to reach the stage."[88]

A few weeks later came the start of the German spring offensive that started in March 1918 and made life hazardous across a wide area. It affected another project that Lena had devised after visiting Paris and hearing regrets expressed that Allied troops had nowhere they could go for entertainment in their own language. She secured the use of a theatre near the Gare Saint-Lazare and the first show went ahead on 29 June 1918, but it coincided with a period when Paris came under enemy bombardment. All leave for the troops was cancelled and many people fled to safer areas.

As Allied forces stood against the German armies, the tide of war began to turn in their favour and Concerts at the Front continued to stage performances through the last months of the war. When the end of hostilities came on 11 November 1918, one of Lena's repertory companies was due to perform in Belgium and she soon found herself travelling on an overcrowded train from Paris to Lille, having queued for hours to obtain the necessary permits and visas for the group. The train journey gave her an opportunity to see for herself the devastation the war had wrought and she was struck not only by "miles of destroyed villages" and devastated countryside but above all by the "terrible silence" after the intensity of artillery fire during the war. The more she thought about it all, the more she felt what she termed "a nausea quite indescribable."[89]

The following spring a Concerts at the Front group made its first visit to Cologne in Germany, where it entertained the Allied occupation force for seven weeks. Other repertory and concert parties performed in Britain at military and naval bases, staging shows for soldiers still hospitalized or recently repatriated, some of whom had been prisoners of war and "were in a great state of excitement at being again on British soil."[90] Lena listened to their tales "of wretchedness, of cruelty, and hunger," but she also saw the relief and happiness felt by so many of them now that they were able to put the nightmare of war behind them.

As 1919 progressed, Lena Ashwell attended memorial services for men who had not returned from the battlefields, and the first Easter after the war saw her giving a memorable recital of passages from the Bible. She used her notable talent for recitation during a special performance of the music and words of writers, poets and composers killed in the war, including George Butterworth and Rupert Brooke.[91] Lena then directed her efforts into repatriating her Concerts at the Front performers. She set up the Lena Ashwell Demobilization and Reconstruction Fund to help the 600 or so men and women who had worked with her in France and further afield. Grateful returning soldiers participated in a "Concerts at the Front Week" in Britain from 24 February to 1 March 1919, raising the necessary money for the concerts to continue until demobilization was completed in July 1919. It was only then, as Lena Ashwell wrote, that "our work with the armies was over."[92]

Summing up the experience of being in the war zone among men who faced death daily, Lena described it as "so overwhelming, so moving, so terrible that one's littleness was stunned and could not find expression." It was, she wrote, almost impossible to put into words "a world in arms – suffering, wounded, muddy, weary, smiling, and tortured" or to "try to give even a small expression – that is beyond description."[93] She paid tribute to her musicians and performers, remembering two in particular who had lost their lives. Singers Frederick Taylor and Emily Pickford died two months after the Armistice when their car went off the road into the River Somme during a spell of icy weather.[94]

The gratitude of the thousands of soldiers, medical staff, patients and war workers who were entertained by Concerts at the Front was clear from letters and testimonials. Among them were two that Lena Ashwell particularly cherished. An article in *Hospital* magazine paid tribute thus: "It would probably be true to say that these concert-parties have actually saved lives. Unquestionably, they have brightened those of thousands of our soldiers just when they most needed diversion."[95]

There was also a letter dated 17 June 1917 from the men of fifteen divisions of the British Third Army. It spoke of their "deep appreciation" of the concerts they had enjoyed, which "helped us to realize again that we are fighting for the Empire, Home and Beauty, and for all they mean in the life of mankind." Such conviction had helped them to carry on the fight "to a victorious end" and "a just and enduring peace," and they described Lena Ashwell as nothing less than "the fairy godmother of us all, and we are proud and grateful to be able to look you in the face today, and to say from full hearts, 'Madam, we thank you.'"[96]

The accolades Lena received were a fitting tribute to an outstanding woman whose early life in Ontario helped to shape her. Although her choice of career meant that Britain became her base, ties of family and friendship ensured that Canada and its people remained close to her heart. As someone who was always conscious of the thousands of men "going forward with a smile to death," and the mass of suffering humanity that she witnessed during her time on Western Front, Lena Ashwell led Concerts at the Front through the years of adversity, bringing enjoyment, hope and healing to those who desperately needed them.[97] She always believed that "beautiful music, happiness and laughter in the midst of so much pain and desolation, nerve-racking noise and ugliness" had a therapeutic power out of all proportion to its simplicity.[98] More than a century after the end of the "Great War," as it often called, the music associated with it is still familiar today as a legacy of the first conflict to be "entwined with popular culture."[99] Lena Ashwell's service to the Allied troops during a dark time was a tribute to her personally, to all those who were a part of Concerts at the Front, and to the difference that one woman made to so many lives.

CHAPTER 12

WOMEN WITH A MISSION (3)

"One of those rare individuals"

JULIA GRACE WALES, PACIFIST AND PEACE ACTIVIST

Sleep brings no more of its old release
From all the cares of day;
Restless we toss, and pray for peace;
Guns thunder while we pray.
When shall the madness pass? Till then
Our hearts beat time with marching men.[1]

"HOPE OF ESCAPE FROM INDEFINITELY CONTINUING A SELF-DESTRUCTIVE STRUGGLE": A PLAN FOR PEACE

Pacifism and peace activism during the war were concepts at odds with popular opinion and official propaganda. Yet amid all the fervour and jingoism that accompanied the outbreak of the First World War in 1914, there were people in the belligerent and neutral nations who believed that taking up arms was not the answer. Such people included those who objected to military service for reasons of conscience, those who rejected war, violence and loss of life, and others who sought ways of solving national and international problems by non-military means.[2]

In Britain, London society hostess Lady Ottoline Morrell and her husband, Philip, were among a group of confirmed pacifists. Ottoline Morrell foresaw the likely consequences of the war and "the horror of what it meant," recognizing that "poverty, want, suffering, chaos" would affect every aspect of life and sweep away all that had gone before.[3] Also in London was Rosika Bédy-Schwimmer, a twenty-six-year-old Hungarian feminist and suffragist who was working as press secretary to the International Woman Suffrage Alliance. Unable to return to her own country after the declaration of war, she felt no sense of nationalism and took the wider view that

> women's rights, men's rights, human rights – all are threatened by the ever-present spectre of war so destructive now of human material and moral values as to render victory indistinguishable from defeat.[4]

In Germany Clara Zetkin, a leader of the socialist women's movement in her country, believed that "when the men kill, it is up to us women to fight for the preservation of life," while across the Atlantic Jane Addams, vice-president of the National American Women's Suffrage Association, was a firm advocate of peace not only to preserve human life, but also to "do away with war as a natural process."[5] In Canada feminist and peace activist Alice Chown of Kingston, Ontario, had been exploring different aspects of social reform, and after the nation entered the First World War she continued to hope that there were "Canadians who believe that the time has come in the world's development when ideas, intelligence and good-will should take the place of force in settling disputes between individuals and nations."[6]

Among those who shared that belief was a young woman from St. Andrews in Quebec who was lecturing in English at the University of Wisconsin. Julia Grace Wales was deeply disturbed by press reports of the early phase of the war, especially given the number of fatalities among civilians and troops alike. Peace advocates in Europe and North America had already begun to discuss ways to bring hostilities to an end, and the more the young Canadian considered the matter, the more convinced she became of the need to find a non-violent way of solving international disputes.

Julia, who was generally known by her second name, Grace, was the daughter of a Canadian physician whose encouragement of her English studies at McGill University and Harvard had led to her choice of teaching as a career. Described by a magazine reporter as "a small, slight little lady, hardly more than a girl," with a "quiet and unassuming" manner, Grace Wales was a supporter of both the suffragist movement and the Woman's Peace Party, an American feminist and pacifist organization that was the first of its kind in the United States to make use of direct action.[7] The war news and the fact that the parents of some of her students were German immigrants only added to Grace's discomfort, and by the end of 1914 she had formulated a plan which, in her view, offered some chance of shortening the fighting. Many people told themselves the war could not last beyond Christmas, but with greater understanding of the lethality of modern warfare it became increasingly obvious that the conflict stood every chance of becoming a long battle of attrition.

Grace entitled her plan "Continuous Mediation Without Armistice," and it began by asking the following question:

> Can a means be found by which a conference of the neutral powers may bring the moral forces of the world to bear upon the present war situation, and offer to the belligerents some opportunity, involving neither com-

mittal to an arbitrary programme nor compromise of the convictions for which they are fighting, to consider the possibility of peace?[8]

It urged the United States, as the largest neutral nation, to set up an international conference to which all the other non-belligerent countries could send delegates. The conference would sit for the duration of the war and by continuous and independent mediation, with or without armistice and if necessary without the specific permission of the belligerents, put before the warring powers "reasonable propositions" based on principles most favourable to the establishment of a permanent peace. It would also invite suggestions from them which could form "some basis of settlement which may appeal to all as worthy of consideration." Well reasoned and expressed, Grace Wales's mediation plan offered each of the belligerents the "hope of escape from indefinitely continuing a self-destructive struggle."[9]

This was a new approach in international relations. Accepted practice took the line that a mediating power or powers would offer their services at the start of a conflict and be ready to bring the warring nations together at any time they might wish, or that they should become involved only when they were sure of meeting with success. The new proposal envisioned that neutral countries should unite, thereby demonstrating their impar-

Julia Grace Wales (1881-1957) was a Canadian academic who devised the Wisconsin Plan, a proposal to convene a conference of representatives from neutral nations who would work to find a solution to the First World War by peaceful means. She was invited to be a member of the Ford Peace Expedition in 1915 and worked tirelessly in Europe as part of the peace efforts of the neutral nations until the USA entered the war in 1917. She later resumed her academic career, which included a period teaching in Britain, and remained a committed supporter of resolving conflict by peaceful means. (Library and Archives Canada, PA-182511)

tiality, and continue to offer their services irrespective of how many times they might be rejected, in the hope of bringing the protagonists to the peace table.[10]

Grace Wales made it clear that the plan was the development of an idea "which has occurred independently to others" besides herself, and a notion that was "in the air the world over."[11] Women of the countries at war were sharing their concerns by writing to one another and to newspapers. One letter, sent by the women of England to the women of Germany and Austria, expressed the sentiment that "our very anguish unites us." It urged everyone to "hold to our faith in peace and goodwill among nations," so that all efforts could be made "with appeal to Wisdom and Reason." The letter received a reply from some 160 German women who believed that ladies of all nations shared a love of "justice, civilization and beauty," and that they could maintain solidarity with their British counterparts in the belief that "really civilized women never lose their humanity."[12]

The Grace Wales proposal for "Continuous Mediation without Armistice" was presented to the Wisconsin Peace Society, with copies forwarded to a number of influential people across the United States, including those close to the president, Woodrow Wilson. It received an endorsement from a leading pacifist, Professor David Jordan of Stanford University, who declared it "the most forceful and practical thing I have yet seen," and he recommended that it be presented at a National Peace Conference in Chicago in February 1915. Grace declined an invitation to attend the event, deciding that her proposal, by now known as the "Wisconsin Plan," might be more favourably received if presented by a man. She did, however, take part in a convention held in Washington, D.C., where she met Jane Addams.[13] As one of the invited speakers, Grace presented a well received and "most convincing argument" for her peace initiative.[14] The Chicago conference acclaimed it enthusiastically and passed a resolution that a delegation present it to President Wilson.[15]

As news of the proposal spread, it attracted widespread support. When a group of Belgian, Dutch, German and British suffragists met in Amsterdam to organize an International Congress of Women, scheduled to take place in The Hague in April 1915, Grace Wales was among those invited. Knowing she would be able to put forward her idea to the delegates, she was among forty-two North American women who set off from Hoboken, New Jersey, on 15 April 1915 on the SS *Noordam*. Everyone was aware of the dangers of German submarine activity in the waters around the British Isles, but despite the risks there was consensus that no chance to advance the cause of peace should be overlooked. Angela Morgan, a journalist who travelled with the

On board the *Noordam*. North American delegates to the 1915 International Congress of Women at the Hague sailed to Europe on the SS *Noordam*. They proved to be a lively, active group and were among 1,100 delegates from both neutral and belligerent countries who attended the conference. (Library of Congress)

delegates, described the group as "brimful of energy" and a force to be reckoned with.[16]

As she talked to people during the voyage, Angela Morgan recognized a "special ability and genius" in some of them. This was hardly surprising given that they included women of the calibre of Jane Addams and Emmeline Pethick-Lawrence, a prominent British suffragist.[17] Also present was Canadian Laura Hughes, niece of Canada's Minister of Militia, Colonel Sam Hughes. He had apparently told Laura, "I am trying to end the war and bring peace by sending my boy to the trenches and my girl to the peace process."[18]

Among those singled out by Morgan as "peculiarly adapted to deal with the great peace problem" was Grace Wales, whom the journalist described as "slim almost to fragility, with the eyes of a dreamer and thinker." She perceived "the sheer strength of an intellect illumined by spiritual vision," and formed the opinion that "Miss Wales must be regarded as one of those rare individuals who arise when the times have need of them."[19] Grace impressed her colleagues to the extent that before they reached Europe they had "virtually accepted" her plan as representative of their main principles, and had voted unanimously to have it translated into four languages for distribution at the congress.[20]

Jane Addams (1860-1935), the daughter of the founder of the Illinois Republican Party, became an activist and reformer and a notable figure in the history of social work and women's suffrage in the United States. In 1910 she was awarded an honorary master of arts degree by Yale University and in 1915 she was elected national chairman of the Woman's Peace Party. Addams was invited to preside over the International Congress of Women in The Hague that year, following which she travelled throughout Europe meeting with leaders, citizen groups and wounded soldiers from both sides. As the elected president of the International Committee of Women for a Permanent Peace, she continued her work throughout the war, travelling frequently to Europe and Asia. Her leadership and visits to war-torn regions were cited in nominations for the Nobel Peace Prize, which she was awarded in 1931. (Library of Congress)

The sea journey was without incident until the *Noordam* neared England. British naval officers came aboard, exercising their right to visit and search vessels from neutral countries that were within British territorial waters. The *Noordam* remained at anchor for four days within sight of the famous white cliffs of Dover, during which time the passengers were not permitted to go ashore. Fortunately, just as everyone was becoming anxious about missing the start of the congress, they were allowed to proceed to Rotterdam, where a Dutch committee of hospitality was waiting to greet them.

The International Congress of Women or Women's Peace Congress, as it was also known, took place from 28 April to 1 May 1915, with more than 1,100

women present. There were representatives from neutral and belligerent nations, among them women from almost half the world's suffrage societies. The countries attending included Austria, Belgium, Canada, Denmark, Germany, Great Britain, Hungary, Italy, the Netherlands, Norway, Sweden and the United States. French delegates were conspicuous by their absence as a protest about the event being held while their nation was under attack, but sent a letter of support. The assembly, in the words of Dr. Aletta Jacobs, president of the Dutch Executive Committee, was meeting to "protest against war and to suggest steps which may lead to warfare becoming an impossibility in the future."[21] It also sought to promote the rights of women to claim their place in the government of the world.

Under the chairmanship of Jane Addams delegates dealt with matters of business in the morning, held committee meetings in the afternoon and were involved in public events in the evening. Agreement at the outset prohibited any discussion of who was to blame for the war or how it was being waged. Instead, the focus was on preparations for a permanent peace and how this goal could be reached. The following two premises were held to be fundamental: (1) that international disputes should be resolved by peaceful means, and (2) that the parliamentary franchise that entitled men to vote should be extended to women.[22]

Grace Wales was an active participant in the discussions that took place within the official proceedings of the congress and at social events arranged

At The Hague, 1915. The International Congress of Women was held in April 1915 with more than 1,110 delegates in attendance. The meeting was presided over by American Jane Addams, and this photograph shows her (facing page, sixth from the left) with other officers of the congress. (LSE Library, public domain)

by the Dutch hosts. She felt that people were initially reluctant to speak out for fear of causing offence, but as time went on "we gained confidence," she wrote, and "our brains were kept so busy we had no time to realize our feelings."[23] Resolutions were passed on matters such as action towards peace and principles of permanent peace; international cooperation; women and war; women's representation at the peace conference that would follow the war; women's enfranchisement; and the education of children. Despite some unsympathetic press coverage, the congress, in the words of American delegate Emily Balch, demonstrated "the most active will for unity I have ever felt in an assemblage," and she paid tribute to the "beautiful spirit of the brave, self-controlled women who dared ridicule and every sort of difficulty" to take part in it.[24]

The resolutions committee of the congress accepted Grace Wales's plan for continuous mediation without an armistice, and at the final session on 1 May 1915 Rosika Schwimmer, the Hungarian peace worker, moved a resolution on mediation. Grace Wales seconded the motion, arguing that "what we have to do is to think all together ... and our ideas must be coordinated if we are to arrive at truth. If there is one thing we need not be afraid of doing, it is thinking honestly. If the peoples of the world will begin to think, they will begin to be safe." In her concluding statement, she told those assembled that, "if we desire with all our hearts to find out the truly right way, nothing can prevent us from finding it."[25] The resolution was passed as follows:

> The International Congress of Women resolves to ask the neutral countries to take immediate steps to create a conference of neutral nations which shall without delay offer continuous mediation. The Conference shall invite suggestions for settlement from each of the belligerent nations and in any case shall submit to all of them simultaneously, reasonable proposals as a basis for peace.[26]

"SOMETHING THAT HAS NOT YET BEEN TRIED IN THIS WAR":
A CONFERENCE OF NEUTRAL NATIONS

To deliver the resolution to the warring and neutral nations it was agreed that envoys, chosen and funded by the International Committee of the Women's Peace Congress, be appointed from among the countries represented at The Hague. Those selected would prepare reports on their findings, which would form the basis of further action. Grace Wales was among those chosen, and together with a British delegate, Chrystal MacMillan, she was asked to go to Denmark, Norway and Sweden.[27] As British subjects the two women were unable to take the regular overland route from Amsterdam, which crossed German territory. Instead, they secured passage on a Dutch freighter whose captain would only agree to transport them one at a time.

Grace travelled first and left the Netherlands in mid-May 1915, using the voyage to write her personal account of the congress. It was a time for reflection, with feelings running high because of the sinking of the *Lusitania* a week or so earlier. Grace tried to remain objective but the obvious dangers of sea travel together with stormy weather and seasickness, prompted her to wonder "what on earth brought insignificant, cowardly me, of all people, here on this boat, on this crazy enterprise?" She knew the answer was the very thing that had lured her to Europe in the first place: "the sheer pushing force of an idea," which "must conquer, not a force of arms." What was needed, she maintained, was honest communication and having "all the truth courageously out in the open."[28]

At Copenhagen Grace found accommodation at the Woman's Reading Club. When she explained that she had just come from The Hague, one French guest "threw up her hands, rolled her eyes" and praised Grace effusively for her courage. She was soon busy making calls, following up introductions and finding her way around the city. "Oh, these open-air cafés, and the long luminous evenings!" she enthused.[29] She met the U.S. Ambassador, Maurice Egan, outlined the congress resolution as "something that has not yet been tried in this war," and found Mr. Egan a good listener who complimented her on her "courageous and sincere" approach. At the same time, he felt obliged to point out the practical difficulties. "How are you going to get any of the foreign offices to listen to this?" he queried. Grace replied that "we were not talking about getting everything settled at once, only about beginning to think." "Why not" she asked, "begin now to scrap it out intellectually? There is perfectly good quarrelling to be had that way – just as good as with our fists." Even if their viewpoints differed, Egan told her that he appreciated her "passion for peace" and gave her a pink carnation as a parting gift. She left feeling more strongly than ever that humanity "ought to and could find a way to think before it destroys itself."[30]

Grace managed to secure an appointment at the British Embassy, where she found her reception very guarded. Sympathetic in manner but firmly of the opinion that the war could not stop "until Belgium is free," the official who met her smiled doubtfully and agreed to read her pamphlet but insisted, "I don't see what we diplomats can do to help." Grace pressed the point that "if we want to find a way out, we will find it." The meeting made clear to her the challenges, particularly with regard to diplomatic staff who, she said, "can't help all the time trying to justify themselves." She concluded that "the more I see this whole business, the less I feel like throwing stones at anybody and the more sorry I feel for all concerned." What was required, she believed, was "a little courage and a little positive constructive faith."[31]

On 30 May 1915 the young Canadian boarded another ship bound for the Norwegian capital city of Christiania (modern-day Oslo). Following "an adventurous trip" to get there, Grace's busy schedule included an audience with King Haakon VII, who was "most affable and talked ever so long." Grace also discussed her ideas with Mansfeldt Findlay, the head of the British mission in Norway.[32] She described that meeting as "the most uphill interview I have ever had" and said that she was given to understand that "all efforts for peace were foolish and wrong." "Isn't it all a matter of ideas of how to get into communication," she retorted, seeking to break the impasse of opposing viewpoints. "Don't think me unfriendly to peace," replied Findlay, but Grace found that "there wasn't any way to get at him, that he was inside a stone wall." In her view there were "many such [men] in every country" who were "good sort of men too – thoroughly honest, brave, reliable," but the problem remained that "they all want peace but they take the way that leads to war."[33]

After reaching her final destination, Stockholm, on 2 June 1915 and meeting Knut Wallenburg, Sweden's foreign minister, Grace Wales returned to Christiania. There she made another important contact with a Norwegian member of the Inter-Parliamentary Union, a global organization of national parliaments which worked to safeguard peace and bring about democratic change through dialogue and action. As she booked her return passage to North America, Grace felt nostalgic for home and ready to leave her "wild adventures, tearing around strange cities in automobiles and talking to diplomats." She looked forward to the "quietness and routine" of her teaching job at the University of Wisconsin but her homeward voyage had its eventful moments.[34] As her ship, the *Hellig Olav*, headed northwest, it was stopped by a British cruiser and taken to Stornoway, the capital of the Hebridean islands of Harris and Lewis. After being searched, the ship was allowed to continue on its way but Grace felt ill and was found to have jaundice. She spent much of the voyage in bed, and on arrival at New York went straight to Quebec to spend the summer with her family.

While Grace Wales enjoyed a quiet interlude, some of her closest associates from the International Congress of Women, including Chrystal MacMillan and Rosika Schwimmer, were in America working with Jane Addams and Emily Balch. Like Grace, they had gone as envoys to a number of European cities and their findings indicated that "the creation of a continuous conference of neutral nations might provide the machinery which would lead to peace."[35] Among the belligerent countries there was an assurance that "such an initiative would not be resented," one minister even asking, "What are the neutrals waiting for?" Other reactions from "men in the high councils of the great nations" indicated an appreciation of what the Women's Peace Congress was attempting to do. "Yours is the sanest proposal that has been brought to this office in the last six months," was the reaction attributed to one government official, whilst another felt it would be "of the greatest importance to finish the fight by early negotiation rather than by further military efforts, which would result in more and more destruction and irreparable loss."[36]

Overall, there was a sense that a conference of neutral nations "would not be opposed" as a medium for the settlement of the war provided that the co-operation of the United States, as the largest of the neutrals, could be obtained. American peace organizations had been trying to persuade President Wilson to endorse the Wisconsin Plan, and Clara Ford, wife of automobile manufacturer Henry Ford, supported a campaign to urge the president to convene such a conference. Efforts continued with the widespread circulation of the plan in pamphlet form and a meeting between the director of the American Peace Society, Louis Lochner, and Woodrow Wilson on 12 November 1915. Lochner urged the president to summon a neutral conference

Rosika Bédy-Schwimmer (1877-1948) was born in Hungary to a Jewish family. An accomplished linguist, she found it hard to find work that would enable her to live independently and began to take an active part in women's issues, supporting the causes of feminism and suffrage and becoming an active member of the International Woman Suffrage Alliance. Schwimmer was working in London when war broke out and in 1915 was a delegate at the International Congress of Women at The Hague. Later that year she was instrumental in convincing Henry Ford to launch his peace expedition. She remained committed to peace efforts and in 1918 became one of the world's first female ambassadors on behalf of the new Hungarian Republic. (LSE Library, public domain)

but it was clear that there were important issues and concerns for Wilson to consider.

Elsewhere, interest in the idea was gaining momentum. Rosika Schwimmer met Henry Ford and impressed him so much that he invited her to his home at Dearborn in Michigan. After hearing more about Grace Wales and her plan for continuous mediation, Ford decided to meet other members of the group and to talk to President Wilson himself. The irrepressible Schwimmer spoke at length to Clara Ford about the role of women in putting an end to war and saving human lives. While the Hungarian peace activist headed to Washington with a delegation "representing the women of war-torn Europe," Clara Ford announced that she wanted to "foster a demonstration enabling American women to go on record as favouring a conference of neutral nations" that would work towards "a just settlement of the great European tragedy." Her husband decided that he would support such efforts and that any peace initiative would "command world-wide attention if it were launched from New York."[37]

"WE'RE GOING TO TRY TO GET THE BOYS OUT OF THE TRENCHES BY CHRISTMAS": THE FORD PEACE EXPEDITION

In addition to being a famous industrialist and inventor, Henry Ford was also a humanitarian who opposed the idea of war. He regarded it as a terrible waste of life and resources and "unjustifiable." "We who can ought to help in the right direction," he said, but decided before doing so to consult with President Wilson on 22 November 1915.[38] According to Louis Lochner, Ford told the president that he had decided to back the resolution of the International Congress of Women and urged Wilson to "take the necessary steps for the appointment of a neutral commission" to go to Europe. Ford pledged to cover the costs, and when Wilson impressed upon him that as the head of a neutral nation "I must also preserve neutrality of judgement," Ford had his answer ready. "If you feel you can't act," he told the president, "I will."[39]

Ford intended to take "a shipful of American delegates to Europe" and at a press conference on 23 November 1915 told a large audience of reporters that "a man should try to do the greatest good to the greatest number." Furthermore, he said, "we're going to try to get the boys out of the trenches by Christmas." As the leader of the peace expedition, he confirmed that "our object is to stop war for all times."[40]

At the University of Wisconsin Grace Wales, whose every spare moment during the past months had been devoted to peace work, was nearing the end of the autumn semester when she received a telegram from Henry Ford

Henry Ford (1863-1947) was an American business magnate and industrialist who founded the Ford Motor Company. As the creator of the mass production assembly line, he developed an automobile that average middle-class families could afford, thereby profoundly affecting life in the twentieth century. Ford opposed war and military intervention and agreed to fund and lead a peace expedition to Europe in 1915. He continued to support peace efforts until the USA declared war on Germany in 1917. (Library of Congress)

inviting her to join him and his expedition on board the *Oscar II*, the vessel he had hired. The ship would sail from New York on 4 December 1915 bound for Christiania, Stockholm and Copenhagen, and Ford made his intentions clear. "I am calling leading men and women of the European nations to join us en route," he said, "and at some central point to be determined later, establish an international conference dedicated to negotiations leading to a just settlement of the war."[41] "The time has come," continued the message, for those few men and women with "courage and energy, irrespective of the cost in personal convenience, money, sacrifice and criticism" to free "the goodwill of Europe" and enable it to assert itself "for peace and justice."[42]

Grace accepted Ford's invitation and received a very positive response from Louis Lochner of the American Peace Society, whom Ford had employed to assist him with the expedition. Lochner told Grace, "we need every ounce of your brains," and he promised to send her funds to cover her travel costs.[43] When she arrived at New York, Henry and Clara Ford and their entourage were installed at the Biltmore Hotel, a palatial new establishment that boasted the latest in design and luxury. "Such a place," enthused Grace when she saw it, was "top notch for grandeur."[44]

The Fords' suite was a hive of activity with people coming and going, phones ringing and reporters poised to take down the latest news about the upcoming trip. Although she was taken aback at the "massive confusion," surrounding everything, Grace told her parents that she was "in the middle of a more exciting adventure than I ever even dreamed of" and foresaw the mission as an opportunity to hasten "government action … What we are after is disarmament."[45] She also made it clear that she and Rosika Schwimmer, who was to be "technical adviser" to the expedition, would remain in the background as nationals of belligerent nations in the war. It was important that the expedition be seen as impartial, and the two women intended to give their support to Jane Addams, who was "well-known abroad" as someone "safe and neutral."[46]

The *Oscar II*, a Scandinavian America Line ship, was moored at Hoboken and a huge crowd gathered to wish it well on its voyage. Henry Ford boarded amid cheers and the press were delighted to learn that the vessel was equipped with a Marconi wireless telegraph that would keep them in touch with what was being called the Ford Peace Expedition. As the *Oscar II* left on the bright and bitterly cold afternoon of 4 December, a brass band played "For He's a Jolly Good Fellow" and reporters prepared articles under such headlines as "Henry Ford Hires Ark to Carry Dove to Warring Nations" and "Little Old Ford Party Sailing Right Along."[47] Ford had invited some sixty journalists to travel with the expedition, most of whom did not take the enterprise seriously and were no doubt amused to see one newspaper describe it as "The Ford Crusade of Cranks to Mind Other People's Business."[48]

The eighty delegates accompanying Henry Ford were, according to Grace Wales, "for the most part people of character, intelligence and soundness of motive."[49] She was sharing a cabin with two women, one of whom, Inez Boissevain, thought Grace attractive, good-hearted and possessed of a sharp intellect.[50] Both Boissevain and the third occupant of the cabin, Alice Park,

Inez Milholland Boissevain (1886-1916) was a suffragist, labour lawyer, socialist, correspondent and public speaker, who greatly influenced the women's movement in America. A law graduate who practised in New York, she was involved in various organizations, including the National American Women's Suffrage Association, and was invited by Henry Ford to join his Peace Expedition in 1915. In 1916 she toured the west of America as a speaker on women's rights but was suffering from pernicious anaemia. She collapsed during a speech, was hospitalized and died on 25 November 1916. (Library of Congress)

The Peace Ship. In December 1915 Henry Ford set off for Europe with the aim of setting up an international conference dedicated to negotiations "leading to a just settlement of the war." He and his group travelled on the SS *Oscar II*, seen here, intending to visit Stockholm, Christiania (modern-day Oslo) and Copenhagen, capital cities of neutral countries. Ford left the expedition soon after reaching Norway, but the majority of the group completed their planned tour. (Public domain)

were pacifists and suffragists, and Grace found they had much in common.[51] Alice regaled Grace with her recollection of surviving the San Francisco earthquake in 1912. On her first evening at sea, Grace was seated beside Henry Ford at dinner and described him as "a most simple sincere man" who seemed to possess "a childlike faith in his plan to shorten the war." "He has no affectations," she noted, and "looks you straight in the face when he talks to you. Everyone on the ship is head over ears in love with him."[52]

Despite rough weather the *Oscar II* kept to its sailing schedule. The delegates filled their time with lectures, discussions and meetings, and Grace Wales assisted with clerical duties. One hot topic of conversation was the fact that Woodrow Wilson had recently been re-elected for a second term as U.S. president. In his inaugural address he announced a shift in attitude towards the war and asked Congress to "strengthen the armed forces so that the nation can care for its own security" and "make sure of entire freedom to play the impartial role in this hemisphere and in the world which we all believe to have been providentially assigned to it."[53] This statement threw the peace mission delegates into a state of upheaval and emotions ran high enough to warrant a "cooling off" period of several days. Further heated discussion centred upon the proposal that delegates should sign a petition supporting Henry Ford's quest for peace, endorsing a policy of international disarmament and calling on Americans to oppose the "dangerous policy of preparedness."[54]

Amid the unrest Grace chose to take a philosophical view. She regarded people's sentiments as proof that "we are all human and we all have vital convictions." Although "every conceivable difficulty has had to be faced and wrestled with," she said, "we seem to have come out on top so far as our spirit and unity are concerned." For her own part, she recognized that "I am having experiences that are worth everything – that are a revelation of great things."[55] Her optimism was well founded and by the time the *Oscar II* entered British waters on 13 December 1915, things had settled down and the formerly sceptical journalists were demonstrating a growing belief in the enterprise.

The ship was escorted by a British cruiser to Kirkwall, capital of the Shetland Islands, where it was inspected and held for twenty-four hours. The friendly harbour master told Ford and his group that people in Britain looked "very kindly upon the Ford Peace Expedition" and regarded it as a "sincere effort to stop the war" but did not think it would be successful. Even so the average man, it seemed, hoped "somethin' good'll come of your brave attempt."[56] On 18 December the *Oscar II* crossed the North Sea with the crew watchful for floating mines and enemy submarines. The vessel arrived safely at Christiansand on the south coast of Norway, where Henry Ford hosted a party and told Scandinavian journalists that "every nation in the world will soon look upon the American peace pilgrimage as taking the initiative in stopping history's worst war."[57]

Although southern Norway was in the throes of exceptionally cold weather and the expedition received a rather mixed press reception, the meetings and events arranged for Ford and his "peace pilgrims" were well attended. Unfortunately, many of the delegates soon became ill with colds or influenza, including Henry Ford himself, who remained confined to his hotel room and unable to throw off what seemed to be a combination of both. The expedition's doctor informed Ford that he was not well enough to undertake the next stage of the journey and should either go to a Norwegian health resort until he recovered, or return to America. After consideration Ford chose the latter, even though Louis Lochner and Rosika Schwimmer told him "the world would think he had abandoned the expedition and its purpose" almost as soon as it had reached Europe.[58]

Ford slipped away quietly and unexpectedly on 23 December 1915, his departure known only to a few people who decided to say nothing until the expedition was on its way to Sweden. After a difficult twenty-hour journey in record cold weather, the rest of the party reached Stockholm on Christmas Eve. Having spent a considerable amount of time working out how to break the news of Ford's departure, Rosika Schwimmer and Louis Lochner issued a statement saying their leader was "temporarily absent on doctor's orders" and that he was appointing a committee of seven people as his surrogates.[59] He had put Rosika Schwimmer in charge of selecting the committee members and clearly had confidence in her ability as a leader, even though she had "no status in Europe as a peacemaker" and her autocratic style of management was the cause of friction.[60]

Despite Ford's absence the atmosphere at Stockholm's Grand Hotel was festive, and Grace Wales told her parents, "We are having as thrilling adventures as ever befell mortals." Her first Christmas in Scandinavia did not disappoint her and the expedition's visit to Sweden was a success.[61] At meetings every mention of a desire to find an early end to the war was met with tumultuous applause on the part of the Swedes, who were normally "not a demonstrative lot."[62] As the peace delegates prepared to move on to Denmark, no fewer than 1,500 people gathered at the train station to see them off.

Another cordial welcome awaited them in Copenhagen, which proved to be the liveliest venue of the entire trip. News of their arrival spread and even the Russian press covered their activities. Despite a wartime ruling that prohibited public meetings, members of Denmark's Council of Women found a way around the restriction and receptions were held. It was not long before one senior newspaper owner declared that "the peace pilgrims have won all Danish hearts."[63] Grace Wales was invited to an afternoon event hosted by Maurice Egan, the American ambassador she had met on her previous visit, and received a warm welcome.

With the Netherlands as the final destination of the "peace pilgrims," the question arose of how best to reach it. Travelling by sea on a neutral vessel meant facing the dangers of mines and submarines, whilst going overland would involve crossing Germany. After a diplomatic approach to the German government, permission was granted for the Ford Peace Expedition to cross its territory in a sealed train. Its members reached The Hague without incident on 8 January 1916, where a large reception committee had assembled to welcome them. The initiative garnered praise from the Dutch parliament and, despite scepticism in the Dutch press at the "highly idealistic character" of the venture, newspapers urged their readers to "recognize the fine thought which inspires the party" and to welcome the fact that "it comes to embittered Europe to preach words of conciliation."[64]

"THE SENTIMENT WE HAVE AROUSED ... WILL SHORTEN THE WAR": THE NEUTRAL CONFERENCE ON CONTINUOUS MEDIATION, 1916

Away from the challenges and disagreements that continued to occur, and which Grace Wales described as "a tempest in a teapot," the expedition committee turned its attention to arrangements for a Neutral Conference on Continuous Mediation, planned for the spring of 1916.[65] Six permanent delegates were selected from each of the following nations: Denmark, the Netherlands, Norway, Sweden, Switzerland and the USA. They came from a variety of backgrounds that included national and municipal politics, academe, the church, the legal profession, the fields of publishing, engineering and medicine, and women's suffrage organizations. After a vote, Stockholm was chosen as the location of the conference and delegates pledged to "devise a peace settlement based on the abolition of armaments and a system of international justice that would protect the rights and freedom of all peoples."[66]

This done, the Ford Peace Expedition was officially disbanded and except for those who would be directly involved in the forthcoming conference – Rosika Schwimmer, Louis Lochner and Grace Wales among them – the remaining members of the mission prepared for their journey home to the United States. Everyone agreed that peace had been "the most talked-of thing in Europe" and drew attention to the fact that Henry Ford had indeed "got peace talk going now!"[67] Ford, from whom nothing had been heard since his return to America, issued a statement confirming that he had left the expedition "because I had a slight touch of the grippe." According to Lochner, regardless of how Ford's sudden departure had been interpreted, the man himself did not "regret a single thing I have done" and remained firm in his belief that "the sentiment we have aroused by making the people think will shorten the war."[68] Swedish writer Ellen Key, in a letter to all members of the mission, said she believed the expedition would "remain in the memory of mankind as an example of the dauntless faith which has achieved the truly great deeds in this world."[69]

As preparations for the Neutral Conference went ahead, Grace Wales left The Hague on 22 January 1916 on a freighter bound for the Swedish port of Gothenburg. She had charge of the Peace Expedition's equipment and papers and undertook the voyage with trepidation, especially when near the Kiel Canal, a waterway through the German state of Schleswig-Holstein that links the North Sea to the Baltic Sea, the ship was stopped by a German cruiser. Grace had her first encounter with officers of the Imperial German Navy and it was "with relief," she said, that the freighter was allowed to proceed and "we saw through a grey mist, the wild and forbidding coast of Sweden."[70] From there she travelled to Stockholm and was soon back at the Grand Hotel, which had been selected as the conference venue. While the American and Scandinavian delegates – among the first to arrive – informally opened proceedings, Louis Lochner went to Switzerland hoping to secure that country's participation.

As she helped to prepare for the conference, Grace found time to appreciate the Grand Hotel. The main meeting room, elegant and spacious, had an air of grandeur. Smaller adjoining rooms served as offices for a secretariat, a library and a publicity department, where Grace would be working. The outlook from her "luxurious room" convinced her that she had "one of the finest views in Europe." She could see a curving waterway with barges, an arching bridge, church spires, towers and gabled rooftops, the parliament buildings and the royal palace, all set against a background of snowy hills. Whether in a "blaze of sunlight" or lit by a "bluish-green Alpine glow in the sky" at sunset, Grace was captivated by Stockholm in its many moods. Inside the hotel the constantly changing international clientele intrigued her, and she concluded that it was "the best place to meet."[71]

The weeks before the conference began were filled with hard work, and the busy Miss Wales was "astonished to find how well I stand this mad life."[72] Henry Ford sent a friend, Gaston Plantiff, to take charge of financial matters and Rosika Schwimmer soon found herself at the centre of a quarrel with his staff. In the midst of the wrangling Grace formed her own conclusion about how decisions and executive powers should be handled, and as a result felt "more comfortable than I had for weeks." She briefed Louis Lochner on the situation as soon as he returned from Switzerland, and when he approached Rosika Schwimmer with a number of grievances, she resigned on 27 February 1916.[73]

The following day, just a week after the German attack on Verdun began, the unofficial Neutral Conference on Continuous Mediation opened. In attendance were five delegates each from Denmark, the Netherlands, Norway, Sweden and Switzerland, and two from the United States. One third of the delegates were women, half of whom had been at the Hague congress the previous year. Debates centred on issues such as nationality, freedom of the seas, economic matters, disarmament, propaganda and the development of peace proposals. Having resigned from her position, Rosika Schwimmer did not appear officially but "daily influenced those delegates who sought her advice."[74]

Grace worked in the conference office and reflected a good deal on her primary concern that the final vote and resolutions should be "heard in all the countries by all the people."[75] As the programme proceeded, it was agreed that a committee would draft an appeal to the belligerent nations. It took six weeks to agree a final document, which in the opinion of Louis Lochner represented an honest attempt to initiate the discussion of peace terms among the warring and neutral nations.

The appeal, which was submitted for "sympathetic consideration," offered seven principles covering territorial issues, economic competition, freedom of the seas, parliamentary control of foreign policy to prevent secret treaties and diplomacy, and the establishment of an international organization to which all nations would submit agreements on disarmament and disputes for arbitration. The final principle incorporated the suggestion that a "World Congress" of "all nations focusing on the political and spiritual freedom of subject nationalities" should participate in the eventual peace conference. The document concluded with a call for the end of "international anarchy" and for "enduring peace for all mankind" by means of "the institution of an international order of justice."[76] The final version of the Appeal to the Belligerents was published in full in the neutral countries and accepted for publication in the following warring nations: Australia, Germany, Great Britain, Italy and Russia. Copies were sent by mail to parliaments and foreign ministries, generating far wider publicity than the conference had expected. As such, the document marked the start of discussion across the nations.

"THE POSSIBILITY OF RESTORING PEACE IN EUROPE": THE FORD INTERNATIONAL PEACE COMMISSION, 1916-1917

Grace Wales continued her work with the Neutral Conference whose ongoing efforts, financed by Henry Ford, concentrated on mediation, scientific enquiry, publicity and propaganda. The central committee of the conference received a message from Ford, who wanted to move its headquarters to The Hague, where it could work at "quiet mediation," one representative per country.[77] A compromise was reached by which Dutch representatives would be based in The Hague, the Swiss in Berne and the Scandinavians in Stockholm. While the three offices planned rallies, parades, peace demonstrations and gatherings, Grace Wales wrote the text of publicity leaflets distributed at the various events. For the summer of 1916 she rented an apartment in a pleasant area of Stockholm and enjoyed more of a social life although, as she emphasized to her family, "nobody has had time for twosomes or flirtations."[78]

Back in the United States, Henry Ford appeared to be following the progress of the peace work in Europe and took a particular interest in disarmament. Louis Lochner was tasked with delivering letters prepared by Ford's office to the leaders and heads of state of the belligerent nations, as well as to Pope Benedict XV in Rome. These letters set out "certain views," wrote Ford, "which I hold regarding the possibility of restoring peace in Europe," and included the request that Louis Lochner be granted a meeting so that he could take away with him "any suggestions that may come of the audience." Lochner returned to Europe in November 1916, confident that "there would be smooth sailing."[79]

The committee members of the Neutral Conference forged ahead with their work and gathered data that could be useful in any future peace negotiations. It was clear that the work now needed to be "built upon a much larger and more international scale," and the decision was taken to terminate the conference in its existing form. Its members were invited to become part of an international commission to be based in The Hague, but "broadened out to include men and women throughout Europe."[80] The proposal had Henry Ford's approval and continued financial backing, and the new organization, to be known as the Ford International Peace Commission, declared in its first communiqué that its task would be the "creation of an intelligent opinion as to the conditions of a lasting peace."[81]

Having overseen this change Louis Lochner returned to the business of delivering Henry Ford's letters. Efforts at mediation were showing signs of promise and on 12 December 1916 events on the international stage took a surprising turn when Germany issued a peace note, which it claimed was "prompted by the desire to avoid further bloodshed and make an end to the atrocities of war." The note, something of a contradiction in terms, confirmed that Germany and its allies proposed "to enter forthwith into peace negotiations" but that they were "resolved to continue to a victorious end."[82] A few days later President Wilson issued his own peace note, which was quoted by the *New York Herald* in an article entitled "1916: Peace May Be Near." "The president," it said, had "astonished the world" by suggesting "that the time has come for paving the way to peace," and for confirmation of the views of the belligerent nations "as to the terms on which hostilities might be concluded."[83]

The Wilson peace note received widespread support. Grace Wales "drew a long breath of relief," for "it seemed to me," she wrote, "that the essence of all that we have struggled for was in that."[84] There was a positive feel to the start of 1917 as the newly-formed Ford International Peace Commission attempted to bring together representatives from Britain and Germany who might be willing to talk to one another, if not in person then through some neutral organ. Louis Lochner, meanwhile, was summoned by Henry Ford to return to the USA, where the two men met with President Wilson to discuss the idea of a league of nations and how such a body might be founded.

On 22 January 1917 President Wilson addressed the Senate, proposing that rather than form a system of alliances such as had existed at the start of the war, a new approach be taken with the formation of a "community of power," which would act in the common interest. He called for a peace that would not leave "resentment, a bitter memory," and this approach seemed to resemble the Neutral Conference's Appeal to the Belligerents and to echo Grace Wales's idea of a peace league and an ending to hostilities that would not involve "humiliation under duress." She modestly took little credit for her original plan, describing it as "a mere drop in the bucket" in the process towards "a great world movement."[85]

"THE WORLD MUST BE MADE SAFE FOR DEMOCRACY": AMERICA'S ENTRY INTO THE WAR

An optimistic Louis Lochner was in Washington on 1 February 1917, awaiting another meeting with President Wilson, when news broke of Germany's announcement of further unrestricted submarine warfare. When Lochner spoke to the president, Wilson declared that if a peaceful solution could be found he wished it "with all my heart," but having considered the situation, the following day he informed Congress that moves to sever relations with Germany were in motion. America was headed for war, and "we must stand behind the President," Henry Ford told Lochner.[86] On 7 February 1917 Lochner learned that Ford had decided to discontinue funding the peace work in Europe, a move that Grace Wales saw as "inevitable" given that their efforts had to be "technically neutral" and would no longer be perceived as such.[87] An emissary from the Ford Motor Company was sent to close the Peace Commission's European offices, but all those who had been involved in the Neutral Conference on Continuous Mediation believed its work had been "worth while."[88]

On 6 April 1917 the United States declared war on Germany. A few days earlier President Wilson addressed Congress, citing Germany's violation of its pledge to suspend submarine warfare in the North Atlantic and its attempt to lure Mexico into an alliance against America. "The world must be made safe for democracy," he said, and the vote that followed four days later was overwhelmingly in favour of war. Grace Wales felt President Wilson had "taken the final – the sooner or later inevitable – step" only because "he must." As she told her sister,

> It seems to me that it is far better for America … to enter the war with a good motive than to stay out with a bad one. Her decision to fight means for her on the whole a long step forward even with respect to pacifism. It means the taking up of international responsibility. It means new and cordial relations with members of the Entente. These are inestimable gains.[89]

As they took stock of this far-reaching development, those who had been involved in the peace initiatives believed they had helped to awaken people to the realities of the prevailing politics and systems of government, and the fact that "the only road to lasting peace lies in the control by the people of their own destinies."[90]

The First World War lasted a further seventeen months. On 8 January 1918 in a speech to Congress, President Wilson included what became known as the "Fourteen Points," a statement of principles of peace that would be used as a basis for negotiations to end the First World War. When Louis Lochner wrote an account of his work with the Ford Peace Expedition and the Neutral Conference on Continuous Mediation, he felt that he and his colleagues had succeeded in formulating a programme that bore "a striking resemblance to all later programmes for peace issued, either from governmental or private sources." In Lochner's opinion, it was the Appeal to the Belligerents that "foreshadowed the famous Fourteen Points in a manner that does credit to the inexperienced group of international pacifists sitting daily around the green table of the Grand Hotel at Stockholm." Although most of the "Fourteen Points" were rejected by several of the victorious Allies when they attended the post-war peace conference, President Wilson's call for a world organization that would provide some system of collective security was incorporated into the Treaty of Versailles that was signed on 28 June 1919. The organization would later be known as the League of Nations.[91]

Julia Grace Wales left Sweden in May 1917 and returned to her teaching post at the University of Wisconsin. After spending the best part of three years working for peace on a continent embroiled in war and having questioned at times the impetus that had taken her there, she remained firm in her intention to "keep working for world organization" with the certainty that "we must ... hold firmly to that 'ultimate optimism' that can keep the work strong for years or decades or centuries if need be."[92] Some of her colleagues had seen enough of the suffering in Europe to convince them that "even the risk of going to jail for their convictions was none too great to undertake."[93] For this exceptional Canadian, however, the pen remained her chosen means of expression and Grace Wales continued to espouse and promote the cause of peace for many years to come.

CHAPTER 13

WOMEN WITH A MISSION (4)

"All the reward an artist could hope for"

MARY RITER HAMILTON, ARTIST ON THE WESTERN FRONT

The lark has ceased his singing,
The wheat is trodden low,
And in the blood-stained garden,
No more the lilies blow.

And where green poplars trembled
Stand shattered trunks instead,
And lines of small white crosses
Keep guard above the dead.[1]

"BEAUCOUP CELEBRATION EVERYWHERE": THE ARMISTICE, 1918

On 4 August 1914, the day Britain declared war on Germany, Rudyard Kipling noted in his wife's diary, "Incidentally, Armageddon begins."[2] On 11 November 1918 when the fighting ceased and silence fell across the Western Front, the realization dawned on soldiers and civilians alike that Kipling's vision of slaughter and suffering was finally at an end.

The news spread like wildfire and newspapers everywhere filled their front pages with the glad tidings. "The Day of Victory" read the headline of the London *Daily Telegraph*, which published the full terms of the Armistice agreed between the Allies and Germany, and pointed out that the German Kaiser, Wilhelm II, had fled to Holland looking "haggard and broken down."[3] In France *Le Figaro* carried the front page news that "*l'Allemagne a Capitulé: Joie Nationale*" (Germany has Surrendered: National Joy) and in the United States, the *New York Times* simply told its readers "Armistice Signed, End of the War." In Canada the news was blazoned across the front pages of newspapers from coast to coast with the *Vancouver Daily Sun* announcing "Peace! Germany Surrenders" and the *Manitoba Free Press* declaring "Huns Quit: War is Over." The *Globe* of Toronto proclaimed that "Germany Throws Up Her Hands" while in the Niagara, the *Erie Daily Times* seemed to sum things

Armistice Day. When hostilities ended on 11 November 1918 after more than four years, people in Canada were overjoyed. Here huge crowds fill the main streets in Toronto, bringing traffic to a standstill as tickertape rains down from windows above the throng. There were similar scenes across the nation. (Toronto Public Library)

up well with its banner heading, "War Has Been Won and Peace is Here: Civilization Saved."[4]

In French cities enthusiastic crowds paraded through the streets waving flags and streamers. Every window in Paris was decorated, and in restaurants, cafés and bars "smiles wreathed every face."[5] That evening the city turned on its lights after the years of darkness, and dancing re-awakened a sense of gaiety. The ladies of the famous *Folies Bergères* appeared on stage draped in the flags of the Allies, and Canadian journalist Elizabeth Montizambert, who witnessed the celebrations, described them as part of "an unforgettable time" that would "never be effaced."[6]

In London jubilation and excitement brightened a day that was "grey and chill with a threat of rain." The streets filled with office workers, servicemen, flag-waving women and happy groups of people singing songs and linking arms. Taxicabs, omnibuses and motor cars were packed with soldiers and civilians "shouting, yelling, singing snatches of songs." Crowds swept towards Buckingham Palace hoping to catch a glimpse of the king and queen, and Mary MacLeod Moore was among them. It was a day, she said, that celebrated the "greatest victory in history" over the "most dishonourable, the most cruel and the most brutal and gross of enemies."[7] Housewife Ethel Bilbrough, who had recorded in her diary every significant event in the war, wrote triumphantly, "'*the day*' has come at last!" and savoured the fact that "we have won the war, and glory, honour and victory is ours."[8] Like Paris, London switched on its lights again for that first evening of peace, symbolizing what everyone hoped would be a brighter future.[9]

The mood was similar in North American cities, and for people in the east of the continent the fact that the news arrived in the early morning did nothing to dampen the mood. Throngs of people gathered in downtown New York, thousands gathered in Ottawa to celebrate and sing "The Maple Leaf Forever," and munitions workers in Toronto paraded up Yonge Street beating tin pans and blowing whistles. As toasts were drunk to peace, a swift homecoming for the troops and absent friends and comrades, author Lucy Maud Montgomery wrote in her diary, "The world's agony has ended." She

Desolation. This scene at Courcelette, where Canadian troops were involved in bitter fighting in the autumn of 1916, was typical of the war-torn landscape found on the Western Front at the end of the war. (Library and Archives Canada, PA-000639)

had been dreaming of an end to the fighting since the day, just over a month earlier, when she had heard that Germany and Austria were "suing for peace." It was news which, as she wrote, should be written "in letters of gold."[10]

Among voluntary workers, medical staff and civilians throughout the war zone there was relief and rejoicing. At No. 3 British General Hospital in Le Tréport, QAIMNS Sister Edith Appleton commented, "Peace! Thank God for that!" while Canadian nurse Ella Mae Bongard at American Base Hospital No. 2 near Étretat recorded that "We can't believe it" and "everyone is so excited that the work is in a mix up." She and her colleagues "marched through the village streets carrying lighted torches and with our army capes inside out to show the scarlet lining." It was "hard to believe that the awful slaughter is over after four years," she concluded.[11] Canadian nurse Hannah Lister, still working near the French city of Toul, remembered how the silence that followed the ceasefire "seemed weird, after so much noise." The rest of the day was declared a holiday and there was "beaucoup celebration everywhere."[12]

Soldiers still serving on the Western Front were tired, worn down and scarcely able to comprehend that the war was over. According to Major R. Macleod, an officer of the Royal Horse Artillery who viewed the situation pragmatically, there was

> little elation at the armistice. After all it was only a cessation of hostilities. The German army was defeated but not destroyed, and fighting might start again if the peace terms could not be agreed. We were thankful for the chance of a rest.[13]

It was elated French civilians who, according to Lieutenant-Colonel Agar Adamson of the Princess Patricia's Canadian Light Infantry, encouraged his regiment to celebrate and "managed to make a good many of the men drunk." Inebriated or not, they had survived the war and, as the colonel wrote to his wife, Mabel, "It must be a relief to women all over the world with relations in the line out here to feel the casualty list is closed."[14]

The former theatres of war did not empty straightaway. There were troops still on duty and former inhabitants trying to return to towns and villages that were damaged, in ruins or even obliterated. They and many others needed help, including civilians who had been held in labour camps and were in "a shocking condition, vermin-infested, exhausted, emaciated." Victims of the Spanish influenza continued to need medical care, and newly released prisoners-of-war were returning from captivity with stories of having survived on little more than "cattle cabbage and water."[15] Ahead lay the lengthy process of repatriating soldiers, clearing the battlefields, rebuilding communities destroyed by the fighting and resettling their inhabitants.

To those whose homes had been in areas of heavy fighting on the Western Front, what had once been familiar was scarcely recognizable. Transformed over the past four years into a grim and desolate wasteland, large tracts of land had been churned up countless times and were filled with bomb craters, dead and stunted trees, detritus, abandoned equipment and the remains of those who had fought and died there. Some might say it was no place for anyone with artistic sensibilities, yet one such Canadian woman ventured there only a few months after the Armistice.

"THE FIRST NOTABLE STEP UP THE STAIRWAY OF FAME":
AN ARTIST IN THE MAKING

Early in 1919 transatlantic liners resumed their scheduled services, and in April of that year a ship left New York for France. Among its passengers was a fifty-year-old artist from western Canada, Mary Riter Hamilton, who was travelling to Europe on a mission for which she was uniquely qualified.

Born on 7 September 1868, Mary had begun her life at Teeswater, Ontario, and later moved with her homesteading parents to Clearwater in south-central Manitoba. After receiving training as a milliner and relocating to Port Arthur, she married Charles Watson Hamilton, a dry goods merchant. The couple suffered the tragedy of a stillborn son, and when Charles died unexpectedly after contracting influenza, Mary found herself a widow after only four years of marriage. She was alone, but money she inherited from her late husband gave her the means to pursue an interest she had nurtured since childhood.

Mrs. Hamilton decided to focus her time and energy on her "innate longing to paint" and moved to Winnipeg, hoping to make a career as an artist.[16] In pursuit of her aim to be completely self-supporting Mary took up decorative china painting, an art form popular at the time. She acquired a studio and offered tuition in that style of painting, at the same time attending classes for her own artistic development. Landscape and sepia drawing were two of her chosen options, which she studied with three well-known Toronto artists: E. Wyly Grier, George Agnew Reid and Mary Hiester Reid. The years from 1894 to 1901 marked a period when Canadian women were starting to make their mark in music and graphic arts, and by 1901 the aspiring artist had the time and financial means to switch from china painting to fine art. Mary Riter Hamilton knew that study at a European art school with recognized instructors was essential to her future as a painter, and in the company

No ordinary artist. Mary Riter Hamilton (1868-1954) was fifty years old when she went to paint the former battlefields of the Western Front. This photograph of her was likely taken around or soon after that time, and seems to give an indication of the focus and resolution that enabled her to complete more than three hundred paintings and drawings before she returned to Canada. (Courtesy of Ron Riter)

of two friends she decided to explore her talent in a totally new environment.

Mary and her companions left Canada on 4 August 1901 bound for Germany. In taking this step she was very much a woman of her time as she sought, along with many others, not only her rightful place in society but also the freedom to be independent. Travelling and studying overseas were becoming an accepted part of life, and European and American art schools were opening their doors to women students. The young Canadian began her formal training in Berlin with Franz Skarbina, an Italian professor at the Academy of Fine Arts. Skarbina was a notable figure in the artistic community, whose interest in the Impressionist movement was assimilated into his teachings. He vetted his students carefully, and after three months of instruction he told Mary Riter Hamilton that she had "the gift" to become an artist. She later remembered Skarbina's assurance that she would succeed, "if I kept on trying."[17]

The prospect of studying and painting amid the beauty and history of other European cities such as Paris and Venice proved irresistible. Mary undertook a sketching tour to the beautiful Italian city of canals, which lived up to her expectations, and in 1903, after some months in Holland, she decided to base herself in Paris. The French capital was enjoying its golden era, or "*Belle époque*," as a centre of artistic, musical and theatrical innovation. With thriving theatres, galleries, music halls, restaurants, *bistros* and cafés, it seemed to offer Mary Riter Hamilton "all she sought," and she soon found herself among aspiring artists from around the world.[18] Having secured accommodation and studio space in the 6th district or *arrondissement*, which was in the heart of the Left Bank and considered the quintessential Parisian neighbourhood, Mary enrolled in art classes at several private academies. Among those which accepted women was the Colarossi academy, a progressive art school popular with overseas students.

In addition to regular tuition, there were sketching assignments and Mary revisited Holland and Venice, producing several canvases that were purchased by patrons in Canada. As she studied landscape painting, portraiture and still life, she became aware of the importance of her work finding favour with academic juries, since this could result in it being shown in one of Paris's annual exhibitions. These high-profile *salons* attracted critics whose reviews could do much to raise an artist's status at home and abroad, and Mary put her capacity for concentrated hard work to good use. The long winter days were "filled with incessant labor," she said, declaring that "nine hours a day of unremitting toil" was nothing unusual.[19] The effort paid dividends, and in 1905 and 1906 her work appeared in the *Salon des Artistes Français*, an association of French painters and sculptors. As one journalist later wrote, it proved to be her "first notable step up the stairway of fame."[20]

After her success at the Paris *salon*, she returned to Canada in 1906 to show some of her work, and an exhibition in Winnipeg proved to be "one of the most worthy ever seen in this city."[21] Mary offered classes that showcased the techniques she had learned in Berlin and Paris and acquired an enthusiastic following. A further display of her work at Toronto towards the end of 1906 marked her as a rising star in the Canadian artistic community.

As pleasing as it was to gain recognition at home, the lure of Europe proved too strong and in 1907 Mary Riter Hamilton was once more on her travels. Perhaps missing the stimulus and excitement of being in and around the European cities she loved, she returned to Paris, later visiting Florence, Vienna and the Spanish Pyrenees to paint and sketch. Her work drew compliments from a British critic, E. A. Taylor, in *Studio*, a well known magazine. He praised Mary's "strong and sincere" oil paintings and the special appeal and "quiet charm" of her watercolours, where as far as he was concerned, "her greatness lies."[22]

La Ville-Lumière or "City of Lights," as Paris was known, remained Mary's base until 1911, and after having her work displayed at two more prominent *salons*, she was described as among the most successful Canadian artists in the city.[23] When she returned to Canada later that year, Mary took with her not only her growing reputation, but also the latest in ideas and techniques. She set about arranging exhibitions in eastern Canada, targeting Toronto, Ottawa and Montreal. It was a time when painters like herself who had trained in Europe were questioning traditional approaches and starting to follow new trends. Mary's shows impressed the critics, who observed in her compositions the influence of Impressionism and the fact that she was "masterful in colouring, adroit in draughtsmanship" and "poetic" in her treatment of "atmosphere and sentiment."[24] Mary borrowed elements from the Impressionist and Post-Impressionist schools, using "bright, rich colours, dramatic light and shadow, and long, loose brush strokes that conveyed rather than defined meaning."[25]

When her work was shown in Montreal it was under the patronage of Prime Minister Robert Borden, and while it was on display in Ottawa, the *Ottawa Journal* declared that Mary Riter Hamilton – as a new and exciting talent – had "a brilliant future before her."[26] Such was her success that the governor-general, the Duke of Connaught, bought three of her canvases and his daughter, Princess Patricia, invited Mary to paint at Rideau Hall. Patronage at this level was significant, especially for an artist who was keen to make Canadians aware of the exciting new work being done in Europe.

Winnipeg prepared to mount another show of Mary's paintings in May 1912, and local newspapers used the opportunity to press for an art gallery to be built in that city. The idea became a reality and the Winnipeg Museum of Fine Arts opened in December 1912, making it the first civic art gallery in Canada. By then the artist herself had decided to spend time in western Canada, where she completed a sketching tour of the Rockies. She continued to Vancouver Island and opened a studio in Victoria. A number of prominent local women supported her and her work, two of them being Margaret Hart, wife of British Columbia's chief coroner, and Rosalind Young, who was married to the provincial secretary and minister of education. Groups such as the Women's Canadian Club and the University Women's Club encouraged Mary, who valued the assistance she received because it was, in her view, "almost impossible to live in Canada by art alone." "Not only is it a matter of money," she said, "but of appreciation."[27] Yet despite such limitations, Mary was by now "an artist of reputation" and was not short of work. In addition to her students and private commissions, she accepted a proposal to paint a series of portraits of British Columbia's lieutenant-governors.[28]

"ONE MUST SEE IT ALL IN ORDER TO REALIZE JUST WHAT THIS TERRIBLE WAR HAS DONE": MARY RITER HAMILTON'S MISSION

After war broke out in 1914, Mary Riter Hamilton felt a strong desire to be of service in Europe but "the way seemed closed."[29] A group of official war artists were commissioned to record the First World War on canvas but Mary was not among them. Creating a lasting record of what was taking place on the Western Front was part of an initiative masterminded by newspaper magnate Sir Max Aitken, later Lord Beaverbrook, who was head of the Canadian War Records organization. It was initially set up to register the nation's war casualties but Aitken expanded its brief to include the preservation of war diaries of Canadian units and the engagement of photographers, cinematographers and artists to document front-line scenes for posterity. As conditions in the war zone were considered too harrowing for women, only male artists were eligible to work there and their female counterparts were limited to the home front.[30]

Aware of this restriction, Mary nevertheless applied to become a war artist in France and Belgium, believing there would be work for her at the rear of the battle areas, "the details for which can only be collected on the spot at the present time."[31] Although she had a clear sense of what she could accomplish, the fact that she was a woman and distant from the majority of selected artists living and working in the Toronto-Montreal corridor likely placed her beyond consideration. There was also the fact that her approach as an artist differed from that of others appointed, including members of the future Group of Seven.[32] Among them were Arthur Lismer, F. H. Varley and A. Y. Jackson, the latter serving with the 60th Battalion, CEF, as the first official war artist. Their inclination was not to make their work "an emotional experience" but rather to produce paintings "within the Canadian 'national' style, which they were in the process of creating." Mary Riter Hamilton, on the other hand, was motivated to paint "through her emotions instead of her training," an approach which "would generally appear to be important in the progress towards 'modernity' in Canadian art" but may, at that time, have resulted in her being "ignored."[33]

Given this situation, Mary directed her efforts into the war effort at home. She helped at fund-raising shows and events, donated paintings to patriotic organizations and undertook "whatever relief work synchronized with her fine talents."[34] This included volunteering with the Canadian Red Cross Society and the Belgian consulate, through which she learned the extent of the devastation being suffered in that country.

With the signing of the Armistice on 11 November 1918 the Amputation Club of British Columbia, a body set up to assist returning servicemen who had lost limbs in the fighting, invited Mary to go to the former battlefields to paint "that portion of the front line in France held by the Canadian Corps." This would involve recording the "actual ground over which Canadian sol-

diers struggled with the enemy" while "the terrain is still unaltered by reconstruction activities."[35] Such scenes, committed to canvas, would be included
in a new veterans' magazine entitled the *Gold Stripe*.

After the appalling numbers of casualties sustained in the war, the idea of
finding some means of remembering those who were lost became important,
and "commemoration was a universal preoccupation" in the post-war period. The *Gold Stripe* planned to include articles by veterans, photographs, art,
memorabilia and other contributions that would, as its subtitle explained,
form "a tribute to those who were killed, wounded and maimed in the Great
War."[36] Its managing editor was James Alexander Paton, a newspaper owner
and political figure in British Columbia who had served with the 72nd Battalion, CEF, on the Western Front.

Mary's Riter Hamilton's commission had to be completed before the task
of clearing and rebuilding the ruined battlefield areas began in earnest. She
knew she had a short time to prepare and that she would be working as an
independent artist, albeit with backing from official quarters. Her exclusion
as an official war artist had, in fact, freed her from any restrictions and she
could act as she saw fit. Mary had a good understanding of the kind of environment in which she would have to work, yet she seemed to relish not
only the chance to portray something important but also to take on a challenge that promised to be remarkable.

By mid-March 1919 Mary was crossing Canada by train on her way to
New York with no idea of when she would return. She admitted to a friend
that she felt "too weary to think" but began to revive by the time she reached
Ottawa, where she had to tackle further bureaucracy and acquire a passport,
permission to visit the battlefield areas and letters of introduction to Canadian military personnel in Europe.[37] At Rideau Hall she was invited to tea
with the governor-general, the Duke of Devonshire, who was interested to
learn of her plans.

At New York, Mary's point of transatlantic departure, she knew she would
have "ten days there – they [the U.S. Immigration Department] demand it,"
she wrote.[38] Once her ship sailed the sea crossing to France went smoothly,
and on arrival at Le Havre Mary stepped ashore armed with an official note
sanctioning her mission and a letter of introduction to a Canadian liaison
officer, Lieutenant-Colonel G. Grassie Archibald. He would smooth her way
and put her in touch with Lieutenant-General Sir Arthur Currie, commander-in-chief of the Canadian forces, who was still in France.

Before travelling to the battlefields Mary stopped in Paris, where she could
revisit old haunts and old friends. She was glad to be back in the country

where she had found recognition as an artist, and anticipated there would be interest in her project as well as a "personal and general appreciation for good work." This meant a lot to her, since she believed it was "indispensable" to have "a really intelligent" understanding of "what craftsmanship and art mean."[39]

From Paris Mary moved on to an area that had been an active part of the war zone. She found lodgings near Arras in the Pas-de-Calais region, where a refugee family gave her their attic "full of shell holes," which, they said, "wasn't fit for a dog." Despite its drawbacks Mary succeeded in making her garret "the best I can" and decided it was "a godsend" as a place to work.[40] Despite the cold spring weather she set off to visit places where Canadians had fought: the Ypres Salient, the Somme, Vimy Ridge, Passchendaele and the communities liberated in the last months of the war. Mary described how, when she first saw Vimy Ridge, scene of Canada's notable victory in April 1917,

> snow and sleet were falling, and I was able to realize what the soldiers had suffered. If as you and others tell me, there is something of the suffering and heroism of the war in my pictures it is because at that moment the spirit of those who fought and died seemed to linger in the air. Every splintered tree and scarred clod spoke of their sacrifice.[41]

As she explained, "I was glad to have seen it under hard conditions." It was important "to get the spirit of it," she said, yet when she tried to put her feelings into words she found it "quite impossible … to give you my impression simply because I am too deeply impressed."[42]

By 9 June 1919, with the help of military transport, Mary had reached Camblain l'Abbé, where she stayed at a Canadian camp that was due to close, and met General Currie. From there she retraced her steps to the Vimy Ridge area and, aware that she needed to be as self-sufficient as possible, managed to reach it without any offer of transport. There was a village at the foot of the ridge where she found shelter in huts that had been built by the Canadians, but it was clearly not a place where she could stay for long owing to the lack of readily available food supplies and other facilities. Despite the primitive living conditions she wrote to a friend that "I wish I could transport you here, for one must see it all in order to realize just what this terrible war has done." That very realization made her task "so tense owing to the nature of it," she explained, "and besides I have had such great distances to go" to reach the locations she wanted to sketch and paint.[43]

A painter at work. Mary Riter Hamilton is seen here at her easel, near Souchez, France, and accompanied by two dogs. During her time overseas, she travelled widely throughout the Western Front, portraying different aspects of the former war zone as well as its post-war regeneration. (Courtesy of Ron Riter)

Mary lived in huts or other temporary accommodation for varying periods and came to terms with the fact that she had taken on a rough, uncertain way of life. She also had to deal with shortages of money and the mail service from Canada, which was still very slow. She was as pragmatic and resourceful as she could be, but as time went by she felt further removed from everyday life and wrote fewer letters. Driven by a sense of urgency that impelled her from one place to another in search of the work she had to do, the hard-working artist was interviewed by a journalist who described her practice of painting quickly and with intensity, stopping only to prepare fresh paint or to eat, almost "with the air of one who resented the interruption."[44] Photographs taken at the time show Mary at her easel in different locations accompanied by one, sometimes two, dogs, who clearly became her companions and brightened what was an otherwise solitary existence.

As Canadian troops continued to be withdrawn from France, Mary Riter Hamilton was increasingly left to her own devices and when she became ill after "trying to do too much knowing my time is short," she was taken in by a kind woman who lived in a chateau near Arras.[45] Following her recovery, Mary was given access to a former army hut along with permission to move it "where I like." "It is mighty cold and uncomfortable," she told a writer for the *Gold Stripe*, "but I intend remaining until I finish the work I came here to do."[46] When she was ready to transfer to a new location, "20 Chinamen" appeared and picked up her hut "just as it stood," she said, "and carried it over."[47] According to Mary there were "about eighty thousand Chinese with the British," undertaking work they had been contracted to do.[48]

The Chinese men were mainly poor farmers from two communities in the eastern Shandong province, many of whom had been enticed to sign a three-year work contract. They had started to arrive on the Western Front in 1917, brought there to tackle demolition work, clearing the battlefields, and other essential but arduous jobs. Via the YMCA there were personnel from China who undertook mission work and helped the labourers with letters, civil rights and practical aspects of their lives in Europe.

The camps that housed these workers consisted mainly of large Nissen huts that could accommodate up to 500 men, but many also slept outside on cold, wet ground and were prone to respiratory diseases.[49] Seeing the conditions they faced daily, Mary Riter Hamilton gained an appreciation of the work they took on, which included finding and removing unexploded shells and mines; clearing roads, canals and other waterways; and above all, recovering and burying human remains. She saw for herself the reality of such risky and taxing tasks, which needed no small amount of courage. There were times when Mary needed it herself, citing the occasion when she was painting a blighted tree at St. Julien in Belgium and "narrowly escaped being blown to bits by a pile of ammunition recently taken from the cleared ground." This and similar dangers were events she appeared to regard as "merely a part of the day's work."[50]

"OPPRESSED BY THE VAST, LEVEL PLAIN OF DEATH": THE REALITY OF THE WESTERN FRONT IN 1919

The civilian population, who had begun to return to war-torn areas after the Armistice, soon encountered the workers from China. Although relations between the two groups were satisfactory at first, things started to change noticeably after the withdrawal of British and Canadian troops during 1919 led to a relaxation of discipline. Homesickness understandably affected the Chinese men, not to mention the hazardous and deeply disturbing nature of what they were required to do. Those Belgians who were trying to rebuild the village of Dickebusch, south west of Ypres, reported that their efforts were hampered by "front wreckers and especially the Chinese," who "ran away from their camps and easily found guns and grenades."[51] Stories, even if hearsay, began to circulate and eyewitness reports asserted that "armed gangs of

Chinese wandered the area," inspiring "more fear than joy." Belgian civilian Gabriella Vanpeteghem maintained that they knew how to fire weapons and that during the day "people were even afraid to go outdoors." In the same area at the former village of Zillebeke, where everything "had been shot to pieces" and food had to be "cooked with water taken from shell holes," a local man, Louis Garrein, reported that some of the Chinese were "dangerous lads. At night they burgled the people living in wooden huts."[52]

The French city of Arras was another troubled area populated by "hooligans," where shots could sometimes be heard after dark. Mary Riter Hamilton came to know of such places, and when one friend from Paris visited she expressed shock at "the nightmare perils of a woman alone in such a situation."[53] There is no doubt that many of those who found themselves in parts of the former war zone were deeply affected by their situation in one way or another. The Chinese labourers had been promised a quick return home but were retained far longer to continue their unenviable work, and as one American missionary who was present at the time admitted, "their lot has been intolerable." Considering that they daily faced danger, deprivation, hostility and illness on a strange continent, they still managed to do what was asked of them.[54]

In this climate of tension and uncertainty Mary Riter Hamilton toiled long and hard to complete her work, taking minimal time off to collect mail and supplies in Paris. She described in letters how she had lost weight, how her accommodation remained tenuous and how she was experiencing financial shortages. Although she felt a sense of isolation she was, in actual fact, far from being alone as a woman in the former war zone. There were others who had come in search of missing husbands in the hope they might still be alive or who desired to know where a loved one had been killed, and some who simply wished to see for themselves what the war zone was like. Nor was Mary the only artist there; an Australian, Evelyn Chapman, was also working in the region and Olive Mudie-Cook, a British artist, painted the Somme River Valley in 1919. Evelyn Chapman had something in common with Mary Riter Hamilton in that their subject matter covered not just the destruction wrought by the war, but also the renewal of everyday life that followed it.[55]

Mary may also have been aware that in 1919 there were several hundred British women employed in the former battlefield areas as drivers to those handling the general clearance and reconstruction work.[56] However, the solitary nature of Mary's mission and her need to go wherever there were scenes of relevance compelled her to continue her "intensely interesting" peripatetic life, as she referred to it. She was experiencing "hardships such as no-

Sanctuary Wood. Mary Riter Hamilton spent a good deal of time working in the former Ypres Salient. This painting shows woodland that was the scene of fighting in 1915 and 1917 and bordered high ground close to Ypres. It was completed by Mary Riter Hamilton in 1920. (Oil on plywood. Library and Archives Canada, C-104742)

one could imagine while away from all help and living among the peasants, walking many miles, doing without food."[57] Others might have given up, but Mary Riter Hamilton had no intention of doing so "until I finish the work I came here to do."[58] As she explained,

> I made up my mind that where our men went under so much more dreadful conditions I could go, and I am very proud to have been able even in a small way to commemorate the deeds of my country men, and especially if possible to lend a helping hand to the poor fellows like those of the Amputation Club who will be long, long sufferers from the war."[59]

In the desolate landscape, Mary found a great deal of subject matter. The extent of it becomes clearer through accounts such as that of Nursing Sister Mabel Clint, who went to the battlefield areas of the Ypres Salient in March

Dug-out on the Somme. In 1919 Mary Riter Hamilton produced this scene of a dug-out on the former Somme battlefield in France, surrounded by the damage and detritus of war. (Oil on cardboard. Library and Archives Canada, C-104800)

1919. She mentioned seeing "rusty guns, trenches full of water, and debris of war that had not yet been touched," and refugees "standing in silent misery about a few yards of broken ground." Amid the wreckage and destruction, Mabel also described skeletons of horses, rusting weapons, roads that broke down into "squelchy mud" and graveyard after graveyard. After a while she "became so oppressed by the vast, level plain of death, that it seemed hard to believe that any had escaped alive."[60] Brigadier-General Edward Morrison of the Canadian Field Artillery further elaborated on what a battlefield looked like after the Canadians had been in action at the St Eloi craters in 1916. He described how "every inch" of the ground had been

> churned up by shell fire until you had to clamber over hillocks of mud mixed with debris, abandoned accoutrements, pieces of soldiers, busted sandbags – here a tangle of scrap iron that might be an old sewing machine

Mount St. Eloi. Canadian troops were involved in a battle here in 1916, just south of Ypres, and Mary Riter Hamilton painted the place in 1919-1920. The graveyard below the high ground gives an indication of the casualties suffered, and today the nearby Ridge Wood Commonwealth War Graves Commission cemetery contains 595 graves. (Oil on plywood. Library and Archives Canada, C-101318)

but was all that was left of a motor lorry, – there a broken windowframe – which was all that remained to show where a brick house had been.[61]

After another two years of war, such remains would have suffered further disturbance and destruction, contributing to the overall desolation of the region by 1919.

Those who worked for the Imperial (later the Commonwealth) War Graves Commission, which had the enormous task of setting up cemeteries and arranging for the proper burial and marking of the thousands of war dead, also saw similar scenes. Among them was the British architect Sir Edwin Lutyens, who felt deeply what he described as "the obliteration of all human endeavour and achievement." To him it was "beyond imagination and all so inexplicable that it makes writing difficult." As he embarked on the work of designing a memorial that would form part of each new cemetery, he could only conclude that "what humanity can endure and suffer is beyond belief."[62]

Mary Riter Hamilton was constantly surrounded by such sights, evidence of the shocking reality of what soldiers had endured while they lived and fought in Kipling's Armageddon. The *Gold Stripe* paid tribute to her work, as follows: "The service being done to Canada and to the memory of the men who met death on the battlefield, by the work which is being carried out by this artist under great difficulties, is very great."[63]

"THE MOST IMPRESSIVE RECORD THAT HAS BEEN MADE OF THE AFTERMATH OF THE WAR": RECOGNITION AND REWARD

As Mary began to send canvases to Canada for exhibits in Vancouver and Victoria, people were able to see the Western Front as she portrayed it. The dates and locations of her compositions during the period 1919 to 1921 are in themselves a record of the areas where she painted. In 1919 she worked mainly in the three main battlefield areas mentioned earlier – the Ypres Salient, Vimy Ridge and the Somme – and the area around Cambrai. She continued her work into the following year, revisiting the Somme to concentrate in more detail on that area before moving to the Ypres area and the Flanders countryside. She returned to those locations in 1921 to extend her range of subject matter.

Beyond the landscape of war, Mary also depicted particular features she came across – trenches, pill boxes, gun-pits, observation posts, mine craters, abandoned vehicles and artillery, and plank roads constructed by the Canadians as a result of their pioneer past. A number of Mary's canvases also

Petit Vimy and Vimy village from the Lens-Arras Road. On 9 April 1917 Vimy Ridge was the scene of an outstanding Canadian victory, and this scene shows the nearby village and surrounding terrain. It was painted in 1919, probably soon after Mary Riter Hamilton arrived on the Western Front. (Oil on canvas. Library and Archives Canada, C-105607)

portrayed isolated graves and larger graveyards as they existed before the Imperial War Graves Commission built its cemeteries. She also depicted scenes in ruined towns and villages, aspects of the work of clearing the battlefields and specific events such as market day amid the ruins of Ypres or Cambrai, the first post-war barge on a river, and people walking through previously dangerous areas which had been made safe. What Mary Riter Hamilton conveyed in such compositions was not just the destruction wrought, but a sense of hope and regeneration after the years of annihilation.

At times the artist felt the need to leave the war zone. She took time away from her easel to help the Canadian Red Cross deliver food to children in some of the damaged French villages and to work at a studio in Paris arranged for her by friends. There she was able to reconnect with the creative life of the city and produce etchings, pastels or oil compositions from some of her drawings. She possessed what was described as an "unusual versatility," and the "freedom of treatment" of her subject matter revealed a "spiritual quality that conveys the artist's feelings."[64]

Mary Riter Hamilton was accomplishing her mission, but its arduous nature was taking its toll. Her living conditions and "an almost desperate penchant for overwork" meant that by 1920 her health was suffering.[65] It was clear that she could no longer continue without rest and better nutrition. Her situation was not helped by the fact that she was experiencing further "ongoing aggravation over money" which made it difficult to purchase supplies and pay for accommodation.[66] Such fluctuations in fortune meant that at one point Mary was forced to find shelter with the YMCA at Cambrai, whilst a little later she had the means to stay at a comfortable hotel at Ypres, which by her own admittance was "costing me far too much" but which lifted her spirits after a period of austerity.[67] The worry, however, remained that her finances would again become "dangerously low" and insufficient for her needs.[68]

As 1920 gave way to 1921, Mary was to be found in Brussels, where she was forced to spend time after suffering rheumatism. To pay for her artist's materials she had been going without comforts of any kind, yet once she felt better and her energy returned, her output continued apace. By the time she finished all the work she wanted to do, Mary Riter Hamilton would have completed some 350 works of art consisting of sketches in charcoal, pencil and chalk, as well as oil and watercolour paintings on cardboard, plywood and canvas.

Reward for such dedication was not long in coming, and in 1922 Mary was delighted to learn that her battlefield paintings were to be exhibited in the foyer of the Paris Opera House. The *montage* was being organized to commemorate the spring 1918 Allied offensive and focus on the successful Allied operations in the Somme region. At a special ceremony the artist received the award of *Les Palmes Académiques* or Order of Academic Palms.[69] Apart from the *Légion d'Honneur*, this was the highest distinction that France had to give, and Mary was the only Canadian to be thus honoured.[70] It was well-deserved acknowledgment of her bravery and dedication as an artist who had worked in some of the most dangerous areas of the Western Front.

"I seem to have made good," Mary wrote modestly to her friend Margaret Hart, but in reality this accolade was a significant milestone in her career.[71] The exhibit attracted attention internationally and led to a meeting with an

American journalist, Frederick G. Falla, who interviewed Mary at her Paris studio in the summer of 1922. Falla described her as follows:

> Among the women who have most enduringly written their name on the history of the war, there are few whose record is likely to last longer or stir more deeply the imagination of future generations than the one created by Mary Riter Hamilton.[72]

For many bereaved families, Falla highlighted the fact that Mary's paintings would provide them with "their only vision of that corner of the world on which their loved ones looked for the last time." He also confirmed that her collection of battlefield paintings was considered by French art critics to be "the most impressive record that has been made of the aftermath of the war."[73]

There was further recognition, with the showing of Mary's work at the *Société Nationale des Beaux-Arts* and the *Société des Artistes* in Paris, while at Amiens her paintings were prominent in an exhibit to raise funds for a memorial in that area. With buyers purchasing some of her compositions, Mary's financial worries receded temporarily only to return a few months later. She continued to walk a tightrope, below which lay the spectre of penury, and she admitted that she "never could have had the courage" to complete her mission, "had I not had an ideal."[74]

Troubled with continuing health problems, including a loss of sight in one eye, Mary refused to feel downcast and thanks to the generous support of friends, she was able to move into a small attic in Paris, where she admitted it was "wonderful to have a fire and hot water."[75] Despite her challenges, one thing had become clear to her. "I am not selling pictures though I do need the money," she told one of her contacts in Victoria, for to do so would seem "like betraying a sacred trust."[76]

Mary Riter Hamilton returned to Canada in 1926, having decided to donate the bulk of her work to the Public Archives of Canada. This decision did not come without a cost, but despite her financial difficulties and an offer from a potential buyer in Montreal to purchase all her Western Front art, Mary kept her resolve. "It is," she explained, "my great wish to give this collection of pictures to the Canadian Government, if it be deemed worthy of acceptance." She added only the proviso that the government should

> take complete charge of them, give them a permanent home, protect the rights of reproduction, and use them in every possible way for the benefit of the war veterans, their dependants and the dependants of those who died.[77]

In a letter to Arthur Doughty, the Dominion Archivist, under whose care her work would be lodged, Mary said that the "great facts of the war would remain, and I could add nothing but my pictures to the essential tragedy and meaning of it all." She expressed her belief that if she had not recorded what she had seen, "something was in danger of being lost."[78] As a result, Mary Riter Hamilton's paintings and drawings, which were born of her talent, dedication and a depth of feeling for what she experienced, have been preserved for posterity. As Mary herself said, "I know that anything of worth or anything of beauty which may be found in the pictures themselves reflects only dimly the visions which came then; the visions which came from the spirit of the men themselves."[79]

Mary knew she had completed her work in France and Belgium not a moment too soon. The former Western Front underwent the changes she had foreseen, with new homes, buildings and roads taking shape along with cemeteries erected by the Imperial War Graves Commission. Under the direction of Sir Fabian Ware and with the help of three of the most eminent architects of the day – Sir Edwin Lutyens, Sir Herbert Baker and Sir Reginald Blomfield – the job of designing and building them was under way by the summer of 1921. Each cemetery was modelled on a plan that consisted of a walled enclosure with uniform headstones in a garden setting, and integral to each one was a Cross of Sacrifice designed by Blomfield representing the faith of the majority, and a Stone of Remembrance created by Lutyens to represent those of all faiths, or of none.

In all, 1,665 cemeteries were constructed in France and 385 in Belgium but because of the nature of the fighting on ground that had been taken and retaken by both sides, many of the dead had no known grave. Their names were recorded on memorials to the missing: 54,896 British and Commonwealth soldiers who were lost in the Ypres Salient before 15 August 1917; 73,412 troops missing on the Somme; and 34,888 officers and men missing at Ypres between 16 August 1917 and the end of the war. In addition, a beautiful memorial on Vimy Ridge lists the names of some 11,160 Canadian soldiers who died in France and have no known grave.

The ravaged landscape and war damage that Mary Riter Hamilton recorded have long disappeared, but those who visit the battlefield areas today continue to be moved by the cemeteries, memorials and remains of places where so many men suffered, endured and perished. Mary's work in France and Belgium has arguably received more attention than all that she accomplished during the rest of her career. Behind it is a story of extraordinary courage, commitment and self-sacrifice that earned her unique status as a woman artist and made her bequest to what is now Library and Archives Canada a national treasure in perpetuity.

What Mary achieved was best summed up by her as follows: "To have been able to preserve some memory of what this consecrated corner of the world looked like after the storm is past, is a great privilege and all the reward an artist could hope for."[80] The result is a remarkable and moving record of the places where Canada's troops fought and died more than one hundred years ago. It is also a poignant reminder of the price that has been paid by Canadians to preserve liberty and their "fair, dear land," their "true north, strong and free."[81]

CHAPTER 14

Epilogue

Reflection, Renewal, Repatriation and Remembrance

> *For Death goes to and fro upon the earth –*
> *It follows in the wake of marching men;*
> *And we who knew the olden peace and mirth,*
> *Will never, never, know the same again.*
> *The scented wind across the boughs of May*
> *Brings but the memory of some yesterday.*[1]

"WE SEEM TO HAVE PASSED THROUGH DANTE'S INFERNO":
THE AFTERMATH

The First World War resulted in between 15 and 19 million deaths and some 23 million wounded.[2] It also led to economic and political collapse, the fall of several monarchies and the end of an established order and way of life. In its wake, many people felt world-weary, "woebegone and maimed," by a life-changing event they would never forget.[3] Soldiers who had survived the trenches, nurses who had cared for countless sick and damaged men, refugees who had lost their homes and communities, civilians who had devoted themselves to the war effort – all were left to contemplate the tragedy of 1914 to 1918, and to mourn the dead of a generation.

Among those who had voiced deep concerns at the outset was British pacifist Lady Ottoline Morrell. She felt it had been "almost too ghastly to have lived through," and acknowledged that "we seemed to have passed through the portal of Dante's Inferno." Remembering that in 1914 she had been told that "modern warfare was so terrible that it could not go on beyond a few weeks," what followed had seemed like a continuing nightmare.[4] In Canada Lucy Maud Montgomery pondered the fact that although "the world's agony has ended," there remained the all-important question of what kind of legacy would emerge from so much death and destruction.[5]

In London journalist Mary MacLeod Moore used her *Saturday Night* column to write on the subject and the terrible price paid in terms of lives. In the light of that sacrifice, it was understandable that people needed to give

"Old Bill" returns to the Western Front. In the months following the Armistice, people began visiting the battlefields. Here the famous First World War cartoonist Captain Bruce Bairnsfather depicts his main character, "Old Bill," walking the ground with his wife. The characteristic humour shines through, just as it did during the war. (From "Fragments from France" No. 1. by permission of Tonie and Valmai Holt)

meaning to it and as far as Mary was concerned, all those in the Allied countries who had given their lives were "part of the fabric of a new and better and nobler world." They had died not just for victory, but also to

> give the world new standards, or rather to revive the old, and to make the world cleaner and better. If Peace means all this, either now or as the nations slowly grow, then we may well rejoice. But we have suffered too much and too long to greet Peace with wild gaiety. These men and boys who have passed into another life while this was still so sweet have gained us the victory. We owe it to them to use well the freedom they won.[6]

In similar vein Canadian suffragette and social reformer Nellie McClung, who felt that the "stern old world has pounded many lessons into proud young hearts," hoped that the "clear, sacrificial fire" of war "may have purified us, burned away the dross, and prepared us for simpler living and simpler pleasures."[7] Nursing Sister Constance Bruce asked the question, "Can anything good come out of this war?" She decided that the answer would come with the passing of time, "when, from the fields of death there spring fair flowers, which free-born children will gather with joy. Then those who have passed will smile."[8]

In January 1919 politicians and dignitaries gathered at Versailles near Paris for the conference that would officially end the war. Some 66,000 Canadians had lost their lives and almost 173,000 had been wounded during the conflict, and the nation's record on the battlefield secured it a place at the peace table.[9] Prime Minister Sir Robert Borden was among those in attendance and he invited the commanding officer of the Canadian Corps, Lieutenant-General Sir Arthur Currie, to be present as an observer. Despite having to watch over his wife, Lucy, who contracted the influenza virus, Sir Arthur was able, on behalf of all Canadian troops, to share in the sense of pride at Canada's inclusion as a separate signatory to the peace treaty. The First World War, for a nation that had now been recognized as a "distinct entity within the British Empire," would come to be regarded by many as Canada's coming of age.[10]

It was a time for giving thanks and acknowledging debts of gratitude. The Belgians were anxious to recognize the help they had received and when Canadian troops passed through Belgian territory on their way to and from tours of duty with the Allied occupation force in Germany, church bells rang, people gathered in the streets to cheer them and they were shown "that kindliness and hospitality that are the outstanding characteristics of the Belgians."[11] At the end of January 1919 the burgomaster of Liège was "anxious to pay homage to the Canadians" and asked if they would stage a military parade in his city. It took place on 4 February 1919, accompanied by massed bands and watched by enthusiastic crowds who waved them along to shouts of "*Vive les Canadiens.*"[12]

As post-war demobilization proceeded, the early months of peace were a time for romance. For some, relationships begun before the war could finally be resumed. For others, liaisons that had started during the war now came to fruition, and Nursing Sister Ethel Upton commented that "scores of our nurses are marrying every week."[13] Couples who had survived the odds of a husband being killed in action could contemplate a future together, and this was the case for Captain Kenneth Edmiston of the 19th Alberta Dragoons and his wife, Mary, who had followed her fiancé to England in 1914. Having married in January 1915 at All Saints parish church, Netheravon, Wiltshire, Kenneth crossed to France with his unit a month later, while Mary remained in Britain. The pair were reunited in March 1919.[14]

A wartime wedding. The marriage of Lieutenant Kenneth Edmiston of the 19th Alberta Dragoons and Miss Mary Allen of Ottawa took place at the parish church of All Saints, Netheravon, Wiltshire, on 3 January 1915. It was attended by all ranks of the regiment and Edmiston's troop formed a traditional guard of honour with swords. (*The War Pictorial,* 1915)

For another couple, the end of the war brought a reunion and a belated and rather unusual honeymoon. Captain William (Bill) Godfrey, a chaplain in the 236th Infantry Battalion, CEF, invited his wife, Clementina, to join him in Belgium. They had not seen one another for more than two years and in March 1919 they met again in Brussels. In the interim Clementina had done war work at home, including six months at Halifax helping in a huge relief operation after the tragic explosion of 6 December 1917 – the result of a collision between two ships carrying munitions – that destroyed a large part of the city. The Godfreys "stayed in a chateau in the village of Overyssche near the Belgian capital for three weeks," recalled Clementina, "before taking the train trip to Lens, Vimy and Arras." From those places they went on "walking tours of the battlefield areas," and she admitted that "I would not have missed the trip over there for anything. Not many couples have a 'honeymoon' like that."[15] While her husband completed his service as chaplain to soldiers who were patients at No. 12 Canadian General Hospital at Bramshott in Surrey, Clementina remained with him. In July 1919 the two were finally able to return to Sackville, New Brunswick, where they had married in December 1916.

In all, some 253,000 Canadian soldiers were repatriated together with 50,000 dependents.[16] Canadian nurses and war workers were gradually released from duty, among them United States Army Nurse Corps nurses Ella Mae Bongard and Hannah Lister, who left France early in 1919 and described their delight on reaching the United States. Hannah's spirits lifted at the sight of Staten Island, after which "finally Old Liberty came into view," she wrote in her diary, looking forward to seeing her family in Canada.[17] French Flag Nursing Corps nurse Agnes Warner arrived at New York at the end of February 1919 together with another colleague, Helen McMurrich. Both had received awards for their war service, including the *Croix de Guerre*, and when the two women reached their home town of Saint John, New Brunswick, it was to a warm welcome. At a reception in her honour Agnes told those present that it had been "a great privilege to do her part."[18]

Canadian hospitals in France began to wind down, and it was May 1919 when Nursing Sisters Laura Holland and Mildred Forbes were discharged from the Canadian Forestry Corps Hospital in the Jura mountains. They had nursed many men during the influenza epidemic and enjoyed some leave on the French Riviera, where the "warm sunny days & brightness" were a welcome contrast to "mud and living more & less uncomfortably for over three years."[19] Around the same time No. 3 Canadian General Hospital finally closed its doors, and Mabel Clint was among the nurses who sailed for home with a convoy of convalescent men on the SS *Megantic*. As the ship entered the Gulf of St. Lawrence in early June 1919, "never had the River looked so beautiful," she commented, but it proved to be an eventful homecoming. The *Megantic* ran over some submerged ice and started to list, but prompt action ensured no significant damage was sustained. Its safe arrival at Quebec City marked the end of overseas service for Mabel and the other passengers, whose feelings at seeing their homeland again were hard to put into words.[20]

Mabel Adamson closed the Belgian Canal Boat Fund in the spring of 1919. King Albert of the Belgians conferred upon her the *Médaille de la Reine Elisabeth* (Queen Elisabeth Medal) in recognition of "the kind and valuable assistance you have personally given to the Belgian Refugees and the Belgian soldiers during the war."[21] Accompanied by her younger son, Anthony, Mabel returned to Canada preceded by her husband, Lieutenant-Colonel Agar Adamson. She missed seeing the colonel and the rest of the PPCLI parading through the streets of Ottawa on a bright, sunny March day, but somewhere in the welcoming crowds was socialite Ethel Chadwick. Her war years had been spent working and fund-raising for the CRCS, the National

Committee of Women for Patriotic Service and other worthy causes. As she noted in her diary, the Princess Pats "came back but not the six hundred" who had left in 1914. There were just thirty-nine men left from the original unit, and as far as Ethel was concerned their dead comrades were "not lost though, but living in imperishable time, in Canada's story. Ideals for the generation to come."[22]

The work of the CRCS Information Bureau was, by its very nature, prolonged by the needs of Canada's servicemen and their families. Lady Julia Drummond and her dedicated team remained at their desks until every task was signed off, making it the late summer of 1919 before Julia reached Montreal. It was a bittersweet homecoming, no doubt assuaged by the prospect of seeing her four-year-old grandson and taking up the reins of the busy life she had left behind nearly five years earlier.

"TRIFLES AT HOME ARE GOING TO SEEM VERY PETTY": ADJUSTING TO A NEW WORLD

After the gigantic military struggle that had at times seemed overwhelming, adjustment to everyday life was not easy. During her tenure as Matron of No. 2 Canadian CCS in France, Mildred Forbes had foreseen problems. "I'm afraid many of us are going to be changed so much that ordinary existence is going to be very trying," she wrote. "We have seen such tremendous things going on that trifles at home are going to seem very petty."[23] Significantly for women, the past four years of conflict had been a time when, in the words of social reformer Nellie McClung, they had been "made to feel their responsibility" and had contributed effectively to the war effort by being "organized in some way."[24] Another writer and activist, Mrs. Alec Tweedie, took the view that thanks to the war "the world has discovered women and women have found themselves."[25] Force of circumstances had "liberated many women from their own hearth," enabling them to taste greater independence, broaden their horizons and play a vital part at home and overseas. They could also take pride in the fact that, as British Prime Minister David Lloyd George stated, it was "the women of the Allied nations who made victory possible."[26]

What they had seen and experienced had changed many of them, leaving them with recollections that inevitably intruded. In the case of VAD Frances Cluett, she knew that "some of the misery" she had witnessed would "ever live in my memory" and that "I shall always have sad sights in my eyes."[27] When she reflected on her wartime service, Mildred Forbes could not forget those who had made the supreme sacrifice, while Grace Morris, who had spent time in England and suffered the loss of one of her brothers, felt unsure about how to pick up the threads of her life again. For her, there was a sense of "not belonging to a world that had changed too much."[28]

Grace and those like her had to navigate their way in what felt like new and unfamiliar conditions. While Canada re-evaluated its position after its hardest four years since nationhood, there was a sense of bleakness to life as families mourned their lost loved ones. At the same time the war had cut across an established way of life, mobilizing the nation's women and introducing them to new and fulfilling roles. It had contributed to the speeding up of certain trends such as the movement towards women's suffrage, the most notable impact on their lives coming when many of them were granted the federal franchise on 24 May 1918.[29] Yet despite such changes, there was no fundamental transformation of their position in society, and the extent to which the war could be said to have been a catalyst for greater gender equality was debatable. Although gains were modest overall, a widespread desire for greater freedom and independence on the part of a few daring young women would lead to the emergence of the so-called "flappers" of the 1920s, who expressed themselves more unconventionally through fashion, smoking in public and drinking alcohol at parties.[30]

In terms of employment, women's work in a variety of jobs during the war had contributed significantly to the functioning of Canadian society. Those wartime efforts, however, did not change the established system and after hostilities ended women were encouraged, or forced, to give way to ex-servicemen seeking work. Although they lost many of the economic gains they had made, changes in attitudes towards single working women continued, as did a slow trend towards the pursuit of secondary education on the part of those who were unskilled. And for women who had already completed further education, a range of new opportunities and career paths made it possible for them to change direction or build on their wartime work experience. It was therefore no accident that the First World War generation of Canadian women numbered some who later reached positions of note.

With the arrival of the 1930s and the conditions of the Depression, the outlook for women was destined to suffer a setback. Wages fell dramatically and priority in terms of jobs was given to men with families to support. The emphasis during those challenging years was on women resuming and maintaining their traditional place in the home, and it would take another war for society to achieve further progress in lessening discrimination and re-evaluating female roles.[31]

"IN THE COMPANY OF SISTERS": POST-WAR LIVES

Among the hard-working heroines whose experiences have featured in this book, the outstanding war record of Canada's nurses gave their profession a tremendous boost. It was honoured in October 1919 at a service in St Paul's Church, Bloor Street East, Toronto, an occasion held in "loving commemoration of The Nursing Sisters of the Canadian Army Medical Corps who died in that service during the Great War, and of Nursing Sister Edith Cavell who was put to death by the enemy at Brussels, October 12th 1915."[32]

Matron-in-Chief Margaret Macdonald, as the first woman in the British Empire to hold that rank, emerged as a leader in the field of military nursing. She was awarded the Florence Nightingale medal, the highest international distinction a nurse can achieve, for "exceptional courage and devotion to the wounded, sick or disabled or to civilian victims of a conflict or disaster."[33] She assisted in the reorganization of the CAMC under its new title, the Royal Canadian Army Medical Corps, and in 1920 she became honorary president of a new body, the Overseas Nursing Sisters Association of Canada. In August 1926 Margaret Macdonald was at the Hall of Honour of the Parliament buildings in Ottawa to unveil the memorial dedicated to the nurses of Canada who served and gave their lives in the First World War. After a long and distinguished career, she retired to her home town of Bailey's Brook, Nova Scotia, where she died on 7 September 1948 at the age of seventy-five.

Matron Ethel B. Ridley, who had discharged the responsible position of Principal Matron in charge of Canadian nurses in France, was made a Companion of the Order of the British Empire and awarded the Royal Red Cross, 1st Class. Others who also received that award were Nursing Sister Edith Hegan, who served at the Anglo-Russian Hospital, Assistant Matron Sophie Hoerner and her superior Matron Katherine MacLatchy of No. 3 Canadian General Hospital, and Nursing Sister Mildred Forbes. The Royal Red Cross, 2nd Class, was awarded to Nursing Sisters May Bastedo, Mabel Clint, Helen Fowlds, Laura Gamble, Laura Holland and Florence Hunter. In all, a total of 317 Royal Red Cross awards were made to Canadian nurses during the First World War.

Sophie Hoerner returned to Canada at the end of 1918. She went back to Saranac Lake in New York state, where she had worked before the war, and in 1919 she married Dr. James W. Price, a physician with a practice in the town. Sophie spent the rest of her life there and died in 1961, aged eighty-five. Katherine MacLatchy went home to Grand Pré in Nova Scotia, and later served as Matron of Cogswell Street Military Hospital and Camp Hill Hospital, Halifax. She was a member of the Graduate Nurses' Association of Nova

Scotia until 1932, and served as honorary president in 1922. MacLatchy, who remained single, was ninety-five when she died in 1969.

Mabel Clint resumed her nursing career and was an advocate for better working conditions in her profession. She became executive secretary and registrar of the Association of Registered Nurses of the Province of Quebec, a post she held until 1929. As someone who enjoyed writing, she produced articles, a novel and an account of her First World War service. Mabel died on 17 March 1939 at Sainte-Anne-de-Bellevue, where she had been a patient at the local military hospital for several months. According to a friend, Mabel's passing followed a heart attack which she suffered on reading the news of Germany's invasion of Czechoslovakia. For some of those who had lived through the First World War, the spectre of another conflict with the old adversary was too much to bear.

Following her posting to Salonika, Laura Gamble, who was twice mentioned in despatches before receiving her Royal Red Cross, was recalled to Canada as Matron of St. Andrew's Military Hospital in Toronto. After the war she worked in the public health sector and became director of the Bureau of Nursing, Toronto Department of Health. As a president of the Nursing Sisters Association of Canada she was held in high regard, and a post-war reference described her as "intelligent, tactful and sympathetic, possesses good judgement and always proved an amiable and willing co-worker." Laura died at Toronto General Hospital, where she had trained, on 21 March 1939.[34]

Nursing Sister Clare Gass returned to Canada in December 1918 and continued working with the CAMC. After her demobilization she took up social work and was among the first to enrol for a new course being offered by McGill University. After completing it and subsequently studying medical social work at Simmons College in Boston, Clare went on to become the head of the Department of Social Work at the Western Division of Montreal General Hospital. The city remained her base for the rest of her career, and in 1923 she made a commemorative visit to France, travelling on the same ship that had taken her to Britain in 1915. Clare did not marry and died in 1968, the much-loved aunt of numerous nieces and nephews.

Mildred Forbes, who, in addition to her Royal Red Cross, had been mentioned in despatches for her work with No. 2 Canadian CCS, was awarded the French *Médaille des Épidémies en Argent*. She and Laura Holland chose similar career paths, the two friends studying social welfare at Boston's Simmons College. Following their graduation in 1920, they both worked at Montreal General Hospital, where Mildred headed a new department of public health and Laura became a social service worker. Having suffered bouts of ill health following the dysentery she contracted at Lemnos, Mildred never fully re-covered. She was hospitalized in December 1920 and died on 21 January 1921, a delayed casualty of the war.

Laura Holland subsequently moved to Toronto, where she became direc-tor of nursing with the Ontario division of the Canadian Red Cross Society. A year later she was promoted to superintendent, and her rise continued in 1923 with a new appointment as director of the welfare division of the To-ronto Department of Public Health. Laura transferred to Vancouver in 1927, where she revolutionized the Children's Aid Society and oversaw new legis-lation concerning children, adoption procedures and unmarried parents. Throughout the 1930s and 1940s she transformed child welfare in the prov-ince and in 1934 was awarded the Order of the British Empire. Laura ended her career as the first woman adviser to the provincial minister of health and welfare. She also lectured in nursing and social welfare at University of Brit-ish Columbia, which awarded her an honorary degree. She died in 1956 and her work in social welfare is still "influential and remembered."[35]

Helen Fowlds returned to Canada in 1919, where she continued nurs-ing with the CAMC until her demobilization. On 25 April 1921 she married Captain Gerald Marryat, who had served during the war with the Canadian Engineers. They lived at Hastings in Ontario, where Helen became a well-known local historian. She died in 1965. May Bastedo continued her nursing career after the war and passed away in 1953. Constance Bruce, Mabel's col-league at Lemnos and Salonika, married and by 1924, as Mrs. Constance Nes-bitt, was living in India with her Royal Air Force husband. In 1927 an article in *Canadian Nurse* magazine reported her as having sailed with her young son for Australia, where she expected "to reside in future."[36]

Of the Canadians who served with the United States Army Nurse Corps, Ella Mae Bongard returned to her home at Picton, Ontario. She met Lieu-tenant Wilfred Scott, who had also served overseas, and the couple were married on 12 December 1921. Ella Mae and Wilfred had two sons, both of whom served in the Second World War, and she died in 1987 at the age of ninety-five. Edith Anderson remained in France until 1919, helping to care for influenza cases and many others who needed ongoing medical treatment. When she passed through war-ravaged areas of France at the start of her journey back to America, she could not help looking "over the shell torn fields" and reflecting on "the millions of dollars in property destroyed to say nothing of the tremendous loss of life."[37] After her return to Canada, Edith resumed her life at the Six Nations Reserve, where she married Claybran Monture in 1920. The couple raised four children, and Edith continued to work as a nurse until she was well into her seventies. She was the last survivor of her wartime unit and when she died in 1996 at the great age of 105, she was believed to be the oldest remaining nurse from the First World War. Charlotte Edith Anderson Monture's service in France is part of the Six Nations' cultural memory of that conflict, and she is remembered and honoured for it.

After leaving Russia in August 1917, Nursing Sister Dorothy Cotton went to England as acting Matron of the IODE Hospital for Officers near London's Hyde Park. She was posted to Canada in October 1918 and became Matron of Camp Hill Military Hospital at Halifax. Dorothy was demobilized and left the CAMC in July 1919, but a year later she accepted an invitation to join a two-year civilian nursing project in Romania,* where she was invited to lead a group of nurses from Montreal to Bucharest. They were to establish a training school at the city's Coltea Hospital and it was due to Lady Muriel Paget of the Anglo-Russian Hospital and her friendship with Queen Marie of Romania that the Canadians were selected for this work. An unfortunate lack of progress with the project proved frustrating, and Dorothy Cotton decided to accept another assignment with the Rockefeller Institute in Paris. On her return to Canada she completed a diploma in public health and began work in Saskatchewan with the Victorian Order of Nurses. Eventually returning to Montreal, Dorothy lived there with her sister Elsie and ran a gift shop for a considerable time. She died on 12 August 1977 at the age of ninety-one.

Nursing Sister Gertrude Gilbert of No. 4 Canadian Ambulance Train returned to Boston, where she had completed her training. She spent a year at a city hospital and then went north to undertake pioneering work at a small mining town in Alaska. While there, she developed health problems from which she was not able to recover. Gertrude decided to go back to her original home at St. Thomas in Ontario, where she died in 1922. In 1929 a room in the Nurses School at Boston Children's Hospital was dedicated to her, to honour "the Memory of an Heroic Nurse."[38]

Alice Swanston returned to her home city of Calgary, where she continued her nursing career at a veterans' hospital. She married and took her turn as a president of the Overseas Nursing Sisters Association of Canada. When she died in 1981, Alice was in her ninety-seventh year. Newfoundland nurse Bertha Forsey married a decorated war veteran and moved to Saskatoon. They raised four children and in 1939 Bertha again put on her nurse's uniform when she was presented to King George VI and Queen Elizabeth during their royal tour of Canada. Two of Bertha's sons served in the Second

* The country was spelled Roumania or Rumania until 1975, when it changed to the present spelling.

World War, as did her daughter Grace, who was a trained nurse and went overseas with her mother's encouragement.

For Blanche Lavallée and her friend Lieutenant Henri Trudeau, there was a happy ending to their friendship begun during the First World War. After Blanche's health necessitated her return to Canada late in 1917, she recovered and the following year went to America to help the United States Army Nurse Corps in its attempts to secure officer status for its members. In 1919 she learned that her wartime service in France had been recognized by the award of the *Médaille des Épidémies* from the French government, and she went on to work for the Red Cross, pursuing her interest in enhancing the status of nurses and women in general.[39]

Henri Trudeau was repatriated to Canada in March 1919 and the couple resumed their relationship, which blossomed over the next few years. Blanche and Henri were married in 1924 and had four daughters. Henri chose to pursue his future career in the Canadian army and rose to the rank of brigadier. In 1940 he was appointed commander of the 12th Military District at Regina, Saskatchewan, where Blanche became a pillar of the local branch of the CRCS. She died in 1969.

Agnes Warner, although glad to return to her home town of Saint John in March 1919, was not in the best of health. After more than three years with the French Flag Nursing Corps, the final months of the war had taken her into forward areas of the fighting and left her weakened and unwell. After recovering somewhat on her return to

Blanche Lavallée in America.
In 1918 Nursing Sister Blanche Lavallée, back in Canada and recovered from health problems, went with a colleague to the United States to support the efforts of American military nurses to obtain officer status. She is seen here (right) in New York. (Library of Congress. No. 2016869131)

North America, she completed a number of speaking engagements, during which she admitted that she had "said farewell to the most interesting period of my life." She felt as if she had been able to "realize" herself and hoped that "I don't shrivel up again when they no longer need me."[40] The fact that Agnes was now in her late forties and had been left depleted by the rigours of nursing in France and Belgium led to her decision to take semi-retirement. She did some work for the Saint John Health Centre and maintained contact with many of her former French patients and their families. In April 1926 she went to New York to seek treatment for an unnamed illness at the Presbyterian Hospital, where she had trained, but was unable to recover. She died there on 23rd of that month.

Dr Irma LeVasseur finally returned to Canada in 1922 and resumed her medical career. Her work in Serbia and France contributed to her professional development as a pioneer in pediatric medicine and in 1923, together with other doctors, she founded the *Hôpital de l'Enfant-Jésus*. Irma later established a school and the *Hôpital des Enfants Malades*, which cared for children with disabilities. When the Second World War broke out, Dr. LeVasseur became a medical examiner of female recruits for the Canadian army. After her death in Quebec City in 1964, a scholarship was established in her name by the Quebec *Sécretariat à la Condition Féminine*. In 2008 she was named a Person of National Historic Significance by the Canadian government.

Of the women who undertook volunteer work overseas, some resumed their previous careers while others used their wartime experience to train for new employment as dietitians, physiotherapists or masseuses. One, Mary Thomas, who had served as a VAD in England and France, applied to medical school and in 1926 became a physician, making her "unique among veteran Canadian VADs."[41] Other former volunteers took up the challenge of a career in an unrelated field such as broadcasting, university administration, recreational work or travel. For those who wished to remain active as voluntary workers in Canada, a new VAD structure enabled them to become general service staff, nursing assistants and function trainers.

Among the VADs mentioned in this book, Isabel Bell-Irving, who married Captain Ben Sweeny in 1917, returned with him to Vancouver, where they raised five children. Leah McCarthy went back to Toronto and soon found romance with Lieutenant-Colonel Ian Sinclair. He was the young former commanding officer of the 13th Battalion, CEF, and in 1914 had been an engineering student at the University of Toronto. Ian Sinclair ended the war having seen a great deal of service and been awarded the Military Cross and the Distinguished Service Order.[42] Leah and Ian married in 1920.

Two career-minded VADs were Frances Cluett and May Bird. Frances continued working overseas as a VAD nursing assistant until 1920, after which she headed home to upgrade her teaching qualification. She then assumed charge of the school in Belleoram, Newfoundland, where she had worked before the war. Frances never married but helped raise a nephew after her brother Arthur was widowed. She died in 1969 at the age of eighty-six. May Bird studied for a nursing degree and graduated in 1924. She became one of the most senior nurses at Western University Hospital and was responsible for training student nurses. After working at Sunnybrook Hospital in Toronto, May became a public health nurse, both in the city and with the Muskoka Health Unit. She died in January 1977 at the age of eighty-seven.

VAD ambulance driver Grace MacPherson made the long homeward journey to Vancouver in the winter of 1919, having spent several months in London working to replenish her finances and "decompress" after her time in France. Back in Canada, she initially found it difficult to detach herself from her wartime life and her fellow Canadians struck her as "cold and undemonstrative." She encouraged them to "wake up" and "welcome home the troops who had fought for King, country and the people of Canada."[43] Grace accepted an offer of employment with the Department of Soldiers' Civil Re-establishment, where she met Major David Livingstone, an engineer who had served overseas with the Canadian Mounted Rifles. The couple married and moved to northern British Columbia, where David was in charge of building branch lines for the CPR. They raised a family, and Grace continued to be active in community and veterans' affairs. She died in 1979.

Among other Canadian war workers, Julia Henshaw returned to Vancouver to resume a life of writing, exploring and pursuing her interest in the flora of British Columbia, on which subject she had published several books before the war. As a popular speaker, she gave lectures at home and overseas on topics that included Canada's rivers, mountains and national parks. In 1925 she served as a director of the Canadian National Parks Association and received invitations to address such organizations as the Royal Society of Arts, the Royal Scottish Geographic Society and the Victoria League. Julia continued to write until her death in 1937 at the age of sixty-eight, and left a legacy of books and articles. Having made her own significant contribution to the war effort overseas, she had always acknowledged the "great work" accomplished by women on the home front during the conflict. She is remembered not only for her fearless war work, but also as one of British Columbia's leading botanists.

Lady Emily Perley remained in London with her husband until his term as high commissioner came to an end in 1922. On 27 July 1921 the French president, Georges Clemenceau, awarded her the *Médaille de la Reconnaissance Française*. On the accompanying certificate it was noted that having taken on the job of recruiting nursing staff for one of the French Red Cross organizations, the *Société de Secours aux Blessés Militaires*, Lady Perley had "acquitted this difficult task with devotion, zeal and competence."[44] After the Perleys returned to Canada, Sir George continued his political career, serving as minister without portfolio in the government of Prime Minister R. B. Bennett. He died in 1938 and Lady Emily survived him by ten years.

Marguerite Gault, who undertook voluntary work in France, returned to Canada knowing the war had claimed the life of her mother, Frances Stephens, one of the victims of the sinking of the *Lusitania*. Her marriage to Hamilton Gault did not survive the war years and they went their separate ways, apparently due to an affair between Marguerite and another officer. Both parties later remarried, Marguerite to an Italian "war ace," Count Luigino Falchi. She died in 1930.[45]

Mabel Adamson, acknowledging the experiences that she and her husband Agar had undergone during their time overseas, decided to supervise the building of a new home, "a stucco covered brick house with stone curly Flemish gables" for both of them "to remind them of their war."[46] Agar, however, found it difficult to settle down after his years of active service and their younger son, Anthony, felt that "both my parents in their separate ways were war casualties."[47] Spending the summers with Mabel at Port Credit and the winters separately in Ottawa or London, Agar was unable to find an occupation that suited him and turned instead to a lively social life that lasted until his death in 1929 following a flying accident. Mabel, who put her creative talents to work by opening a pottery studio, died in 1943 and was buried at Port Credit beside her husband.

Lady Julia Drummond's involvement with the Canadian Red Cross Society lasted long after the war. She travelled a good deal in Europe, at times for pleasure but often to the headquarters of the International Committee of the Red Cross at Geneva. She received many invitations to official events in the post-war years and was present at a service held on 11 November 1920 at Westminster Abbey to unveil the grave of the Unknown Warrior.[48] On 8 July 1923 she was at St. Julien in Belgium for the unveiling and dedication of a Canadian memorial to the men who had fought and died there during the Second Battle of Ypres. In the years 1924 to 1929, she travelled widely to destinations such as Algeria, Egypt, Greece, Malta, Palestine, Syria and Turkey.[49]

In 1936 Julia Drummond returned to Europe for the dedication of the magnificent Canadian war memorial at Vimy Ridge in France. She recorded her impressions of the occasion, describing how "the aspiration, the sorrow, the hope which this Memorial represents are of the Eternal." By that time, with fascism growing stronger by the year and worrying signs of another war on the horizon, she was reminded that it was the sacrifice of so many young men in the First World War "which has saved us." She prayed "in their name ... that war may cease and love may be all in all," but it was not to be. Britain declared war against Germany on 3 September 1939 and a week later, Canada followed suit.[50] Julia Drummond died in June 1942, in the middle of the second major conflict of her lifetime, and one that she had hoped would never happen.

With her First World War work accomplished, the energetic and committed Lena Ashwell chose in the years that followed to focus on the theatre as a means of helping society recover and move forward from the conflict. She was convinced that "art is not a luxury" but rather "part of the very fibre of our national life."[51] After writing an account of her Concerts at the Front project, in 1922 Lena began to plan a new repertory company which subsequently became known as the Lena Ashwell Players. It was composed of people who had worked for her in the war zone, and she created it "in memory of those who fought, and the great army of those who died, and of those still with us who have come back to the bitter struggle for existence."[52] Well into her later years, Lena maintained her belief in drama as a way of stimulating positive attitudes, and the British Poet Laureate John Masefield dedicated his *Sonnets of Good Cheer* to the Lena Ashwell Players. He cited their leader, with her "courage, to keep the thing going, in the midst of adversity" as the source of his inspiration.[53] Beyond all that she achieved, Lena continued to be haunted by her memories of the First World War. She died on 13 March 1957.

Peace activist Julia Grace Wales continued her academic career as a lecturer at the University of Wisconsin. In 1920 she was granted a teaching fellowship at London University, making her the first North American woman to receive this award. She undertook Shakespearean research at the universities of London and Oxford, and later taught at Girton and Newnham Colleges, University of Cambridge. After returning to Wisconsin, she completed her Ph.D. in 1926 and became Assistant Professor of English.

Grace Wales taught until 1947. She never married and never relinquished her interest in the peace movement. In her spare time she continued to write pacifist articles and others with a religious theme. Together with her mother and younger sister, she co-authored an anthology of poems which was published in 1935, followed in 1942 by a book, *Democracy needs education*. After her retirement Grace returned to the family home at St. Andrews East in Quebec. Having celebrated her seventy-sixth birthday on 14 July 1957, she died the following day.

With the main collection of her war art in the safe custodianship of the Public Archives of Canada, from 1926 onwards Mary Riter Hamilton resumed her career as an artist. Her work, which found its way to art galleries, museums and private collections across the nation, continued to win widespread acclaim but after the prolonged and intense hardship of her mission to France and Belgium, Mary no longer felt the drive to continue with her earlier style of painting. For a time she turned to something quite different – the creation of dress accessories – before moving to Vancouver in 1929, where she opened a studio.

In 1948 declining health led to her retirement, and in March 1952 the Women's Auxiliary to the Vancouver Art Gallery and the Women's Volunteer Service Bureau sponsored an exhibition of Mary's work, which received prominent newspaper coverage. The *Vancouver Province* chose to announce the event under the title "Bygone Fame Reclaimed Here for Brilliant Woman Artist," and when Mary died in 1954 the *Vancouver Sun* paid tribute to her as "Canada's first woman artist." She was buried at Port Arthur, Ontario, beside the grave of her husband, Charles.[54]

For Canadian journalists Mary MacLeod Moore, Elizabeth Montizambert and Beatrice Nasmyth, the shadow of the First World War lingered well beyond 1918. Beatrice was invited to report on the Versailles peace conference and headed to France for the duration of the proceedings. After marrying, she and her husband, Guy Furniss, decided that Canada offered better employment opportunities than post-war Britain. They both found work, Guy in newspaper sales and Beatrice writing articles for *Modern Woman*, a British magazine. They had two children and their son Harry served as a pilot with the Royal Canadian Air Force in the Second World War. Beatrice outlived her husband by fourteen years and died in 1977.

Mary MacLeod Moore continued to live and work in London, writing for *Saturday Night* and the *Sunday Times*. In 1919 she published a book entitled *The Maple Leaf's Red Cross: The War Story of the Canadian Red Cross Overseas*, which remains a valuable record of the contributions of Canadian women to the success of the Canadian Red Cross Society. In June 1923, after more than a decade of working for the *Sunday Times*, Mary married its editor, Leonard Rees. The pair, already well known in London literary circles, hosted many prominent and influential people and after Leonard's death in 1932, Mary remained on the staff of the paper until 1940. She died in London in 1960.

Elizabeth Montizambert moved from Paris to London, where the *Montreal Gazette* asked her to be its London editor. She continued to pursue her interest in art, fashion and the theatre and wrote a book and a guidebook about the city, featuring it regularly in her monthly column for the *Gazette*. Elizabeth returned often to France to visit friends and familiar haunts, and when war broke out in 1939 she again found herself writing articles about wartime life. Having completed her last column in December 1944 she retired to the country, where she died in 1964. She and her two colleagues had been intrepid writers, war correspondents and "adventurers in a dangerous age" that had seen them witness one "cataclysmic drama" in their lifetime, only to be faced twenty years later with another.[55]

Prominent among those who had blazed a trail during the First World War, Roberta MacAdams became the first woman in the British Empire to introduce and successfully pass a piece of legislation that gave legal recognition to a veteran's organization, the Great War Next-of-Kin Association. At the end of the war she chaperoned British war brides to Canada and assisted them through her work with the Alberta Soldier Settlement Board. She joined the staff of the Khaki University, an educational extension programme for soldiers, and her position in the provincial legislature led to the setting up of a teacher training school in Edmonton. Roberta married Albertan lawyer Harvey Price and moved to Calgary with her husband and son. She continued to be active in educational and women's organizations until her death in 1959.

Margaret "Madge" Robertson Watt, who introduced the Women's Institute movement in Britain, was appointed a Member of the Order of the British Empire by King George V in 1919. After the Armistice she went to France and worked with the British Red Cross Society to help sick and wounded civilians. Following her return to British Columbia, Madge became president of the WI's provincial advisory board and from that time onwards she put her weight behind the idea of an international organization of rural women. She was instrumental in arranging a major conference in 1929 and a new body, the Associated Countrywomen of the World, was launched with Madge as its first president. In the decade preceding the Second World War she remained very active, visiting WI branches in many countries. When she died in 1948 at the age of eighty, Margaret Robertson Watt was lauded as a visionary who believed that women could, and should, demonstrate their leadership abilities and assist others to realize their potential. In 2007 she was named a Person of National Historic Significance by the Canadian government.

Of those civilian women who recorded their observations on the war and followed its events in detail, Lucy Maud Montgomery published the eighth novel in her "Anne of Green Gables" series in 1921. It was described by one historian as "in some ways her most interesting book," and she entitled it *Rilla of Ingleside*. With the focus on Anne's daughter, Bertha Marilla "Rilla" Blythe, and the life of her family and community during the war years, it proved to be virtually the only Canadian work of fiction that described everyday life on the home front from "direct personal experience" and in "well observed detail."[56]

Grace Morris of Pembroke, Ontario, having spent time in Britain during the war years, returned home to help with the war effort in her locality. In 1919 she became engaged to Major Stuart Thorne of the 1st Canadian Tun-

Victory Parade. In June 1919 representatives of the victorious Allied forces gathered in London to take part in a great parade before King George V and other dignitaries. Among them was a contingent of VADs who, in this artist's impression, are marching past cheered by enthusiastic onlookers. (Author's collection)

Étaples Commonwealth War Graves Commission Cemetery. Designed by British architect Sir Edwin Lutyens, this beautiful cemetery is the largest of its kind in France. Among its 11,516 graves are to be found those of the Canadian nurses killed in May 1918 during a German air attack on No. 1 Canadian General Hospital. (Photograph by Dianne Graves)

nelling Company, who had returned from France to begin a job with Ontario Hydro. Unfortunately Thorne's wartime service had adversely affected his health and not long before their wedding he collapsed and died of a heart condition resulting from trench fever suffered in 1916. With her father's encouragement Grace decided to pursue a career in architecture and joined a practice in Toronto as an apprentice architect. In so doing, she became the first women in the city to take up such a position.[57]

Grace worked on the design of houses and in due course found lasting happiness with James J. Craig, a partner in the firm that employed her. On 29 December 1923 the couple were married and they raised three children. With the outbreak of the Second World War, James went overseas to help set up the Canadian Armoured Corps Reinforcement Unit. During his absence Grace, in addition to caring for her growing family, returned to the drawing board to develop her talents as an artist and designer. She also wrote an account of her family and its experiences during the First World War, still seeking to find true reconciliation with the tragedy of that time. "I am alone still," she wrote, conjecturing that, "in this tragic world there must be a purpose. Perhaps for me it is that I must live to see that the names of the men who gave their lives for this beautiful country should not be forgotten."[58]

They were not, and every year on 11 November all those who lost their lives during the First World War and later conflicts are remembered at services and ceremonies throughout Britain, Canada and other Allied countries. Most of the Canadian women who were killed or died doing their duty overseas rest in cemeteries in Britain and France. Among them, the nurses and medical staff who lost their lives during the German air raids on base hospitals in May and June 1918 lie at Étaples Commonwealth War Graves Commission (CWGC) cemetery on the north French coast. It is a place of quiet beauty overlooked by a striking memorial designed by Sir Edwin Lutyens.

In the case of Matron Jessie Jaggard and Nursing Sister Frances Munro, who died at Lemnos, Robert Peck, Canada's ambassador to the Hellenic Republic, unveiled a new memorial plaque in their memory at Portianos CWGC cemetery on 17 April 2015. Not only does it honour them, but it is also a reminder of the valiant work of all the medical staff who served there, "without whose dedication many more servicemen would have died."[59]

The names of the nursing sisters who were lost at sea when HMCHS *Llandovery Castle* was torpedoed in June 1918 are recorded on local or family memorials. There are also plaques in their memory at the Elizabeth Garrett Anderson Hospital in London and on a memorial at Point Pleasant Park, Halifax.

When the First World War came to an end on 11 November 1918, church bells in cities, towns and villages across Canada rang in celebration. One hundred years later on 11 November 2018 those bells were heard once again in a country-wide event entitled the "Bells of Peace" that began to the sound of bagpipes at Cape Spear in Nova Scotia and ended on Vancouver Island. The author was present as the bells tolled at sunset from the tower of St. James the Apostle Anglican Church at Perth, Ontario, "cutting through the evening shade, literally echoing the past 100 years before."[60] Those who gathered to commemorate the peace and honour the fallen were reminded that "with each pealing of the bells, we will remember them."[61]

* * * * *

The surviving diaries, letters, memoirs, recollections and service records of some of the Canadian women who served overseas enable us to gain an insight into their war effort, to acknowledge their courage and endurance and to respect their dedication. More than a century later, their stories testify to the fact that Canada's women went out into a world engulfed in a terrible war, determined to make a difference. What they accomplished speaks for itself.

A history of Canadians in the First World War, written in its aftermath, pays tribute to the nation's troops. It also discusses the contribution made by women and speaks of their "heroic sacrifices of time and money," their "whole-hearted acceptance of war's burden" and their conviction that "Canada's cause and the cause of the civilized world should triumph."[62] It has been said that the war could not have been waged "were it not mothered" by such women who strove, "in the company of sisters," to play their part.[63] In doing so at a time when their quest for independence and greater freedom was still breaking new ground, the First World War proved to be a notable event in their history and development. Their involvement in the nation's support of its troops over more than four years of conflict, and their strides in the post-war world to find new ways forward and greater self-expression, left an important marker on the long road towards the self-determination that Canadian women were to achieve in the future.

Bells of peace. On 11 November 2018 church bells rang out across Canada at dusk to mark the 100th anniversary of the Armistice, as they had done in 1918. This photograph shows the spire of St. James's Anglican Church, Perth, Ontario, whose bells chimed one hundred times to mark that special anniversary. (Photograph by Dianne Graves)

Endnotes

ARCHIVAL SOURCES – ABBREVIATIONS

AM	Archives of Manitoba
ANS	Archives of Nova Scotia
AO	Archives of Ontario
BCAV	British Columbia Archives, Victoria
CWM	Canadian War Museum, Military History Research Centre, Ottawa
GMA	Glenbow Museum and Archives, Calgary, Alberta
GMMH	Guelph Museums, McCrae House
IWM	Imperial War Museum, London
IFFM	In Flanders Fields Museum Kenniscentrum, Ypres
LAC	Library and Archives Canada, Ottawa
LWRM	Lincoln and Welland Regiment Museum, St. Catharines
McCM	McCord Museum of History, Montreal
MUA	McGill University Archives
MUL	McGill University Library
MUOL	McGill University, Osler Library of the History of Medicine
MUN	Memorial University of Newfoundland Centre for Newfoundland Studies,
MVTM	Mississippi Valley Textile Museum, Almonte
DHHO	National Defence Headquarters, Ottawa, Directory of History and Heritage
PAL	Port Alberni Library, British Columbia
TUA	Trent University Archives
UBCA	University of British Columbia Archives
WMA	Whitehern Museum and Archives, Hamilton

Chapter 1. Prelude to Armageddon : The Coming of War, 1914

1 From "Canada's Answer" by Elspeth Honeyman, in John W. Garvin, ed. *Canadian Poems of the Great War* (Toronto, 1918), 91.

2 Winston Churchill, *The World Crisis: 1911-1914* (Toronto, 1923), 129; Lady Ottoline Morrell, quoted in Kirsty McLeod, *The Last Summer: May to September 1914* (London, 1983), 101.

3 McLeod, *The Last Summer*, 12-13.

4 Harold Macmillan, *The Winds of Change 1914-1939* (London, 1966), 59.

5 Sandra Gwyn, *Tapestry of War: A Private View of Canadians in the Great War* (Toronto, 1992), 12.

6 Ethel Chadwick, quoted in Gwyn, *Tapestry of War*, 19; Diary of Ethel Chadwick, 2 August 1914, MG30 D258, Ethel Chadwick Papers, LAC.

7 Lucy Maud Montgomery, 5 August 1914 in Mary Rubio and Elizabeth Waterston, *The Selected Journals of L.M. Montgomery, Volume II 1910-1921* (Don Mills, 2003), 150.

8 The Ottoman Empire controlled a good deal of Western Asia, north Africa and southwestern Europe from the 14th to the early 20th century. It joined the First World War on the side of the Central Powers and after its defeat and partitioning, lost its Middle Eastern territories. A successful Turkish war of independence led to the founding of the modern Republic of Turkey in 1923.

9 M.B. Clint, *Our Bit: Memories of War Service by a Canadian Nursing Sister* (Montreal, 1934), 3.

10 Wilfrid Laurier, House of Commons Debates, 12 January 1910, 1735, LAC.

11 *Globe and Mail*, "Scenes of Patriotism in Several Cities," 5 August 1914.

12 *Winnipeg Free Press*, 5 August 1914.

13 D.L. Matthews, ed. *The Oslers During World War One* (Gravenhurst, Ontario, 1999), 49-51.

14 Mary Tuer, Diary of a European Tour, 29-31 July 1914, 1-4 August 1914, 75-1001, Tuer Papers, TUA.

15 Mary Tuer to 'Daisy', 6 September 1914, 75-1001, Tuer Papers, TUA.

16 Elizabeth Montizambert, "Causerie de Paris," *Montreal Gazette*, 25 August 1914, 8 September

1914. She wrote her column for the *Gazette* under the pseudonym 'Antoinette'.

17 Mary MacLeod Moore, "London Letter," *Saturday Night Magazine*, 29 August 1914. Mary used the pseudonym 'Pandora' for her *Saturday Night* articles.

18 Kate Adie, *Fighting on the Home Front: The Legacy of Women in World War One* (London, 2013), 239-240.

19 Debbie Marshall, *Firing Lines: Three Canadian Women Write the First World War* (Toronto, 2017), 85, 19. Canada soon established its own system of press censorship.

20 Anna Maria Tremonti in Marshall, *Firing Lines*, 10.

21 *Winnipeg Free Press*, 16 August 1914.

22 Lady Grace Julia Drummond, quoted in Donald MacKay, *The Square Mile: Merchant Princes of Montreal* (Vancouver and Toronto, 1987), 157.

23 Colonel Fortesque Duguid, *The Official History of the Canadian Forces in The Great War 1914-1919, Volume 1, Part 1* (Ottawa, 1938), 41.

24 Cyril C. Allinson, "John McCrae: Poet, Soldier, Physician," 88, Reference Collection , GMMH.

25 Elizabeth Montizambert, "Causerie de Paris," *Montreal Gazette*, 18 September 1914, 28 September 1914.

26 Grace Morris Craig, *But This is Our War* (Toronto, 1981), 27.

27 Lucy Maud Montgomery, 5 August 1914, in Rubio and Waterston, *The Selected Journals of L.M. Montgomery, Vol. II*, 150.

28 Ottoline Morrell, *Ottoline: The Early Memoirs of Lady Ottoline Morrell*, (London, 1963), 260, 262.

29 Ralph Allen, *Ordeal by Fire: Canada 1910-1945* (Toronto, 1961), 1.

30 From a speech by Sir Wilfrid Laurier to the Canadian Club, Ottawa, 18 January 1904. The phrase was quickly simplified to "The twentieth century belongs to Canada."

31 R. Douglas Francis, Richard Jones, Donald B. Smith, *Destinies: Canadian History Since Confederation*, (Toronto, 2008) 156, 179. It is estimated that by 1912 one in every eight adult Canadian women belonged to a women's group and of this figure, the majority were middle class, middle-aged, English-speaking Protestants.

32 Francis, Jones, Smith, *Destinies: Canadian History Since Confederation*, 182.

33 Francis, Jones, Smith, *Destinies*, 186.

34 Andrew Macphail, *Official History of The Canadian Forces in The Great War 1914-1919: The Medical Services* (Ottawa, 1925), 226.

35 Anon., *Canada in the Great World War*, Vol. VI (Toronto, 1921), 81.

36 The term "War Establishment" referred to the full wartime complement of equipment, vehicles and manpower required for a military unit.

37 Clint, *Our Bit*, 4.

38 Ibid., 5.

39 Clare Gass, 6 May 1915, in Susan Mann, ed. *The War Diary of Clare Gass 1915-1918* (Montreal, 2000), 9.

40 Diary of Florence Hunter, 26 September 1914, 58A 1 235.1, Florence Hunter Papers, CWM.

41 Allinson, "John McCrae: Poet, Soldier, Physician," 88, Reference Collection, GMMH.

42 Kate Reid, quoted in MacKay, *The Square Mile*, 182.

43 Iona Carr, *A Story of the Canadian Red Cross Society Information Bureau in The Great War* (Toronto, 1920), 4.

44 Clint, *Our Bit*, 6-7.

45 Ibid., 7.

46 Guy Drummond to Julia Drummond, 30 September 1914. PO15/FO1, Drummond Family Fonds, McCM.

47 Clint, *Our Bit*, 7.

48 Morris Craig, *But This is Our War*, 27.

49 Diary of Ethel Chadwick, 4 October 1914, 31 August 1914, MG30 D258, LAC.

50 Captain Agar Adamson, 12 October 1914, in N.M. Christie, ed., *Letters of Agar Adamson* (Nepean, Ontario, 1997),11-12.

51 *The Times*, 15 October 1914, 1; Austin Harrison, "The Coming of the Canadians," *Canada in Khaki*, Second Edition, 1918, 17-18.

52 Adie, *Fighting on the Home Front*, 31.

53 Michael Bliss, *Sir William Osler: A Life in Medicine* (Toronto, 1999), 407.

54 Fleur Cowles, *1913: The Defiant Swansong* (London, 1967), 13, 30.

55 Maurice Baring, *Flying Corps Headquarters 1914-1918* (London, 1985), 14.

56 Winifred L.B. Tower, Journal 26 July to October 1914, and "Some Diary Notes, October 1914 to February 1916," 18, P476, IWM.

57 Katherine M. Wilson-Simmie, *Lights Out: A Canadian Nursing Sister's Tale* (Belleville, Ontario, 1981), 13-14.

58 Clint, *Our Bit*, 4; Beatrice Nasmyth, "Canadian Soldier Lads See World's Metropolis," *Daily Province*, 27 November 1914.

59 Marshall, *Firing lines*, 93.

60 On 1 October 1914, the Commissioner of the Metropolitan Police ordered that throughout the London area bright exterior lighting was to be extinguished or dimmed, and that street lighting had to be partly covered with black paint.

61 Second Lieutenant Don Brophy, 20 December 1915, in Brereton Greenhous, ed., *A Rattle of Pebbles: The First World War Diaries of Two Canadian Airmen* (Ottawa, 1987), 6.

62 Jerry White, *Zeppelin Nights: London in the First World War* (London, 2015), 39, 125. The first enemy air raid in Britain took place on 19 January 1915 over East Anglia.

63 Sister K.E. Luard, quoted in Anne Powell, *Women in the War Zone: Hospital Service in the First World War* (Stroud, 2013), 95-96.

64 The Right Hon. L.S. Amery, *My Political Life*, Vol. 2 (London, 1939), 42.

65 Clint, *Our Bit*, 18.

66 In February 1915 the Canadian medical units on Salisbury Plain proceeded to the French towns of Étaples and Le Tréport as No. 1 and No. 2 Canadian General Hospitals, which would form part of a network of Allied base hospitals located on or near to the north French coast.

67 Ethel M. Bilbrough, *My War Diary 1914-1918*, (London, 2014), 153.

68 Ibid., 19.

69 Vera Brittain, *Testament of Youth: An Autobiographical Study of the Years 1900-1925* (London, 2014), 98.

70 Lucy Maud Montgomery, 1 January 1915, in Rubio and Waterston, *The Selected Journals of L.M. Montgomery, Vol. II*, , 159.

71 Winston Churchill, *The World Crisis*, 10-11; verse from "The Hour (Midnight, August 4, 1914)" by James B. Fagan, quoted in Clint, *Our Bit*, 2.

Chapter 2. "How will it all end and what will become of us all?" Medical Service – The Western Front and England, 1914-1915

1 From "The New Year, 1917 A.D." by Minnie Hallowell Bowen, in Garvin ed., *Canadian Poems of the Great War*, 28.

2 Reverend Albert Woods to his wife, quoted in William D. Mathieson, *My Grandfather's War: Canadians Remember the First World War 1914-1918* (Toronto, 1981), 136.

3 Donald E. Graves, *Always Ready: A History of the Royal Regiment of Canada* (Toronto, 2017), 138.

4 Ibid., 138.

5 Reverend Albert Woods to his wife, quoted in Mathieson, *My Grandfather's War*, 135.

6 Sophie Hoerner to 'Mollie', 12 May 1915, MG30 E290, Sophie Hoerner Papers, LAC.

7 Shawna M. Quinn, *Agnes Warner and the Nursing Sisters of the Great War* (Fredericton, 2010), 27.

8 QAIMNS nurses regarded themselves as very much part of the military medical machine even though they had no official status within the British armed forces, and were unsuccessful in their attempts to acquire it. Most nurses from Newfoundland, which at that time was not part of Canada, served with the QAIMNS.

9 The USANC recruited some 20,000 registered nurses for war service, and more than 10,000 served overseas.

10 Quinn, *Agnes Warner*, 27. The unit in question was funded by Mary Borden Turner, a wealthy American.

11 Reference dated July 1916, R11203-G-1-E, Alice E. Isaacson Papers, LAC.

12 Tim Cook, *At the Sharp End: Canadians Fighting The Great War 1914-1916*, Vol. 1 (Toronto, 2007), 205.

13 Sophie Hoerner letter to 'Madeleine', 12 September 1915, MG30 E290, Sophie Hoerner Papers, LAC.

14 Cynthia Toman, *Sister Soldiers of the Great War: The Nurses of the Canadian Army Medical Corps* (Vancouver, 2016), 36.

15 Sophie Hoerner to 'Mollie', 12 May 1915, MG30 E290, LAC.

16 John McCrae to Janet McCrae, 12 March 1916. MG30 D209, Micro. A-1103, John McCrae Papers, LAC.

17 Macphail, *Official History of The Canadian Forces in The Great War*, 214, 216.

18 Jack Davey to 'Kate' 15 December 1915, Historic Collection of the Bromley Court Hotel, Bromley, Kent, UK.

19 Clint, *Our Bit*, 97.

20 Toman, *Sister Soldiers of the Great War*, 73.

21 Agnes Warner, 3 August 1914, quoted in Quinn, *Agnes Warner*, 45.

22 Agnes Warner to her mother, 2 August 1914, 23 August 1914, in Quinn, *Agnes Warner*, 66-67.

23 Donald Jack, *Rogues, Rebels and Geniuses: The Story of Canadian Medicine* ,(Toronto, 1981), 345, 348; Service Record of Dr. Margaret Parks, File 7603-S010, RG150 Accession 1992-93/166, LAC.

24 Service Record of Dr. Margaret E. MacKenzie, File B6979-S037, RG 150 Accession 1992-93/166, LAC. Dr. MacKenzie served as a nurse until 1919.

25 Clint, *Our Bit*, 21, 24.

26 Sophie Hoerner to 'Mollie', 4 July 1915, MG30 E290, LAC.

27 Edith Hudson, "'War Memoirs' of Miss Edith Hudson," 21, in "Military Nursing Service World War 1, 1914-1918," RG64-7-21, folder 21, MUA.

28 Constance Bruce, *Humour in Tragedy: Hospital Life behind Three Fronts by a Canadian Nursing Sister* (London, [1918]), 5-7.

29 *Pictou Advocate*, 14 August 1914.

30 Susan Mann, *Margaret Macdonald: Imperial Daughter* (Montreal, 2005), 100.

31 Mann, *Margaret Macdonald*, 104, 107-108.

32 Mary MacLeod Moore, "London Letter," *Saturday Night Magazine*, 16 January 1915.

33 Agnes Warner to her mother, 23 August 1914, in Quinn, *Agnes Warner*, 67.

34 Report by Nursing Sister J. Cameron Smith on a visit to Moore Barracks, 19-21 July 1916, 2, MG30 E45, Margaret Macdonald Papers, LAC.

35 Bruce, *Humour in Tragedy*, 11.

36 Helen Fowlds to her mother, 30 March 1915, 69-001, Series I, box 1, Helen Fowlds Marryat Papers, TUA.

37 Helen Fowlds to her mother, 5 April 1915, 69-001, I/1, Helen Fowlds Marryat Papers, TUA.

38 Bruce, *Humour in Tragedy*, 12-13.

39 Sophie Hoerner to 'Mollie', 26 May 1915, MG30 E290, LAC.

40 Daniel J. Dancocks, *Welcome to Flanders Fields, The First Canadian Battle of The Great War: Ypres 1915* (Toronto, 1988), 188.

41 "War Memoirs of Miss Edith Hudson," RG64-7-21 82, folder 21, MUA.

42 Anonymous. *A War Nurse's Diary: Sketches from a Belgian Field Hospital* (New York, 1918), 99.

43 Agnes Warner, 14 August 1916, in Quinn, *Agnes Warner*, 119.

44 Cook, Tim. *No Place to Run: The Canadian Corps and Gas Warfare in the First World War.* (Vancouver, 1999), 21.

45 Anon. "Gas poisoning" The Nursing Times XI, 524 (15 May 1915), 585.

46 Desmond Morton, *When Your Number's Up: The Canadian Soldier in the First World War*, (Toronto, 1993), 193.

47 Clint, *Our Bit*, 43.

48 "Letters from the Front: Three Days of Our Work," in Mary Plummer, ed. *With the First Canadian Contingent* (London, 1915), 62.

49 Clare Gass, 6 July 1915, in Mann, *The War Diary of Clare Gass*, 39.

50 William Boyd, *With A Field Ambulance at Ypres: Being letters written March 7-August 15 1915* (Toronto, 1916), 25.

51 Sophie Hoerner to 'Mollie', 8 July 1915, 2 July 1915, MG30 E290, LAC.

52 Sophie Hoerner to 'A.G.N', 1 August 1915, MG30 E290, LAC.

53 Terry Bishop Stirling, "Such Sights One Will Never Forget: Newfoundland Women and Overseas Nursing in the First World War," in Glassford and Shaw, *A Sisterhood of Suffering and Service*, 126.

54 Anne E. Ross, Narrative, 10, MG30 E446, Anne E. Ross Papers, LAC.

55 Laura Holland letter to her mother, 21 July 1915, Laura Holland Fonds, Correspondence Series (CS) 1-15, UBCA.

56 John McCrae to Janet McCrae, 14 June 1915, MG30 D209, Micro A-1977, John McCrae Papers, LAC.

57 Wilson-Simmie, *Lights Out*, 88.

58 Maysie Parsons, quoted in Bishop Stirling "Such Sights One Will Never Forget," in Glassford and Shaw, *A Sisterhood of Suffering and Service*, 136.

59 Letter from Mabel Joice dated 1 June 1916, published in *The Cobourg World*, 7 July 1916.

60 Letter from Mabel Joice to Pearl Cornelius, *The Cobourg World*, 24 November 1915.

61 Mary Burns to Theodora Paynter, 22 April 1916, M-6245, Box 1, File 2, Theodora Paynter McKay Papers, GMA.

62 Letter from Mabel Joice to Pearl Cornelius, *The Cobourg World*, 24 November 1916.

63 Laurence Binyon, comp. *For Dauntless France: An account of Britain's aid to the French wounded and victims of the War*, (London, n.d.), 36.

64 Ibid., 27 September 1915, 65.

65 Sophie Hoerner to 'Mollie', 23 October 1915, MG30 E290, LAC.

66 "Matron Maclatchy's Recollections," 25 October 1915, quoted in Mann, *The War Diary of Clare Gass*, 244.

67 Clare Gass, 25 October 1915, in Mann, *The War Diary of Clare Gass*, 74.

68 Wilson-Simmie, *Lights Out*, 148.

69 Ibid., 51.

70 Clare Gass, 4 July 1915, in Mann, *The War Diary of Clare Gass*, 38.

71 Sophie Hoerner to 'Mollie', 4 July 1915, MG30 E290, LAC.

72 Ibid., 18 March 1916, 108.

73 Helen Fowlds to her mother, 9 April 1915, 69-001, I/1, TUA.

74 "Matron MacLatchy's Recollections," quoted in Mann, *The War Diary of Clare Gass*, 248.

75 Sophie Hoerner to 'Mollie', 25 November 1915, MG30 E290, LAC. These rules were maintained throughout the war, even during demobilization.

76 Agnes Warner, 23 September 1915, 3 October 1915, in Quinn, *Agnes Warner*, 94-96.

77 Ibid., 3 October 1915, 96.

78 Service record of Janet McGregor MacDonald, B6735-S019, RG150 Accession 1992-93/166, LAC.

79 Wilson-Simmie, *Lights Out*, 152.

80 Bruce, *Humour in Tragedy*, 5.

81 Clare Gass, 25 December 1915, in Mann, *The War Diary of Clare Gass*, 89.

82 Ibid.; Sophie Hoerner to 'Janet', 13 December 1915, MG30 E290, LAC.

Chapter 3. "A hospital alone shows what war is": Medical Service – The Western Front and England, 1916-1919

1 From "Our Day," by Isabel Ecclestone Mackay in Garvin, ed., *Canadian Poems of the Great War*, 136.

2 Clare Gass, 25 December 1915, in Mann, *The War Diary of Clare Gass*, 89.

3 Agnes Warner, 22 February 1916, in Quinn, *Agnes Warner*, 107.

4 Ibid., 3 May 1916, 114.

5 Clare Gass, 8 June 1916, in Mann, *The War Diary of Clare Gass*, 123.

6 Adie, *Fighting on the Home Front*, 176.

7 "Military Nursing," *Canadian Nurse*, Vol. 213, No. 8 (1917), 482.

8 "October Meeting 1939," 58A 1 264, Alice Swanston Ironside Papers, CWM.

9 Dr. J.J. Danby, quoted in G.W.L. Nicholson, *Canada's Nursing Sisters* (Toronto, 1975), 81.

10 Anon. *No. 7 (Queen's) Canadian General Hospital, March 26th 1915-November 15th 1917* (London, 1918), 33-35; Mary MacLeod Moore, "Canadian Women War Workers Overseas," *Canadian* magazine, Vol. 52, January 1919, 38.

11 Wilson-Simmie, *Lights Out*, 127, 129-130.

12 Ibid., 156-157.

13 Morton, *When Your Number's Up*, 191-192.

14 John McCrae to David McCrae, 4 July 1916, MG30 D209, Micro-1103, LAC.

15 Sophie Hoerner to 'Carrie', 10 June 1915, MG30 E290, LAC.

16 Edward Archibald to his wife, 21 July 1916, 3 February 1916, MS545/4, 1916 (1) and (3), Edward Archibald Papers, MUOL.

17 Toman, *Sister Soldiers*, 201-202.

18 Wilson-Simmie, *Lights Out*, 117.

19 Edward Morrison to John McCrae, 3 December 1916, MG30 D209, Micro A-1977, LAC.

20 Marshall, *Firing Lines*, 138-140.

21 Elizabeth Montizambert, "Causerie de Paris," *Montreal Gazette*, 11 May 1916.

22 Marie Lavallée to Blanche Lavallée, 22 June 1915, CA ON00093 96/5-1, Series 1, Blanche Lavallée Fonds, DHHO.

23 Marie Lavallée to Blanche Lavallée, 22 December 1915, 31 December 1915, CA ON00093 96/5-1, Series 1, Blanche Lavallée Fonds, DHHO.

24 Sherrell Branton Leetooze, *WW1 Nursing Sisters of Old Durham County* (Bowmanville, 2014), 75.

25 Marshall, *Firing Lines*, 164.

26 Wendy Moore, *Endell Street: The Trailblazing Women Who Ran World War One's Most Remarkable Military Hospital* (London, 2020), 203; service record of Dr. Frances Evelyn Windsor, RG150 Acc. 1992-93/166, Box 10492-25, LAC.

27 Moore, *Endell Street*, 217; Adie, *Fighting on the Home Front*, 116.

28 Laura Holland to her mother, 3 September 1916, Laura Holland Fonds, CS 2-19, UBCA.

29 Clare Gass, 4 September 1916 in Mann, *The War Diary of Clare Gass*, 139.

30 Mabel Joice to Pearl Cornelius, 30 October 1916, *The Cobourg World*, 24 November 1916.

31 Ethel M. Bilbrough, 14 December 1916, in Bilbrough, *My War Diary*, 190.

32 Clare Gass, 25 December 1916 in Mann, *The War Diary of Clare Gass*, 153.

33 Laura Holland to her mother, 27 December 1916, Laura Holland Fonds, CS 2-40, UBCA.

34 Anne E. Ross, Narrative, 10-11, MG30 E446, Anne E. Ross Papers, LAC.

35 Beatrice Kilbourne, quoted in "Diaries Reveal Harrowing Experiences of First World War Nursing Sisters," *Vancouver Courier*, 20 March 2015; John McCrae to Geills Kilgour 4 February 1917, MG30 D209, Micro A-1103, LAC.

36 The Royal Red Cross was introduced by Queen Victoria in 1873 as an award to military nurses for exceptional service and devotion to duty. In November 1915, it was expanded to include two classes: First, or Member (RRC), and Second or Associate (ARRC). Laura Holland was awarded the Royal Red Cross Second Class.

37 Laura Holland to her mother, 4 March 1917, Laura Holland Fonds, CS 2-54, UBCA. Queen Alexandra was the widow of King Edward VII and mother of King George V.

38 The Hon. Ian Mackenzie, quoted in W.W. Murray, *The Epic of Vimy* (Ottawa, 1936), 95.

39 Diary of Alice Isaacson, 11 April 1917, R11203-0-1-E, LAC.

40 Beatrice Kilbourne, quoted in "Diaries Reveal Harrowing Experiences of First World War Nursing Sisters," *Vancouver Courier*, 20 March 2015.

41 Alice Isaacson diary, 24 July 1917, R11203-0-1-E, LAC; Edith Appleton, 19 August 1918, in Cowen, *A Nurse At The Front*, 242.

42 Editorial, *British Journal of Nursing*, Vol. 54, 15 May 1915, 423.

43 Sophie Hoerner to 'Mollie', 11 October 1915, MG30 E290, LAC.

44 Wilson-Simmie, *Lights Out*, 35.

45 Henri Trudeau to Blanche Lavallée, 4 December 1915, 18 November 1916, CA ON00093 96/5-1 Series 2, Georges Alexandre Henri Trudeau Fonds, DHHO.

46 Ibid., 22 August 1916.

47 Sophie Hoerner to 'Mollie', 12 May 1915, MG30 E290, LAC; Edna Howey, quoted in Toman, *Sister Soldiers*, 174.

48 Philip Gibbs, "I Saw Passchendaele Taken," *The Great War – I Was There*, Part 35 (London, 1938), 1402.

49 Mary MacLeod Moore, "London Letter," *Saturday Night Magazine*, 15 December 1917.

50 Mildred Forbes to Cairine Wilson, 17 July 1917, 29 August 1917, Cairine Reay Wilson Papers, R-5278-4-1-E, Microfilm reel H-2299, LAC.

51 Mildred Forbes to Cairine Wilson, 11 October 1917, Cairine Wilson Papers, Micro. H-2299, LAC.

52 Luella Denton to Mrs McArthur, 7 October 1917, www.greyroots.com/story/canadian-nursing.sister.

53 Diary of Hannah Lister, 23-30 September, 2-4 November, 7 December 1917. 58E 2 3.6, Hannah Lister Fonds, CWM.

54 Ella Mae Bongard, 9 December 1917, in Eric Scott, ed. *Nobody Ever Wins a War: The World War 1 Diaries of Ella Mae Bongard*, (Ottawa, 1998), 24.

55 Florence McPhedran (1878-1934) went to England during the First World War with her two young daughters. In her efforts to work as a war correspondent she lobbied Canadian Prime Minister Robert Borden to be allowed to go to France. The reports she wrote while touring the lines of communication were forwarded to the Toronto *Daily Star*.

56 Mary MacLeod Moore, "Somewhere in France, the Veil Lifted," *Saturday Night Magazine*, 26 January 1918.

57 Beatrice Nasmyth, "Lifts the Curtain on Life of Canadian Troops on Soil of France," *Daily Province*, 16 February 1918.

58 Marshall, *Firing Lines*, 170-180.

59 Clare Gass, 24 December 1917 in Mann, *The War Diary of Clare Gass*, 186; Ella Mae Bongard, 24 December 1917 in Scott, ed., *Nobody Ever Wins A War*, 26.

60 Dianne Graves, *A Crown of Life: The World of John McCrae* (Montreal, 2012), 280.

61 Clare Gass, 1 January 1918, in Mann, *The War Diary of Clare Gass*, 186-187.

62 Diary of Alice Isaacson, 1 January 1918, R11203-O-1-E, LAC.

63 Bertha Forsey, in Bishop Stirling, "Such Sights One Will Never Forget," in Glassford and Shaw, *A Sisterhood of Suffering and Service*, 134, 139.

64 Ella Mae Bongard, 2 February 1918, in Scott, ed., *Nobody Ever Wins A War*, 30.

65 Clare Gass, 19-20 March 1918, in Mann, *The War Diary of Clare Gass*, 189-190.

66 Ibid., 24 March 1918, 191.

67 Ibid., 10 April 1918, 24 April 1918, 5 May 1918, 193-195.

68 Anne E. Ross, Narrative, 12, MG30 E446, LAC; Ella Mae Bongard, 31 March 1918 in Scott, ed. *Nobody Ever Wins a War*, 35.

69 Ella Mae Bongard, 31 March 1918, 6-7 April 1918 in Scott,ed. *Nobody Ever Wins a War*, 35-36.

70 Clare Gass, 7 May 1918, in Mann, *The War Diary of Clare Gass*, 193-195.

71 Katherine Macdonald to her family, 18 May 1918, 58A 1 114.9, Katharine Macdonald Fonds, CWM.

72 Elizabeth Montizambert, "Causerie de Paris," *Montreal Gazette*, 27 April 1918.

73 Ibid., 20 May 1918.

74 Diary of Hannah Lister, 20 May 1918, 31 May 1918, 18-19 June 1918, 58E 2 3.6, CWM.

75 Charlotte Edith Anderson, 15 February 1918 in Terri L. Monture Wicks, ed. *Diary of A War Nurse, American Expeditionary Force 1918* (n.d., 1996), 8.

76 Ibid., 16 June 1918, 27.

77 Mary MacLeod Moore, "London Letter," *Saturday Night Magazine*, 27 April 1918.

78 Ibid., 4 May 1918.

79 Ella Mae Bongard, 21 July 1918, in Scott, ed., *Nobody Ever Wins a War*, 51.

80 Service record of Dr Margaret Parks, RG150 Acc. 1992-93/166, B7603-S010, LAC.

81 Diary of Hannah Lister, 12 September 1918, 58E 2 3.6, CWM.

82 Anne E. Ross, Narrative, 13, MG30 E446, LAC.

83 Service record of Georgina Pope, RG150 Acc.1992-93/166. B7901-S051. LAC.

84 Macphail, *The Medical Services*, 127.

85 Ibid.

86 Diary of Gertrude Gilbert, 20 August 1918, 22-23 August 1918, 58A 1 22.12, Gertrude Gilbert Fonds, CWM.

87 Ibid., 29-30 August 1918.

88 Ibid.

89 Diary Book X, 16 September 1917, MG30 E155, R2480-0-2-E, Roger F. Clarke Papers, LAC.

90 Diary of Gertrude Gilbert, 2 October 1918, 58A 1 22.12, Gertrude Gilbert Fonds, CWM.

91 Ibid., 24-25 October 1918.

92 Diary of Hannah Lister, 21 October 1918, 58E 2 3.6, CWM; Mildred Forbes to Cairine Wilson, 31 October 1918, Cairine Wilson Papers, Micro. H-2299, LAC.

93 Diary of Gertrude Gilbert, 23 November 1918, 58E 2 3.6, CWM.

94 Ibid., 17 January 1919, 3 March 1919.

95 Service records of Victoria Hennan (B4268-S014), Matilda Green (B3781-S054) and Evelyn McKay (B6924-S054). RG150 Acc. 1992-93/166, LAC.

96 Clint, *Our Bit*, 115.

97 War Diary of No. 1 CGH, May 1918, RG9, III, Vol 3746, No. 51-17-1, LAC.

98 Captain T.W. Ballantyne to Mrs. Macdonald, 29 May 1918, 58A 1 114.9, Katherine Macdonald Fonds, CWM.

99 Katherine Macdonald to her family, 18 May 1918, 58A 1 114.9, CWM.

100 Margaret Macdonald to Mrs. Macdonald, 6 June 1918, 58A 1 114.9, CWM.

101 Captain T.W. Ballantyne to Mrs. Macdonald, 29 May 1918, 58A 11.114.9, CWM.

102 Nicholson, *Canada's Nursing Sisters*, 99; unnamed newspaper obituary notice for Nursing Sister Katherine Macdonald, 58A 1 114.9, CWM. The reference to a "crown of life" comes from Revelation, Chapter 2, verse 10: "Be Thou faithful unto death, and I will give thee a crown of life."

103 Report by Matron Ethel B. Ridley, 26 May 1918, 58A 1 114 9, CWM, Katherine Macdonald Fonds.

104 Clint, *Our Bit*, 117.

105 Nicholson, *Canada's Nursing Sisters*, 94. The Military Medal was awarded to personnel of the British Army and other arms of the British forces, and to personnel of other Commonwealth countries below commissioned rank. Established in 1916, it recognised acts of bravery and devotion to duty under fire.

106 Graves, *A Crown of Life*, 302.

107 Erich Maria Remarque, *All Quiet on the Western Front*, (London, 1929), 266.

Chapter 4. "A chapter, unique in its joys and sorrows" Medical Service in the Eastern Mediterranean

1 From "Out There" by Elspeth Honeyman, in Garvin ed., *Canadian Poems of the Great War*, 93.

2 Laura Holland to her mother, 8 (11) August 1915, Laura Holland Fonds, CS 1-18a, UBCA.

3 Alan Moorehead, *Gallipoli* (London, 1959), 35.

4 Col. G.W.L. Nicholson, *Canadian Expeditionary Force 1914-1919* (Ottawa: 1964), 497.

5 Clint, *Our Bit*, 50.

6 Alice K. Ross, quoted in Toman, *Sister Soldiers*, 80.

7 Clint, *Our Bit*, 52.

8 Anne E. Ross, Narrative, 7, MG30 E446, LAC.

9 Vera Brittain, *Testament of Youth*, 270. Vera chronicled her experiences during the First

World War in this best-selling memoir, first published in 1933.

10 Laura Holland to her mother, 8 (11) August 1915, Laura Holland Fonds, CS 1-18a, UBCA. Laura often started her letters and added sections on subsequent dates. In this case she started her letter on 8 August and the extract quoted was written on 11 August 1915.

11 Bruce, *Humour in Tragedy*, 21.

12 Clint, *Our Bit*, 57.

13 Macphail, *The Medical Services*, 296.

14 Clint, *Our Bit*, 57.

15 Ibid., 59.

16 Ibid.

17 War Diary of No. 1 Canadian Stationary Hospital, 8 September 1915, RG9-III-B-2, Vol. 3747, LAC; Macphail, *The Medical Services*, 296.

18 Wilson-Simmie, *Lights Out*, 75, 65; Clint, *Our Bit*, 62.

19 Clint, *Our Bit*, 62.

20 Bruce, *Humour in Tragedy*, 25.

21 Macphail, *The Medical Services*, 297.

22 Diary of Florence Hunter, August 1915, 18, 58A 1 235.1, CWM.

23 Wilson-Simmie, *Lights Out*, 74.

24 Laura Holland to her mother, 25 September 1915, Laura Holland Fonds, CS 1-24, UBCA.

25 Helen Fowlds to her mother, 16 September 1915, 69-001, I/1, TUA.

26 Mabel Clint, *Our Bit*, 63. Her phrasing likely derived from the first three lines of "The Soldier" by British poet, Rupert Brooke, who himself died on his way to Gallipoli.

27 Clint, *Our Bit*, 61-62.

28 Bruce, *Humour in Tragedy*, 36.

29 Ibid., 35, 37.

30 Ibid., 34.

31 Wilson-Simmie, *Lights Out*, 79.

32 Ibid., 64.

33 Anne E. Ross, Narrative, 7, MG30 E446, LAC; Laura Holland to her mother, 20 September 1915, Laura Holland Fonds, CS 1-23, UBCA.

34 Wilson-Simmie, *Lights Out*, 80.

35 Mildred Forbes to Cairine Wilson, 22 October 1915, Cairine Wilson Papers, Micro. H-2299, LAC.

36 Laura Holland to her mother, 20 September 1915, Laura Holland Fonds, CS 1-23, UBCA.

37 Clint, *Our Bit*, 65.

38 Ibid.

39 Wilson-Simmie, *Lights Out*, 92.

40 Bruce, *Humour in Tragedy* 5, 38, 28.

41 Ibid., 37-38, 60.

42 Ibid., 42.

43 Ibid., 75.

44 Wilson-Simmie, *Lights Out*, 64.

45 Clint, *Our Bit*, 71.

46 Toman, *Sister Soldiers*, 88.

47 Diary of Florence Hunter, 15 November 1915, 20, 58A 1 235.1, CWM.

48 Helen Fowlds to her mother, 28 December 1915, 69-001, I/1, TUA.

49 Bruce, *Humour in Tragedy*, 43.

50 Helen Fowlds to her mother, 19 December 1915, 69-001, I/1, TUA. Anzac Cove and Suvla Bay, to which Helen refers, were Allied landing sites on the Gallipoli peninsula.

51 Diary of Florence Hunter, 31 January 1916, 58A 1 235.1, CWM.

52 Wilson-Simmie, *Lights Out*, 100.

53 Laura Holland to her mother, 28 (22) January 1916, Laura Holland Fonds, CS 1-41, UBCA.

54 Bruce, *Humour in Tragedy*, 43-45.

55 Report, "No. 1 Canadian Stationary Hospital," Folder XII, MG30 E45, Margaret Macdonald Papers, LAC.

56 Lieutenant-General Sir Alfred Keogh to Major-General G. Carleton Jones, 15 September 1915, in Nicholson, *Canadian Expeditionary Force 1914-1919*, 498.

57 From "The Sisters Graves at Lemnos" by Vera Brittain, *The Oxford Magazine*, 11 May 1917. The title of the poem was later amended to "The Sisters Buried at Lemnos."

58 Victoria Wallace, Director General of the Commonwealth War Graves Commission. www.canadainternational.gc.ca/greece/eyes_abroad/fallen nurses.

59 Private O. Waller, quoted in article, "'The Nurse of the Mediterranean' in the Eyes of the ANZACS" by Albert Galea, *The Malta Independent on Sunday*, 11 November 2018, 10-11.

60 Laura Holland to her mother, 17 (26) August 1916, Laura Holland Fonds, CS 1-23, UBCA.

61 Diary of Laura Gamble, 13 November 1916, MG30 E510, Laura Gamble Papers, LAC. St. Patrick's Hospital, Malta, opened on 15 August 1915 and eventually expanded to 1,168 beds. It closed on 27 April 1917.

62 Vera Brittain, *Testament of Youth*, 276.

63 Ibid., 274.

64 Private Sidney Scowcroft, quoted in article "'The Nurse of the Mediterranean' in the Eyes of the ANZACS" by Albert Galea, *The Malta Independent on Sunday*, 11 November 2018, 10-11.

65 Vera Brittain, quoted in Anne Powell, *Women in the War Zone*, 322.

66 Brian Douglas Tennyson, *The Canadian Experience of the Great War: A Guide to Memoirs*, (Lanham, Maryland, 2013), Note 1421, 313.

67 Mabel lucas, quoted in Toman, *Sister Soldiers*, 204.

68 Toman, *Sister Soldiers*, 169.

69 Luella Denton, quoted in Toman, *Sister Soldiers*, 90; Diary of Laura Gamble, 13 November 1916, MG30 E510, Laura Gamble Papers, LAC.

70 Bruce, *Humour in Tragedy*, 17.

71 Laura Holland to her mother, 17 (26) August 1916, Laura Holland Fonds, CS 2-18, UBCA.

Chapter 5. "Quite different to the work we had in France": Medical Service in Greece, the Balkans and the Middle East

1 From "Canada to England, July 1st, 1917" by Horace Bray, in Garvin, ed., *Canadian Poems of the Great War*, 36.

2 Nicholson, *Canada's Nursing Sisters*, 72-73.

3 Dr. H.C.L. Lindsay, "In Salonika," *The Gold Stripe*, Vol. 1, 132-133.

4 May Bastedo, "My Trip Abroad," 16 November 1915, 58A 1 2.1, May Bastedo Fonds, CWM.

5 Ruby Peterkin to 'Rene', undated but presumed November 1915, MG30 E160, LAC.

6 Ruby Peterkin to her family, 3 December 1915, MG30 E160, Ruby Peterkin Papers, LAC.

7 May Bastedo, "My Trip Abroad," 20 December 1915, 58A 1 2.1, May Bastedo Fonds, CWM.

8 Ibid., 29 December 1915, 31 December 1915.

9 Dr. H.C.L. Lindsay, "In Salonika," *The Gold Stripe*, Vol. 1, 134.

10 Laura Holland to her mother, 11 March 1916, Laura Holland Fonds, CS 1-53, UBCA.

11 Diary of Laura Gamble, 7 January 1916, MG30 E510, LAC.

12 Ibid., 27 March 1916.

13 Helen Fowlds to her mother, 11 March 1916, 69-001, I/1, TUA.

14 Mildred Forbes to Cairine Wilson, 11 March 1916, Cairine Wilson Papers, Micro. H-2299, LAC.

15 Laura Holland to her mother, 5 March 1916, Laura Holland Fonds, CS 1-50, UBCA.

16 Constantine Fraser, "Speaking Volumes," in *Slightly Foxed: The Real Reader's Quarterly*, No. 54, Summer 2017, 48. This expression can be translated to mean "before the term existed."

17 Laura Holland to her mother, 5 July 1916, Laura Holland Fonds, CS 2-13, UBCA.

18 Nicholson, *Nursing Sisters of Canada*, 72; Helen Fowlds to her mother, 22 April 1916, 69-001, I/1, TUA.

19 Helen Fowlds to her mother, 22 April 1916, 69-001, I/1, TUA.

20 Laura Holland to her mother, 7 May 1916, Laura Holland Fonds, CS 2-3, UBCA.

21 May Bastedo to her family, 25 May 1916, 58A 1 2.1, CWM.

22 Laura Holland to her mother, 4 June 1916, Laura Holland Fonds, CS 2-8, UBCA.

23 Ibid.

24 Diary of Laura Gamble, 6 June 1916, 31 August 1916, MG30 E510, LAC.

25 Mildred Forbes to Cairine Wilson, 22 June 1916, Cairine Wilson Papers, Micro. H-2299, LAC.

26 Bruce, *Humour in Tragedy*, 57.

27 Ibid., 22 July 1916.

28 Nicholson, *Canada's Nursing Sisters*, 76.

29 Helen Fowlds to her mother, 19 May 1916, 69-001, I/1, TUA; Mildred Forbes to Cairine Wilson, 7 August 1916, Cairine Wilson Papers, Micro.

H-2299, LAC; Laura Holland to her mother, 31 May 1916, Laura Holland Fonds, CS 2-7, UBCA.

30 Laura Holland to her mother, 7 May 1916, 21 May 1916, 24 June 1916, Laura Holland Fonds, CS 2-3, 2-5, 2-12, UBCA.

31 Ruby Peterkin to 'Rene', 14 April 1916, MG30 E160, LAC.

32 Ruby Peterkin to 'Rene', 2 February 1916, MG30 E160, LAC. The Victoria Cross was, and still is, the highest award for valour "in the face of the enemy" made to British armed forces.

33 Bruce, *Humour in Tragedy*, 62.

34 Dr. H.C.L. Lindsay, "In Salonika," *The Gold Stripe*, Volume 1, 135.

35 Laura Holland to her mother, 4 June 1916, Laura Holland Fonds, CS 2-8, UBCA; Bruce, *Humour in Tragedy*, 59-60, 62.

36 Bruce, *Humour in Tragedy*, 63.

37 Georgi Kolenko to Florence Hunter, 16 December 1916, 58A 1 235.1, CWM.

38 Bruce, *Humour in Tragedy*, 63-64.

39 Dr. H.C.L. Lindsay, "In Salonika," *The Gold Stripe*, Vol. 1, 135.

40 J. Johnston Abraham, *Surgeon's Journal: the Autobiography of J. Johnston Abraham* (Melbourne, 1957), 143, 147-148.

41 Abraham, *Surgeon's Journal*, 134.

42 Albiny Paquette, *Hon. Albiny Paquette: Soldat, Médecin, Maire, Député-Ministre: 33 années à la législature de Québec: Souvenirs d'une vie de travail et de bonheur*, (Montreal, 1977), 30-31; Pauline Gill, *Docteure Irma: l'Indomptable* (Quebec, 2008), 372.

43 In 1900 pneumonia, influenza, tuberculosis and enteritis were the main causes of death in the United States, and children under five accounted for forty per cent of all deaths from these infections.

44 Albiny Paquette, www.fondationlionelgroulx.org/Irma-LeVasseur-et-les.html.

45 Passenger Lists, Lusitania Resource, www.rmslusitania.info.

46 Catherine Travis, quote from "Progress and Permanence: Women and the New Brunswick Museum 1880 to 1980," http://women and museum.com/ctravis.htm.

47 The Scottish Women's Hospitals for Foreign Services (SWH), was founded in 1914 and was one of the largest volunteer medical groups in the war. Its units provided trained staff and ancillary workers and by 1918, the organization had sent help to France, Russia, Salonika, Serbia, Malta, Roumania and Corsica.

48 Anon., "Diary of a Red Cross Nurse in Serbia," in *The Canadian Nurse*, Volume 13, No. 7, July 1917, 359.

49 Dr. Elsie Inglis, quoted in Powell, *Women in the War Zone*, 178. Dr Inglis, a suffragist and qualified doctor from Edinburgh, organized the Serbian unit of the SWH which treated patients

throughout the typhus epidemic and stayed on to cope with hundreds of wounded men during the Serbian Army's retreat.

50 Anon., "Diary of a Red Cross Nurse in Serbia," in *The Canadian Nurse*, Volume 13, No. 7, July 1917, 361-367. In the event, nothing came of the German claim.

51 Marshall, *Firing Lines*, 127.

52 "Progress and Permanence: Women and the New Brunswick Museum 1880 to 1980". http://women and museum.com/ctravis.htm.

53 Pauline Gill, *Docteure Irma: l'Indomptable* (Quebec, 2008), title page.

54 Irma LeVasseur, quoted in www.fondation-lionelgroulx.org/Irma-LeVasseur-et-les.html.

55 Paquette, *Hon. Albiny Paquette*, 35.

56 Wilson-Simmie, *Lights Out*, 56.

57 Bruce, *Humour in Tragedy*, 18-19.

58 Ibid., 18.

59 Helen Fowlds to her mother, 16 August 1915, 69-001, I/1, TUA.

60 Laura Holland to her mother, 11 February 1916, Laura Holland Fonds, CS 1-45, UBCA.

61 Ibid., 12 February 1916, CS 1-46.

62 Mary McNaughton letter to the *Cobourg World*, August 1915, in Percy Climo, *A Collection of World War 1 Letters as published in The Cobourg World Newspaper, 1914-1919* (Colbourne, Ontario, 1985), 186, 188.

63 Nicholson, *Canada's Nursing Sisters*, 66-67.

64 Ibid., 67.

65 Mary McNaughton letter to the *Cobourg World*, August 1915, in Climo, *A Collection of World War 1 Letters* , 188.

66 Elsie D. Collis, no date given, quoted in Toman, *Sister Soldiers*, 91.

67 Powell, *Women in the War Zone*, 207-212.

68 Adie, *Fighting on the Home Front*, 111.

69 Laura Holland to her mother, 11 February 1916, Laura Holland Fonds, CS 1-45, UBCA; Helen Fowlds to her mother, 15 February 1916, 69-001,I/1, TUA.

70 Mary Bird to her father, 28 June 1916, 31 July 1916, 58A 1 221.4, Mary Bird Fonds, CWM.

71 Laura Holland to her mother, 14 (16) February 1916, Laura Holland Fonds, CS 1-47, UBCA. Phlebitis is a condition in which a vein becomes inflamed.

72 Clint, *Our Bit*, 82.

73 Ibid., 84.

74 Ibid.

75 Ibid., 83.

76 Diary of Lieutenant Harold Price in Greenhous, ed., *A Rattle of Pebbles*, xii.

77 Ida Jefferson, quoted in Powell, *Women in the War Zone*, 308, 310.

78 Diary of Harold Price, 1 February 1918 in Greenhous, ed. *A Rattle of Pebbles*, 261.

79 Ibid., 1 February 1918, 261.

80 Ibid., 3 February 1918, 262.

81 Ida Jefferson, quoted in Powell, *Women in the War Zone*, 308, 310.

Chapter 6. Caregiving in "the realm of politics and diplomacy": Medical Service in Russia

1 From "Out of the West" by Cuthbert Goodridge MacDonald, in Garvin, ed., *Canadian Poems of the Great War*, 118.

2 Anon. *The Russian Diary of an Englishman, Petrograd, 1915-1917*, (London,1919), x.

3 Marie Brown, *Russia and Revolution: The Promise and the Performance* (Glasgow, 1979), 41.

4 Caroline Moorehead, *Dunant's Dream: War, Switzerland and the History of the Red Cross* (London, 1999), 232.

5 Ibid.

6 Alexander Chancellor, "A Forgotten Hospital that was the British Empire's Gift to our Russian Allies," 16 April 1916, www.spectator.co.uk/article/long-life-14-april-2016.

7 Ibid. Muriel Paget (née Finch-Hatton) CBE, (1876-1938) was the daughter of the 12th Earl of Winchelsea and the wife of Richard Paget, later Baron Paget of Cranmore.

8 Michael Harmer, *The Forgotten Hospital* (Chichester, 1982), 5.

9 Although the British Red Cross and the Order of Saint John of Jerusalem in England supported the Anglo-Russian Hospital through large donations, its status was ambiguous as it was neither an official military hospital nor an official Red Cross hospital.

10 Diary of Sarah Macnaughtan, 24 November 1915, quoted in Powell, *Women in the War Zone*, 155-156.

11 Lady Sybil Grey (1882-1966) was the second daughter of Albert, 4th Earl Grey. She was extremely well travelled and had lived in Canada from 1904-1911 while her father was governor general.

12 Simon Boyd, *Lady Sybil: Empire, War and Revolution* (Kendal, 2017), 123.

13 Sir Lawrence Jones, quoted in Boyd, *Lady Sybil*, xv.

14 Sophie Hoerner to her mother, 26 September 1915, MG30 E290, LAC.

15 The regiment was named after Princess Patricia, its honorary colonel and the daughter of Prince Arthur, Duke of Connaught, who was Canada's governor-general in 1914.

16 Postcard from Kathleen Rosamond to Jessie Cotton, 31 October 1915, Rosamond Family Papers, MVTM.

17 Countess Olga Poutiatine was the daughter of a Russian nobleman and a British heiress. She was born and raised in Moscow but was living in Britain with her mother when the war began. Countess Olga had volunteered for work in a British hospital but dreamed of going back to work in Russia, which she was now able to do.

18 The Gulf of Riga is a bay on the Baltic Sea that lies between Latvia and Estonia. The city of Riga, present-day capital of Latvia was, at the time of the First World War, the fifth largest city in the Russian Empire.

19 Diary of Dorothy Cotton, 7 November 1915, 11 November 1915, MG30 E464, Dorothy Cotton Papers, LAC.

20 Ibid., 14-15 November 1915.

21 Dorothy Cotton, "A Word Picture of the Anglo-Russian Hospital, Petrograd," The Canadian Nurse, 22:9, September 1926, 486.

22 Ibid., 486.

23 Ibid., 487.

24 Diary of Dorothy Cotton, 24 November 1915, MG30 E464, LAC.

25 Dorothy Cotton to her mother, 24 November 1915. MG30 E464, LAC.

26 Sybil Grey, quoted in Boyd, Lady Sybil, 131.

27 Moorehead, Dunant's Dream, 235.

28 Boyd, Lady Sybil, 131.

29 Ibid., 133.

30 Dorothy Cotton to Elsie Cotton, 5 December 1915, MG30 E464, LAC.

31 Anon, The Russian Diary of an Englishman, 17.

32 Dorothy Cotton to her mother, 24 November 1915, postcard to Charles Cotton, 28 November 1915, MG30 E464, LAC.

33 Dorothy Cotton to her mother, 24 November 1915, MG30 E464, LAC.

34 Dorothy Cotton to Elsie Cotton, 5 December 1915, MG30 E464, LAC.

35 Ibid.

36 Anon., The Russian Diary of an Englishman, 16, 18-19.

37 Sybil Grey, quoted in Boyd, Lady Sybil, 154; Dorothy Cotton, letter to 'Bob' (Robert Fetherstonhaugh), 16 December 1915, "War Diaries and Letters: Dorothy Cotton," Fetherstonhaugh Papers, MUL.

38 Dorothy Cotton, quoted in Toman, "Eyewitness to Revolution," in Jane Brooks and Christine E. Hallett, One Hundred Years of Wartime Nursing Practices, 1854-1953 (Manchester, 2015), 132. The Honourable Etheldreda Mary Lindley, née Fraser (1872-1949), was a daughter of Simon Fraser, 13th Baron Lovat. Her husband, the Honourable Francis Oswald Lindley, was a British diplomat who had served in numerous locations in Europe and the Middle East before being appointed to Petrograd in 1915.

39 Dorothy Cotton to her mother, 25 December 1915, MG30 E464, LAC.

40 Ibid., 25 January 1916.

41 Toman, Sister Soldiers, 91. Throughout her service with the Anglo-Russian Hospital, Dorothy Cotton was on secondment from the CAMC nursing service.

42 Dorothy Cotton to her mother, 25 January 1916, MG30 E464, LAC.

43 Sarah Macnaughtan diary, 24 November 1915, quoted in Powell, Women in the War Zone, 157.

44 Sybil Grey, quoted in Boyd, Lady Sybil, 162; Moorehead, Dunant's Dream, 235.

45 Sybil Grey, quoted in Boyd, Lady Sybil, 162.

46 Dorothy Cotton to her mother, 25 January 1916, MG30 E464, LAC.

47 Diary of Dorothy Cotton, 1 February 1916, MG30 E464, LAC.

48 Dorothy Cotton, Report III, 20, MG30 E464, LAC.

49 Cotton, "A Word Picture of the Anglo-Russian Hospital, Petrograd," The Canadian Nurse, 22:9, September 1926, 486; Daily Graphic, 22 February 1916, 1.

50 Dvinsk was one of a number of names in various languages used to identify the city known today by its Latvian name, Daugavpils.

51 Diary of Dorothy Cotton, 15 February 1916, MG30 E464, 22.

52 Dorothy Cotton to her mother, 5 April 1916, MG30 E464, LAC.

53 Dorothy Cotton to her mother, 4 April 1916, MG30 E464, LAC.

54 Dorothy Cotton, letter to "Bob," 16 December 1915, "War Diaries and Letters: Dorothy Cotton," Featherstonhaugh Papers, MUL. The term "Sister Buttons" derived from the fact that the uniform of CAMC nurses included a double row of buttons on the dress.

55 Vilna was the Russian, Latvian and Hebrew name for the city known today as Vilnius, capital of Lithuania.

56 Dorothy Cotton to her mother, 30 April 1915, MG30 E464, LAC.

57 Dorothy Cotton to "Traddles," 1 May 1916, MG30 E464, LAC.

58 Dorothy Cotton to Mary Rosamond, 4 May 1916. MG30 E464, LAC.

59 Diary of Dorothy Cotton, May 1916, 57-58, MG30 E464, LAC.

60 Diary of Dorothy Cotton, 10 June 1916, 35, MG30 E464, LAC.

61 Sybil Grey, quoted in Boyd, Lady Sybil, 193-184.

62 Diary of Dorothy Cotton, 14 June 1916, 39-40, MG30 E464, LAC.

63 Boyd, Lady Sybil, 184.

64 Ibid., 186-187.

65 Dorothy Cotton to Elsie Cotton, 17 June 1916, MG30 E464, LAC.

66 Sybil Grey, quoted in Boyd, Lady Sybil, 188.

67 Dorothy Cotton postcard to Ross Cotton, 12 June 1916, MG30 E464, LAC.

68 Agar Adamson to Mabel Adamson, 14 June 1916, in Christie, The Letters of Agar Adamson, 188.

69 Elsie Cotton to Dorothy Cotton, 29 June 1916, MG30 E464, LAC.

70 Sybil Grey quoted in Boyd, Lady Sybil, 189.

71 Diary of Dorothy Cotton, June 1916, 26-38,

MG30 E464, LAC; Sybil Grey, quoted in Boyd, *Lady Sybil*, 190.

72 Lady Muriel Paget to her husband, 12 August 1916, quoted in Powell, *Women in the War Zone*, 297-300.

73 Nicholson, *Canada's Nursing Sisters*, 91. Gertrude Squire's term of service also included several weeks with a field hospital in Russia's Caucasus region.

74 Syra Timasheff to Dorothy Cotton, 1916 (no exact date given), MG30 E464, LAC.

75 Agar Adamson to Mabel Adamson, 16 September 1916, in Christie, *Letters of Agar Adamson*, 220.

76 Dorothy Seymour, quoted in Powell, *Women in the War Zone*, 301.

77 Ibid., 303.

78 Dorothy Cotton to Elsie Cotton, 1 March 1917, MG30 E464, LAC.

79 Ibid., 4 March 1917.

80 Ibid.

81 Edith Hegan, 15 March 1917, in Powell, *Women in the War Zone*, 354. A "shilling shocker" was a novel of crime or violence that cost a shilling to buy and was very popular in the Victorian era.

82 Edith Hegan, "The Russian Revolution from a Hospital Window," *Harper's Monthly Magazine*, 135 (1918), 557.

83 Ibid.

84 Dorothy Cotton to Elsie Cotton, 4 March 1917, MG30 E464, LAC.

85 Ibid.

86 Dorothy Cotton to Elsie Cotton, 12 March 1917, MG30 E464, LAC.

87 Ibid.

88 Dorothy Seymour, quoted in Powell, *Women in the War Zone*, 354.

89 Ibid.

90 Ibid. After being moved to Yekaterinburg in the Ural mountains, the czar, czarina and their children were shot and killed in July 1918 by Bolshevik troops.

91 Toman, "Eyewitness to Revolution," in Brooks and Hallett, *One Hundred Years of Wartime Nursing Practices*, 136.

92 Cotton, "A Word Picture of the Anglo-Russian Hospital, Petrograd". *The Canadian Nurse*, 22: 9, September 1926, 488.

93 Toman, "Eyewitness to Revolution," in Brooks and Hallett, *One Hundred Years of Wartime Nursing Practices*, 125.

94 Ibid., 138.

Chapter 7. "The courage displayed by the nursing staff matched that of the greatest heroes of the war": Medical Service at Sea

1 From "Freedom" by Albert Durrant Watson, in Garvin, ed., *Canadian Poems of the Great War*, 249.

2 Arthur Banks, *A Military Atlas of the First World War*, (Barnsley, 1989), 236.

3 Translation of announcement published in the *Reichsanzeiger* (the official newspaper of the German Reich), 4 February 1915, quoted in Sir Julian S. Corbett, *Naval Operations*, Vol. II, (Nashville, 1997), 260-261. The statement refers to the fact that on 31 January 1915 the British government instructed British ships to fly neutral flags in the war zone, presumably for the purpose of avoiding recognition by German naval vessels.

4 Emily Edwardes, November 1916, quoted in "Diaries reveal harrowing experiences of First World War nursing sisters," *Vancouver Courier*, 20 March 2015.

5 Wilson-Simmie, *Lights Out*, 58. According to the London *Times* of 6 September 1915, not all the men aboard the *Royal Edward* were lost. A published Admiralty casualty list stated that of a total of 1,367 officers and men who had embarked on the *Royal Edward* at Avonmouth, 13 officers and 851 troops were missing, believed drowned.

6 Ibid., 16, 18. Despite these precautions, the *Hesperian* was torpedoed and sunk several months later on 4 September 1915 by the German submarine *U-20*, the same U-Boat that had attacked the *Lusitania*.

7 Diary of Hannah Lister, August 1917, 26-28, 58E 2 3.6, CWM.

8 Diary of Ella Mae Bongard, 15-16 October 1915 in Scott, *Nobody Ever Wins A War*, 13.

9 By mid-August 1918, a total of thirteen British hospital ships had been sunk in British or French waters, the Aegean and the Mediterranean, plus several others belonging to Allied nations. This left many people outraged.

10 Wilson-Simmie, *Lights Out*, 115. The vessel in question, HMHS *Anglia*, was later struck in the English Channel by a mine laid by the German submarine UC-5, one mile east of Folkestone Gate.

11 Beatrice Kilbourn, 20 February 1917, in "Diaries Reveal Harrowing Experiences of First World War Nursing Sisters," *Vancouver Courier*, 20 March 2015.

12 Wilson-Simmie, *Lights Out*, 55.

13 Diary of May Bastedo, 28-29 October 1915, 58A 1 2.1, CWM.

14 May Bastedo to her mother, 20 November 1915, 58A 1 2.1, CWM.

15 Diary of Laura Gamble, 28 October 1915, 47, MG30 E510, LAC. Her mention of a "maxim," referred to the German Maxim 08 machine gun.

16 Report on Gallipoli, *Canadian Nursing and Hospital Review*, January 1922, 32. At Gallipoli hospital ships were requested by the Turkish military high command to remain beyond the range of fire, or they would not be responsible for their safety.

17 Lieutenant N. King Wilson quoted in Mathieson, *My Grandfather's War*, 139-140.

18 Hague Convention X, 1907, Article IV.

19 Macphail, *The Medical Services*, 242.

20 *Amiral* Carl Scheer, quoted in Macphail, *The Medical Services*, 242.

21 Unnamed nurse, quoted in *Canadian Nursing and Hospital Review*, January 1922, 32.

22 Wilson-Simmie, *Lights Out*, 54.

23 Leetooze, *WW1 Nursing Sisters of Old Durham County*, 40.

24 T.H. Potts, "The Last Voyage Westward of H.M.H.S. 'Llandovery Castle,'" *The Gold Stripe*, Vol. 1, xxxv-xxxvi, xxxviii.

25 Ibid., xxxvi, xxxviii, xl.

26 Service records of Major Alistair Fraser, B3275-S007, and Lieutenant James Fraser, B3284-S002, RG150, Acc. 1992-93/166, LAC.

27 Biographical information for Rena McLean, *Dictionary of Canadian Biography*: www.biographi.ca/mclean_rena_maude.

28 https://rememberingfirstworldwarnurses.blogspot.com.

29 The term "mentioned in despatches" related to a member of the armed forces whose gallant or meritorious service in the face of the enemy warranted the inclusion of their name in an official report prepared by their superior officer, and sent to the high command.

30 Official Report of the Sinking of the "Llandovery Castle" as issued to the press by the Hon. The Minister, Overseas Military Forces of Canada, 6, RG24 Vol. 1868, File FN-WW1-48, LAC.

31 Ibid.

32 Ibid., 3.

33 Ibid., 3-4.

34 Sergeant Knight, "The Sinking of HMHS Llandovery Castle," courtesy of Lori Douglas and Port Alberni Library, 1-2.

35 Ibid., 4.

36 Official Report of the Sinking of the "Llandovery Castle," 8, RG24 Vol. 1868, File FN-WW1-48, LAC.

37 Ibid.

38 Knight, "The Sinking of HMHS Llandovery Castle," 5.

39 Service record of Margaret Marjory Fraser, B3287-S053, RG150, Acc. 1992-93/166, LAC.

40 *The Times*, 2 July 1918, 1. The "Fastnet" referred to the Fastnet Rock, which stands in the Atlantic Ocean and forms the most southerly point of Ireland.

41 *Halifax Chronicle Herald*, 2 July 1918, 1; *Toronto Star*, 2 July 1918, 2.

42 Mildred Forbes to Cairine Wilson, 24 July 1918, Cairine Wilson Papers, Micro. H-2299, LAC.

43 Service record of Sophie Mary Hoerner, B4418-S041, RG150 Accession 1992-93/166, LAC.

44 General George Tuxford, quoted in Bruce Cane, *It Made You Think of Home: The Haunting Journal of Deward Barnes, EEF: 1916-1919*. Toronto: 2004, 228.

45 Official Report of the Sinking of the "Llandovery Castle," 8, RG24 Vol. 1868, File FN-WW1-48, LAC.

46 Knight, "The Sinking of HMHS Llandovery Castle," 5.

47 Ibid., 8.

48 Claude Mullins, *The Leipzig Trials: An Account of the War Criminals' Trials and a Study of German Mentality* (London, 1921), 110.

49 Mullins, *The Leipzig Trials*, 127.

50 Ibid., 115, 132.

51 Ibid., 117-118.

52 Ibid., 119.

53 Ibid., 126.

54 Ibid., 127.

55 Jürgen Matthäus, "The Lessons of Leipzig: Punishing German War Criminals after The First World War," 17, in Patricia Herbert and Jürgen Matthäus ed., *Atrocities on Trial: Historical Perspectives on the Politics of Prosecuting War Crimes* (Lincoln, Nebraska, 2008).

56 Service records of the nursing sisters listed, RG150 Accession 1992-93/166, LAC.

57 Paul Ciufo quoted in www.llandoverycastle.ca/creative-team.

58 www.eventfinda.co.nz/2018/armistice-day-centenary-service/auckland/parnell; Memorandum sent to next-of-kin by Colonel G. Carleton Jones, 28 June 1918, quoted in Nicholson, *Canada's Nursing Sisters*, 96.

59 From "To Our Immortal Dead" by S. Morgan-Powell in Garvin, ed., *Canadian Poems of the Great War*, 159.

60 Margaret Macdonald to W.R. Landon, 12 May 1922, MG30 E45, File correspondence 1923, LAC. Of those Canadian nurses who served with the Imperial nursing services, 183 later enlisted with the CAMC.

61 Ibid.

62 Wording from the Sisters' Memorial, Hall of Honour, Parliament Hill, Ottawa.

Chapter 8. "If only you knew what a comfort you are to us, dear Madame": Civilian Volunteer Work

1 From "Our Day" by Isabel Ecclestone Mackay, in Garvin, ed., *Canadian Poems of the Great War*, 136.

2 Anon, *Canada in the Great World War*, Vol. VI (Toronto, 1921), 176.

3 Mabel Adamson, 27 October 1914, quoted in Gwyn, *Tapestry of War*, 109.

4 Gwyn, *Tapestry of War*, 109.

5 Cunard poster "Europe via Liverpool," sailings from 1 May 1915 to 4 June 1915, author's collection.

6 According to Lusitania Resource, www.rmslusitania.info, there were sixty passengers of British nationality resident in Canada who travelled 1st Class, 236 in 2nd Class and sixty-four in 3rd Class.

7 Passenger lists, Lusitania Resource, www.rmslusitania.info.

8 Ibid.

9 Lusitania Resource, www.rmslusitania.info.

10 The body of Frances Stephens was recovered and later transported to Canada. However, the *Hesperian*, the ship which took the body, was torpedoed and sunk by the same submarine that sank the *Lusitania*. Therefore, by the worst of coincidences, Mrs Stephens was twice a victim of *U-20*.

11 *Globe and Mail*, 10 May 1915.

12 Eyewitness account of Sarah Lohden, 2nd class passenger list, Lusitania Resource, www.rmslusitania.info; Lady Marguerite Allan, *Globe and Mail*, 9 May 1915.

13 Lady Marguerite Allan, *Globe and Mail*, 9 May 1915.

14 Mary MacLeod Moore, "London Letter," *Saturday Night*, 5 June 1915.

15 Ian Hugh Maclean Miller, *Our Glory and Our Grief: Torontonians and the Great War* (Toronto, 2002), 45.

16 White, *Zeppelin Nights*, 100, 102.

17 Adie, *Fighting on the Home Front*, 156.

18 Sir Henry Lucy, quoted in Adie, *Fighting on the Home Front*, 56.

19 Lord Northcliffe, quoted in Adie, *Fighting on the Home Front*, 25.

20 Anon, *Canada in the Great World War*, Vol. VI, 181.

21 *London Gazette*, 7 June 1918, 6718; Grace's Guide to British Industrial History, www.gracesguide.co.uk/C._A._Vandervell_and_Co. The award of Member of The Most Excellent Order of the British Empire was established in June 1917. It rewards contributions to the arts and sciences, public service and work with charitable and welfare organizations. There are five levels: Member (MBE), Officer (OBE), Commander (CBE), Knight or Dame Commander (DBE), and Knight or Dame Grand Cross (GBE).

22 Jane Robinson, *A Force to be reckoned with: A History of the Women's Institute* (London, 2011), 17, 24-25.

23 Entry for Sir George Perley, *Dictionary of Canadian Biography*, Volume 16 (Toronto/Montreal, 2003).

24 Anon., *Canada in The Great World War*, Vol. II (Toronto, 1919), 212; Mary MacLeod Moore," Canadian Women War Workers Overseas" *The Canadian* Vol. 52, No. 3 (January 1919), 26.

25 Moore, "Canadian Women War Workers Overseas," 42.

26 Ibid., 43.

27 Eleanor McLaren Brown quoted in Anon., *Canada in The Great World War*, Vol. VI, 207-208.

28 Plummer, *With the First Canadian Contingent*, Introduction, 5.

29 Sarah Glassford, *Marching as To War: The Canadian Red Cross Society 1885-1939*,(Ph.D. dissertation, 2007), 61.

30 Anon., *Canada in the Great World War*, Vol. II, 200.

31 The money was eventually used to pay for twenty ambulances and a wing of a naval hospital in Britain.

32 Sarah Glassford, *Mobilizing Mercy: A History of the Canadian Red Cross* (Montreal, 2017), 16-17.

33 Anon. *Canada in the Great World War*, Vol. II, 191.

34 Glassford, *Mobilizing Mercy*, 62-63.

35 The honorary secretary of the Committee of Management of the Canadian Nurses' Club in London, quoted in Anon., *Canada in the Great World War*, Vol. VI, 214.

36 Binyon, *For Dauntless France:* , 31.

37 White, *Zeppelin Nights*, 138-139.

38 Adie, *Fighting on the Home Front*, 34.

39 *The Tatler*, 9 May 1917. The show took place on 11 May 1917.

40 Although Canada did not use Red Cross personnel in its military medical service, the CRCS undertook the selection of nurses who were deployed by the British Red Cross Society in its hospitals or convalescent homes.

41 Glassford, *Mobilizing Mercy*, 88.

42 Ibid., 113.

43 Marshall, *Firing Lines*, 123-126, 83-85.

44 Mary MacLeod Moore, "London Letter," *Saturday Night*, 26 August 1918.

45 Agar Adamson, quoted in Gwyn, *Tapestry of War*, 158.

46 Anon., *Canada in the Great World War*, Vol. VI, 182-183.

47 Henrica Belson in *The Record*, 15 February 1915, 4, LWRM.

48 Gwyn, *Tapestry of War*, 108.

49 Gwyn, *Tapestry of War*, 427; Agar Adamson to Mabel Adamson, 12 March 1915, 10 March 1915, 17 March 1915, 1 February 1916, 6 March 1915, MG30 E149, Adamson Papers, LAC; Anthony Adamson, *Wasps in the Attic* (Published privately, 1988), 223, 209.

50 *The Canadian Annual Review for 1917*, 508; Gwyn, *Tapestry of War*, 107.

51 *The Canadian Annual Review for 1917*, 508.

52 Andrew P. Hyde, *The First Blitz: The German Air Campaign against Britain 1917-1918* (Barnsley, 2002), 89.

53 Bilbrough, 25 May 1917, *My War Diary*, 195-196.

54 Edwin Lutyens to Emily Lutyens, 9 September 1915 in Clayre Percy and Jane Ridley, *The Letters of Edwin Lutyens* (London, 1985). 315.

55 Adie, *Fighting on the Home Front*, 96.

56 Ibid., 121.

57 Lucile Jones to Agar Adamson, 21 June 1916, in Christie, *Letters of Agar Adamson*, 188.

58 Binyon, *For Dauntless France*, 118.

59 Ibid., 371.

60 Anon., *Canada in the Great World War*, Vol. VI, 185.

61 Binyon, *For Dauntless France*, 197.

62 Mary MacLeod Moore, *Maple Leaf's Red Cross: The Story of the Canadian Red Cross Overseas* (London, 1919),161-162.

63 Ibid., 178, 180.

64 Ibid., 162-163.

65 "Matron MacLatchy's Recollections" quoted in Mann, *The War Diary of Clare Gass*, 247; Binyon, *For Dauntless France*, 220.

66 Moore, *The Maple Leaf's Red Cross*, 177-178.

67 Anon.,*Canada in the Great World War*, Vol. VI, 186; Diary of Grace MacPherson, 15 June 1917, 58A 1.284.9, Grace MacPherson Papers, CWM.

68 The Countess of Bessborough, quoted in Adie, *Fighting on the Home Front*, 97.

69 Adie, *Fighting on the Home Front*, 98. An estaminet was a small cafe selling alcoholic drinks.

70 Anon., *Canada in the Great World War*, Vol. VI, 185.

71 Ibid.

72 Anon., *Canada in the Great World War*, Vol. VI, 188.

73 Ibid., 184-185.

74 Elizabeth Montizambert, "Causerie de Paris," *Montreal Gazette*, 15 July 1915

75 Ibid., 24 November 1917.

76 The *Médaille de la Reconnaissance Française* or Medal of French Gratitude was created in July 1917 and awarded to civilians. It was intended to express the gratitude of the French government to those who had aided wounded or disabled refugees, or who had carried out an act of exceptional dedication in the presence of the enemy during the First World War.

77 Daphne Bramham, "Julia Henshaw: A Unique Woman of the War," *Vancouver Sun*, 8 September 2014.

78 Anon., *Canada in the Great World War*, Vol. VI, 190; Donald E. Graves, *Field of Glory: The Battle of Crysler's Farm, 1813* (Toronto: 1999), dedication. The *Croix de Guerre* is a French military decoration, introduced in 1915 and awarded during the First World War to those military personnel, French or part of foreign military forces allied to France, who distinguished themselves by acts of heroism. The medal itself consists of a cross on two crossed swords.

79 John McCrae to Janet McCrae, 18 April 1915, MG30 D209, Micro A-1977, LAC.

80 Adie, *Fighting on the Home Front*, 210.

81 Letter from Florens Rod, published in *The Tablet*, 19 June 1915, 20; Belgian Canal Boat Fund poster, MG30 E149, Adamson Papers, Vol. 6, LAC.

82 Gwyn, *Tapestry of War*, 126.

83 Adamson, *Wasps in the Attic*, 194-195.

84 Gwyn, *Tapestry of War*, 128-129.

85 Ibid., 130.

86 Belgian Canal Boat Fund appeal, December 1917, MG30 E149, Vol. 8, LAC; Anon., *A War Nurse's Diary: Sketches from a Belgian Field Hospital* (New York, 1918), 54.

87 Anon., *A War Nurse's Diary*, 54.

88 Adamson, *Wasps in the Attic*,192; Mabel Adamson to her mother, 15 September 1915, MG30 E149, Vol. 2, LAC.

89 Ibid.

90 Adie, *Fighting on the Home Front*, 184-185.

91 Mabel Adamson to her mother, 1 November 1915, MG30 E149, Vol. 3, LAC.

92 Ibid., 3 December 1915. Lady Dorothie Fielding was the daughter of Lord Denbigh, and became a highly decorated volunteer nurse and ambulance driver with Dr. Munro's unit in Belgium.

93 Esther McNeil to Mabel Adamson, 11 February 1916, MG30 E149, Vol. 4, LAC.

94 Letter from Sister Marie Joseph, Mother Superior, quoted in Adamson, *Wasps in the Attic*, 180.

95 Agar Adamson to Mabel Adamson, April 1917, in Adamson, *Wasps in the Attic*, 220.

96 Ibid., 209.

97 Belgian Canal Boat Fund appeal, December 1917, MG30 E149, Vol. 8, LAC.

98 *Canadian* magazine, Vol. 52, January 1919, 37.

Chapter 9. It was enough to have had "the privilege of being of service": Volunteers in Uniform

1 From "Canada to England, July 1st, 1917" by Horace Bray in Garvin, ed. *Canadian Poems of the Great War*, 35.

2 Adie, *Fighting on the Home Front*, 55.

3 Ibid., 283.

4 Vera Laughton Matthews, quoted in Adie, *Fighting on the Home Front*, 283. The WRNS in the First World War was active from 1917-1919.

5 Linda J. Quiney, "Gendering Patriotism: Canadian Volunteer Nurses as the Female 'Soldiers' of the Great War" in Sarah Glassford, *A Sisterhood of Suffering and Service* (Vancouver, 2013), 6.

6 Ibid., 118.

7 Linda J. Quiney, *This Small Army of Women: Canadian Volunteer Nurses and the First World War* (Vancouver, 2017), 62.

8 Adie, *Fighting on the Home Front*, 108.

9 Quiney, "Gendering Patriotism," 197.

10 Toman, *Sister Soldiers*, 42-43. Applicants could train with the British Red Cross Society (BRCS) or present their Canadian St. John Ambulance qualification in the hope that they would be accepted as VAD nursing assistants.

11 Quiney, *This Small Army of Women*, 17.

12 White, *Zeppelin Nights*, 145.

13 Bessie Hall to her mother, 2 October 1918, MG1 Vol. 661, No. 8, McGregor-Miller Collection, ANS. The British Red Cross VAD uniform featured a blue dress and red cross in the centre of a white apron. Bessie's description indicates she was a St. John Ambulance VAD. Their uniform was grey with a plain white apron and an armband emblazoned with the eight-pointed Order of St. John.

14 Report of wartime nursing read at CNATN Convention, July 1919, in *The Canadian Nurse*, September 1919, 1977.

15 Powell, *Women in the War Zone*, 72.

16 Katherine Furse, quoted in Powell, *Women in the War Zone*, 73-74.

17 Quiney, *This Small Army*, 8.

18 Quiney, *This Small Army*, 8-9.

19 Ibid., 5-6, 60-61.

20 *The Varsity* magazine, 1 November 1916, 1; Toman, *Sister Soldiers*, 191.

21 Violet Wilson interview c. 1970, Voice of the Pioneer, LAC.

22 Daphne Read, ed. *The Great War and Canadian Society: An Oral History* (Toronto, 1978), 125.

23 Read, ed., *The Great War and Canadian Society*, 125.

24 Frances Cluett to her mother, 29 March 1917, in Bill Rompkey and Bert Riggs. *Your Daughter Fanny: The War Letters of Frances Cluett, VAD* (St Johns, 2006), 72.

25 Bordon Reid, ed. *Poor Bloody Murder: Personal Memoirs of the First World War* (Oakville, 1980), 166. Leah McCarthy wrote her account under her married name, Mrs. Ian Sinclair.

26 Rompkey and Riggs. *Your Daughter Fanny*, xxviii; Quiney, *This Small Army*, 170.

27 Elizabeth O'Kiely, *Gentleman Air Ace: The Duncan Bell-Irving Story* (Madeira Park, BC, 1992), 79.

28 O'Kiely, *Gentleman Air Ace*, 84; Karen Syrett, "Lady Ridley's Hospital for Officers at 10 Carlton House Terrace" 21, RAMC/555, Wellcome Library.

29 Robert A.J. McDonald, "He Thought He was the Boss of Everything: Masculinity and Power in a Vancouver Family," *BC Studies*, No. 132, Winter 2001-2002, 51, 20.

30 Syrett, "Lady Ridley's Hospital," 22-23.

31 O'Kiely, *Gentleman Air Ace*, 137.

32 Ibid., 87.

33 Quiney, *This Small Army*, 117.

34 By 1918 the age limits had been relaxed to between twenty-one and forty-eight years in order to meet demand.

35 Annie Wynne-Roberts, quoted in Charles Lyons Foster, ed., *Letters from the Front: Being a Record of the Part Played by Officers of the Bank in the Great War, 1914-1919* (Toronto, 1920). Volume 1, 184.

36 Frances Cluett to her mother, 7 May 1917, Frances Cluett Collection-174. File 2.02.001, MUN.

37 Ibid., 8 June 1917.

38 Linda J. Quiney, "Assistant Angels: Canadian Voluntary Aid Detachment Nurses in the Great War," *Canadian Bulletin of Medical History*, Vol. 15, 1998, 199.

39 *Daily News* article, quoted in Adie, *Fighting on the Home Front*, 196.

40 Mary Bird to 'Cath,' 8 May 1918, 58A 1 221.4, Mary Bird Fonds, CWM.

41 Anon., *Canada in the Great World War*, Volume VI, 187.

42 Jean Marita Sears interview, 23 July 1974, "Voice of the Pioneer," LAC.

43 Binyon, *For Dauntless France*, 17; Moore, *The Maple Leaf's Red Cross*, 183.

44 Gertrude Arnold "The Search for Missing Men and Other Stories of a Canadian V.A.D.," *Maclean's Magazine*, November 1919, 27.

45 Olive Dent, quoted in Powell, *Women in the War Zone*, 125.

46 Violet Wilson interview c. 1970, "Voice of the Pioneer," LAC.

47 Binyon, *For Dauntless France*, 13, 15.

48 Quiney, *This Small Army*, 97.

49 Quiney, "Canadian Voluntary Aid Detachment Nurses". 199.

50 Diary of Grace MacPherson, 7-11 August 1916, 58A 1.284.12, Grace MacPherson Fonds, CWM.

51 Diary of Grace MacPherson, 17 August 1916, 18 September 1916, 58A 1.284.12, Grace MacPherson Fonds, CWM.

52 Ibid., 28 March 1917.

53 Ibid., 12 April 1917.

54 Grace E. MacPherson, "With A Motor Ambulance," *The Gold Stripe*, Volume 3, 81.

55 Ibid., 81.

56 Ibid., 81-82; Diary of Grace MacPherson, 19 April 1917, 58A 1 284.12, CWM.

57 Diary of Grace MacPherson, 5 May 1917, 8 June 1917, 58A 1 284.12, CWM.

58 Ibid., 12 April 1916.

59 Ibid., 8 June 1917.

60 Ibid., 15 June 1917.

61 Ibid., 8 June 1917, 26 September 1917, 8 September 1917, 4 November 1917.

62 Ibid., 10 February 1918, 10 March 1918, 13 March 1918, 23 March 1918; Grace E. MacPherson, "With A Motor Ambulance," 84.

63 Diary of Grace MacPherson, 11 April 1918, 20 May 1918, 58A 1 284.12, CWM; Grace E. MacPherson, "With A Motor Ambulance," 83-84.

64 Quiney "Assistant Angels," 201.

65 Moorehead, *Dunant's Dream*, 222; Quiney, *This Small Army*, 148.

66 Quiney, *This Small Army*, 180.

67 Mary Bird to the Misses Bird, 15 October 1915, 58A 1 221.4, Mary Bird Fonds, CWM.

68 Mary Bird to her family, 15 October 1915, 58A 1 221 4, CWM.

69 Mary Bird to the Misses Bird, 9 May 1916, 58A 1 221 4, CWM.

70 Ibid.

71 Mary Bird to her family, 15 October 1915, 58A 1 221 4, CWM.

72 Mary Bird to her father, 30 October 1915, 58A 1 221 4, CWM.

73 Sybil Grey, 25 July 1918 in Boyd, *Lady Sybil*, 340.

74 Dame Maud McCarthy quoted in *Canada in the Great World War*, Vol. VI, 182.

75 Grace MacPherson, "Draft for Article in Gold Stripe," 58A 1 284.12, CWM.
76 Quiney, *This Small Army*, 167.
77 Anon. *Canada in The Great World War*, Vol. II, 143.
78 Ibid., Vol. VI, 138.
79 Ibid., Vol. VI, 148.
80 Adie, *Fighting on the Home Front*, 96.
81 Anon., *Canada in the Great World War*, Vol. VI, 147.
82 Captain Edward Baker, 1910, https://www.fany.org.uk/history/wwi/overview.
83 Anon., *Canada in the Great World War*, Vol. II, 108-109.
84 Adie, *Fighting on the Home Front*, 182.
85 Katie Snyder, "With the F.A.N.Y.'s in France," *The Gold Stripe*, Volume 2, 129.
86 https://www/fany.org.uk/history/wwi/overview.
87 Snyder, "With the F.A.N.Y.'s in France," 129.
88 Ibid.
89 Anon., *Canada in the Great World War*, Vol. VI, 183.
90 Adie, *Fighting on the Home Front*, 284.
91 From "The Girl Behind the Man Behind the Gun," by Wilson MacDonald, in Garvin, ed., *Canadian Poems of the Great War*, 119.
92 Quiney, *This Small Army*, 180; "War Conditions in the Nursing World" *The Canadian Nurse*, October 1918, 1312; Anon., *Canada in the Great World War*, Vol. VI, 188.
93 Binyon, *For Dauntless France*, 15-17
94 Syrett, "Lady Ridley's Hospital," 24.
95 Quiney, *This Small Army*, 100, 178. The deaths were all apparently the result of complications resulting from influenza.
96 Diary of Sybil Johnson, 18 July 1918, Sybil Johnson Collection-201. File 2.03.002, MUN.
97 Binyon, *For Dauntless France*, 15-17; Quiney, *This Small Army*, 129.

Chapter 10. "A splendid courageous devotion": Lady Grace Julia Drummond, "Mother" to the Canadian Forces

1 From "The Mothering Heart" by Blanche E. Holt Murison, in Garvin ed., *Canadian Poems of the Great War*, 163.
2 Georges Vanier to his mother, 20 September 1916, in Deborah Cowley, ed., *Georges Vanier: Soldier: Wartime Letters and Diaries 1915-1919* (Toronto, 2000), 165.
3 "Montreal's Patriotic Women," *The Globe*, 17 August 1914.
4 Iona Carr, *A Story of the Canadian Red Cross Society Information Bureau in The Great War* (Toronto, 1920), 4.
5 The "Square Mile" is a nostalgic name given to a Montreal neighbourhood that developed mainly between 1850 and 1930 in the west-central part of the city on the slopes of Mount Royal. It housed an English-speaking elite that included some of Canada's wealthiest and most influential people.
6 Henry James Morgan, ed. *Types of Canadian Women*, Vol. 1 (Toronto, 1903), 94.
7 Coronation invitation, PO15/CO2.1, Drummond Family Fonds, McCM.
8 Caroline Andrew and Beth Moore Milroy, eds., *Life Spaces: Gender, Household, Employment* (Vancouver, 1988), 71-72.
9 Julia Drummond, note on speech to Women's Canadian Club 12 December 1907, PO15/CO6, Drummond Family Fonds, McCM.
10 Untitled document on Guy Drummond, PO15/FO1, 2, McCM.
11 Iona Carr, *A Story of the Canadian Red Cross Information Bureau*, Foreword, 4.
12 Interview with Julia Drummond, *Family Herald and Weekly Star*, 21 January 1920, 11.
13 Carr, *A Story of the Canadian Red Cross Information Bureau*, 9.
14 Ibid.
15 Ibid.
16 At the start of the twentieth century the Hamburg-Amerika Line ship *Deutschland* won the Blue Riband for the fastest crossing of the Atlantic on three occasions. During the war many of the company's vessels were destroyed and those that survived were handed over to the Allies as reparation.
17 Matthews, ed., *The Oslers During World War One*, 148.
18 Mary MacLeod Moore, "Canadian Women War Workers Overseas" *The Canadian*, Vol. 52, No. 3 (January 1919), 741.
19 Dancocks, *Welcome to Flanders Fields*, 98-99.
20 R.C. Fetherstonhaugh, *The 13th Battalion Royal Highlanders of Canada 1914-1919* (Canada, 1925), 41.
21 Ibid., 41.
22 Guy Drummond to Julia Drummond, 22 April 1915, PO15/F4.3, McCM.
23 Leaflet, "Personal Protection Against Gas," (London, 1938), 9.
24 J.A. Currie, The Red Watch: With 1st Canadian Division in Flanders (Toronto, 1916), 225.
25 Guy Drummond to Julia Drummond, 22 April 1915, PO15/F4.3, McCM.
26 Telegram to Julia Drummond, 22 April 1915, PO15/CO5, McCM.
27 Julia Drummond to Guy Drummond, 25 April 1915, PO16/FO4, McCM.
28 Julia Drummond address to the Ottawa branch of the Women's Canadian Club. Undated newspaper clipping, PO15/CO6, McCM.
29 Mary MacLeod Moore, London Letter, *Saturday Night*, 29 May 1915.
30 Sermon, "Life for Ever and Ever," Canadian Memorial Service, 10 May 1915, 3,5, PO15/CO5.1, Drummond Family Fonds, McCM.

31 Cynthia Asquith, *Lady Cynthia Asquith Diaries, 1915-1918*, 8 May 1915, (London, 1968), 121.

32 Bilbrough, *My War Diary 1914-1918*, 145.

33 Talbot Papineau to Caroline Papineau, 30 May 1915, MG30 E52, Vol. 2, Papineau Papers, LAC.

34 Gwyn, *Tapestry of War*, 205.

35 Carr, *A Story of the Canadian Red Cross Information Bureau*, 14.

36 Thomas Rivers Bulkeley, an officer of the Scots Guards, had met his wife, Evelyn, in Canada when he was an aide to the Duke of Connaught and she was lady-in-waiting to the Duchess. The couple married in 1913 and had a son in January 1914. On 22 October 1914 Rivers Bulkeley was killed in action near Ypres.

37 Carr, *A Story of the Canadian Red Cross Information Bureau*, 75-77.

38 Ibid., 76.

39 Ibid., 76, 8.

40 Ibid., 9.

41 Ibid., 74.

42 Mary MacLeod Moore to Rev. Calvin Mcquesten, 10 March 1916, Box 04-007, Reverend Calvin McQuesten correspondence, WMA.

43 Ibid., 74-75.

44 Agar Adamson to Mabel Adamson, in Christie, *The Letters of Agar Adamson*, 9 January 1917, 252. The Overseas Club, for British subjects around the world, promoted comradeship and service to the British Empire among its members. The Ladies Empire Club catered to women visiting London and encouraged student travel throughout the Empire.

45 Mary MacLeod Moore, "Canadian Women War Workers Overseas" *The Canadian* Vol. 52, No. 3 (January 1919), 739.

46 Lieutenant Leonard Richardson to his parents, 11 January 1918 in Elizabeth Richardson-Whealy, ed., *Pilot's Log: The log, diary, letters and verse of Lt. Leonard A. Richardson, Royal Flying Corps 1917-1918* (St. Catharines, 1998), 64.

47 Macphail, *Official History of The Canadian Forces in The Great War*, 342.

48 Morris Craig, *But This is Our War*, 94.

49 Hyde, *The First Blitz*, 57.

50 Captain Bruce Bairnsfather, *Bullets and Billets* (New York, 1917), 182, 180.

51 Macphail, *Official History of The Canadian Forces in The Great War*, 347-348.

52 George V. Bell, quoted in Mathieson, *My Grandfather's War*, 158.

53 Mary McLeod Moore, *The Story of the King George and Queen Mary Maple Leaf Club. London: 1915-1919* (London, ?1919), 5.

54 George V. Bell, quoted in Mathieson, *My Grandfather's War*, 177.

55 Macphail, *Official History of The Canadian Forces in The Great War*, 291.

56 Carr, *A Story of the Canadian Red Cross Information Bureau*, 76.

57 Moore, *The Story of the King George and Queen Mary Maple Leaf Club*, 6.

58 Sian Evans, *Mrs Ronnie: The society hostess who collected kings* (London, 2013), 55.

59 Moore, *The Story of the King George and Queen Mary Maple Leaf Club*, 7.

60 Earl Grey was a much respected former governor general of Canada, and Lord Milner was an eminent British statesman and colonial administrator.

61 Ibid., 6, 8.

62 Ibid., 9; Macphail, *Official History of The Canadian Forces in The Great War*, 348.

63 Diary of Her Majesty Queen Mary, 11 February 1917, quoted in Evans, *Mrs. Ronnie*, 75.

64 Moore, *The Story of the King George and Queen Mary Maple Leaf Club*, 11.

65 *The Dead Horse Corner Gazette*, magazine of 3rd Canadian Infantry Brigade, June 1916, quoted in Moore, *The Story of the King George and Queen Mary Maple Leaf Club*, 10.

66 Moore, *The Story of the King George and Queen Mary Maple Leaf Club*, 20.

67 Ibid., 25.

68 "The Maple Leaf Club and its Equipment," *The Globe*, 18 February 1916.

69 Moore, *The Story of the King George and Queen Mary Maple Leaf Club*, 11.

70 Sir William Hearst, address at Massey Hall, Toronto, October 1916, F6, MU1312, B253642, Envelope 2, Hearst Papers, AO.

71 Moore, *The Story of the King George and Queen Mary Maple Leaf Club*, 11.

72 Carr, *A Story of the Canadian Red Cross Information Bureau*, 76.

73 Bilbrough, *My War Diary*, 212.

74 In its final phase, the Information Bureau had had to move from Cockspur Street to larger premises in London's West End, where it was based until August 1919.

75 A.L. Baden to Julia Drummond, 8 August 1918, PO15/CO5.1, McCM.

76 The British Red Cross Society Medal was given to members of the British Red Cross (CRCS included) and VAD nurses who volunteered for a thousand hours of service or for a period of one year during the First World War. The Red Cross Medal of Merit (Serbia) was awarded to men and women, both Serbian and foreign nationals, in recognition of exceptional services rendered to the Serbian Red Cross in time of war or peace.

77 The Order of St. John of Jerusalem is a British order of chivalry instituted in 1888 under royal charter. Found throughout the Commonwealth, the USA, Ireland and Hong Kong, its mission is the prevention of sickness and injury and the worldwide enhancement of health and well-being.

78 Julia Drummond, *Family Herald and Weekly Star*, 21 January 1920, 11, PO15/CO6, McCM.

79 Carr, *A Story of the Canadian Red Cross Information Bureau*, Foreword, 5.

80 Ibid., Foreword, 6.

81 Ibid.

82 Julia Drummond, *Family Herald and Weekly Star*, 21 January 1920, 11, CO15/CO6, McCM.

83 Carr, *A Story of the Canadian Red Cross Information Bureau*, 8, Foreword, 5.

84 Earl Grey to Julia Drummond, 3 January 1917, PO15/CO5, McCM.

Chapter 11. "Bringing laughter, hope and healing": Lena Ashwell and "Concerts at the Front"

1 Verse from "Carry On" by Robert W. Service, in Garvin, ed., *Canadian Poems of the Great War*, 215.

2 Lena Ashwell, "A Year's Music at the Front," *Strand Magazine*, Vol. 51, January to June 1916, 261.

3 "Miss Ashwell's Success," *The Ottawa Journal*, 11 March 1903, 7; Lena Ashwell, *Myself a Player* (London, 1936), 13.

4 "Miss Ashwell's Success," *The Ottawa Journal*, 11 March 1903, 7.

5 Lena Ashwell, *Modern Troubadours: A Record of the Concerts at the Front* (London, 1922), 47. Columbine is the common name for Aquilegia, a plant found in woods, meadows and at higher altitudes throughout the Northern Hemisphere.

6 "Miss Ashwell's Success," *The Ottawa Journal*, 11 March 103, 7. The Bishop Strachan School was founded in 1867 and continues to this day as an Anglican day and boarding school for girls.

7 The English actress Ellen Terry (1847-1928) was one of the most popular stage performers in Britain and North America. She played many great Shakespearean roles during the twenty-four years she worked as the leading lady of Sir Henry Irving, the celebrated actor and theatre-manager. Their partnership was one of the most famous in the history of the British theatre.

8 Margaret Leask, *Lena Ashwell: actress, patriot, pioneer* (Hatfield, 2012), 1.

9 "Miss Ashwell's Success," *The Ottawa Journal*, 11 March 1903, 7.

10 Lena Ashwell, *Myself a Player*, 79; "Miss Ashwell's Success," interview, *The Ottawa Journal*, 11 March 1903, 7.

11 Leask, *Lena Ashwell*, 26.

12 *Evening Standard*, 14 May 1906.

13 *New York Times*, 7 October 1906.

14 The actor-producer Sir Herbert Beerbohm-Tree, was the half-brother of the writer and caricaturist, Sir Max Beerbohm.

15 Leask, *Lena Ashwell*, 79.

16 After Roger Pocock wrote his report of the Russo-Japanese War he became convinced of the need for British subjects travelling the frontiers of the world to bring back information of interest to the state. He later became the founder of the Legion of Frontiersmen of the Commonwealth.

17 Leask, *Lena Ashwell*, 97.

18 Ibid., 101-103.

19 *Manchester Guardian*, 13 November 1913.

20 Leask, *Lena Ashwell*, 108.

21 Elizabeth Robins quoted in Naomi Paxton, *Stage Rights: The Actresses' Franchise League, activism and politics 1908-58* (Manchester, 2018), 172.

22 Jack Stickney to his mother, 17 December 1914, Jack Stickney Papers, Box 1, UBCA.

23 Adamson, *Wasps in the Attic*, 226.

24 Ashwell, *Modern Troubadours*, 5.

25 Leask, *Lena Ashwell*, 109. Lady Corisande Rodney (1870-1943), formerly the wife of George, 7th Baron Rodney, visited France very early in the war and saw the general lack of decent leisure facilities for the troops. It was at her suggestion that the YMCA built recreation huts in France, and during the war she supervised the work of women volunteers for the YMCA in that country.

26 Ashwell, "A Year's Music at the Front," *Strand Magazine*, 258.

27 Ibid., 257.

28 Ibid., 257; Ashwell, *Modern Troubadours*, 6.

29 Ibid.

30 Lena Ashwell, *Topical Times* 6 October 1894.

31 Ashwell, *Modern Troubadours*, 7.

32 Ada L. Ward, "Entertaining at the Front" *The Gold Stripe*, Volume 1, 49.

33 Ashwell, *Modern Troubadours*, 7.

34 Leask, *Lena Ashwell*, 21.

35 Ashwell, "A Year's Music at the Front," *Strand Magazine*, 258.

36 Ibid., 258.

37 Theodore Flint to Lena Ashwell, 21 February 1915, in Leask, *Lena Ashwell*, 117.

38 Ashwell, *Modern Troubadours*, 10.

39 Ashwell, "A Year's Music at the Front," *Strand Magazine*, 261.

40 After the war, Elsie Griffin went on to become the lead suprano of the D'Oyly Carte Opera Company.

41 "In a General Hospital in France: Miss Lena Ashwell's Concert Parties," *The Hospital*, 28 August 1915, 455.

42 Ashwell, "A Year's Music at the Front," *Strand Magazine*, 258.

43 Ibid.

44 Leask, *Lena Ashwell*, 21; *Echo and Evening Chronicle*, 24 March 1915.

45 Erik Larson, *Dead Wake: The Last Crossing of the Lusitania* (New York, 2015), 116, 299.

46 Ashwell, *Modern Troubadours*, 12.

47 Ada L. Ward, "Entertaining at the Front," *The Gold Stripe*, Vol. 1, 51; Ashwell, "A Year's Music at the Front," *Strand Magazine*, 260-261. Lena Ashwell also cited cases where music helped patients to regain both speech and memory.

48 Ashwell, "A Year's Music at the Front," *Strand Magazine*, 259-261.

49 Elsie Illingworth, *Huddersfield Weekly Examiner*, 20 October 1915.

50 Ada L. Ward, "Entertaining at the Front," *The Gold Stripe*, Vol. 1, 49.

51 Ibid., 50.

52 Ashwell, "A Year's Music at the Front," *Strand Magazine*, 260.

53 Mann, *The War Diary of Clare Gass*, 8 August 1915, 18 October 1915, 16 November 1915, 51, 71, 81.

54 Ashwell, "A Year's Music at the Front," *Strand Magazine*, 260.

55 "Visit of HH Princess Victoria of Schleswig-Holstein to France commencing 12 August 1915" in David H. Smith, *The Forgotten Angels: History of the YMCA Women's Auxiliary, Part One*, 5-6, 10.

56 Daisy Godfrey, quoted in "WW1 Lena Ashwell parties: Shining a Light on the young women who brought music to the trenches," *The Daily Telegraph*, 4 August 2014.

57 *Daily Sketch*, 20 September 1915.

58 *Loughton Advertiser* 18 September 1915.

59 Ada L. Ward, "Entertaining at the Front," *The Gold Stripe*, Volume 1, 51.

60 Leask, *Lena Ashwell*, 133.

61 Ada L. Ward, "Entertaining at the Front," *The Gold Stripe*, Volume 1, 52.

62 Ashwell, *Modern Troubadours*, 73.

63 *The Red Triangle*, 30 June 1916.

64 Ashwell, *Modern Troubadours*, 11.

65 Ashwell, "A Year's Music at the Front," *Strand Magazine*, 260.

66 Lena Ashwell, *Pearson's Magazine*, June 1916.

67 *Halifax Daily Guardian*, 3 March 1919; Kate Adie, *Fighting on the Home Front*, 221.

68 Ashwell, *Modern Troubadours*, 152.

69 Ibid., 153.

70 Ibid., 164-165.

71 Ibid., 141.

72 "Boys Our Hearts Are With You," written in 1916, Acc, PR1977-182, Keystone Archives, UM. The Khaki Girls of Winnipeg were part of the Women's Volunteer Reserve.

73 Ashwell, *Modern Troubadours*, 2.

74 Ibid., 177-178,

75 Marshall, *Firing Lines*, 160.

76 Ibid., 161.

77 Cicely Hamilton, *Life Errant* (London, 1935), 131.

78 Ashwell, *Modern Troubadours*, 152.

79 Ibid., 142.

80 Ibid., 171.

81 Ibid.

82 *The Tatler*, 4 July 1917. Lady Diana Manners was a celebrated beauty who, before the First World War, socialised with a group of intellectuals known as "The Coterie."

83 Leask, *Lena Ashwell*, 141.

84 Ashwell, *Modern Troubadours*, 2; Article, "Laughing to Hide Our Tears," *Illustrated Sunday Herald*, 28 March 1915.

85 Leask, *Lena Ashwell*, 142. The Labour Corps, inaugurated in 1915, accepted men who were medically unfit for front line service. They undertook a wide range of work such as building and maintaining roads and railways, digging trenches, repairing and salvaging items for re-use and felling timber. Their contribution is not often acknowledged.

86 *Daily Graphic*, 27 August 1917.

87 *Evening News*, 22 October 1917.

88 Leask, *Lena Ashwell*, 149.

89 Ashwell, *Modern Troubadours*, 198-200.

90 Ibid., 194-195.

91 George Butterworth (1885-1916) was an English composer best known for his orchestral pieces. He was commissioned in the Durham Light Infantry and in August 1916 was awarded the Military Cross for capturing a series of trenches near Pozières but was killed before receiving the award. Rupert Brooke (1887-1915), was an English poet known for his war sonnets. He enlisted in 1914, was commissioned into the Royal Naval Volunteer Reserve and sailed for Gallipoli in February 1915. On the way, he developed sepsis following an infected mosquito bite, died and was buried on the Greek island of Skyros.

92 Ashwell, *Modern Troubadours*, 208.

93 Ibid., 2.

94 Adie, *Fighting on the Home Front*, 221.

95 "In a General Hospital in France: Miss Lena Ashwell's Concert Parties," *The Hospital*, 28 August 1915, 456.

96 Ashwell, *Modern Troubadours*, 140.

97 Ibid., 2.

98 "Touring Parties and Arts Advocacy 1914-1919" by Margaret Leask, in Mander, Andrew, ed., *British Theatre and the Great War 1914-1919* (Basingstoke, 2015), 251.

99 Adie, *Fighting on the Home Front*, 4.

Chapter 12. "One of those rare individuals": Julia Grace Wales, Pacifist and Peace Activist

1 From "Between The Waking and The Sleeping" by Elizabeth Roberts MacDonald in Garvin, ed. *Canadian Poems of the Great War*," 115.

2 Integral to pacifism is the belief that violence of any kind is unjustifiable, and that all disputes should be settled by peaceful means. https://en.oxforddictionaries.com.

3 Morrell, *Ottoline*, 260-262.

4 Rosika Bédy-Schwimmer, www.azquotes.com/quote/957937.

5 Clara Zetkin, www.aspiringquotes.us/quotes/rioh_Z3KVUiqt; Jane Addams, https//quotefancy.com/quote/1061003.

6 Chown, *The Stairway*, xlvii.

7 Carol Lawrence, "The Canadian Girl Who Won World-wide Fame," *Woman's Century*, July 1916, MG30 C238, Vol. 1, Julia Grace Wales Papers, LAC.

8 Julia Grace Wales, "Continuous Mediation without Armistice," 3. MG30 C238, Vol. 1, Julia Grace Wales Papers, LAC.

9 Ibid.

10 Lochner, Louis P., *America's Don Quixote: Henry Ford's Attempt to Save Europe* (London, 1924), 5-6.

11 Julia Grace Wales, "Continuous Mediation Without Armistice," cover page, MG30 C238, Vol. 3, LAC.

12 Mary Jean Woodard Bean, *Julia Grace Wales: Canada's Hidden Heroine and the Quest for Peace 1914-1918* (Ottawa, 2005), 52-53.

13 Jane Addams (1860-1935) was a feminist, a leader of women's suffrage and a pioneeing American settlement activist and reformer. She became involved in the peace movement and in January 1915, was elected national chairman of the Women's Peace Party. After the 1915 International Congress of Women she was elected president of the International Committee of Women for Permanent Peace, which later developed into the Women's International League for Peace and Freedom. Addams became a major figure in domestic and international peace movements and in 1931 she was awarded the Nobel Peace Prize.

14 Ibid., 56.

15 Although President Wilson did not receive the delegation on the grounds that he had more requests than he could reasonably deal with at the time, Julia Grace Wales's Plan for Continuous Mediation was forwarded to him in the form of a resolution by the Wisconsin Legislature.

16 Angela Morgan, "The Women's Congress at The Hague," *Christian Work*, 22 May 1915, 661-662.

17 Baroness Emmeline Pethick-Lawrence (1867-1954) was a British suffragist and women's rights activist. She was a member of the Suffrage Society and became treasurer of the Women's Social and Political Union, founded in 1906. Together with her husband, she launched the publication *Votes for Women*, in 1907. Her name, together with those of other supporters of women's suffrage, appears on the plinth of a statue unveiled in London's Parliament Square in 2018.

18 Woodard Bean, *Julia Grace Wales*, 66. Sam Hughes's son, Garnet Hughes, served on the Western Front and rose to the rank of major-general. Laura Hughes, a feminist, socialist and pacifist, was the daughter of Sam's brother, James Hughes.

19 Morgan, "The Women's Congress at The Hague," *Christian Work*, 22 May 1915, 661.

20 Ibid., 662.

21 Woodard Bean, *Julia Grace Wales*, 84.

22 Ibid., 87.

23 Julia Grace Wales to the International Committee of Women for Permanent Peace, 4-5 June 1915, 7. MG30 C238, Vol. 1, LAC.

24 Jane Addams, Emily G. Balch, Alice Hamilton, *Women at the Hague: The International Congress of Women and its Results* (New York, 1915),

15. Emily Greene Balch (1876-1961) was a sociologist, pacifist and Professor of Political Economy and Political and Social Science at Wellesley College, Massachusetts. She became a Quaker in 1921 and played a prominent role in the Women's International League for Peace and Freedom, based in Geneva. In 1946, after many years working for peace and disarmament, Balch was awarded the Nobel Peace Prize.

25 Report of the International Congress of Women at The Hague, 28 April to 1 May 1915, quoted in Woodard Bean, *Julia Grace Wales*, 104.

26 Addams, Balch, Hamilton, *Women at the Hague*, 152.

27 Jessie Chrystal MacMillan (1872-1937) was a Scottish barrister, liberal politician, feminist and pacifist. She actively campaigned for women's right to vote and was one of the founders of the Women's International League for Peace and Freedom. In 1919, she was a delegate at the Paris Peace Conference. After the passing of an act that year which allowed women to enter the legal profession, she applied to the Middle Temple to become a barrister and was called to the bar in 1924.

28 Julia Grace Wales to the International Committee, 4-5 June 1915, 7, 5. MG30 C238, Vol. 1, LAC.

29 Ibid., 8.

30 Ibid., 8-9.

31 Ibid., 13-15.

32 Sir Mansfeldt de Cardonnel Findlay (1861-1932) was a British diplomat who served in Europe, Constantinople and Buenos Aires. With the outbreak of war in 1914, Findlay grappled with complex problems that included the naval blockade of Germany, and was knighted for his services in 1916. Although Grace Wales refers to meeting "the Ambassador," the head of a British diplomatic mission overseas at that time normally held the title of Envoy Extraordinary and Minister Plenipotentiary, who was ranked below an ambassador.

33 Julia Grace Wales to the International Committee, 15-17. MG30 C238, Vol. 1, LAC.

34 Ibid., 20.

35 From statement "Issued by Envoys of the International Congress of Women at the Hague to the Governments of Europe, and the President of the United States." MG30 C238, Vol. 4, LAC.

36 Ibid.

37 Lochner, *America's Don Quixote* 17.

38 Henry Ford interview, 22 August 1915, quoted in Lochner, *America's Don Quixote*, 2.

39 Lochner, *America's Don Quixote*, 26.

40 Ibid., 27.

41 Henry Ford's telegram to Julia Grace Wales, Scrapbook of Ford Peace Expedition, 1, MG30 C238, Vol. 1, LAC.

42 Ibid.

43 Julia Grace Wales to her family, 28 November 1915, MG30 C238, Vol. 1, LAC.

44 Julia Grace Wales to her family, 3 December 1915, MG30 C238, Vol. 1, LAC.

45 Barbara S. Kraft, *The Peace Ship: Henry Ford's Pacifist Adventure in the First World War* (New York, 1978), 92; Julia Grace Wales to her family, 3 December 1915, MG30 C238, Vol. 1, LAC.

46 Julia Grace Wales to her family, 3 December 1915, MG30 C238, Vol. 1, LAC.

47 Scrapbook of Ford Peace Expedition, 2, 8, MG30 C238, Vol. 1, LAC.

48 Ibid., 5.

49 Julia Grace Wales to her family, 3 December 1915. MG30 C238, Vol. 1, LAC.

50 Inez Milholland Boissevain (1886-1916) was labour lawyer, public speaker, suffragist and correspondent. She greatly influenced the women's movement in America as an active member of various organisations including the National American Women's Suffrage Association. She wrote for the *New York Herald Tribune* as a correspondent during the war and after suffering from pernicious anaemia, died at Los Angeles in November 1916 while on a speaking tour.

51 Californian Alice Locke Parke (1861-1961) was a notable suffragist and advocate of women's rights. As a member of the Women's Suffrage Association for sixty years, she campaigned for a range of issues including birth control, sex education in schools and labour unionism. She was also a leader of the Women's International League for Peace and Freedom.

52 Julia Grace Wales to her family, 3 December 1915, MG30 C238, Vol. 1, LAC.

53 Woodard Bean, *Julia Grace Wales*, 191.

54 Ibid., 193.

55 Julia Grace Wales to her family, 26 December 1915, MG30 C238, Vol. 1, LAC.

56 Lochner, *America's Don Quixote*, 76-77.

57 Ibid., 79.

58 Kraft, *The Peace Ship*, 156.

59 Ibid., *The Peace Ship*, 159.

60 Ibid., 156.

61 Julia Grace Wales to her family, 22 December 1915, 1, MG30 C238, Vol. 1, LAC.

62 Lochner, *America's Don Quixote*, 95.

63 Ibid., 100-101, 98.

64 Ibid., 112.

65 Julia Grace Wales to Anna Letitia 'Tita' Wales, 20-26 February 1917, 1, MG30 C238, Vol. 4, LAC.

66 Kraft, *The Peace Ship*, 180.

67 Lochner, *America's Don Quixote*, 122.

68 Ibid., 117. At this point, Ford appointed his private secretary, Ernest Liebold, to oversee financial and other practical matters relating to the peace work in Europe,

69 Ibid., 236.

70 Julia Grace Wales, Ford Peace Expedition Memoir, Section M, 1, MG30 C238, Vol. 2, LAC.

71 Julia Grace Wales to her family, 26 January 1916, MG30 C238, Vol. 2, LAC.

72 Ibid.

73 Julia Grace Wales, Ford Peace Expedition Memoir, Section K, MG30 C238, Vol. 2, LAC.

74 Kraft, *The Peace Ship*, 217.

75 Ibid., 213-214.

76 Ibid., 222.

77 Lochner, *America's Don Quixote*, 208.

78 Julia Grace Wales to her family, 14 November 1916, MG30 C238, Vol. 1, LAC.

79 Lochner, *America's Don Quixote*, 183, 185.

80 Ibid., 190.

81 Ibid., 190.

82 *New York Times*, 13 December 1916, 1.

83 *New York Herald*, 23 December 1916, 1.

84 Julia Grace Wales to her family, 7 February 1917, MG30 C238, Vol. 1, LAC.

85 Ibid.

86 Lochner, *America's Don Quixote*, 219-220.

87 Julia Grace Wales to her family, 7 February 1917, MG30 C238, Vol. 1, LAC.

88 Lochner, *America's Don Quixote*, 224.

89 Julia Grace Wales to 'Tita', 20-26 April 1917, MG30 C238, Vol. 1, LAC.

90 Lochner, *America's Don Quixote*, 228-229.

91 Ibid., 151.

92 Julia Grace Wales to her family, 7 February 1917, MG30 C238, Vol. 1, LAC.

93 Lochner, *America's Don Quixote*, 229.

Chapter 13. "All the reward an artist could hope for" : Mary Riter Hamilton, Artist on the Western Front

1 From "In a Belgian Garden" by F.O. Call, in Garvin, ed., *Canadian Poems of the Great War*, 39.

2 Rudyard Kipling, 4 August 1918, postscript, quoted in Lord Birkenhead, *Rudyard Kipling* (New York, 1978), 258.

3 *Daily Telegraph*, special edition 11-14 November 1918.

4 Front page headlines from *Le Figaro*, *The New York Times*, *The Vancouver Daily Sun*, *The Manitoba Free Press*, *The Globe*, *The Erie Daily Times*, 11 November 1918.

5 Clint, *Our Bit*, 122.

6 Elizabeth Montizambert, "Causerie de Paris," *Montreal Gazette*, 18 December 1918.

7 Mary MacLeod Moore, 11 November 1918, quoted in Marshall, *Firing Lines*, 197.

8 Bilbrough, *My War Diary*, 11 November 1918, 221.

9 Michael MacDonagh, *London During the Great War: The Memories of a Journalist* (London, 1935), 329-330.

10 Lucy Maud Montgomery, 11 November 1918, 6 October 1918 in Rubio and Waterston, *The Selected Journals of L.M. Montgomery, Volume II*, 274, 269.

11 Edith Appleton, 12 November 1918, in Cowen, ed., *A Nurse at the Front*, 263; Bongard, *Nobody Ever Wins A War*, 58.

12 Diary of Hannah Lister, 11 November 1918, 152, 58E 2 3.6, CWM.

13 *An Artillery Officer in the First World War* by Colonel R. MacLeod, D.S.O., M.C., 224.

14 Christie, *Letters of Agar Adamson*, 11 November 1918, 12 November 1918, 348-349.

15 Quinn, *Agnes Warner*, 139; Diary of Gertrude Gilbert, 17 November 1918, 21 November 1918, 58A 1 22.12, CWM.

16 J.E.M. Bruce, "Mary Riter Hamilton," *The Gold Stripe*, Vol. 2, 22.

17 Angela E. Davis and Sarah M. McKinnon, *No Man's Land: The Battlefield Paintings of Mary Riter Hamilton, 1919-1922* (exhibition catalogue), 8, BCAV.

18 The 'Belle Epoque' was a period in the history of the western world that is normally regarded as lasting from the end of the Franco-Prussian War in 1871, until the start of the First World War.

19 Kathryn A. Young and Sarah M. McKinnon, *No Man's Land: The Life and Art of Mary Riter Hamilton* (Winnipeg, 2017), 45.

20 Bruce, "Mary Riter Hamilton," *The Gold Stripe*, Vol. 2, 22.

21 "Mrs. Hamilton's Picture Exhibit," *Town Topics*, 23 June 1906.

22 Robert Amos, *Mary Riter Hamilton 1873-1954*. Victoria: Art Gallery of Greater Victoria, 1978. Exhibition catalogue, 10, BCAV.

23 Bruce, "Mary Riter Hamilton," *The Gold Stripe*, Vol. 2, 23.

24 W. Garland Foster, "Coals to Newcastle: Art another Canadian Product – Mary Riter Hamilton. A Canadian Artist Whose Work Attests the Fact." *The Western Home Monthly*, May 1930, 49.

25 Young and McKinnon, *Mary Riter Hamilton*, 9.

26 Ibid., 62.

27 Anne Anderson Perry, "Artists and Their Doings: O Canada! What of Art! Noted Woman Painter and Patriot speaks of our National Needs." *Western Women's Weekly*, Vol. 2, No. 8, 1 February 1919, 4.

28 Young and McKinnon, *Mary Riter Hamilton*, 75.

29 Ibid., 77.

30 This limitation, however, enabled women artists to expand their work to include non-traditional areas such as industry and armament manufacture in which women took over work normally done by men who were away on active service.

31 Terresa McIntosh, "Other Images of War: Canadian Women War Artists of the First and Second World Wars." M.A. Thesis, Carleton University, 1990, 16.

32 The Group of Seven, founded in Toronto in 1920, was an organization of self-proclaimed artists most of whom made their living working as commercial artists. After their first exhibition in 1920 at the Toronto Art Gallery, they came to identify themselves as a national school of Canadian landscape painters.

33 Angela E. Davis, "Mary Riter Hamilton:, Manitoba Artist 1873-1954." *Manitoba History*, Number 11, Spring 1986, 25.

34 Madge MacBeth, "One of Our Last War Workers Comes Home," *Toronto Star Weekly*, 20 February 1926.

35 Bruce, "Mary Riter Hamilton: An Artist Impressionist on the Battlefields of France," *The Gold Stripe*, Vol. 3, 11.

36 Jay Winter, *Sites of Memory, Sites of Mourning* (Cambridge, 2014), 28; *The Gold Stripe*, Vol. 1, title page.

37 Mary Riter Hamilton to Margaret Hart, 25 March 1919, quoted in Young and McKinnon, *Mary Riter Hamilton*, 81.

38 Ibid.

39 Perry, "Artists and Their Doings," *Western Women's Weekly*, 1 February 1919, 4.

40 Mary Riter Hamilton to Margaret Hart, 7 May 1919, quoted in Young and McKinnon, *Mary Riter Hamilton*, 90-91.

41 Frederick G. Falla, "Dauntless Canadian Woman Tells of Grim Experiences While Painting the Nightmare Land of the Somme," Paris: McClure Newspapers Syndicate, 10 September 1922, BCAV.

42 Bruce, "Mary Riter Hamilton: An Artist Impressionist on the Battlefields of France," *The Gold Stripe*, Vol. 3, 12.

43 Mary Riter Hamilton to Mrs. H.E. Young, 9 June 1919, quoted in Young and McKinnon, *Mary Riter Hamilton*, 94.

44 Madge MacBeth, "One of Our Last War Workers Comes Home," *Toronto Star Weekly*, 20 February 1926.

45 Young and McKinnon, *Mary Riter Hamilton*, 91.

46 Bruce, "Mary Riter Hamilton: An Artist Impressionist on the Battlefields of France," *The Gold Stripe*, Vol. 3, 12.

47 Mary Riter Hamilton to Mrs. Taylor, 29 July 1919. quoted in Young and McKinnon, *Mary Riter Hamilton*, 95.

48 Ibid., 95.

49 Shirley Frey, "The Chinese Labour Corps of World War One: Forgotten Ally, Imperialist Partner." Collection of the ICCLC, IFFM.

50 Macbeth, "One of Our Last War Workers Comes Home," *Toronto Star Weekly*, 20 February 1926.

51 Dominic Dendooven, "Living Together: Belgian Witness Accounts of the Chinese Labour Corps," 6. Collection of the ICCLC, IFFM.

52 Ibid., 6-7; Louis Garrein, "Living Together: Belgian Witness Accounts of the Chinese Labour Corps," 6-7. Collection of the ICCLC, IFFM.

53 Young and Mckinnon, *Mary Riter Hamilton*, 106.

54 Gregory James, "Murder and Mayhem in the Chinese Labour Corps," 21. Collection of the ICCLC, IFFM.

55 Young and McKinnon, *Mary Riter Hamilton*, 103.

56 Gregory James, "Murder and Mayhem in the

Chinese Labour Corps," 1. Collection of the IC-CLC, IFFM.

57 Bruce, "Mary Riter Hamilton: An Artist Impressionist on the Battlefields of France," *The Gold Stripe*, Vol. 3, 12.

58 Angela Davis, "Mary Riter Hamilton: An Artist In No-Man's-Land," *The Beaver*, October-November 1989, 12.

59 Falla, "Dauntless Canadian Woman Tells of Grim Experiences," 10 September 1922, BCAV.

60 Clint, *Our Bit*, 136-140.

61 Edward Morrison to 'Mimosa,' 7 April 1916, MG30 E81, E.W.B. Morrison Papers, LAC.

62 Clayre Percy and Jane Ridley, *The Letters of Edwin Lutyens* (London, 1985), 350.

63 Bruce, "Mary Riter Hamilton: An Artist Impressionist on the Battlefields of France," *The Gold Stripe*, Vol. 3, 12.

64 *The Ladies Review*, supplement to *The Week* (Victoria), 6 December 1913, 1;*Montreal Gazette*, 8 February 1912, 8; *Toronto Star*, 22 November 1912, 2.

65 Amos, *Mary Riter Hamilton 1873-1954*, 12.

66 Young and McKinnon, *Mary Riter Hamilton*, 101, 99.

67 Mary Riter Hamilton to Margaret Hart, 15 February 1920, quoted in Young and McKinnon, *Mary Riter Hamilton*, 99.

68 Mary Riter Hamilton to Margaret Hart, September 1920 quoted in Young and McKinnon, *Mary Riter Hamilton*, 101.

69 The *Ordre des Palmes Académiques* was instituted in 1808 by the Emperor Napoleon. It is a national order bestowed by the French nation on distinguished academics and those who have given valuable service to universities, science and education. The decoration was divided into two classes (1) *Officier de l'Instruction Publique*, which entitled the recipient to wear a badge of golden palms on a purple ribbon, and (2) *Officier d'Académie* with silver palms.

70 The *Légion d'Honneur* is the highest French decoration, established in 1802 by Napoleon Bonaparte and awarded to those who have rendered distinguished civil or military service.

71 Mary Riter Hamilton to Margaret Hart, 20 June 1922, quoted in Young and McKinnon, *Mary Riter Hamilton*, 108.

72 Falla, "Dauntless Canadian Woman Tells of Grim Experiences," 10 September 1922, BCAV.

73 Ibid.

74 Mary Riter Hamilton to Margaret Hart, 29 June 1922, quoted in Young and McKinnon, *Mary Riter Hamilton*, 108.

75 Mary Riter Hamilton to Margaret Hart, 7 February 1923, 25 July 1923, quoted in Young and McKinnon, *Mary Riter Hamilton*, 109.

76 Mary Riter Hamilton to Margaret Hart, 29 June 1922, quoted in Young and McKinnon, *Mary Riter Hamilton*, 108; Madge MacBeth, "One of

Our Last War Workers Comes Home," *Toronto Star Weekly*, 20 February 1926.

77 Amos, *Mary Riter Hamilton 1893-1954*, 14, BCAV.

78 Mary Riter Hamilton to Arthur Doughty, 27 July 1926, RG37-B, R1185-15-3-E, Sir Arthur Doughty Papers, LAC.

79 Ibid.

80 Falla, "Dauntless Canadian Woman Tells of Grim Experiences," 10 September 1922, 10, BCAV.

81 Canadian National Athem, "O Canada," Verse 1.

Chapter 14. Epilogue: Reflection, Renewal, Repatriation and Remembrance

1 From "Yesterday" by Virna Sheard, in Garvin, ed., *Canadian Poems of the Great War*, 224.

2 Nadège Mougel, "World War 1 Casualties," Centre Européen Robert Schumann, 2011, 1.

3 Lady Diana Manners, quoted in McLeod, *The Last Summer*, 164.

4 Morrell, *Ottoline*, 279.

5 Lucy Maud Montgomery, 11 November 1918, in Rubio and Waterston, *The Selected Journals of L.M. Montgomery*, Volume II, 274.

6 Mary MacLeod Moore, "London Letter," *Saturday Night*, 26 July 1919.

7 Nellie McClung, quoted in "How War changed Everything for Alberta's Women," *Calgary Herald*, 19 June 2014; Nellie McClung, quoted in Gwyn, *Tapestry of War*, 164.

8 Bruce, *Humour in Tragedy*, 67.

9 veterans.gc.ca/eng/remembrance.

10 A.M.J. Hyatt, *General Sir Arthur Currie: A Military Biography*, 7; Arthur Meighen, quoted in Macmillan, *The Winds of Change*, 109.

11 Col. W.W. Murray, *History of the 2nd Canadian Battalion in the Great War 1914-1919* (Ottawa, 1936), 336.

12 Ibid., 339.

13 Ethel Upton, quoted in Toman, *Sister Soldiers*, 173.

14 Service record of Captain K. Edmiston, RG150 Acc. 1992-93/166, B2831-S001, LAC.

15 David Pierce Beatty, *Memories of The Forgotten War* (Port Elgin, 1986), 49.

16 Nicholson, *Canada's Nursing Sisters*, 98.

17 Ella Mae Bongard, *Nobody Ever Wins A War*, 11 February 1919, 65.

18 Quinn, *Agnes Warner*, 142.

19 Mildred Forbes to Cairine Wilson, 25 January 1919, MG27 IIIC6, Micro H-2299, LAC.

20 Clint, *Our Bit*, 172.

21 Adamson, *Wasps in the Attic*, 231. The *Médaille de la Reine Elisabeth* was a Belgian decoration created in October 1916 by royal decree. It was awarded to both Belgians and foreign nationals who rendered exceptional service to the country by working and caring for suffering Belgian victims of the war for one year or more prior to 10 September 1919.

22 Diary of Ethel Chadwick, 19 March 1919, MG30 D258, LAC.

23 Mildred Forbes to Cairine Wilson, 24 July 1918, MG27 IIIC6, Micro. H-2299, LAC.

24 Michelle Swann and Veronica Strong-Boag, "Mooney, Helen Letitia (McClung)," in *Dictionary of Canadian Biography*, Vol. 18, Toronto/Montreal: University of Toronto/Université Laval, 2003.

25 Laura Doan, *Disturbing Practices: History, Sexuality, and Women's Experience of Modern War* (Chicago, 2013), 142.

26 Gwyn, *Tapestry of War*, 438; Anon., *Canada in the Great World War*, Vol. VI, 213.

27 Frances Cluett in Stirling "Such Sights One Will Never Forget," in Glassford and Shaw, *A Sisterhood of Suffering and Service*, 142.

28 Morris Craig, *But This Is Our War*, Epilogue, 1.

29 Francis, Jones, Smith, *Destinies*, 243. In Canada, the introduction of votes for women began provincially in 1916 and was followed by the sanctioning in 1918 of the right to vote federally for all females who were British citizens over the age of twenty-one.

30 Ibid., 273.

31 Ibid., 271-272, 301, 322.

32 Order of Service, 58A 1 266.1, Edna Lena Moore Fonds, CWM. The forty-four names of the Canadian nurses who died during the war were shown on the order of service. British nurse Edith Cavell (1865-1915) cared for the wounded of both sides and helped some 200 Allied soldiers escape from German-occupied Belgium. She was arrested, tried for treason, found guilty by a court martial and shot by a German firing squad.

33 The Florence Nightingale medal is also awarded for exemplary service in the areas of public health or nursing education.

34 Laura Gamble Department of National Defence reference, 28 May 1921, MG30 E510, LAC. The Overseas Nursing Sisters Association of Canada later extended its membership and changed its title to the Nursing Sisters Association of Canada.

35 McKenzie, ed., *War Torn Exchanges*, 215.

36 Toman, *Sister Soldiers*, 52.

37 Wicks, ed. *Diary of a War Nurse*, 30.

38 *The Boston Herald*, 17 May 1929, 58A 1 22.12, CWM.

39 The *Médaille d'Honneur des Épidémies* was a French medal instituted in 1885 as a consequence of a cholera epidemic. Issued by what later became the Department of Public Health, it was awarded to anyone who had participated in combatting or preventing an epidemic.

40 Quinn, Agnes Warner, 148.

41 Quiney, *This Small Army*, 182-183.

42 The Military Cross is a British award given to captains or officers of lower rank up to warrant officers. It recognizes acts of exemplary gallantry during active land operations against an enemy. The Distinguished Service Order, established by Queen Victoria in 1886, is awarded for distinguished or meritorious service by officers of the armed forces during wartime. At the time of the First World War, Canadians and other troops of what became the British Commonwealth were eligible for these awards.

43 Grace MacPherson, "With a Motor Ambulance," *Gold Stripe*, Vol. 3, 84.

44 Statement of award to Lady Emily Perley, MG27 II D12(e) Vol. 15, Part 2, Perley Papers, LAC.

45 Article, "Marriage Invalid Defence Contends," *Montreal Gazette*, 29 September 1931.

46 Adamson, *Wasps in the Attic*, 237.

47 Ibid., 232.

48 On 11 November 1920 the remains of an unknown British soldier, which had been brought back from the former Western Front, were buried in Westminster Abbey with full military honours.

49 Information from passport of Lady Julia Drummond, PO15/CO1, McCM.

50 Julia Drummond "Vimy: A Remembrance," 5, PO15/CO6, McCM.

51 Leask, *Lena Ashwell*, 151.

52 Lena Ashwell, "The Artistic Growth of the Soldier," *Sunday Evening Telegraph*, 2 March 1919.

53 John Masefield, *Sonnets of Good Cheer to the Lena Ashwell Players, From Their Well-Wisher* (Bath, 1926), preface.

54 *Vancouver Province*, 1 March 1952; *Vancouver Sun*, 15 April 1954.

55 Marshall, *Firing Lines*, 274, 20.

56 Gwyn, *Tapestry of War*, 165.

57 Morris Craig, *But This is Our War*, 144; Macmillan, *The Winds of Change*, 51.

58 Morris Craig, *But This is Our War*, 145.

59 Victoria Wallace, Director-General of the Commonwealth War Graves Commission. www.canadainternational.gc.ca/greece/eyes_abroad_fallen nurses.

60 *Perth Courier*, "Peace Rings True in Community," 15 November 2018

61 Barry Boyce, Perth Royal Canadian Legion, quoted in "Peace Rings True in Community," *Perth Courier*, 15 November 2018.

62 Anon., *Canada in The Great World War*, Vol. VI, 177-178.

63 Ibid., 176; From "Keeping Warm" by Betsy Struthers, *Censored Letters* (Oakville, 1984), 35.

Bibliography

PRIMARY SOURCES
Archives of Manitoba
    Keystone Archives Acc. PR1977 Sheet Music
Archives of Nova Scotia
    MG1 Volume 661 McGregor-Miller Collection
Archives of Ontario
    F6 MU1312, B253642, Hearst Fonds
British Columbia Archives
    ND249 H355 A4, Mary Riter Hamilton papers
British Library
    British Newspaper Archive
Canadian War Museum, Ottawa, Military History Research Centre
    58A 1 114.9, Katherine Macdonald Fonds
    58A 1 2.1, May Bastedo Fonds
    58A 1 22.12, Gertrude Gilbert Fonds
    58A 1 221.4, Mary Bird Fonds
    58A 1 235.1, Florence Hunter Fonds
    58A 1 264.1, Alice Swanston Ironside Fonds
    58A 1 266.1, Edna Lena Moore Fonds
    58A 1 284.12, Grace MacPherson Fonds
    58E 2 3.6, Hannah Lister Fonds
Glenbow Museum and Archives, Calgary, Alberta
    M-6245, Theodora Paynter Mackay Papers
Guelph Museums, McCrae House
    Cyril C. Allinson, unpublished manuscript: "John McCrae: Poet, Soldier, Physician"
Imperial War Museum, London
    P476, Winifred L.B. Tower, "Journal" 26 July to October 1914, and "Some Diary Notes,
        October 1914 to February 1916"
In Flanders Fields Museum, Ypres, Belgium
    Kenniscentrum
        Records of the International Conference on the Chinese Labour Corps during the
            First World War
Library and Archives Canada, Ottawa
    Manuscript Group
        MG27 II D12(e) Volume 15, Lady Emily Perley Papers
        MG27 IIIC6, Cairine Reay Wilson Papers
            R5278-4-1-E, Mildred Forbes correspondence, Microfilm reel H-2299)
        MG30 C238, Julia Grace Wales Papers
        MG30 D209, John McCrae Papers (Microfilm reels A-1103, 1977)
        MG30 D258, Ethel Chadwick Papers

MG30 E45, Margaret Macdonald Papers, Vol. 10

MG30 E52, Talbot Papineau Papers (Items 4 and 5, correspondence)

MG30 E81, E.W.B. Morrison Papers

MG30 E149, Adamson Papers, Vols. 2, 3, 4, 6, 7

MG30 E155, Roger F. Clarke Papers, Diary Book X.

MG30 E160, Ruby Peterkin Papers

MG30 E290, Sophie Hoerner Papers

MG30 E446, Anne E. Ross Papers, Narrative of Services

MG30 E464, Dorothy Cotton Papers

MG30 E510, Laura A. Gamble Papers

R11203-O-1-E, Alice E. Isaacson Papers

RG9-III-B-2, Volume/Box No. 3746. War Diary, No. 1 Canadian General Hospital 1914-1919

RG9-III-B-2, Volume/Box No. 3747. War Diary, No. 1 Canadian Stationary Hospital, 1914-1919

RG24 Volume 1868 File FN-WW 1-48.
    Official Report of the Sinking of the "Llandovery Castle" as issued to the press by the Hon. The Minister, Overseas Military Forces of Canada.

RG27-B, R1185-15-3-E. Sir Arthur Doughty Papers

RG150 Accession 1992-93/166. First World War service records. Voice of the Pioneer audio files Violet Wilson, 9861, Acc.1981-0111

McCord Museum of History, Montreal

    PO15, Drummond Family Fonds

        File C, Lady Grace Julia Drummond

        File F, Guy Melfort Drummond

McGill University Archives

    "Military Nursing Service World War 1, 1914-1918"

    RG64-7-21, "War Memoirs of Miss Edith Hudson"

McGill University Library

    Rare Books and Special Collections

        R.C. Fetherstonhaugh, "War Diaries and Letters: Dorothy Cotton"

    Osler Library of the History of Medicine

        MS545/4 Edward Archibald Fonds

            Letters of Edward Archibald, 1906-1941

        P100 Sir William Osler Papers

            Folder 326, Lady Grace Osler correspondence

Memorial University of Newfoundland

    Centre for Newfoundland Studies

        Frances Cluett Collection-174. File 2.02.001

Mississippi Valley Textile Museum Archives, Almonte

    Rosamond family Papers

National Defence Headquarters, Ottawa

    Directory of History and Heritage

        CA ON00093 96/5-1 Series 1, Blanche Olive Lavallée Fonds

        CA ON00093 96/5-1 Series 2, Georges Alexandre Henri Trudeau Fonds

Port Alberni Library, British Columbia

    Document: "The Sinking of HMHS Llandovery Castle, 1920"

Trent University Archives

    75-1001 Mary Tuer Papers

    69-001 Helen Fowlds Marryat Papers, Series I, Box 1

University of British Columbia Archives
    Laura Holland Papers. Correspondence Series, Boxes 1-2
    Jack Stickney Papers, Box 1
Whitehern Museum and Archives, Hamilton
    Reverend Calvin McQuesten correspondence. Box 04-007

Privately Held Material
Cotton and Rosamond Family Papers, held by Barry and Anne Roxburgh of Lanark, Ontario.
Memoir, *An Artillery Officer in the First World War* by Colonel R. MacLeod, D.S.O., M.C. held by Sue and Lindsay Court of Beaminster, England.

Published Letters, Diaries and Memoirs
Abraham, J. Johnston. *Surgeon's Journal: the Autobiography of J. Johnston Abraham.* Melbourne: Heinemann, 1957.
Adamson, Anthony. *Wasps in the Attic.* Published privately, 1988.
Addams, Jane, Emily G. Balch, Alice Hamilton. *Women at The Hague: The International Congress of Women and its Results.* New York: The Macmillan Company, 1918.
Anon. *Canada in the Great World War*, Toronto: United Publishers of Canada Ltd., Vol. II, 1919, Vol. III, 1919, Vol. VI, 1921.
Anon. *The Russian Diary of an Englishman, Petrograd, 1915-1917.* London: William Heinemann, 1919.
Anon. *A War Nurse's Diary: Sketches from a Belgian Field Hospital.* New York: The Macmillan Company, 1918.
Ashwell, Lena. *Modern Troubadours: A Record of the Concerts at the Front.* London: Gyldendal, 1922.
———. *Myself A Player.* London: Michael Joseph, 1936.
Bairnsfather, Bruce. *Bullets and Billets.* New York: G.P. Putnam's Sons, 1917.
Bilbrough, Ethel M. *My War Diary 1914-1918.* London: Ebury Press, 2014.
Boyd, William, *With a Field Ambulance at Ypres: Being letters written March 7–August 15 1915.* Toronto: The Musson Book Company, 1916.
Brittain, Vera. *Testament of Youth.* London: Virago, 1978.
Bruce, Constance. *Humour in Tragedy: Hospital Life behind Three Fronts by a Canadian Nursing Sister.* London: Skeffington and Son [1918].
Cane, Bruce. *It Made You Think of Home: The Haunting Journal of Deward Barnes, CEF, 1916-1919.* Toronto: Dundurn Press, 2004.
Carr, Iona K. *A Story of the Canadian Red Cross Information Bureau During The Great War.* Toronto: Canadian Red Cross, 1920.
Chown, Diana, ed. *The Stairway.* Toronto: University of Toronto Press, 1988.
Clint. M.B. *Our Bit: Memories of War Service by a Canadian Nursing Sister.* Montreal: Barwick Ltd., 1934.
Cooper, Lady Diana. *The Rainbow Comes and Goes, Volume 1.* London: Rupert Hart-Davis, 1958.
Cowen, Ruth, ed. *A Nurse at the Front: The First World War Diaries of Sister Edith Appleton.* London: Simon and Schuster UK Ltd., 2013.
Craig, Grace Morris. *But This Is Our War.* Toronto: University of Toronto Press, 1981.
Currie, J.A. *The Red Watch: With 1st Canadian Division in Flanders.* Toronto: McClelland & Stewart, 1916.
Foster, Charles Lyons, ed. *Letters from the Front: Being a Record of the Part Played by Officers of the Bank in the Great War, 1914-1919.* Volumes 1 and 2. Toronto: Southam Press, 1920.

Greenhous, Brereton, ed. *A Rattle of Pebbles: The First World War Diaries of Two Can-adian Airmen.* Ottawa: Minister of Supply and Services, 1987.

Hamilton, Cicely. *Life Errant.* London: J.M. Dent, 1935.

Harmer, Michael. *The Forgotten Hospital.* Chichester: Springwood Books Ltd., 1982.

Mann, Susan, ed. *The War Diary of Clare Gass 1915-1918.* Montreal: McGill-Queen's University Press, 2000.

Moore, Mary MacLeod. *Maple Leaf's Red Cross: The Story of the Canadian Red Cross Overseas.* London: Skeffington & Son Ltd., 1919.

———. *The Story of the King George and Queen Mary Maple Leaf Club. London: 1915-1919.* London, n.d. ?1919.

Morrell, Ottoline. *Ottoline: The Early Memoirs of Lady Ottoline Morrell.* London, Faber and Faber, 1963.

Murray, W.W. *The Epic of Vimy.* Ottawa: The Legionary, 1936.

Paquette, Albiny. *Hon. Albiny Paquette: Soldat, médecin, maire, député, ministre: 33 années à la législature de Québec: Souvenirs d'une vie de travail et de bonheur.* Montreal: n.d., 1977.

Quinn, Shawna M. *Agnes Warner and the Nursing Sisters of the Great War.* Fredericton: Goose Lane Editions, 2010.

Plummer, Mary, ed. *With the First Canadian Contingent.* London: Hodder & Stoughton, 1915.

Richardson-Whealy, Elizabeth, ed. *Pilot's Log: The Log, Diary, Letters and Verse of Lt. Leonard A. Richardson, Royal Flying Corps 1917-1918.* St. Catharines, Ontario: Paul Heron Publishing Ltd., 1998.

Rompkey, Bill, and Bert Riggs. *Your Daughter Fanny: The War Letters of Frances Cluett, VAD.* St. John's, Newfoundland: Flanker Press, 2006.

Rubio, Mary, and Elizabeth Waterston. *The Selected Journals of L.M. Montgomery, Volume II 1910-1921.* Toronto: Oxford University Press, 2003.

Scott, Eric, ed. *Nobody Ever Wins a War: The World War 1 Diaries of Ella Mae Bongard, R.N.* Ottawa: Janeric Enterprises, 1997.

Wicks, Terri L. Monture, ed. *Diary of a War Nurse, American Expeditionary Force, 1918.* 1996.

Wilson-Simmie, Katherine M. *Lights Out: A Canadian Nursing Sister's Tale.* Belleville, Ontario: Mika Publishing Company, 1981.

SECONDARY SOURCES

Books

Adie,Kate. *Fighting on the Home Front: The Legacy of Women in World War One.* London: Hodder & Stoughton, 2013.

Allen, Ralph. *Ordeal by Fire: Canada 1910-1945.* Toronto: Doubleday, 1961.

Amery, The Rt. Hon. L.S. *My Political Life.* 2 volumes. London: Hutchinson, 1953.

Andrew, Caroline and Beth Moore Milroy, eds. *Life Spaces: Gender, Household, Employment.* Vancouver: UBC Press, 1988.

Anon. *A History of No. 7 (Queen's) Canadian General Hospital, March 26th, 1915-Nov. 15th, 1917.* London: C.W. Falkner, 1918.

Banks, Arthur. *A Military Atlas of the First World War.* Barnsley: Leo Cooper, 1989.

Baring, Maurice. *Flying Corps Headquarters 1914-1918.* London: Ashford, Buchan & Enright, 1985.

Bean, Mary Jean Woodard. *Julia Grace Wales: Canada's Hidden Heroine and the Quest for Peace 1914-1918.* Ottawa: Borealis Press, 2005.

Beatty, David Pierce. *Memories of the Forgotten War: The World War I Diary of Pte. V.E. Goodwin*. Port Elgin, New Brunswick: Baie Verte Editions, 1986.

Binyon, Laurence, comp. *For Dauntless France: An Account of Britain's Aid to the French Wounded and Victims of the War*. London: Hodder & Stoughton, n.d.

Bliss, Michael. *William Osler: A Life in Medicine*. Toronto: University of Toronto Press, 2000.

Boyd, Simon. *Lady Sybil: Empire, War and Revolution*. Kendal: Hayloft Publishing Ltd., 2017.

Brooks, Jane and Christine E. Hallett. *One Hundred Years of Wartime Nursing Practices, 1854-1953*. Manchester: Manchester University Press, 2015.

Brown, Marie. *Russia and Revolution: The Promise and the Performance*. Glasgow: Blackie and Son, 1979.

Christie, Norm, ed. *The Letters of Agar Adamson*. Ottawa: CEF Books, 1997.

Churchill, Winston. *The World Crisis: 1911-1914*. Toronto: The Macmillan Company of Canada, 1923.

Climo, Percy. *A Collection of World War 1 Letters as Published in The Cobourg World Newspaper, 1914-1919*. Colborne, Ontario, 1985.

Cook, Tim. *At the Sharp End: Canadians Fighting the Great War 1914-1916*. Toronto: Penguin Group, 2007.

———. *No Place to Run: The Canadian Corps and Gas Warfare in the First World War*. Vancouver: UBC Press, 2000.

———. *The Secret History of Soldiers: How Canadians Survived the Great War*. Canada: Allen Lane, 2018.

Corbett, Sir Julian S. *Official History of the War. Naval Operations – Volume II*. Nashville, Tennessee: The Battery Press Inc., 1997.

Cowles, Fleur. *1913: The Defiant Swansong*. London: Weidenfeld & Nicholson, 1967.

Cowley, Deborah, ed. *Georges Vanier: Soldier: Wartime Letters and Diaries 1915-1919*. Toronto: Dundurn Press, 2000.

Dancocks, Daniel J. *Welcome to Flanders Fields, The First Canadian Battle of the Great War: Ypres 1915*. Toronto: McClelland and Stewart, 1988.

Doan, Laura. *Disturbing Practices: History, Sexuality, and Women's Experience of Modern War*. Chicago: University of Chicago Press, 2013.

Duguid, A. Fortesque. *The Official History of the Canadian Forces in the Great War 1914-1919, Volume 1, Part 1*. Ottawa: J.O. Patenaude, 1938.

Dumont, Micheline, Michèle Jean, Marie Lavigne, Jennifer Stoddart. *Quebec Women: A History*. Toronto: Women's Press, 1987.

Evans, Siân. *Mrs Ronnie: The Society Hostess Who Collected Kings*. London: National Trust Books, 2013.

Fetherstonhaugh, R.C. *The 13th Battalion Royal Highlanders of Canada 1914-1919*. Canada: The 13th Battalion Royal Highlanders of Canada, 1925

Francis, R. Douglas, Richard Jones, Donald B. Smith. *Destinies: Canadian History Since Confederation*. Toronto: Nelson Education, 2008.

Gill, Pauline. *Docteure Irma: l'Indomptable*. Québec: Québec Loisirs, 2008.

Glassford, Sarah, and Amy J. Shaw, eds. *A Sisterhood of Suffering and Service: Women and Girls of Canada and Newfoundland during the First World War*. Vancouver: UBC Press, 2012,

Glassford, Sarah. *Mobilizing Mercy: A History of the Canadian Red Cross*. Montreal: McGill-Queen's University Press, 2017.

Graves, Dianne. *A Crown of Life: The World of John McCrae*. Montreal: Robin Brass Studio, 2012.

Graves, Donald E. *Always Ready: A History of the Royal Regiment of Canada*. Toronto: The Royal Regiment of Canada Association, 2017.

————. *Field of Glory: The Battle of Crysler's Farm, 1813*. Toronto: Robin Brass Studio, 1999.

Gwyn, Sandra. *Tapestry of War: A Private View of Canadians in the Great War*. Toronto: Harper Collins, 1992.

Herbert, Patricia and Matthäs, Jurgen, ed. *Atrocities on Trial: Historical Perspectives on the Politics of Prosecuting War Crimes*. Lincoln: University of Nebraska Press, 2008.

Hyatt, A.M.J. *General Sir Arthur Currie: A Military Biography*. Toronto: University of Toronto Press, 1987.

Hyde, Andrew P. *The First Blitz: The German Air Campaign against Britain 1917-1918*. Barnsley: Leo Cooper, 2002.

Imperial Order Daughters of the Empire. *The IODE in War time, a Record of Women's Work for King and Empire*. Publisher not identified, ?Toronto, 1919.

Jack, Donald. *Rogues, Rebels and Geniuses: The Story of Canadian Medicine*. Toronto: Doubleday Canada Ltd., 1981.

Kluckner, Michael. *Toronto the Way It Was*. Toronto: Whitecap Books, 1988.

Kraft, Barbara S. *The Peace Ship: Henry Ford's Pacifist Adventure in the First World War*. New York: Macmillan Publishing Co., 1978.

Larson, Erik. *Dead Wake: The Last Crossing of the Lusitania*. New York: Crown Publishers, 2015.

Leask, Margaret. *Lena Ashwell: Actress, Patriot, Pioneer*. Hatfield: University of Hertfordshire Press, 2012.

Leetooze, Sherrell Branton. *WW1 Nursing Sisters of Old Durham County*. Bowmanville: Lynn Michael-John Associates, 2014.

Leonhard, Jörn. *Pandora's Box: A History of the First World War*. Cambridge, Massachusetts, and London, England: The Belknap Press of Harvard University Press, 2018.

Litalien, Michel. *Dans la tourmente: Deux hôpitaux militaires canadiens-français dans la France en guerre (1915-1919)*. Outremont (Québec): Editions Athéna, 2003.

Lochner, Louis P. *America's Don Quixote: Henry Ford's Attempt to Save Europe*. London: Kegan Paul, Trench, Trubner & Co., 1924.

MacDonagh, Michael. *London During the Great War: The Memories of a Journalist*. London: Eyre & Spottiswood, 1935.

MacKay, Donald. *The Square Mile: Merchant Princes of Montreal*. Vancouver and Toronto: Douglas & McIntyre, 1987.

Macmillan, Harold. *The Winds of Change 1914-1939*. London: Macmillan, 1966.

Macphail, Sir Andrew. *Official History of the Canadian Forces in the Great War 1914-1919: The Medical Services*. Ottawa: F.A. Acland, 1925.

Mann, Susan. *Margaret Macdonald: Imperial Daughter*. Montreal: McGill-Queen's University Press, 2005.

Marshall, Debbie. *Firing Lines: Three Canadian Women Write the First World War*. Toronto: Dundurn Press, 2017.

Mathieson, William D. *My Grandfather's War: Canadians Remember the First World War 1914-1918*. Toronto: Macmillan of Canada, 1981.

Matthews, D.L., ed. *The Oslers During World War One*. Gravenhurst, Ontario: The Artstract Co., 1999.

Maunder, Andrew, ed. *British Theatre and the Great War, 1914-1919*, Basingstoke: Palgrave Macmillan, 2015.

McClung, Nellie L. *In Times Like These*. Toronto: University of Toronto Press, 1972.

McLeod, Kirsty. *The Last Summer: May to September 1914*. London: Collins, 1983.

Miller, Ian Hugh Maclean, *Our Glory and Our Grief: Torontonians and the Great War*. Toronto: University of Toronto Press, 2002.

Moore, Mary MacLeod. *The Story of the King George and Queen Mary Maple Leaf Club, 1915-1919*. London: s.n., 1919.

Moorehead, Alan. *Gallipoli*. London: Arrow, 1959.

Moorehead, Caroline. *Dunant's Dream: War, Switzerland and the History of the Red Cross*. London: Harper Collins, 1999.

Morgan, Henry James, ed. *Types of Canadian Women*. Volume 1. Toronto: William Briggs, 1903.

Moore, Wendy. *Endell Street: The Trailblazing Women Who Ran World War One's Most Remarkable Military Hospital*. London: Atlantic Books, 2020

Morton, Desmond. *When Your Number's Up: The Canadian Soldier in the First World War*. Toronto: Random House of Canada, 1993.

Mullins, Claude. *The Leipzig Trials: An Account of the War Criminals' Trials and a Study of German Mentality*. London: H.F. & G. Witherby, 1921.

Murray, Col. W.W. *History of the 2nd Canadian Battalion in the Great War 1914-1919*. Ottawa: The Historical Committee, 2nd Battalion, C.E.F. 1947.

———. *The Epic of Vimy*. Ottawa: The Legionary, 1936.

Nicholson, Col. G.W.L. *Canadian Expeditionary Force 1914-1919*. Ottawa: Department of National Defence, 1964.

———. *Canada's Nursing Sisters*. Toronto: Hakkert, 1975.

O'Kiely, Elizabeth. *Gentleman Air Ace: The Duncan Bell-Irving Story*. Madeira Park: Harbour Publishing, 1992.

Paxton, Naomi. *Stage Rights: The Actresses' Franchise League, Activism and Politics 1908-58*. Manchester: Manchester University Press, 2018.

Percy, Clayre and Jane Ridley. *The Letters of Edwin Lutyens*. London: Collins, 1985.

Powell, Anne. *Women in the War Zone: Hospital Service in the First World War*. Stroud, Gloucestershire: The History Press, 2013.

Quiney, Linda J. *This Small Army of Women: Canadian Volunteer Nurses and the First World War*. Vancouver: UBC Press, 2017.

Read, Daphne, ed. *The Great War and Canadian Society: An Oral History*. Toronto: Hogtown Press, 1978.

Reid, Bordon, ed. *Poor Bloody Murder: Personal Memoirs of the First World War*. Oakville, Ontario: Mosaic Press, 1980.

Remarque, Erich Maria. *All Quiet on the Western Front*. New York: Little Brown & Company, 1929.

Robinson, Jane. *A Force To Be Reckoned With: A History of the Women's Institute*. London: Virago Press, 2011.

Shackleton, Keith R. *Second to None: The Fighting 58th Battalion of the Canadian Expeditionary Force*. Toronto: Dundurn Press, 2002.

Tennyson, Brian Douglas. *The Canadian Experience of the Great War: A Guide to Memoirs*. Lanham, Maryland: Scarecrow Press, 2013.

Toman, Cynthia. *Sister Soldiers of the Great War: The Nurses of the Canadian Army Medical Corps*. Vancouver: UBC Press, 2016.

Urquhart, H.M. *The History of 16th Battalion (the Canadian Scottish) Canadian Expeditionary Force in the Great War, 1914-1919*. Toronto: The Macmillan Company of Canada, 1932.

White, Jerry. *Zeppelin Nights: London in the First World War*. London: Vintage, 2014.

Whitelaw, Liz. *The Life and Rebellious Times of Cicely Hamilton*. Columbus, Ohio: University of Ohio Press, 1990.

Winter, Jay. *Sites of Memory, Sites of Mourning: The Great War in European Cultural History*. Cambridge: Cambridge University Press, 2014.

Wise, S.F. *Canadian Airmen and the First World War*. Toronto: University of Toronto Press, 1980.

Poetry
Garvin, John W., ed. *Canadian Poems of the Great War*. Toronto: McClelland & Stewart, 1918.
Masefield, John. *Sonnets of Good Cheer to the Lena Ashwell Players, From Their Well-Wisher*. Bath: Mendip Press, 1926.
Struthers, Betsy. *Censored Letters*. Oakville, Ontario: Mosaic Press, 1984.
Wetherell, James Elgin, ed. *Later English Poems 1901-1922*. Toronto: McClelland and Stewart, 1922.

Dictionaries
Dictionary of Canadian Biography, Vols. 16, 18. University of Toronto/Université Laval

Exhibition Catalogues
Amos, Robert. *Mary Riter Hamilton 1873-1954*. Victoria: Art Gallery of Greater Victoria, 1978.
Davis, Angela E. and Sarah M. McKinnon. *No Man's Land: The Battlefield Paintings of Mary Riter Hamilton, 1919-1922*. Winnipeg: University of Manitoba, 1992.
The Battlefield Paintings of Mary Riter Hamilton, 1919-1922. Winnipeg: University of Manitoba, 1992.

Newspapers
Boston Herald
Daily Graphic
Daily Malta Chronicle
Daily Sketch
Daily Telegraph
Echo and Evening Chronicle
Erie Daily Times
Evening News
Evening Standard
Family Herald and Weekly Star
Globe and Mail
Halifax Chronicle Herald
Halifax Daily Guardian
Huddersfield Weekly Examiner
Illustrated Sunday Herald
Le Figaro
Loughton Advertiser
Malta Independent on Sunday
Manchester Guardian
Manitoba Free Press
McClure Newspapers Syndicate
Montreal Gazette
New York Herald
New York Times
Ottawa Journal
Perth Courier
Pictou Advocate

Sun (Toronto)
Sunday Evening Telegraph
Sunday Times
The Times
Toronto Daily Star
Toronto Star Weekly
Vancouver Courier
Vancouver Daily Province
Vancouver Sun

Magazines and Periodicals
BC Studies
British Journal of Nursing
Canada in Khaki
Canadian [magazine]
Canadian Annual Review
Canadian Bulletin of Medical History
Canadian Nursing and Hospital Review
Christian Work
Harper's Monthly Magazine
Journal of the CHA
London Gazette
Maclean's
Manitoba History
Pearson's Magazine
Punch
Saturday Night
Slightly Foxed: The Real Reader's Quarterly
Strand Magazine
Studio
Town Topics
The Beaver
The Canadian Nurse
The Dead Horse Corner Gazette
The Gold Stripe
The Hospital
The Nursing Times
The Oxford Magazine
The Record
The Red Triangle
The Spectator
The Tablet
The Varsity
The Week
The Western Home Monthly
Topical Times
Town Topics
Western Women's Weekly
Woman's Century
World

Published Articles and Monographs

Anon. "War Conditions in the Nursing World," *The Canadian Nurse*, Vol. 14, No. 8, October 1918, 1352-1355.

Anon. "Gas Poisoning," *The Nursing Times*, XI, 15 May 1915, 585.

Arnold, Gertrude. "The Search for Missing Men and Other Stories of a Canadian V.A.D," *Maclean's Magazine*, November 1919, 27-28.

Ashwell, Lena. "A Year's Music at the Front," *Strand Magazine*, Volume 51, January-June 1916, 257-261.

Bruce, J.E.M. "Mary Riter Hamilton: An Artist Impressionist on the Battlefields of France," *The Gold Stripe*, No. 3, 1919, 11-12.

Chancellor, Alexander. "A Forgotten Hospital That Was the British Empire's Gift to Our Russian Allies," *The Spectator*, 16 April 2016. www.spectator.co.uk/article/long-life-14 April 2016.

Cotton, Dorothy. "A Word Picture of the Anglo-Russian Hospital, Petrograd," *The Canadian Nurse*, 22:9, September 1936, 486-488.

Davis, Angela E. "Mary Riter Hamilton: An Artist in No-Man's Land," *The Beaver*, October-November 1989, 6-16.

——. "Mary Riter Hamilton: Manitoba Artist 1873-1954," *Manitoba History*, No. 11, Spring 1986, 22-27.

Gibbs, Philip. "I Saw Passchendaele Taken," *The Great War – I Was There*, Part 35, (London, 1938), 1401-1404.

Gunn, Jean. "The Service of Canadian Nurses and Voluntary Aids During the War," *The Canadian Nurse*, Vol. 15, No. 9, September 1919, 1975-1979.

Hegan, Edith. "The Russian Revolution from a Hospital Window," *Harper's Monthly Magazine*, 1918.

MacBeth, Madge, "One of Our Last War Workers Comes Home," *Toronto Star Weekly*, 20 February 1926.

Macdonald, Margaret. "The Canadian Matron-in-Chief on Work in France," *The Canadian Nurse*, Vol. 15, No. 9, September 1919, 1991-1993.

McDonald, Robert A.J. "He Thought He Was the Boss of Everything: Masculinity and Power in a Vancouver Family," *BC Studies, No. 132*, Winter 2001-2002.

Moore, Mary MacLeod. "Canadian Women War Workers Overseas," *The Canadian*, Vol. 52, No. 3 (January 1919), 737-751.

Morgan, Angela. "The Women's Congress at The Hague," *Christian Work*, 22 May 1915.

Mougel, Nadège. "World War 1 Casualties," *Centre Européen Robert Schumann*, 2011, 1-13.

Perry, Anne Anderson. "Artist's and Their Doing: Oh Canada: What of Art," *Western Woman's Weekly*, 1 February 1919, 4-5.

Quiney, Linda J. "Gendering Patriotism: Canadian Volunteer Nurses as the Female 'Soldiers' of the Great War," in Sarah Glassford and Amy J Shaw, ed., *A Sisterhood of Suffering and Service*, 103-125.

——. "Sharing the Halo: Social and Professional Tensions in the Work of World War I Canadian Volunteer Nurses," *Journal of the CHA*, Vol. 9, 1998, 105-124.

——. "Assistant Angels: Canadian Voluntary Aid Detachment Nurses in the Great War," *Canadian Bulletin of Medical History*, Vol. 15, 1998, 189-206.

Smith, David H. *The Forgotten Angels: History of the YMCA Women's Auxiliary, Part One,*. YMCAs of England, Ireland, Scotland and Wales. n.d.

Snyder, Catherine. "With the FANYs in France," *The Gold Stripe* Volume 2, 1919, 129-130.

Stirling, Terry Bishop. "Such Sights One Will Never Forget": Newfoundland Women and Overseas Nursing in the First World War," in Sarah Glassford and Amy J. Shaw, ed., *A Sisterhood of Suffering and Service*, 126-147.

Syrett, Karen. "Lady Ridley's Hospital for Officers at 10 Carlton House Terrace," *RAMC/555*, Wellcome Library, 20-24.

Unpublished Sources

Glassford, Sarah. *Marching as to War: The Canadian Red Cross Society 1885–1939*. Ph.D. dissertation, York University, 2007.

McIntosh, Terresa. *Other Images of War: Canadian Women War Artists of the First and Second World Wars*. M.A. thesis, Carleton University, 1990.

Digital Sources

www.aspiringquotes.us/quotes/rioh_Z3KVUiqt; Jane Addams, https//quotefancy.com/quote/1061003 www.azquotes.com/quote/957937 and quote/902022

www.biographi./ca/en

www.canadainternational.gc.ca/greece/eyes_abroad-coupdoeil/fallen_nurses

https://en.wikipedia.org/wiki/List_of_hospital_ships_sunk_in_World_War_1

www.eventfinda.co.nz/2018/armistice-day-centenary-service/auckland/parnell

www.fondationlionelgroulx.org/Irma-Levasseur-et-les.html

www.gracesguide.co.uk/C._A._ Vandervell_and_Co

www.greyroots.com/archives

faculty/marianopolis.edu/c.belanger/quebechistory/encyclopedia/dd.htm

https//quotefancy.com/quote/1061003

https://rememberingfirstworldwarnurses.blogspot.com.

www.rmslusitania.info

www.spectator.co.uk/article/long-life -14-april-2016

veterans.gc.ca/eng/remembrance

http://womenandmuseum.com/btravis.htm

Index

Stamers, Anna, 141, 152
Stanford University, 246
Staten Island, New York, 294
Steenvorde, Belgium, 122
Stephens, Frances, 156-157, 304
Stewart, Christina, 156
Stickney, Private Jack, 227
Stobart, Mabel St. Clair, 97
Stockholm, Sweden, 252, 255, 259, 261, 263
Stokhod, River, 123
Strachy, Margaret, 171
Suez Canal, 100
Sutton, Captain Fred, 47
Suvla Bay, Gallipoli, 80, 84, 136
Swan River, Manitoba, 140, 152
Swanston, Alice, 45, 300
Sweeny, Captain Ben, 302
Sylvester, Captain E.A., 142-143, 147
Syros, Greece, 132

Taplow, Berkshire, 26, 37, 42
Tasman Sea, 135
Tate, Miss, 172
Tatiana, Grand Duchess, 108, 120
Taylor, Captain, 187
Taylor, E.A., 273
Taylor, Ermine, 208
Taylor, Frederick, 241
Teeswater, Ontario, 271
Templeman, Jean, 152
Terry, Ellen, 224, 226
Texel, Netherlands, 138
The Hague, Netherlands, 246, 250, 259-260, 263
Thomas, Hugh Owen, 26
Thomas, Mary, 302
Thompson, Eleanor, 67
Thompson, Muriel, 200
Thorndike, Sybil, 226
Thorne, Elsie, 197
Thorne, Major Stuart, 308
Tigris River, 104-105
Timasheff, Syra, 124
Tomb of the Unknown Warrior, Westminster Abbey, 304
Toronto, Ontario, 4, 67, 84, 87, 105, 140-141, 152, 156, 162-163, 169, 172, 176, 185, 188, 198, 219, 286, 271, 273-274, 299
Toronto, University of, 28, 34, 185, 302
Toronto Department of Public Health, 298-299
Toronto Women's Patriotic League, 180,
Torquay, Devon, 16
Toul, France, 58, 60, 64, 270
Travis, Dr. Catherine, 97, 99
Trouville, France, 29, 172

Troyes, France, 29
Trudeau, Lieutenant Henri, 53, 301
Tsarskoye Selo, Russia, 125
Tuer, Mary, 4
Turner, Captain William, 232
Tuxford, General George, 146
Tweedie, Mrs. Alec, 295

Union Castle Steamship Line, 138,
Union Steamship Company, 135
United States Army Nurse Corps, 24, 55, 133, 294, 299, 301
University Women's Club, 274
Upton, Ethel, 292
United States
    and foreign policy, 258
    and peace activism, 244, 253
    declaration of war, 1917, 52, 239, 264-265
    goes into combat, 1918, 61

Valcartier, Quebec, 6, 8, 11, 155
Vallée du Denacre, France, 40
Valletta, Malta, 83-84
Valleyfield, Quebec, 67
Vancouver, 4, 37, 67, 173, 186, 191, 299, 302-303
Vancouver Art Gallery, 306
Vancouver Island, 274, 310
Vanier, Georges, 204, 211
Vanpeteghem, Gabriella, 280
Varapaeva, Belarus, 121
Varley, F.H., 275
Venice, Italy, 272
Versailles, France, 292, 306
Victoria, British Columbia, 87, 102, 152, 274
Victoria League, 303
Victoria, Queen, 205, 228
Victorian Order of Nurses, 205, 300
Vienna, Austria, 273
Vilna (Vilnius), Lithuania, 120
Vimy Ridge, France, 277, 284, 305
Vimy village, France, 285, 293
Vittel, France, 60-61
Voluntary Aid Detachment,
    organization and regulations, 182-185
    recruitment, 183
    in Britain and Canada, 110, 182, 185-187
    work in France, 184, 188-194
    work in eastern Mediterranean, 194-197
    work with CAMC, 197
    uniform, 183-184
Von Heimburg, *Oberleutnant-zur-See* Heino, 133
Von Schlieffen, Field Marshal Alfred, 6

Wainwright, Muriel, 194

A native of Kent, England, Dianne Graves studied languages before embarking on a public relations career in international education and travel. She is also the author of *A Crown of Life: The World of John McCrae*, *In the Midst of Alarms: The Untold Story of Women and the War of 1812* and *Redcoats and River Pirates: Sam and Ellen's Adventure at the Windmill*, an historical novel for young readers set on the St. Lawrence River in the 1830s.

Dianne Graves has acted as a consultant on a number of projects, including the CBC documentary series *A People's History of Canada,* and has appeared in several documentary films, notably *John McCrae's War.* She continues to research and write and lives in a 19th-century farmhouse in the scenic Mississippi River Valley of eastern Ontario with her husband, Canadian military historian Donald E. Graves.

In the photograph Dianne Graves attends the annual Remembrance Day parade and ceremonies in Ypres, Belgium.

By the same author

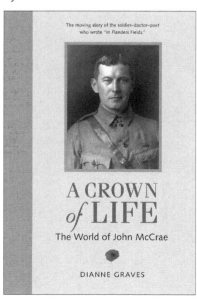

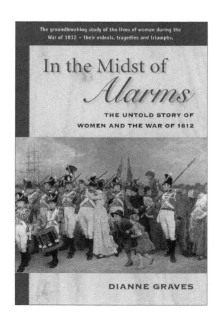